FAO
LEGISLATIVE
STUDY

86

Groundwater in international law
Compilation of treaties and other legal instuments

Stefano Burchi
Kerstin Mechlem

for the
Development Law Service
FAO Legal Office

UNITED NATIONS EDUCATIONAL, SCIENTIFIC AND CUL.....
ORGANIZATION
FOOD AND AGRICULTURE ORGANIZATION OF THE UNITED NATIONS
Rome, 2005

Published jointly by:

Food and Agriculture
Organization of the United
Nations
Viale delle Terme di Caracalla
00100 Rome, Italy

United Nations
Educational, Scientific
and Cultural Organization
7, place de Fontenoy
75007 Paris, France

ISBN 92-5-105231-X

CONTENTS

ACKNOWLEDGEMENTS

The initial research and structuring of relevant material for this publication was carried out by Stefanie Rothenberger, working as a research assistant with the Development Law Service from July through December 2003. Charlotte Oliver took over from Stefanie Rothenberger, working under contract with UNESCO and FAO. The high calibre of Ms Rothenberger's and Ms Oliver's professional input to the project is gratefully acknowledged. In addition, the advice provided by Jacob J. Burke, Senior Officer in the Land and Water Development Division of FAO, on points of hydrogeology issues was highly appreciated.

This publication would not have been possible without the support of the Secretariat of UNESCO's International Hydrological Programme (IHP). Mention is also to be made of Raya Marina Stephan, UNESCO Consultant, for her help and advice.

FOREWORD

Despite the social, economic, environmental and political importance of groundwater, international law has paid relatively little attention to this resource. Groundwater represents about ninety-seven percent of the fresh water resources available, excluding the water locked in the polar ice. It serves the basic needs of more than one-half of the world's population and it is often the only source of water in arid and semi-arid countries. Improvements in pumping technology and growth in industry, agriculture, and global population are leading to ever increasing levels of use of this resource, and to growing reliance on it. Largely as a result of these phenomena, groundwater resources and the social, economic and environmental systems dependent on them have, over the last fifty years, come under pressure from over-abstraction and pollution, seriously threatening their sustainability.

International law has so far only rarely taken account of groundwater. While surface water treaties abound, groundwater is either nominally included in the scope of these instruments, mainly if it is "related" to surface waters, or it is not mentioned at all. Only few legal instruments contain groundwater-specific provisions, and even fewer address groundwater exclusively.

As groundwater quickly emerges from the limelight and gains strategic importance as a source of often high-quality freshwater in the face of the impending water crisis world-wide, the need for rules of international law addressing groundwater management and protection becomes ever more compelling. It is perhaps no coincidence that the United Nations International Law Commission (ILC) has the topic "Shared Natural Resources", comprising groundwater, oil and gas, in its programme of work. In addition, a trend can be detected to increasingly address groundwater in international agreements, non-binding instruments and interstate compacts, from a resource management as well as an environmental perspective.

It is against this backdrop that FAO and UNESCO have joined forces and embarked on this publication project. It brings together a variety of binding and non-binding international law instruments that, in varying degrees and from different angles, deal with groundwater. Its aim is to report developments in international law and to contribute to detecting law in-the-making in this important field.

The publication was prepared by FAO in connection with the UNESCO projects on international waters "Internationally Shared Aquifer Resources Management" (ISARM) and "From Potential Cooperation to Cooperation Potential" (PC–CP).

Stefano Burchi, Senior Legal Officer, and Kerstin Mechlem, Legal Officer, Development Law Service, FAO, are responsible for the scope and structure of the publication, for the selection of legal materials and their arrangement.

Giuliano Pucci
Legal Counsel
FAO

András Szöllösi-Nagy
Deputy Assistant
Director-General for
Natural Resources
Secretary International
Hydrological Programme
(IHP)
UNESCO

LIST OF SELECTED ACRONYMS
AND ABBREVIATIONS

ASEAN	Association of Southeast Asian Nations
Doc.	Document
FAO	Food and Agriculture Organization of the United Nations
GEF	Global Environment Facility
ibid.	ibidem
ILA	International Law Association
ILM	International Legal Materials
IUCN	International Union for Conservation of Nature and Natural Resources
No.	Number
NSAS	Nubian Sandstone Aquifer System
OJ	Official Journal of the European Union
OSS	Observatoire du Sahara et du Sahel Sahara and Sahel Observatory
p.	page
para.	paragraph
(s)	signatory
SASS	Systhème Aquifère du Sahara Septentrional Northwestern Sahara Aquifer System
TIAS	Treaties and Other International Acts Series
UN	United Nations
UN/ECE	United Nations Economic Commission for Europe
UNTS	United Nations Treaty Series
UNESCO	United Nations Educational, Scientific and Cultural Organization
UN	United Nations
Vol.	Volume

I. INTRODUCTION

Scope

This publication contains a variety of international legal instruments on groundwater resources, both transboundary and domestic. The extent to which each instrument covers groundwater varies; some deal exclusively with this resource whereas others contain merely a passing reference to the subject.

Some instruments are binding, others are non-binding. Among the binding ones are global, multi- and bilateral international treaties and agreements, inter-state agreements of Australia and the United States of America and directives of the European Community. The non-binding legal instruments emanate from a variety of governmental and non-governmental sources. While some reflect binding law, others indicate law-in-the-making, or are pointers to the future direction of the international law and policy of groundwater resources.

A predecessor to the present collection is the book International Groundwater Law edited by Ludwik A. Teclaff and Albert E. Utton (London, Rome, New York: Oceana Publishers, Inc., 1981). The instruments included in that book have not been reproduced in this publication.

Arrangement of the Materials

The material included in this publication has been divided in four chapters. Chapter II covers all international agreements which deal exclusively with groundwater resources. Other than those featured in International Groundwater Law, by Ludwik A. Teclaff and Albert E. Utton, only three legal instruments – all multilateral – could be identified. Chapter III contains treaties which include provisions on groundwater within the larger scope of each instrument. These are set out according to their geographic scope from global to multilateral to bilateral. The multilateral instruments, in turn, have been subdivided by geographic scope into regional treaties and treaties concerning a specific river or lake basin. The bilateral treaties have been arranged in alphabetical order, by pairs of states parties. In all, twenty-four legal instruments can be found in this chapter. Chapter IV includes interstate agreements, i.e., legal instruments concluded between member states of a federal country, which either deal exclusively with groundwater or reflect attention to it within their broader scope. One of these was concluded between states of the United States of America, and five by states of Australia. Finally, Chapter V contains other legal instruments: two European Community directives and a proposal for a directive, as well as a selection of eleven non-binding instruments, including three by non-governmental organizations. The proposed European Community Directive on the Protection of Groundwater Against Pollution has exceptionally been included in this publication in view of its apparent relevance, notwithstanding its draft status at the time of going to print.

With the exception already indicated as to bilateral treaties, the legal instruments within each chapter and sub-chapter have been arranged in chronological order.

Presentation of Selected Instruments

The instruments which deal exclusively with a specific aquifer have been reproduced in full. With respect to all other instruments, only those parts which directly or indirectly address groundwater have been retained. The selection of relevant parts inevitably reflects a degree of judgment. In their choice the editors have drawn upon FAO expertise in hydro-geological and related sciences.

As a general rule, provisions concerning institutional arrangements, the settlement of disputes, final clauses, and other matters of a strictly procedural nature have been systematically omitted from this publication. Maps and annexes of highly technical content have not been reproduced either. Whenever entire articles, sections, annexes and maps have been left out, their headings have been retained marked as [ ], so that the reader would have an overview of the full scope of the relevant instrument. Where only part of an article is omitted, it is replaced by an ellipsis (…).

Parties and Entry into Force

The states parties to the Groundwater Agreements (chapter II), to the Bilateral Treaties (chapter III.iii), and to the Interstate Agreements (chapter IV) are indicated immediately before the title of the relevant legal instrument. In view of their large numbers, the states parties and/or signatories to Global Conventions (chapter III.i) and to Multilateral Treaties (chapter III.ii) are listed in a footnote. A distinction is made between states parties and signatories (the latter being identified with an (s)), whenever the information was available to the editors. If known, information on the entry into force of legally binding instruments is provided in a footnote.

Sources and References

FAOLEX, FAO's on-line database of domestic natural resources legislation and international freshwater treaties (http://faolex.fao.org/faolex/index. htm), the International Treaties & Compacts database hosted by Oregon State University (http://mgd.nacse.org/ cgi-bin/qml2.0/watertreaty/ irealJS.qml), other internet sources as well as published international legal materials, notably the United Nations Treaty Series (UNTS) and International Legal Materials (ILM), were used in the research phase of this project. Additional instruments have been obtained through the editors' informal network of resource persons.

Additional Information

The texts of the legal instruments reproduced here are faithful to the texts which have been retrieved from the referenced sources. Obvious spelling errors and other textual errors have not been corrected, but have been highlighted by the word [sic]. Footnotes indicated by an asterisk have been inserted by the editors and are not part of the original texts.

Disclaimer

For all the care and attention to detail the editors have invested in this publication, there can be no pretence of exhaustiveness or of definitiveness to it. Important legal instruments may have been missed in the search, errors of judgment may have been made in the selection of parts of any given legal instrument, or other mistakes may have crept in. The editors invite the readership to flag such errors and omissions to them, in view of a subsequent edition and update of this publication.

II.   GROUNDWATER AGREEMENTS

Chad - Egypt - Libya - Sudan

1.   **Programme for the Development of a Regional Strategy for the Utilisation of the Nubian Sandstone Aquifer System (NSAS) - Terms of Reference For the Monitoring and Exchange of Groundwater Information of the Nubian Sandstone Aquifer System [Tripoli, 5 October 2000]***

For sustainable utilisation of the Nubian Sandstone Aquifer System, consolidation of the existing data and information in such a usable accessible manner and the continuous update of knowledge in the Aquifer Systems should be maintained. In order to accomplish this objective and to assure the exchange and flow of information between the four countries sharing the NSAS. It is herewith, the four countries namely, Chad, Egypt, Libya and Sudan represented by their National Coordinators formulated and signed the following agreements;

Agreement No. 1 – Terms of Reference for the Monitoring and Exchange of Groundwater Information of the Nubian Sandstone Aquifer System [Tripoli, 5 October 2000]†

Consolidated data throughout the implementation of the "Programme for the Development of a Regional Strategy for the utilisation of the Nubian Sandstone Aquifer System" was achieved through a Regional Information System called the Nubian Aquifer Regional Information System (NARIS). This integrated Information System is conceived to fulfill the following tasks:

–   Storing and documenting the different data, covering all fields relevant to the Nubian Sandstone Aquifer System.

–   Processing, analysis and display of basic data.

---

* FAOLEX (FAO legal database online). Reprinted in: Centre for Environment & Development for the Arab Region and Europe (CEDARE), Regional Strategy for the Utilisation of the Nubian Sandstone Aquifer System, Volume IV, Appendix II, Cairo, 2001.
† Ibid.

–   Preparing the input parameters which are needed for the modeling at different scales and calibration of the groundwater model and comparison of the results of modeling with other data for planning and decision making.

–   Provide an easy link between the participating countries through a system ensuring the exchange and flow of information.

Therefore it is herewith agreed that the four countries namely; Chad, Egypt, Libya and Sudan share the data that was consolidated throughout the implementation of the Programme mentioned above and included in the Nubian Aquifer Regional Information System (NARIS) in addition to information on developmental aspects including socio-economic data, management of harsh environment, drilling experiences, meteorological data, .. etc. and also agreed to update this system as specified in the Agreement on Terms of Reference for Monitoring and Data Sharing.

The sharing of this information will be accomplished according to the setup specified below;

Internet Environment - Server and access through internet.

In this protocol the data will be stored on a server and accessed through internet by the four countries through web-based Oracle. A level of security is maintained in this technique, so that access is enabled only to the four countries.

Agreement No. 2 – Terms of Reference for Monitoring and Data Sharing [Tripoli, 5 October 2000]*

For sustainable development and proper management of the Nubian Sandstone Aquifer System, continuous monitoring of the aquifer should be maintained. In order to observe the regional behaviour of the NSAS, monitored parameters of the aquifer should be shared between the concerned countries.

Ibid.

Hence, it is herewith agreed between the four countries sharing the Nubian Sandstone Aquifer System, namely Chad, Egypt, Libya and Sudan, represented by their National Coordinators to monitor and share among them the following information:

– Yearly extraction in every extraction site, specifying geographical location and number of producing wells and springs in every site.

– Representative Electrical Conductivity measurements (EC), taken once a year in each extraction site, followed by a complete chemical analysis if drastic changes in salinity is [sic] observed.

– Water level measurements taken twice a year in the locations shown in the attached maps and tables. The proposed monitoring network is subject to changes upon the feedback of the National Coordinators of the concerned countries.

These measurements should be undertaken within the Nubian Aquifer System and the Post Nubian Aquifer System.

…

[Omitted: Proposed regional well monitoring network, Regional monitoring network in the Nubian Aquifer, Regional monitoring network in the Post Nubian Aquifer]

Algeria - Libya - Tunisia

2.   Establishment of a Consultation Mechanism for the Northwestern Sahara Aquifer System (SASS) [2002]*

…

---

*   Excerpts of the procès verbal (Minutes) of a meeting of representatives of Algeria, Libya and Tunisia held at the Headquarters of the Food and Agriculture Organization of the United Nations (FAO) in Rome, Italy, on 19 and 20 December 2002. The procès verbal was subsequently endorsed by Algeria on 6 January 2003, Tunisia on 15 February 2003 and Libya on 23 February 2003. The Minutes and the subsequent letters of endorsement signified an agreement to establish the Consultation Mechanism. The procès verbal is on file with the editors, in the English and French originals.

Consultation mechanism

…

A consensus has emerged on an *evolutionary approach* that, starting from a simple structure (phase 1), evolves into a more complex and autonomous structure charged with specific functions (phase 2).

[Omitted: Sketch of consultation mechanism - (phase 1)]

Features of consultation mechanism (phase 1)

The consultation mechanism presents the following features:

(i)   *Objective*

To coordinate, promote and facilitate the rational management of the NWSAS water resources.

(ii)   *Structure*

-   *a steering committee* composed of representatives of the national agencies in charge of water resources, acting as national focal points; the committee meets in ordinary session once a year, and in extraordinary session upon the request of one of the three states; sessions are held alternatively in each country; the committee's chairmanship is held by the representative of the host country.

-   *a coordination unit* directed by a coordinator designated by the OSS in consultation with the steering committee;

-   an *ad hoc scientific committee* for evaluation and scientific guidance, to be convened when the need arises.

(iii)   *Legal status*

The coordination unit is administered and hosted by the OSS.

(iv)   *Functions*

- to manage the tools developed under the SASS project (hydrogeologic data base and simulation model);

- to develop and follow-up a reference observation network;

- to process, analyze and validate data relating to the knowledge of the resource;

- to develop databases on socio-economic activities in the region, in relation to water uses;

- to develop and publish indicators on the resource and its uses in the three countries;

- to promote and facilitate the conduct of joint or coordinated studies and research by experts from the three countries;

- to formulate and implement training programmes;

- to update the NWSAS model on a regular basis;

- to devise and formulate proposals relating to the evolution and functioning of the consultation mechanism, and to its operationalization during phase 2.

(v)   *Financing*

Each state bears the operating costs of its own focal point. The functioning of the coordination unit is financed out of subventions and gifts granted to the OSS by the concerned states, cooperating countries, etc.

...

III. WATER RESOURCES AND ENVIRONMENTAL TREATIES CONTAINING PROVISIONS ON GROUNDWATER

i. Global Conventions

3. United Nations Convention to Combat Desertification in those Countries Experiencing Serious Drought and/or Desertification, particularly in Africa [Paris, 17 June 1994]*

The Parties to this Convention,

...

---

* 33 ILM 1328 (1994). Entry into force: 26 December 1996. Parties: Afghanistan, Albania, Algeria, Andorra, Angola, Antigua and Barbuda, Argentina, Armenia, Australia, Austria, Azerbaijan, Bahamas, Bahrain, Bangladesh, Barbados, Belarus, Belgium, Belize, Benin, Bhutan, Bolivia, Bosnia and Herzegovina, Botswana, Brazil, Brunei Darussalam, Bulgaria, Burkina Faso, Burundi, Cambodia, Cameroon, Canada, Cape Verde, Central African Republic, Chad, Chile, China, Colombia, Comoros, Congo, Cook Islands, Costa Rica, Côte d'Ivoire, Croatia, Cuba, Cyprus, Czech Republic, Democratic People's Republic of Korea, Democratic Republic of the Congo, Denmark, Djibouti, Dominica, Dominican Republic, Ecuador, Egypt, El Salvador, Equatorial Guinea, Eritrea, Ethiopia, European Community, Fiji, Finland, France, Gabon, Gambia, Georgia, Germany, Ghana, Greece, Grenada, Guatemala, Guinea, Guinea-Bissau, Guyana, Haiti, Honduras, Hungary, Iceland, India, Indonesia, Iran (Islamic Republic of), Ireland, Israel, Italy, Jamaica, Japan, Jordan, Kazakhstan, Kenya, Kiribati, Kuwait, Kyrgyzstan, Lao People's Democratic Republic, Latvia, Lebanon, Lesotho, Liberia, Libyan Arab Jamahiriya, Liechtenstein, Lithuania, Luxembourg, Madagascar, Malawi, Malaysia, Maldives, Mali, Malta, Marshall Islands, Mauritania, Mauritius, Mexico, Micronesia (Federated States of), Monaco, Mongolia, Morocco, Mozambique, Myanmar, Namibia, Nauru, Nepal, Netherlands, New Zealand, Nicaragua, Niger, Nigeria, Niue, Norway, Oman, Pakistan, Palau, Panama, Papua New Guinea, Paraguay, Peru, Philippines, Poland, Portugal, Qatar, Republic of Korea, Republic of Moldova, Romania, Russian Federation, Rwanda, Saint Kitts and Nevis, Saint Lucia, Saint Vincent and the Grenadines, Samoa, San Marino, Sao Tome and Principe, Saudi Arabia, Senegal, Seychelles, Sierra Leone, Singapore, Slovakia, Slovenia, Solomon Islands, Somalia, South Africa, Spain, Sri Lanka, Sudan, Suriname, Swaziland, Sweden, Switzerland, Syrian Arab Republic, Tajikistan, Thailand, The Former Yugoslav Republic of Macedonia, Timor-Leste, Togo, Tonga, Trinidad and Tobago, Tunisia, Turkey, Turkmenistan, Tuvalu, Uganda, Ukraine, United Arab Emirates, United Kingdom of Great Britain and Northern Ireland, United Republic of Tanzania, United States of America, Uruguay, Uzbekistan, Vanuatu, Venezuela, Viet Nam, Yemen, Zambia, Zimbabwe, as at 31 July 2004.

Reaffirming the Rio Declaration on Environment and Development which states, in its Principle 2, that States have, in accordance with the Charter of the United Nations and the principles of international law, the sovereign right to exploit their own resources pursuant to their own environmental and developmental policies, and the responsibility to ensure that activities within their jurisdiction or control do not cause damage to the environment of other States or of areas beyond the limits of national jurisdiction,

...

Have agreed as follows:

Part I - Introduction

Article 1 - Use of terms

For the purposes of this Convention:

(a) "desertification" means land degradation in arid, semi-arid and dry sub-humid areas resulting from various factors, including climatic variations and human activities;

(b) "combating desertification" includes activities which are part of the integrated development of land in arid, semi-arid and dry sub-humid areas for sustainable development which are aimed at:

    (i)   prevention and/or reduction of land degradation;

    (ii) rehabilitation of partly degraded land; and

    (iii) reclamation of desertified land;

(c) "drought" means the naturally occurring phenomenon that exists when precipitation has been significantly below normal recorded levels, causing serious hydrological imbalances that adversely affect land resource production systems;

(d) "mitigating the effects of drought" means activities related to the prediction of drought and intended to reduce the vulnerability of society and natural systems to drought as it relates to combating desertification;

(e)   "land" means the terrestrial bio-productive system that comprises soil, vegetation, other biota, and the ecological and hydrological processes that operate within the system;

(f)   "land degradation" means reduction or loss, in arid, semi-arid and dry sub-humid areas, of the biological or economic productivity and complexity of rainfed cropland, irrigated cropland, or range, pasture, forest and woodlands resulting from land uses or from a process or combination of processes, including processes arising from human activities and habitation patterns, such as:

    (i)   soil erosion caused by wind and/or water;

    (ii)   deterioration of the physical, chemical and biological or economic properties of soil; and

    (iii)   long-term loss of natural vegetation;

(g)   "arid, semi-arid and dry sub-humid areas" means areas, other than polar and sub-polar regions, in which the ratio of annual precipitation to potential evapotranspiration falls within the range from 0.05 to 0.65;

(h)   "affected areas" means arid, semi-arid and/or dry sub-humid areas affected or threatened by desertification;

(i)   "affected countries" means countries whose lands include, in whole or in part, affected areas;

(j)   "regional economic integration organization" means an organization constituted by sovereign States of a given region which has competence in respect of matters governed by this Convention and has been duly authorized, in accordance with its internal procedures, to sign, ratify, accept, approve or accede to this Convention;

(k)   "developed country Parties" means developed country Parties and regional economic integration organizations constituted by developed countries.

Article 2 - Objective

1.   The objective of this Convention is to combat desertification and
     mitigate the effects of drought in countries experiencing serious
     drought and/or desertification, particularly in Africa, through effective
     action at all levels, supported by international cooperation and
     partnership arrangements, in the framework of an integrated approach
     which is consistent with Agenda 21, with a view to contributing to the
     achievement of sustainable development in affected areas.

2.   Achieving this objective will involve long-term integrated strategies that
     focus simultaneously, in affected areas, on improved productivity of
     land, and the rehabilitation, conservation and sustainable management
     of land and water resources, leading to improved living conditions, in
     particular at the community level.

Article 3 - Principles

In order to achieve the objective of this Convention and to implement its
provisions, the Parties shall be guided, inter alia, by the following:

...

(c) the Parties should develop, in a spirit of partnership, cooperation
     among all levels of government, communities, non-governmental
     organizations and landholders to establish a better understanding of the
     nature and value of land and scarce water resources in affected areas
     and to work towards their sustainable use; and

...

Part II - General provisions

Article 4 - General obligations

...

2.   In pursuing the objective of this Convention, the Parties shall:

...

(d)   promote cooperation among affected country Parties in the fields of environmental protection and the conservation of land and water resources, as they relate to desertification and drought;

...

Article 5 - Obligations of affected country Parties

In addition to their obligations pursuant to article 4, affected country Parties undertake to:

(a)   give due priority to combating desertification and mitigating the effects of drought, and allocate adequate resources in accordance with their circumstances and capabilities;

(b)   establish strategies and priorities, within the framework of sustainable development plans and/or policies, to combat desertification and mitigate the effects of drought;

(c)   address the underlying causes of desertification and pay special attention to the socio-economic factors contributing to desertification processes;

(d)   promote awareness and facilitate the participation of local populations, particularly women and youth, with the support of non-governmental organizations, in efforts to combat desertification and mitigate the effects of drought; and

(e)   provide an enabling environment by strengthening, as appropriate, relevant existing legislation and, where they do not exist, enacting new laws and establishing long-term policies and action programmes.

[Omitted: Article 6 - Obligations of developed country Parties, Article 7 - Priority for Africa, Article 8 - Relationship with other conventions]

Part III - Action programmes, scientific and technical cooperation and supporting measures

Section 1: Action programmes

[Omitted: Article 9 - Basic approach; Article 10 - National action programmes, Article 11 - Subregional and regional action programmes, Article 12 - International cooperation, Article 13 - Support for the elaboration and implementation of action programmes, Article 14 - Coordination in the elaboration and implementation of action programmes]

Article 15 - Regional implementation Annexes

Elements for incorporation in action programmes shall be selected and adapted to the socio-economic, geographical and climatic factors applicable to affected country Parties or regions, as well as to their level of development. Guidelines for the preparation of action programmes and their exact focus and content for particular subregions and regions are set out in the regional implementation Annexes.

[Omitted: Section 2: Scientific and technical cooperation: Article 16 - Information collection, analysis and exchange, Article 17 - Research and development, Article 18 - Transfer, acquisition, adaptation and development of technology; Section 3: Supporting measures: Article 19 - Capacity building, education and public awareness, Article 20 - Financial resources, Article 21 - Financial mechanisms]

Part IV - Institutions
[Omitted: Article 22 - Conference of the Parties, Article 23 - Permanent Secretariat, Article 24 - Committee on Science and Technology, Article 25 - Networking of institutions, agencies and bodies]

Part V - Procedures

[Omitted: Article 26 - Communication of information, Article 27 - Measures to resolve questions on implementation, Article 28 - Settlement of disputes]

Article 29 - Status of Annexes

1.   Annexes form an integral part of the Convention and, unless expressly provided otherwise, a reference to the Convention also constitutes a reference to its Annexes.

2.   The Parties shall interpret the provisions of the Annexes in a manner that is in conformity with their rights and obligations under the articles of this Convention.

[Omitted: Article 30 - Amendments to the Convention, Article 31 - Adoption and amendment of Annexes, Article 32 - Right to vote]

Part VI - Final provisions

[Omitted: Article 33 - Signature, Article 34 - Ratification, acceptance, approval and accession, Article 35 - Interim arrangements, Article 36 - Entry into force, Article 37 - Reservations, Article 38 - Withdrawal, Article 39 - Depositary, Article 40 - Authentic texts]

...

[Omitted: Annex I - Regional implementation Annex for Africa, Annex II - Regional implementation Annex for Asia, Annex III - Regional implementation Annex for Latin America and the Caribbean]

Annex IV

Regional implementation Annex for the northern Mediterranean

Article 1 - Purpose

The purpose of this Annex is to provide guidelines and arrangements necessary for the effective implementation of the Convention in affected country Parties of the northern Mediterranean region in the light of its particular conditions.

Article 2 - Particular conditions of the northern Mediterranean region

The particular conditions of the northern Mediterranean region referred to in article 1 include:

(a)   semi-arid climatic conditions affecting large areas, seasonal droughts, very high rainfall variability and sudden and high- intensity rainfall;

(b)   poor and highly erodible soils, prone to develop surface crusts;

(c)   uneven relief with steep slopes and very diversified landscapes;

(d)   extensive forest coverage losses due to frequent wildfires;

(e)   crisis conditions in traditional agriculture with associated land abandonment and deterioration of soil and water conservation structures;

(f)   unsustainable exploitation of water resources leading to serious environmental damage, including chemical pollution, salinization and exhaustion of aquifers; and

(g)   concentration of economic activity in coastal areas as a result of urban growth, industrial activities, tourism and irrigated agriculture.

Article 3 - Strategic planning framework for sustainable development

1.   National action programmes shall be a central and integral part of the strategic planning framework for sustainable development of the affected country Parties of the northern Mediterranean.

2.   A consultative and participatory process, involving appropriate levels of government, local communities and non-governmental organizations, shall be undertaken to provide guidance on a strategy with flexible planning to allow maximum local participation, pursuant to article 10, paragraph 2 (f) of the Convention.

Article 4 - Obligation to prepare national action programmes and timetable

Affected country Parties of the northern Mediterranean region shall prepare national action programmes and, as appropriate, subregional, regional or joint action programmes. The preparation of such programmes shall be finalized as soon as practicable.

Article 5 - Preparation and implementation of national action programmes

In preparing and implementing national action programmes pursuant to articles 9 and 10 of the Convention, each affected country Party of the region shall, as appropriate:

(a) designate appropriate bodies responsible for the preparation, coordination and implementation of its programme;

(b) involve affected populations, including local communities, in the elaboration, coordination and implementation of the programme through a locally driven consultative process, with the cooperation of local authorities and relevant non-governmental organizations;

(c) survey the state of the environment in affected areas to assess the causes and consequences of desertification and to determine priority areas for action;

(d) evaluate, with the participation of affected populations, past and current programmes in order to design a strategy and elaborate activities in the action programme;

(e) prepare technical and financial programmes based on the information gained through the activities in subparagraphs (a) to (d); and

(f) develop and utilize procedures and benchmarks for monitoring and evaluating the implementation of the programme.

Article 6 - Content of national action programmes

Affected country Parties of the region may include, in their national action programmes, measures relating to:

(a) legislative, institutional and administrative areas;

(b) land use patterns, management of water resources, soil conservation, forestry, agricultural activities and pasture and range management;

(c) management and conservation of wildlife and other forms of biological diversity;

(d)   protection against forest fires;

(e)   promotion of alternative livelihoods; and

(f)   research, training and public awareness.

Article 7 - Subregional, regional and joint action programmes

1.   Affected country Parties of the region may, in accordance with article 11 of the Convention, prepare and implement subregional and/or regional action programmes in order to complement and increase the efficiency of national action programmes. Two or more affected country Parties of the region, may similarly agree to prepare a joint action programme between or among them.

2.   The provisions of articles 5 and 6 shall apply mutatis mutandis to the preparation and implementation of subregional, regional and joint action programmes. In addition, such programmes may include the conduct of research and development activities concerning selected ecosystems in affected areas.

3.   In preparing and implementing subregional, regional or joint action programmes, affected country Parties of the region shall, as appropriate:

(a)   identify, in cooperation with national institutions, national objectives relating to desertification which can better be met by such programmes and relevant activities which could be effectively carried out through them;

(b)   evaluate the operational capacities and activities of relevant regional, subregional and national institutions; and

(c)   assess existing programmes relating to desertification among Parties of the region and their relationship with national action programmes.

Article 8 - Coordination of subregional, regional and joint action programmes

Affected country Parties preparing a subregional, regional or joint action programme may establish a coordination committee composed of representatives of each affected country Party concerned to review progress in combating desertification, harmonize national action programmes, make recommendations at the various stages of preparation and implementation of the subregional, regional or joint action programme, and act as a focal point for the promotion and coordination of technical cooperation pursuant to articles 16 to 19 of the Convention.

Article 9 - Non-eligibility for financial assistance

In implementing national, subregional, regional and joint action programmes, affected developed country Parties of the region are not eligible to receive financial assistance under this Convention.

Article 10 - Coordination with other subregions and regions

Subregional, regional and joint action programmes in the northern Mediterranean region may be prepared and implemented in collaboration with those of other subregions or regions, particularly with those of the subregion of northern Africa.

4.　United Nations Convention on the Law of the Non-navigational Uses of International Watercourses [New York, 21 May 1997]*

The Parties to the present Convention,

Conscious of the importance of international watercourses and the non-navigational uses thereof in many regions of the world,

Having in mind Article 13, paragraph 1 (a), of the Charter of the United Nations, which provides that the General Assembly shall initiate studies and make recommendations for the purpose of encouraging the progressive development of international law and its codification,

Considering that successful codification and progressive development of rules of international law regarding non-navigational uses of international

---

* 36 ILM 710 (1997). Not yet in force. Parties and signatories (s): Côte d'Ivoire (s), Finland, Germany (s), Hungary, Iraq, Jordan, Lebanon, Luxembourg (s), Namibia, Netherlands, Norway, Paraguay (s), Portugal (s), Qatar, South Africa, Sweden, Syrian Arab Republic, Tunisia (s), Venezuela (s), Yemen (s), as at 31 July 2004.

watercourses would assist in promoting and implementing the purposes and principles set forth in Articles 1 and 2 of the Charter of the United Nations,

Taking into account the problems affecting many international watercourses resulting from, among other things, increasing demands and pollution,

Expressing the conviction that a framework convention will ensure the utilization, development, conservation, management and protection of international watercourses and the promotion of the optimal and sustainable utilization thereof for present and future generations,

Affirming the importance of international cooperation and good-neighbourliness in this field,

Aware of the special situation and needs of developing countries, Recalling the principles and recommendations adopted by the United Nations Conference on Environment and Development of 1992 in the Rio Declaration and Agenda 21,

Recalling also the existing bilateral and multilateral agreements regarding the non-navigational uses of international watercourses,

...

Have agreed as follows:

Part I - Introduction

Article 1 - Scope of the present Convention

1.   The present Convention applies to uses of international watercourses and of their waters for purposes other than navigation and to measures of protection, preservation and management related to the uses of those watercourses and their waters.

2.   The uses of international watercourses for navigation is not within the scope of the present Convention except insofar as other uses affect navigation or are affected by navigation.

Article 2 - Use of terms

For the purposes of the present Convention:

(a) "Watercourse" means a system of surface waters and groundwaters constituting by virtue of their physical relationship a unitary whole and normally flowing into a common terminus;

(b) "International watercourse" means a watercourse, parts of which are situated in different States;

(c) "Watercourse State" means a State Party to the present Convention in whose territory part of an international watercourse is situated, or a Party that is a regional economic integration organization, in the territory of one or more of whose Member States part of an international watercourse is situated;

(d) "Regional economic integration organization" means an organization constituted by sovereign States of a given region, to which its member States have transferred competence in respect of matters governed by this Convention and which has been duly authorized in accordance with its internal procedures, to sign, ratify, accept, approve or accede to it.

Article 3 - Watercourse agreements

1. In the absence of an agreement to the contrary, nothing in the present Convention shall affect the rights or obligations of a watercourse State arising from agreements in force for it on the date on which it became a party to the present Convention.

2. Notwithstanding the provisions of paragraph 1, parties to agreements referred to in paragraph 1 may, where necessary, consider harmonizing such agreements with the basic principles of the present Convention.

3. Watercourse States may enter into one or more agreements, hereinafter referred to as "watercourse agreements", which apply and adjust the provisions of the present Convention to the characteristics and uses of a particular international watercourse or part thereof.

4. Where a watercourse agreement is concluded between two or more watercourse States, it shall define the waters to which it applies. Such

an agreement may be entered into with respect to an entire international watercourse or any part thereof or a particular project, programme or use except insofar as the agreement adversely affects, to a significant extent, the use by one or more other watercourse States of the waters of the watercourse, without their express consent.

5.   Where a watercourse State considers that adjustment and application of the provisions of the present Convention is required because of the characteristics and uses of a particular international watercourse, watercourse States shall consult with a view to negotiating in good faith for the purpose of concluding a watercourse agreement or agreements.

Where some but not all watercourse States to a particular international watercourse are parties to an agreement, nothing in such agreement shall affect the rights or obligations under the present Convention of watercourse States that are not parties to such an agreement.

Article 4 - Parties to watercourse agreements

1.   Every watercourse State is entitled to participate in the negotiation of and to become a party to any watercourse agreement that applies to the entire international watercourse, as well as to participate in any relevant consultations.

2.   A watercourse State whose use of an international watercourse may be affected to a significant extent by the implementation of a proposed watercourse agreement that applies only to a part of the watercourse or to a particular project, programme or use is entitled to participate in consultations on such an agreement and, where appropriate, in the negotiation thereof in good faith with a view to becoming a party thereto, to the extent that its use is thereby affected.

Part II - General principles

Article 5 - Equitable and reasonable utilization and participation

1.   Watercourse States shall in their respective territories utilize an international watercourse in an equitable and reasonable manner. In particular, an international watercourse shall be used and developed by watercourse States with a view to attaining optimal and sustainable

utilization thereof and benefits therefrom, taking into account the interests of the watercourse States concerned, consistent with adequate protection of the watercourse.

2.   Watercourse States shall participate in the use, development and protection of an international watercourse in an equitable and reasonable manner. Such participation includes both the right to utilize the watercourse and the duty to cooperate in the protection and development thereof, as provided in the present Convention.

Article 6 - Factors relevant to equitable and reasonable utilization

1.   Utilization of an international watercourse in an equitable and reasonable manner within the meaning of article 5 requires taking into account all relevant factors and circumstances, including:

(a)   Geographic, hydrographic, hydrological, climatic, ecological and other factors of a natural character;

(b)   The social and economic needs of the watercourse States concerned;

(c)   The population dependent on the watercourse in each watercourse State;

(d)   The effects of the use or uses of the watercourses in one watercourse State on other watercourse States;

(e)   Existing and potential uses of the watercourse;

(f)   Conservation, protection, development and economy of use of the water resources of the watercourse and the costs of measures taken to that effect;

(g)   The availability of alternatives, of comparable value, to a particular planned or existing use.

2.   In the application of article 5 or paragraph 1 of this article, watercourse States concerned shall, when the need arises, enter into consultations in a spirit of cooperation.

3. The weight to be given to each factor is to be determined by its importance in comparison with that of other relevant factors. In determining what is a reasonable and equitable use, all relevant factors are to be considered together and a conclusion reached on the basis of the whole.

Article 7 - Obligation not to cause significant harm

1. Watercourse States shall, in utilizing an international watercourse in their territories, take all appropriate measures to prevent the causing of significant harm to other watercourse States.

2. Where significant harm nevertheless is caused to another watercourse State, the States whose use causes such harm shall, in the absence of agreement to such use, take all appropriate measures, having due regard for the provisions of articles 5 and 6, in consultation with the affected State, to eliminate or mitigate such harm and, where appropriate, to discuss the question of compensation.

Article 8 - General obligation to cooperate

1. Watercourse States shall cooperate on the basis of sovereign equality, territorial integrity, mutual benefit and good faith in order to attain optimal utilization and adequate protection of an international watercourse.

2. In determining the manner of such cooperation, watercourse States may consider the establishment of joint mechanisms or commissions, as deemed necessary by them, to facilitate cooperation on relevant measures and procedures in the light of experience gained through cooperation in existing joint mechanisms and commissions in various regions.

Article 9 - Regular exchange of data and information

1. Pursuant to article 8, watercourse States shall on a regular basis exchange readily available data and information on the condition of the watercourse, in particular that of a hydrological, meteorological, hydrogeological and ecological nature and related to the water quality as well as related forecasts.

2.   If a watercourse State is requested by another watercourse State to provide data or information that is not readily available, it shall employ its best efforts to comply with the request but may condition its compliance upon payment by the requesting State of the reasonable costs of collecting and, where appropriate, processing such data or information.

3.   Watercourse States shall employ their best efforts to collect and, where appropriate, to process data and information in a manner which facilitates its utilization by the other watercourse States to which it is communicated.

Article 10 - Relationship between different kinds of uses

1.   In the absence of agreement or custom to the contrary, no use of an international watercourse enjoys inherent priority over other uses.

2.   In the event of a conflict between uses of an international watercourse, it shall be resolved with reference to articles 5 to 7, with special regard being given to the requirements of vital human needs.

Part III - Planned measures

Article 11 - Information concerning planned measures

Watercourse States shall exchange information and consult each other and, if necessary, negotiate on the possible effects of planned measures on the condition of an international watercourse.

Article 12 - Notification concerning planned measures with possible adverse effects

Before a watercourse State implements or permits the implementation of planned measures which may have a significant adverse effect upon other watercourse States, it shall provide those States with timely notification thereof. Such notification shall be accompanied by available technical data and information, including the results of any environmental impact assessment, in order to enable the notified States to evaluate the possible effects of the planned measures.

Article 13 - Period for reply to notification

Unless otherwise agreed:

(a)   A watercourse State providing a notification under article 12 shall allow the notified States a period of six months within which to study and evaluate the possible effects of the planned measures and to communicate the findings to it;

(b)   This period shall, at the request of a notified State for which the evaluation of the planned measures poses special difficulty, be extended for a period of six months.

Article 14 - Obligations of the notifying State during the period for reply

During the period referred to in article 13, the notifying State:

(a)   Shall cooperate with the notified States by providing them, on request, with any additional data and information that is available and necessary for an accurate evaluation; and

(b)   Shall not implement or permit the implementation of the planned measures without the consent of the notified States.

Article 15 - Reply to notification

The notified States shall communicate their findings to the notifying State as early as possible within the period applicable pursuant to article 13. If a notified State finds that implementation of the planned measures would be inconsistent with the provisions of articles 5 or 7, it shall attach to its finding a documented explanation setting forth the reasons for the finding.

Article 16 - Absence of reply to notification

1.   If, within the period applicable pursuant to article 13, the notifying State receives no communication under article 15, it may, subject to its obligations under articles 5 and 7, proceed with the implementation of the planned measures, in accordance with the notification and any other data and information provided to the notified States.

2. Any claim to compensation by a notified State which has failed to reply within the period applicable pursuant to article 13 may be offset by the costs incurred by the notifying State for action undertaken after the expiration of the time for a reply which would not have been undertaken if the notified State had objected within that period.

Article 17 - Consultations and negotiations concerning planned measures

1. If a communication is made under article 15 that implementation of the planned measures would be inconsistent with the provisions of articles 5 or 7, the notifying State and the State making the communication shall enter into consultations and, if necessary, negotiations with a view to arriving at an equitable resolution of the situation.

2. The consultations and negotiations shall be conducted on the basis that each State must in good faith pay reasonable regard to the rights and legitimate interests of the other State.

3. During the course of the consultations and negotiations, the notifying State shall, if so requested by the notified State at the time it makes the communication, refrain from implementing or permitting the implementation of the planned measures for a period of six months unless otherwise agreed.

Article 18 - Procedures in the absence of notification

1. If a watercourse State has reasonable grounds to believe that another watercourse State is planning measures that may have a significant adverse effect upon it, the former State may request the latter to apply the provisions of article 12. The request shall be accompanied by a documented explanation setting forth its grounds.

2. In the event that the State planning the measures nevertheless finds that it is not under an obligation to provide a notification under article 12, it shall so inform the other State, providing a documented explanation setting forth the reasons for such finding. If this finding does not satisfy the other State, the two States shall, at the request of that other State, promptly enter into consultations and negotiations in the manner indicated in paragraphs 1 and 2 of article 17.

3.   During the course of the consultations and negotiations, the State
       planning the measures shall, if so requested by the other State at the
       time it requests the initiation of consultations and negotiations, refrain
       from implementing or permitting the implementation of those
       measures for a period of six months unless otherwise agreed.

Article 19 - Urgent implementation of planned measures

1.   In the event that the implementation of planned measures is of the
       utmost urgency in order to protect public health, public safety or other
       equally important interests, the State planning the measures may, subject
       to articles 5 and 7, immediately proceed to implementation, notwith-
       standing the provisions of article 14 and paragraph 3 of article 17.

2.   In such case, a formal declaration of the urgency of the measures shall
       be communicated without delay to the other watercourse States
       referred to in article 12 together with the relevant data and information.

3.   The State planning the measures shall, at the request of any of the
       States referred to in paragraph 2, promptly enter into consultations and
       negotiations with it in the manner indicated in paragraphs 1 and 2 of
       article 17.

Part IV - Protection, preservation and management

Article 20 - Protection and preservation of ecosystems

Watercourse States shall, individually and, where appropriate, jointly, protect
and preserve the ecosystems of international watercourses.

Article 21 - Prevention, reduction and control of pollution

1.   For the purpose of this article, "pollution of an international
       watercourse" means any detrimental alteration in the composition or
       quality of the waters of an international watercourse which results
       directly or indirectly from human conduct.

2.   Watercourse States shall, individually and, where appropriate, jointly,
       prevent, reduce and control the pollution of an international
       watercourse that may cause significant harm to other watercourse States
       or to their environment, including harm to human health or safety, to

the use of the waters for any beneficial purpose or to the living resources of the watercourse. Watercourse States shall take steps to harmonize their policies in this connection.

3.   Watercourse States shall, at the request of any of them, consult with a view to arriving at mutually agreeable measures and methods to prevent, reduce and control pollution of an international watercourse, such as:

(a)   Setting joint water quality objectives and criteria;

(b)   Establishing techniques and practices to address pollution from point and non-point sources;

(c)   Establishing lists of substances the introduction of which into the waters of an international watercourse is to be prohibited, limited, investigated or monitored.

Article 22 - Introduction of alien or new species

Watercourse States shall take all measures necessary to prevent the introduction of species, alien or new, into an international watercourse which may have effects detrimental to the ecosystem of the watercourse resulting in significant harm to other watercourse States.

Article 23 - Protection and preservation of the marine environment

Watercourse States shall, individually and, where appropriate, in cooperation with other States, take all measures with respect to an international watercourse that are necessary to protect and preserve the marine environment, including estuaries, taking into account generally accepted international rules and standards.

Article 24 - Management

1.   Watercourse States shall, at the request of any of them, enter into consultations concerning the management of an international watercourse, which may include the establishment of a joint management mechanism.

2.   For the purposes of this article, "management" refers, in particular, to:

(a)   Planning the sustainable development of an international watercourse and providing for the implementation of any plans adopted; and

(b)   Otherwise promoting the rational and optimal utilization, protection and control of the watercourse.

Article 25 - Regulation

1.   Watercourse States shall cooperate, where appropriate, to respond to needs or opportunities for regulation of the flow of the waters of an international watercourse.

2.   Unless otherwise agreed, watercourse States shall participate on an equitable basis in the construction and maintenance or defrayal of the costs of such regulation works as they may have agreed to undertake.

3.   For the purposes of this article, "regulation" means the use of hydraulic works or any other continuing measure to alter, vary or otherwise control the flow of the waters of an international watercourse.

Article 26 - Installations

1.   Watercourse States shall, within their respective territories, employ their best efforts to maintain and protect installations, facilities and other works related to an international watercourse.

2.   Watercourse States shall, at the request of any of them which has reasonable grounds to believe that it may suffer significant adverse effects, enter into consultations with regard to:

(a)   The safe operation and maintenance of installations, facilities or other works related to an international watercourse; and

(b)   The protection of installations, facilities or other works from wilful or negligent acts or the forces of nature.

Part V - Harmful conditions and emergency situations

Article 27 - Prevention and mitigation of harmful conditions

Watercourse States shall, individually and, where appropriate, jointly, take all appropriate measures to prevent or mitigate conditions related to an international watercourse that may be harmful to other watercourse States, whether resulting from natural causes or human conduct, such as flood or ice conditions, water-borne diseases, siltation, erosion, salt-water intrusion, drought or desertification.

Article 28 - Emergency situations

1. For the purposes of this article, "emergency" means a situation that causes, or poses an imminent threat of causing, serious harm to watercourse States or other States and that results suddenly from natural causes, such as floods, the breaking up of ice, landslides or earthquakes, or from human conduct, such as industrial accidents.

2. A watercourse State shall, without delay and by the most expeditious means available, notify other potentially affected States and competent international organizations of any emergency originating within its territory.

3. A watercourse State within whose territory an emergency originates shall, in cooperation with potentially affected States and, where appropriate, competent international organizations, immediately take all practicable measures necessitated by the circumstances to prevent, mitigate and eliminate harmful effects of the emergency.

4. When necessary, watercourse States shall jointly develop contingency plans for responding to emergencies, in cooperation, where appropriate, with other potentially affected States and competent international organizations.

Part VI - Miscellaneous provisions

Article 29 - International watercourses and installations in time of armed conflict

International watercourses and related installations, facilities and other works shall enjoy the protection accorded by the principles and rules of international law applicable in international and non-international armed conflict and shall not be used in violation of those principles and rules.

Article 30 - Indirect procedures

In cases where there are serious obstacles to direct contacts between watercourse States, the States concerned shall fulfil their obligations of cooperation provided for in the present Convention, including exchange of data and information, notification, communication, consultations and negotiations, through any indirect procedure accepted by them.

Article 31 - Data and information vital to national defence or security

Nothing in the present Convention obliges a watercourse State to provide data or information vital to its national defence or security. Nevertheless, that State shall cooperate in good faith with the other watercourse States with a view to providing as much information as possible under the circumstances.

Article 32 - Non-discrimination

Unless the watercourse States concerned have agreed otherwise for the protection of the interests of persons, natural or juridical, who have suffered or are under a serious threat of suffering significant transboundary harm as a result of activities related to an international watercourse, a watercourse State shall not discriminate on the basis of nationality or residence or place where the injury occurred, in granting to such persons, in accordance with its legal system, access to judicial or other procedures, or a right to claim compensation or other relief in respect of significant harm caused by such activities carried on in its territory.

Article 33 - Settlement of disputes

1.   In the event of a dispute between two or more Parties concerning the interpretation or application of the present Convention, the Parties

concerned shall, in the absence of an applicable agreement between them, seek a settlement of the dispute by peaceful means in accordance with the following provisions.

2. If the Parties concerned cannot reach agreement by negotiation requested by one of them, they may jointly seek the good offices of, or request mediation or conciliation by, a third party, or make use, as appropriate, of any joint watercourse institutions that may have been established by them or agree to submit the dispute to arbitration or to the International Court of Justice.

3. Subject to the operation of paragraph 10, if after six months from the time of the request for negotiations referred to in paragraph 2, the Parties concerned have not been able to settle their dispute through negotiation or any other means referred to in paragraph 2, the dispute shall be submitted, at the request of any of the parties to the dispute, to impartial fact-finding in accordance with paragraphs 4 to 9, unless the Parties otherwise agree.

4. A Fact-finding Commission shall be established, composed of one member nominated by each Party concerned and in addition a member not having the nationality of any of the Parties concerned chosen by the nominated members who shall serve as Chairman.

5. If the members nominated by the Parties are unable to agree on a Chairman within three months of the request for the establishment of the Commission, any Party concerned may request the Secretary-General of the United Nations to appoint the Chairman who shall not have the nationality of any of the parties to the dispute or of any riparian State of the watercourse concerned. If one of the Parties fails to nominate a member within three months of the initial request pursuant to paragraph 3, any other Party concerned may request the Secretary-General of the United Nations to appoint a person who shall not have the nationality of any of the parties to the dispute or of any riparian State of the watercourse concerned. The person so appointed shall constitute a single-member Commission.

6. The Commission shall determine its own procedure.

7. The Parties concerned have the obligation to provide the Commission with such information as it may require and, on request, to permit the

Commission to have access to their respective territory and to inspect any facilities, plant, equipment, construction or natural feature relevant for the purpose of its inquiry.

8.   The Commission shall adopt its report by a majority vote, unless it is a single-member Commission, and shall submit that report to the Parties concerned setting forth its findings and the reasons therefor and such recommendations as it deems appropriate for an equitable solution of the dispute, which the Parties concerned shall consider in good faith.

9.   The expenses of the Commission shall be borne equally by the Parties concerned.

10.   When ratifying, accepting, approving or acceding to the present Convention, or at any time thereafter, a Party which is not a regional economic integration organization may declare in a written instrument submitted to the Depositary that, in respect of any dispute not resolved in accordance with paragraph 2, it recognizes as compulsory ipso facto and without special agreement in relation to any Party accepting the same obligation:

(a)   Submission of the dispute to the International Court of Justice; and/or

(b)   Arbitration by an arbitral tribunal established and operating, unless the parties to the dispute otherwise agreed, in accordance with the procedure laid down in the annex to the present Convention.

A Party which is a regional economic integration organization may make a declaration with like effect in relation to arbitration in accordance with subparagraph (b).

Part VII - Final clauses

[Omitted: Article 34 - Signature, Article 35 - Ratification, acceptance, approval or accession]

Article 36 - Entry into force

1.   The present Convention shall enter into force on the ninetieth day following the date of deposit of the thirty-fifth instrument of

ratification, acceptance, approval or accession with the Secretary-General of the United Nations.

2.   For each State or regional economic integration organization that ratifies, accepts or approves the Convention or accedes thereto after the deposit of the thirty-fifth instrument of ratification, acceptance, approval or accession, the Convention shall enter into force on the ninetieth day after the deposit by such State or regional economic integration organization of its instrument of ratification, acceptance, approval or accession.

3.   For the purposes of paragraphs 1 and 2, any instrument deposited by a regional economic integration organization shall not be counted as additional to those deposited by States.

[Omitted: Article 37 - Authentic texts, Annex - Arbitration]

ii.   Multilateral Treaties

a.   Regional Treaties

5.   ASEAN Agreement on the Conservation of Nature and Natural Resources [Kuala Lumpur, 9 July 1985]*

[The Contracting Parties]

...

Recognizing the importance of natural resources for present and future generations;

Conscious of their ever-growing value from a scientific, cultural, social and economic point of view;

---

* Reprinted in: Burhenne, Wolfgang E., (ed.), IUCN Environmental Law Centre/FUST Treaty Series - International Environment Law: Multilateral Treaties, Volume V, p. 985:51, Berlin, 1985. Not yet in force. Parties and/or signatories: Negara Brunei Darussalam, Indonesia, Malaysia, Philippines, Singapore, Thailand.

Conscious also that the interrelationship between conservation and socio-economic development implies both that conservation is necessary to ensure sustainability of development, and that socio-economic development is necessary for the achievement of conservation on a lasting basis;

Recognizing the interdependence of living resources, between them and with other natural resources, within ecosystems of which they are part;

Wishing to undertake individual and joint action for the conservation and management of their living resources and the other natural elements on which they depend;

Recognizing that international co-operation is essential to attain many of these goals;

Convinced that an essential means to achieve such concerted action is the conclusion and implementation of an Agreement;

Have agreed as follows:

Chapter I - Conservation and development

Article 1 - Fundamental principle

1. The Contracting Parties, within the framework of their respective national laws, undertake to adopt singly, or where necessary and appropriate through concerted action, the measures necessary to maintain essential ecological processes and life-support systems, to preserve genetic diversity, and to ensure the sustainable utilization of harvested natural resources under their jurisdiction in accordance with scientific principles and with a view to attaining the goal of sustainable development.

2. To this end they shall develop national conservation strategies, and shall co-ordinate such strategies within the framework of a conservation strategy for the Region.

Article 2 - Development planning

1. The Contracting Parties shall take all necessary measures, within the framework of their respective national laws, to ensure that conservation

and management of natural resources are treated as an integral part of development planning at all stages and at all levels.

2.   To that effect they shall, in the formulation of all development plans, give as full consideration to ecological factors as to economic and social ones.

3.   The Contracting Parties shall, where necessary, take appropriate action with a view to conserving and managing natural resources of significant importance for two or several Contracting Parties.

Chapter II - Conservation of species and ecosystems

[Omitted: Article 3 - Species - Genetic diversity, Article 4 - Species - Sustainable use, Article 5 - Species - Endangered and endemic]

Article 6 - Vegetation cover and forest resources

...

(e)   designate areas whose primary function shall be the maintenance of soil quality in the catchment considered and the regulation of the quantity and quality of the water delivered from it;

...

Article 7 - Soil

1.   The Contracting Parties shall, in view of the role of soil in the functioning of natural ecosystems, take measures, wherever possible towards soil conservation, improvement and rehabilitation; they shall, in particular, endeavour to take steps to prevent soil erosion and other forms of degradation, and promote measures which safeguard the processes of organic decomposition and thereby its continuing fertility.

2.   To that effect, they shall, in particular, endeavour to:

(a)   establish land use policies aimed at avoiding losses of vegetation cover, substantial soil losses, and damages to the structure of the soil;

(b)   take all necessary measures to control erosion, especially as it may affect coastal or freshwater ecosystems, lead to siltation of downstream areas such as lakes or vulnerable ecosystems such as coral reefs, or damage critical habitats, in particular that of endangered or endemic species;

(c)   take appropriate measures to rehabilitate eroded or degraded soils including rehabilitation of soil affected by mineral exploitation.

Article 8 - Water

1.   The Contracting Parties shall, in view of the role of water in the functioning of natural ecosystems, take all appropriate measures towards the conservation of their underground and surface water resources.

2.   They shall, to that effect, in particular, endeavour to:

(a)   undertake and promote the necessary hydrological research especially with a view to ascertaining the characteristics of each watershed;

(b)   regulate and control water utilization with a view to achieving sufficient and continuous supply of water for, inter alia, the maintenance of natural life supporting systems and aquatic fauna and flora;

(c)   when planning and carrying out water resource development projects take fully into account possible effects of such projects on natural processes or on other renewable natural resources and prevent or minimize such effects.

[Omitted: Article 9 - Air]

Chapter III - Conservation of ecological processes

Article 10 - Environmental degradation

The Contracting Parties, with a view to maintaining the proper functioning of ecological processes, undertake, wherever possible, to prevent, reduce and control degradation of the natural environment and, to this end, shall endeavour to undertake, in addition to specific measures referred to in the following article:

(a)   to promote environmentally sound agricultural practice by, inter alia, controlling the application of pesticides, fertilizers and other chemical products for agricultural use, and by ensuring that agricultural development schemes, in particular for wetland drainage or forest clearance, pay due regard to the need to protect critical habitats as well as endangered and economically important species;

(b) to promote pollution control and the development of environmentally sound industrial processes and products;

(c) to promote adequate economic or fiscal incentives for the purposes of sub-paragraphs (a) and (b) above;

(d) as far as possible to consider the originator of the activity which may lead to environmental degradation responsible for its prevention, reduction and control as well as, wherever possible, for rehabilitation and remedial measures required;

(e) to take into consideration, when authorizing activities likely to affect the natural environment, the foreseeable interactions between the new activities proposed and those already taking place in the same area, and the result of such interactions on the air, waters and soils of the area;

(f) to pay particular attention to the regulation of activities which may have adverse effects on processes which are ecologically essential or on areas which are particularly important or sensitive from an ecological point of view, such as the breeding and feeding grounds of harvested species.

Article 11 - Pollution

The Contracting Parties, recognizing the adverse effect that polluting discharges or emissions may have on natural processes and the functioning of natural ecosystems as well as on each of the individual ecosystem components, especially animal and plants species, shall endeavour to prevent, reduce and control such discharges, emissions or applications in particular by:

(a) submitting activities likely to cause pollution of the air, soil, freshwater, or the marine environment, to controls which shall take into consideration both the cumulative effects of the pollutants concerned and the self-purificating aptitude of the recipient natural environment;

(b) making such controls conditional on, inter alia, appropriate treatment of polluting emissions; and

(c)   establishing national environmental quality monitoring programmes,
       particular attention being paid to the effects of pollution on natural
       ecosystems, and co-operation in such programmes for the Region as a
       whole.

Chapter IV - Environmental planning measures

Article 12 - Land use planning

1.   The Contracting Parties shall, wherever possible in the implementation
     of their development planning, give particular attention to the national
     allocation of land usage. They shall endeavour to take the necessary
     measures to ensure the integration of natural resource conservation into
     the land use planning process and shall, in the preparation and
     implementation of specific land use plans at all levels, give as full
     consideration as possible to ecological factors as to economic and social
     ones. In order to achieve optimum sustainable land use, they undertake
     to base their land use plans as far as possible on the ecological capacity
     of the land.

2.   The Contracting Parties shall, in carrying out the provisions of
     paragraph 1 above, particularly consider the importance of retaining the
     naturally high productivity of areas such as coastal zones and wetlands.

3.   They shall, where appropriate, co-ordinate their land use planning with
     a view to conserving and managing natural resources of significant
     importance for two or several Contracting Parties.

Article 13 - Protected areas

1.   The Contracting Parties shall as appropriate establish, in areas under
     their jurisdiction, terrestrial, freshwater, coastal or marine protection
     areas for the purpose of safeguarding:

     -    the ecological and biological processes essential to the functioning
          of the ecosystems of the Region;

     -    representative samples of all types of ecosystem of the Region;

     -    satisfactory population levels for the largest possible number of
          species of fauna and flora belonging to those ecosystems;

- areas of particular importance because of their scientific, educational, aesthetic, or cultural interest;

and taking into account their importance in particular as:

- the natural habitat of species of fauna and flora, particularly rare or endangered or endemic species;

- zones necessary for the maintenance of exploitable stocks of economically important species;

- pools of genetic material and safe refuges for species, especially endangered ones;

- sites of ecological, aesthetic or cultural interest;

- reference sources for scientific research;

- areas for environmental education.

They shall, in particular, take all measures possible in their power to preserve those areas which are of an exceptional character and are peculiar to their country or the Region as well as those which constitute the critical habitats of endangered or rare species, of species that are endemic to a small area and of species that migrate between countries of Contracting Parties.

2. Protected areas established pursuant to this Agreement shall be regulated and managed in such a way as to further the objectives for the purpose of which they have been created. Contracting Parties shall, wherever possible, prohibit within such protected areas activities which are inconsistent with such objectives.

3. Protected areas shall include:

(a) National Parks:

    (i) This expression denotes natural areas that are sufficiently large to allow for ecological self-regulation of one or several ecosystems, and which have not been substantially altered by human occupation or exploitation.

(ii)   National Parks shall be placed under public control, their boundaries shall not be altered nor shall any portion of any National Park be alienated except by the highest competent authority.

(iii) National Parks shall be dedicated to conservation and to scientific, educational and recreational uses and the common welfare of the people.

(b)   Reserves:

(i)   This expression denotes areas set aside for the purpose of preserving a specific ecosystem, the critical habitat of certain species of fauna or flora, a water catchment area or for any other specific purpose relating to the conservation of natural resources or objects or areas of scientific, aesthetic cultural, educational or recreational interest.

(ii)   After reserves have been established their boundaries shall not be altered nor shall any portion of such reserves be alienated except by the authority establishing them or by higher authority.

(iii) Reserves shall be dedicated to the purposes for which they have been created and, in the light of the national interests of the Contracting Parties, any activity inconsistent with such purposes shall be prohibited.

4.   Contracting Parties shall, in respect of any protected area established pursuant to this Agreement:

(a)   prepare a management plan and manage the area on the basis of this plan;

(b)   establish, wherever appropriate, terrestrial or aquatic buffer zones that shall be located around protected areas and which, in the case of marine areas, may include coastal land areas or watersheds of rivers flowing into the protected area; in such buffer zones all activities that may have harmful consequences on the ecosystems that such areas purport to protect shall be prohibited or regulated and activities which are consistent with the purpose of the protected area shall be promoted.

5.   Contracting Parties shall, in respect of any protected area established pursuant to this Agreement, endeavour to:

(a)   prohibit the introduction of exotic animal or plant species;

(b)   prohibit the use or release of toxic substances or pollutants which could cause disturbance or damage to protected ecosystems or to the species they contain;

(c)   to the maximum extent possible, prohibit or control any activity exercised outside protected areas when such an activity is likely to cause disturbance or damage to the ecosystems or species that such protected areas purport to protect.

6.   Contracting Parties shall co-operate in the development of principles, objectives, criteria and guidelines for the selection, establishment and management of protected areas in the Region with a view to establishing a co-ordinated network of protected areas throughout the Region, giving particular attention to those of regional importance. An Appendix containing such principles, objectives, criteria and guidelines shall be drawn up in the light of the best scientific evidence as adapted to the conservation requirements of the Region and shall be adopted by a meeting of Contracting Parties.

7.   In addition to the establishment of the protected areas referred to in paragraph 3 of this Article, Contracting Parties shall promote, through the adoption of appropriate measures, the conservation of natural areas by private owners, community or local authorities.

Article 14 - Impact assessment

1.   The Contracting Parties undertake that proposals for any activity which may significantly affect the natural environment shall as far as possible be subjected to an assessment of their consequences before they are adopted, and they shall take into consideration the results of this assessment in their decision-making process.

2.   In those cases where any such activities are undertaken, the Contracting Parties shall plan and carry them out so as to overcome or minimize any assessed adverse effects and shall monitor such effects with a view to taking remedial action as appropriate.

[Omitted: Chapter V - National supporting measures: Article 15 - Scientific research, Article 16 - Education, information and participation of the public, training, Article 17 - Administrative machinery]

Chapter VI - International co-operation

[Omitted: Article 18 - Co-operative activities]

Article 19 - Shared resources

1.　Contracting Parties that share natural resources shall co-operate concerning their conservation and harmonious utilization, taking into account the sovereignty, rights and interests of the Contracting Parties concerned in accordance with generally accepted principles of international law.

2.　To that end, they shall, in particular:

(a)　co-operate with a view to controlling, preventing, reducing or eliminating adverse environmental effects which may result in one Contracting Party from the utilization of such resources in another Party;

(b)　endeavour to conclude bilateral or multilateral agreements in order to secure specific regulation of their conduct in respect of the resources concerned;

(c)　as far as possible, make environmental assessments prior to engaging in activities with respect of shared natural resources which may create a risk of significantly affecting the environment of another sharing Contracting Party or other sharing Contracting Parties;

(d)　notify in advance the other sharing Contracting Party or the other sharing Contracting Parties of pertinent details of plans to initiate, or make a change in, the conservation of utilization of the resource which can reasonably be expected to affect significantly the environment in the territory of the other Contracting Party or Contracting Parties;

(e)　upon request of the other sharing Contracting Party or sharing Contracting Parties, enter into consultation concerning the above-mentioned plans;

(f)   inform the other sharing Contracting Party or other sharing Contracting Parties of emergency situations or sudden grave natural events which may have repercussions on their environment;

(g)   whenever appropriate, engage in joint scientific studies and assessments with a view to facilitating co-operation with regard to environmental problems related to a shared resource, on the basis of agreed data.

3.   Contracting Parties shall especially co-operate together and, where appropriate, shall endeavour to co-operate with other Contracting Parties, with a view to:

(a)   the conservation and management of:

-       border or contiguous protected areas;

-       shared habitats of species listed in Appendix 1;

-       shared habitats of any other species of common concern;

...

Article 20 - Transfrontier environmental effects

1.   Contracting Parties have in accordance with generally accepted principles of international law the responsibility of ensuring that activities under their jurisdiction or control do not cause damage to the environment or the natural resources under the jurisdiction of other Contracting Parties or of areas beyond the limits of national jurisdiction.

2.   In order to fulfil this responsibility, Contracting Parties shall avoid to the maximum extent possible and reduce to the minimum extent possible adverse environmental effects of activities under their jurisdiction or control, including effects on natural resources, beyond the limits of their national jurisdiction.

3.   To that effect, they shall endeavour:

(a)   to make environmental impact assessment before engaging in any activity that may create a risk of significantly affecting the environment or the natural resources of another Contracting Party or the environment or natural resources beyond national jurisdiction;

(b)   to notify in advance the other Contracting Party or Contracting Parties concerned of pertinent details of plans to initiate, or make a change in, activities which can reasonably be expected to have significant effects beyond the limits of national jurisdiction;

(c)   to enter into consultation concerning the above-mentioned plans upon request of the Contracting Party or Contracting Parties in question;

(d)   to inform the Contracting Party or Contracting Parties in question of emergency situations or sudden grave natural events which may have repercussion beyond national jurisdiction.

4.   Contracting Parties shall, in particular, endeavour to refrain from actions which might directly or indirectly adversely affect wildlife habitats situated beyond the limits of national jurisdiction, especially habitats of species listed in Appendix 1 or habitats included in protected areas.

[Omitted: Chapter VII - International supporting measures: Article 21 - Meeting of the contracting parties, Article 22 - Secretariat, Article 23 - National focal points, Chapter VIII: Article 24 - Adoption of protocols, Article 25 - Amendment of the agreement, Article 26 - Appendices and amendments to appendices, Article 27 - Rules of procedure, Article 28 - Reports, Article 29 - Relationships with other agreements, Article 30 - Settlement and disputes, Article 31 - Ratification, Article 32 - Accession, Article 33 - Entry into force, Article 34 - Responsibility of the depositary, Article 35 - Deposit and registration, List of species for Appendix 1 A, List of species for Appendix 1 B]

6.   Convention on Environmental Impact Assessment in a Transboundary Context [Espoo, 25 February 1991]*

The Parties to this Convention,

Aware of the interrelationship between economic activities and their environmental consequences,

Affirming the need to ensure environmentally sound and sustainable development,

Determined to enhance international co-operation in assessing environmental impact in particular in a transboundary context,

Mindful of the need and importance to develop anticipatory policies and of preventing, mitigating and monitoring significant adverse environmental impact in general and more specifically in a transboundary context,

Recalling the relevant provisions of the Charter of the United Nations, the Declaration of the Stockholm Conference on the Human Environment, the Final Act of the Conference on Security and Co-operation in Europe (CSCE) and the Concluding Documents of the Madrid and Vienna Meetings of Representatives of the Participating States of the CSCE,

Commending the ongoing activities of States to ensure that, through their national legal and administrative provisions and their national policies, environmental impact assessment is carried out,

Conscious of the need to give explicit consideration to environmental factors at an early stage in the decision-making process by applying environmental impact assessment, at all appropriate administrative levels, as a necessary tool to improve the quality of information presented to decision makers so that environmentally sound decisions can be made paying careful attention to

---

* 30 ILM 800 (1991). Entry into force: 10 September 1997. Parties and signatories(s): Albania, Armenia, Austria, Azerbaijan, Belarus (s), Belgium, Bulgaria, Canada, Croatia, Cyprus, Czech Republic, Denmark, Estonia, European Community, Finland, France, Germany, Greece, Hungary, Iceland (s), Ireland, Italy, Kazakhstan, Kyrgystan, Latvia, Liechtenstein, Lithuania, Luxembourg, Netherlands, Norway, Poland, Portugal, Republic of Moldova, Romania, Russian Federation (s), Slovakia, Slovenia, Spain, Sweden, Switzerland, The Former Yugoslav Republic of Macedonia, Ukraine, United Kingdom of Great Britain and Northern Ireland, United States of America (s), as at 31 July 2004.

minimizing significant adverse impact, particularly in a transboundary context,

...

Have agreed as follows:

Article 1 - Definitions

For the purposes of this Convention,

(i)   "Parties" means, unless the text otherwise indicates, the Contracting Parties to this Convention;

(ii)   "Party of origin" means the Contracting Party or Parties to this Convention under whose jurisdiction a proposed activity is envisaged to take place;

(iii)   "Affected Party" means the Contracting Party or Parties to this Convention likely to be affected by the transboundary impact of a proposed activity;

(iv)   "Concerned Parties" means the Party of origin and the affected Party of an environmental impact assessment pursuant to this Convention;

(v)   "Proposed activity" means any activity or any major change to an activity subject to a decision of a competent authority in accordance with an applicable national procedure;

(vi)   "Environmental impact assessment" means a national procedure for evaluating the likely impact of a proposed activity on the environment;

(vii)   "Impact" means any effect caused by a proposed activity on the environment including human health and safety, flora, fauna, soil, air, water, climate, landscape and historical monuments or other physical structures or the interaction among these factors; it also includes effects on cultural heritage or socio-economic conditions resulting from alterations to those factors;

(viii) "Transboundary impact" means any impact, not exclusively of a global nature, within an area under the jurisdiction of a Party caused by a proposed activity the physical origin of which is situated wholly or in part within the area under the jurisdiction of another Party;

(ix) "Competent authority" means the national authority or authorities designated by a Party as responsible for performing the tasks covered by this Convention and/or the authority or authorities entrusted by a Party with decision-making powers regarding a proposed activity;

(x) "The Public" means one or more natural or legal persons.

Article 2 - General provisions

1. The Parties shall, either individually or jointly, take all appropriate and effective measures to prevent, reduce and control significant adverse transboundary environmental impact from proposed activities.

2. Each Party shall take the necessary legal, administrative or other measures to implement the provisions of this Convention, including, with respect to proposed activities listed in Appendix I that are likely to cause significant adverse transboundary impact, the establishment of an environmental impact assessment procedure that permits public participation and preparation of the environmental impact assessment documentation described in Appendix II.

3. The Party of origin shall ensure that in accordance with the provisions of this Convention an environmental impact assessment is undertaken prior to a decision to authorize or undertake a proposed activity listed in Appendix I that is likely to cause a significant adverse transboundary impact.

4. The Party of origin shall, consistent with the provisions of this Convention, ensure that affected Parties are notified of a proposed activity listed in Appendix I that is likely to cause a significant adverse transboundary impact.

5. Concerned Parties shall, at the initiative of any such Party, enter into discussions on whether one or more proposed activities not listed in Appendix I is or are likely to cause a significant adverse transboundary impact and thus should be treated as if it or they were so listed. Where those Parties so agree, the activity or activities shall be thus treated.

General guidance for identifying criteria to determine significant adverse impact is set forth in Appendix III.

6. The Party of origin shall provide, in accordance with the provisions of this Convention, an opportunity to the public in the areas likely to be affected to participate in relevant environmental impact assessment procedures regarding proposed activities and shall ensure that the opportunity provided to the public of the affected Party is equivalent to that provided to the public of the Party of origin.

7. Environmental impact assessments as required by this Convention shall, as a minimum requirement, be undertaken at the project level of the proposed activity. To the extent appropriate, the Parties shall endeavour to apply the principles of environmental impact assessment to policies, plans and programmes.

8. The provisions of this Convention shall not affect the right of Parties to implement national laws, regulations, administrative provisions or accepted legal practices protecting information the supply of which would be prejudicial to industrial and commercial secrecy or national security.

9. The provisions of this Convention shall not affect the right of particular Parties to implement, by bilateral or multilateral agreement where appropriate, more stringent measures than those of this Convention.

10. The provisions of this Convention shall not prejudice any obligations of the Parties under international law with regard to activities having or likely to have a transboundary impact.

Article 3 - Notification

1. For a proposed activity listed in Appendix I that is likely to cause a significant adverse transboundary impact, the Party of origin shall, for the purposes of ensuring adequate and effective consultations under Article 5, notify any Party which it considers may be an affected Party as early as possible and no later than when informing its own public about that proposed activity.

2. This notification shall contain, inter alia:

(a) Information on the proposed activity, including any available information on its possible transboundary impact;

(b) The nature of the possible decision; and

(c) An indication of a reasonable time within which a response under paragraph 3 of this Article is required, taking into account the nature of the proposed activity;

and may include the information set out in paragraph 5 of this Article.

3. The affected Party shall respond to the Party of origin within the time specified in the notification, acknowledging receipt of the notification, and shall indicate whether it intends to participate in the environmental impact assessment procedure.

4. If the affected Party indicates that it does not intend to participate in the environmental impact assessment procedure, or if it does not respond within the time specified in the notification, the provisions in paragraphs 5, 6, 7 and 8 of this Article and in Articles 4 to 7 will not apply. In such circumstances the right of a Party of origin to determine whether to carry out an environmental impact assessment on the basis of its national law and practice is not prejudiced.

5. Upon receipt of a response from the affected Party indicating its desire to participate in the environmental impact assessment procedure, the Party of origin shall, if it has not already done so, provide to the affected Party:

(a) Relevant information regarding the environmental impact assessment procedure, including an indication of the time schedule for transmittal of comments; and

(b) Relevant information on the proposed activity and its possible significant adverse transboundary impact.

6. An affected Party shall, at the request of the Party of origin, provide the latter with reasonably obtainable information relating to the potentially affected environment under the jurisdiction of the affected Party, where such information is necessary for the preparation of the

environmental impact assessment documentation. The information shall be furnished promptly and, as appropriate, through a joint body where one exists.

7. When a Party considers that it would be affected by a significant adverse transboundary impact of a proposed activity listed in Appendix I, and when no notification has taken place in accordance with paragraph 1 of this Article, the concerned Parties shall, at the request of the affected Party, exchange sufficient information for the purposes of holding discussions on whether there is likely to be a significant adverse transboundary impact. If those Parties agree that there is likely to be a significant adverse transboundary impact, the provisions of this Convention shall apply accordingly. If those Parties cannot agree whether there is likely to be a significant adverse transboundary impact, any such Party may submit that question to an inquiry commission in accordance with the provisions of Appendix IV to advise on the likelihood of significant adverse transboundary impact, unless they agree on another method of settling this question.

8. The concerned Parties shall ensure that the public of the affected Party in the areas likely to be affected be informed of, and be provided with possibilities for making comments or objections on, the proposed activity, and for the transmittal of these comments or objections to the competent authority of the Party of origin, either directly to this authority or, where appropriate, through the Party of origin.

Article 4 - Preparation of the environmental impact assessment documentation

1. The environmental impact assessment documentation to be submitted to the competent authority of the Party of origin shall contain, as a minimum, the information described in Appendix II.

2. The Party of origin shall furnish the affected Party, as appropriate through a joint body where one exists, with the environmental impact assessment documentation. The concerned Parties shall arrange for distribution of the documentation to the authorities and the public of the affected Party in the areas likely to be affected and for the submission of comments to the competent authority of the Party of origin, either directly to this authority or, where appropriate, through the Party of origin within a reasonable time before the final decision is taken on the proposed activity.

Article 5 - Consultations on the basis of the environmental impact assessment documentation

The Party of origin shall, after completion of the environmental impact assessment documentation, without undue delay enter into consultations with the affected Party concerning, inter alia, the potential transboundary impact of the proposed activity and measures to reduce or eliminate its impact. Consultations may relate to:

(a) Possible alternatives to the proposed activity, including the no-action alternative and possible measures to mitigate significant adverse transboundary impact and to monitor the effects of such measures at the expense of the Party of origin;

(b) Other forms of possible mutual assistance in reducing any significant adverse transboundary impact of the proposed activity; and

(c) Any other appropriate matters relating to the proposed activity.

The Parties shall agree, at the commencement of such consultations, on a reasonable timeframe for the duration of the consultation period. Any such consultations may be conducted through an appropriate joint body, where one exists.

Article 6 - Final decision

1. The Parties shall ensure that, in the final decision on the proposed activity, due account is taken of the outcome of the environmental impact assessment, including the environmental impact assessment documentation, as well as the comments thereon received pursuant to Article 3, paragraph 8 and Article 4, paragraph 2, and the outcome of the consultations as referred to in Article 5.

2. The Party of origin shall provide to the affected Party the final decision on the proposed activity along with the reasons and considerations on which it was based.

3. If additional information on the significant transboundary impact of a proposed activity, which was not available at the time a decision was made with respect to that activity and which could have materially affected the decision, becomes available to a concerned Party before work on that

activity commences, that Party shall immediately inform the other concerned Party or Parties. If one of the concerned Parties so requests, consultations shall be held as to whether the decision needs to be revised.

Article 7 - Post-project analysis

1. The concerned Parties, at the request of any such Party, shall determine whether, and if so to what extent, a post-project analysis shall be carried out, taking into account the likely significant adverse transboundary impact of the activity for which an environmental impact assessment has been undertaken pursuant to this Convention. Any post-project analysis undertaken shall include, in particular, the surveillance of the activity and the determination of any adverse transboundary impact. Such surveillance and determination may be undertaken with a view to achieving the objectives listed in Appendix V.

2. When, as a result of post-project analysis, the Party of origin or the affected Party has reasonable grounds for concluding that there is a significant adverse transboundary impact or factors have been discovered which may result in such an impact, it shall immediately inform the other Party. The concerned Parties shall then consult on necessary measures to reduce or eliminate the impact.

[Omitted: Article 8 - Bilateral and multilateral co-operation, Article 9 - Research programmes, Article 10 - Status of the appendices, Article 11 - Meeting of parties, Article 12 - Right to vote, Article 13 - Secretariat, Article 14 - Amendments to the Convention, Article 15 - Settlement of disputes, Article 16 - Signature, Article 17 - Ratification, acceptance, approval and accession, Article 18 - Entry into force, Article 19 - Withdrawal, Article 20 - Authentic texts]

...

Appendices

Appendix I - List of activities

...

10. Waste-disposal installations for the incineration, chemical treatment or landfill of toxic and dangerous wastes.

...

12. Groundwater abstraction activities in cases where the annual volume of water to be abstracted amounts to 10 million cubic metres or more.

...

14. Major mining, on-site extraction and processing of metal ores or coal.

...

Appendix II - Content of the environmental impact assessment documentation

Information to be included in the environmental impact assessment documentation shall, as a minimum, contain, in accordance with Article 4:

(a) A description of the proposed activity and its purpose;

(b) A description, where appropriate, of reasonable alternatives (for example, locational or technological) to the proposed activity and also the no-action alternative;

(c) A description of the environment likely to be significantly affected by the proposed activity and its alternatives;

(d) A description of the potential environmental impact of the proposed activity and its alternatives and an estimation of its significance;

(e) A description of mitigation measures to keep adverse environmental impact to a minimum;

(f) An explicit indication of predictive methods and underlying assumptions as well as the relevant environmental data used;

(g) An identification of gaps in knowledge and uncertainties encountered in compiling the required information;

(h) Where appropriate, an outline for monitoring and management programmes and any plans for post-project analysis; and

(i)   A non-technical summary including a visual presentation as appropriate (maps, graphs, etc.).

Appendix III - General criteria to assist in the determination of the environmental significance of activities not listed in Appendix I

1.   In considering proposed activities to which Article 2, paragraph 5, applies, the concerned Parties may consider whether the activity is likely to have a significant adverse transboundary impact in particular by virtue of one or more of the following criteria:

(a)   Size: proposed activities which are large for the type of the activity;

(b)   Location: proposed activities which are located in or close to an area of special environmental sensitivity or importance (such as wetlands designated under the Ramsar Convention, national parks, nature reserves, sites of special scientific interest, or sites of archaeological, cultural or historical importance); also, proposed activities in locations where the characteristics of proposed development would be likely to have significant effects on the population;

(c)   Effects: proposed activities with particularly complex and potentially adverse effects, including those giving rise to serious effects on humans or on valued species or organisms, those which threaten the existing or potential use of an affected area and those causing additional loading which cannot be sustained by the carrying capacity of the environment.

2.   The concerned Parties shall consider for this purpose proposed activities which are located close to an international frontier as well as more remote proposed activities which could give rise to significant transboundary effects far removed from the site of development.

Appendix IV - Inquiry procedure

1.   The requesting Party or Parties shall notify the secretariat that it or they submit(s) the question of whether a proposed activity listed in Appendix I is likely to have a significant adverse transboundary impact to an inquiry commission established in accordance with the provisions of this Appendix. This notification shall state the subject-matter of the inquiry. The secretariat shall notify immediately all Parties to this Convention of this submission.

2. The inquiry commission shall consist of three members. Both the requesting party and the other party to the inquiry procedure shall appoint a scientific or technical expert, and the two experts so appointed shall designate by common agreement the third expert, who shall be the president of the inquiry commission. The latter shall not be a national of one of the parties to the inquiry procedure, nor have his or her usual place of residence in the territory of one of these parties, nor be employed by any of them, nor have dealt with the matter in any other capacity.

3. If the president of the inquiry commission has not been designated within two months of the appointment of the second expert, the Executive Secretary of the Economic Commission for Europe shall, at the request of either party, designate the president within a further two-month period.

4. If one of the parties to the inquiry procedure does not appoint an expert within one month of its receipt of the notification by the secretariat, the other party may inform the Executive Secretary of the Economic Commission for Europe, who shall designate the president of the inquiry commission within a further two-month period. Upon designation, the president of the inquiry commission shall request the party which has not appointed an expert to do so within one month. After such a period, the president shall inform the Executive Secretary of the Economic Commission for Europe, who shall make this appointment within a further two-month period.

5. The inquiry commission shall adopt its own rules of procedure.

6. The inquiry commission may take all appropriate measures in order to carry out its functions.

7. The parties to the inquiry procedure shall facilitate the work of the inquiry commission and, in particular, using all means at their disposal, shall:

(a) Provide it with all relevant documents, facilities and information; and

(b) Enable it, where necessary, to call witnesses or experts and receive their evidence.

8.   The parties and the experts shall protect the confidentiality of any information they receive in confidence during the work of the inquiry commission.

9.   If one of the parties to the inquiry procedure does not appear before the inquiry commission or fails to present its case, the other party may request the inquiry commission to continue the proceedings and to complete its work. Absence of a party or failure of a party to present its case shall not constitute a bar to the continuation and completion of the work of the inquiry commission.

10.   Unless the inquiry commission determines otherwise because of the particular circumstances of the matter, the expenses of the inquiry commission, including the remuneration of its members, shall be borne by the parties to the inquiry procedure in equal shares. The inquiry commission shall keep a record of all its expenses, and shall furnish a final statement thereof to the parties.

11.   Any Party having an interest of a factual nature in the subject-matter of the inquiry procedure, and which may be affected by an opinion in the matter, may intervene in the proceedings with the consent of the inquiry commission.

12.   The decisions of the inquiry commission on matters of procedure shall be taken by majority vote of its members. The final opinion of the inquiry commission shall reflect the view of the majority of its members and shall include any dissenting view.

13.   The inquiry commission shall present its final opinion within two months of the date on which it was established unless it finds it necessary to extend this time limit for a period which should not exceed two months.

14.   The final opinion of the inquiry commission shall be based on accepted scientific principles. The final opinion shall be transmitted by the inquiry commission to the parties to the inquiry procedure and to the secretariat.

Appendix V - Post-project analysis

Objectives include:

(a) Monitoring compliance with the conditions as set out in the authorization or approval of the activity and the effectiveness of mitigation measures;

(b) Review of an impact for proper management and in order to cope with uncertainties;

(c) Verification of past predictions in order to transfer experience to future activities of the same type.

[Omitted: Appendix VI - Elements for bilateral and multilateral co-operation, Appendix VII - Arbitration]

7. Convention on the Protection and Use of Transboundary Watercourses and International Lakes [Helsinki, 17 March 1992]*

Preamble

The Parties to this Convention,

Mindful that the protection and use of transboundary watercourses and international lakes are important and urgent tasks, the effective accomplishment of which can only be ensured by enhanced co-operation,

Concerned over the existence and threats of adverse effects, in the short or long term, of changes in the conditions of transboundary watercourses and international lakes on the environment, economies and well-being of the member countries of the Economic Commission for Europe (ECE),

Emphasizing the need for strengthened national and international measures to prevent, control and reduce the release of hazardous substances into the aquatic environment and to abate eutrophication and acidification, as well as

---

* 31 ILM 1312 (1992). Entry into force: 6 October 1996. Parties and signatories (s): Albania, Austria, Azerbaijan, Belarus, Belgium, Bulgaria, Croatia, Czech Republic, Denmark, Estonia, European Community, Finland, France, Germany, Greece, Hungary, Italy, Kazakhstan, Latvia, Liechtenstein, Luxembourg, Netherlands, Norway, Poland, Portugal, Republic of Moldova, Romania, Russian Federation, Slovakia, Slovenia, Spain, Sweden, Switzerland, Ukraine, United Kingdom of Great Britain and Northern Ireland (s), as at 31 July 2004.

pollution of the marine environment, in particular coastal areas, from land-based sources,

Commending the efforts already undertaken by the ECE Governments to strengthen co-operation, on bilateral and multilateral levels, for the prevention, control and reduction of transboundary pollution, sustainable water management, conservation of water resources and environmental protection,

Recalling the pertinent provisions and principles of the Declaration of the Stockholm Conference on the Human Environment, the Final Act of the Conference on Security and Co-operation in Europe (CSCE), the Concluding Documents of the Madrid and Vienna Meetings of Representatives of the Participating States of the CSCE, and the Regional Strategy for Environmental Protection and Rational Use of Natural Resources in ECE Member Countries covering the Period up to the Year 2000 and Beyond,

Conscious of the role of the United Nations Economic Commission for Europe in promoting international co-operation for the prevention, control and reduction of transboundary water pollution and sustainable use of transboundary waters, and in this regard recalling the ECE Declaration of Policy on Prevention and Control of Water Pollution, including Transboundary Pollution; the ECE Declaration of Policy on the Rational Use of Water; the ECE Principles Regarding Co-operation in the Field of Transboundary Waters; the ECE Charter on Groundwater Management; and the Code of Conduct on Accidental Pollution of Transboundary Inland Waters,

...

Emphasizing that co-operation between member countries in regard to the protection and use of transboundary waters shall be implemented primarily through the elaboration of agreements between countries bordering the same waters, especially where no such agreements have yet been reached,

Have agreed as follows:

Article 1 - Definitions

For the purposes of this Convention,

1. "Transboundary waters" means any surface or groundwaters which mark, cross or are located on boundaries between two or more States; wherever transboundary waters flow directly into the sea, these transboundary waters end at a straight line across their respective mouths between points on the low-water line of their banks;

2. "Transboundary impact" means any significant adverse effect on the environment resulting from a change in the conditions of transboundary waters caused by a human activity, the physical origin of which is situated wholly or in part within an area under the jurisdiction of a Party, within an area under the jurisdiction of another Party. Such effects on the environment include effects on human health and safety, flora, fauna, soil, air, water, climate, landscape and historical monuments or other physical structures or the interaction among these factors; they also include effects on the cultural heritage or socio-economic conditions resulting from alterations to those factors;

3. "Party" means, unless the text otherwise indicates, a Contracting Party to this Convention;

4. "Riparian Parties" means the Parties bordering the same transboundary waters;

5. "Joint body" means any bilateral or multilateral commission or other appropriate institutional arrangements for co-operation between the Riparian Parties;

6. "Hazardous substances" means substances which are toxic, carcinogenic, mutagenic, teratogenic or bio-accumulative, especially when they are persistent;

7. "Best available technology" (the definition is contained in Annex I to this Convention).

Part I - Provisions relating to all Parties

Article 2 - General provisions

1. The Parties shall take all appropriate measures to prevent, control and reduce any transboundary impact.

2.   The Parties shall, in particular, take all appropriate measures:

(a)   To prevent, control and reduce pollution of waters causing or likely to cause transboundary impact;

(b)   To ensure that transboundary waters are used with the aim of ecologically sound and rational water management, conservation of water resources and environmental protection;

(c)   To ensure that transboundary waters are used in a reasonable and equitable way, taking into particular account their transboundary character, in the case of activities which cause or are likely to cause transboundary impact;

(d)   To ensure conservation and, where necessary, restoration of ecosystems.

3.   Measures for the prevention, control and reduction of water pollution shall be taken, where possible, at source.

4.   These measures shall not directly or indirectly result in a transfer of pollution to other parts of the environment.

5.   In taking the measures referred to in paragraphs 1 and 2 of this article, the Parties shall be guided by the following principles:

(a)   The precautionary principle, by virtue of which action to avoid the potential transboundary impact of the release of hazardous substances shall not be postponed on the ground that scientific research has not fully proved a causal link between those substances, on the one hand, and the potential transboundary impact, on the other hand;

(b)   The polluter-pays principle, by virtue of which costs of pollution prevention, control and reduction measures shall be borne by the polluter;

(c)   Water resources shall be managed so that the needs of the present generation are met without compromising the ability of future generations to meet their own needs.

6.   The Riparian Parties shall co-operate on the basis of equality and reciprocity, in particular through bilateral and multilateral agreements, in order to develop harmonized policies, programmes and strategies

covering the relevant catchment areas, or parts thereof, aimed at the prevention, control and reduction of transboundary impact and aimed at the protection of the environment of transboundary waters or the environment influenced by such waters, including the marine environment.

7. The application of this Convention shall not lead to the deterioration of environmental conditions nor lead to increased transboundary impact.

8. The provisions of this Convention shall not affect the right of Parties individually or jointly to adopt and implement more stringent measures than those set down in this Convention.

Article 3 - Prevention, control and reduction

1. To prevent, control and reduce transboundary impact, the Parties shall develop, adopt, implement and, as far as possible, render compatible relevant legal, administrative, economic, financial and technical measures, in order to ensure, inter alia, that:

(a) The emission of pollutants is prevented, controlled and reduced at source through the application of, inter alia, low- and non-waste technology;

(b) Transboundary waters are protected against pollution from point sources through the prior licensing of waste-water discharges by the competent national authorities, and that the authorized discharges are monitored and controlled;

(c) Limits for waste-water discharges stated in permits are based on the best available technology for discharges of hazardous substances;

(d) Stricter requirements, even leading to prohibition in individual cases, are imposed when the quality of the receiving water or the ecosystem so requires;

(e) At least biological treatment or equivalent processes are applied to municipal waste water, where necessary in a step-by-step approach;

(f) Appropriate measures are taken, such as the application of the best available technology, in order to reduce nutrient inputs from industrial and municipal sources;

(g) Appropriate measures and best environmental practices are developed and implemented for the reduction of inputs of nutrients and hazardous substances from diffuse sources, especially where the main sources are from agriculture (guidelines for developing best environmental practices are given in Annex II to this Convention);

(h) Environmental impact assessment and other means of assessment are applied;

(i) Sustainable water-resources management, including the application of the ecosystems approach, is promoted;

(j) Contingency planning is developed;

(k) Additional specific measures are taken to prevent the pollution of groundwaters;

(l) The risk of accidental pollution is minimized.

2. To this end, each Party shall set emission limits for discharges from point sources into surface waters based on the best available technology, which are specifically applicable to individual industrial sectors or industries from which hazardous substances derive. The appropriate measures mentioned in paragraph 1 of this article to prevent, control and reduce the input of hazardous substances from point and diffuse sources into waters, may, inter alia, include total or partial prohibition of the production or use of such substances. Existing lists of such industrial sectors or industries and of such hazardous substances in international conventions or regulations, which are applicable in the area covered by this Convention, shall be taken into account.

3. In addition, each Party shall define, where appropriate, water-quality objectives and adopt water-quality criteria for the purpose of preventing, controlling and reducing transboundary impact. General guidance for developing such objectives and criteria is given in Annex III to this Convention. When necessary, the Parties shall endeavour to update this annex.

Article 4 - Monitoring

The Parties shall establish programmes for monitoring the conditions of transboundary waters.

Article 5 - Research and development

The Parties shall co-operate in the conduct of research into and development of effective techniques for the prevention, control and reduction of transboundary impact. To this effect, the Parties shall, on a bilateral and/or multilateral basis, taking into account research activities pursued in relevant international forums, endeavour to initiate or intensify specific research programmes, where necessary, aimed, inter alia, at:

(a)   Methods for the assessment of the toxicity of hazardous substances and the noxiousness of pollutants;

(b)   Improved knowledge on the occurrence, distribution and environmental effects of pollutants and the processes involved;

(c)   The development and application of environmentally sound technologies, production and consumption patterns;

(d)   The phasing out and/or substitution of substances likely to have transboundary impact;

(e)   Environmentally sound methods of disposal of hazardous substances;

(f)   Special methods for improving the conditions of transboundary waters;

(g)   The development of environmentally sound water-construction works and water-regulation techniques;

(h)   The physical and financial assessment of damage resulting from transboundary impact.

The results of these research programmes shall be exchanged among the Parties in accordance with Article 6 of this Convention.

Article 6 - Exchange of information

The Parties shall provide for the widest exchange of information, as early as possible, on issues covered by the provisions of this Convention.

Article 7 - Responsibility and liability

The Parties shall support appropriate international efforts to elaborate rules, criteria and procedures in the field of responsibility and liability.

Article 8 - Protection of information

The provisions of this Convention shall not affect the rights or the obligations of Parties in accordance with their national legal systems and applicable supranational regulations to protect information related to industrial and commercial secrecy, including intellectual property, or national security.

Part II - Provisions relating to Riparian Parties

Article 9 - Bilateral and multilateral co-operation

1. The Riparian Parties shall on the basis of equality and reciprocity enter into bilateral or multilateral agreements or other arrangements, where these do not yet exist, or adapt existing ones, where necessary to eliminate the contradictions with the basic principles of this Convention, in order to define their mutual relations and conduct regarding the prevention, control and reduction of transboundary impact. The Riparian Parties shall specify the catchment area, or part(s) thereof, subject to co-operation. These agreements or arrangements shall embrace relevant issues covered by this Convention, as well as any other issues on which the Riparian Parties may deem it necessary to co-operate.

2. The agreements or arrangements mentioned in paragraph 1 of this article shall provide for the establishment of joint bodies. The tasks of these joint bodies shall be, inter alia, and without prejudice to relevant existing agreements or arrangements, the following:

(a) To collect, compile and evaluate data in order to identify pollution sources likely to cause transboundary impact;

(b) To elaborate joint monitoring programmes concerning water quality and quantity;

(c) To draw up inventories and exchange information on the pollution sources mentioned in paragraph 2 (a) of this article;

(d) To elaborate emission limits for waste water and evaluate the effectiveness of control programmes;

(e) To elaborate joint water-quality objectives and criteria having regard to the provisions of Article 3, paragraph 3 of this Convention, and to propose relevant measures for maintaining and, where necessary, improving the existing water quality;

(f) To develop concerted action programmes for the reduction of pollution loads from both point sources (e.g. municipal and industrial sources) and diffuse sources (particularly from agriculture);

(g) To establish warning and alarm procedures;

(h) To serve as a forum for the exchange of information on existing and planned uses of water and related installations that are likely to cause transboundary impact;

(i) To promote co-operation and exchange of information on the best available technology in accordance with the provisions of Article 13 of this Convention, as well as to encourage co-operation in scientific research programmes;

(j) To participate in the implementation of environmental impact assessments relating to transboundary waters, in accordance with appropriate international regulations.

3. In cases where a coastal State, being Party to this Convention, is directly and significantly affected by transboundary impact, the Riparian Parties can, if they all so agree, invite that coastal State to be involved in an appropriate manner in the activities of multilateral joint bodies established by Parties riparian to such transboundary waters.

4. Joint bodies according to this Convention shall invite joint bodies, established by coastal States for the protection of the marine

environment directly affected by transboundary impact, to co-operate in order to harmonize their work and to prevent, control and reduce the transboundary impact.

5.   Where two or more joint bodies exist in the same catchment area, they shall endeavour to co-ordinate their activities in order to strengthen the prevention, control and reduction of transboundary impact within that catchment area.

Article 10 - Consultations

Consultations shall be held between the Riparian Parties on the basis of reciprocity, good faith and good-neighbourliness, at the request of any such Party. Such consultations shall aim at co-operation regarding the issues covered by the provisions of this Convention. Any such consultations shall be conducted through a joint body established under Article 9 of this Convention, where one exists.

Article 11 - Joint monitoring and assessment

1.   In the framework of general co-operation mentioned in Article 9 of this Convention, or specific arrangements, the Riparian Parties shall establish and implement joint programmes for monitoring the conditions of transboundary waters, including floods and ice drifts, as well as transboundary impact.

2.   The Riparian Parties shall agree upon pollution parameters and pollutants whose discharges and concentration in transboundary waters shall be regularly monitored.

3.   The Riparian Parties shall, at regular intervals, carry out joint or co-ordinated assessments of the conditions of transboundary waters and the effectiveness of measures taken for the prevention, control and reduction of transboundary impact. The results of these assessments shall be made available to the public in accordance with the provisions set out in Article 16 of this Convention.

4.   For these purposes, the Riparian Parties shall harmonize rules for the setting up and operation of monitoring programmes, measurement systems, devices, analytical techniques, data processing and evaluation procedures, and methods for the registration of pollutants discharged.

Article 12 - Common research and development

In the framework of general co-operation mentioned in Article 9 of this Convention, or specific arrangements, the Riparian Parties shall undertake specific research and development activities in support of achieving and maintaining the water-quality objectives and criteria which they have agreed to set and adopt.

Article 13 - Exchange of information between riparian parties

1.   The Riparian Parties shall, within the framework of relevant agreements or other arrangements according to Article 9 of this Convention, exchange reasonably available data, inter alia, on:

(a)   Environmental conditions of transboundary waters;

(b)   Experience gained in the application and operation of best available technology and results of research and development;

(c)   Emission and monitoring data;

(d)   Measures taken and planned to be taken to prevent, control and reduce transboundary impact;

(e)   Permits or regulations for waste-water discharges issued by the competent authority or appropriate body.

2.   In order to harmonize emission limits, the Riparian Parties shall undertake the exchange of information on their national regulations.

3.   If a Riparian Party is requested by another Riparian Party to provide data or information that is not available, the former shall endeavour to comply with the request but may condition its compliance upon the payment, by the requesting Party, of reasonable charges for collecting and, where appropriate, processing such data or information.

4.   For the purposes of the implementation of this Convention, the Riparian Parties shall facilitate the exchange of best available technology, particularly through the promotion of: the commercial exchange of available technology; direct industrial contacts and co-operation, including joint ventures; the exchange of information and

experience; and the provision of technical assistance. The Riparian Parties shall also undertake joint training programmes and the organization of relevant seminars and meetings.

Article 14 - Warning and alarm systems

The Riparian Parties shall without delay inform each other about any critical situation that may have transboundary impact. The Riparian Parties shall set up, where appropriate, and operate co-ordinated or joint communication, warning and alarm systems with the aim of obtaining and transmitting information. These systems shall operate on the basis of compatible data transmission and treatment procedures and facilities to be agreed upon by the Riparian Parties. The Riparian Parties shall inform each other about competent authorities or points of contact designated for this purpose.

Article 15 - Mutual assistance

1. If a critical situation should arise, the Riparian Parties shall provide mutual assistance upon request, following procedures to be established in accordance with paragraph 2 of this article.

2. The Riparian Parties shall elaborate and agree upon procedures for mutual assistance addressing, inter alia, the following issues:

(a) The direction, control, co-ordination and supervision of assistance;

(b) Local facilities and services to be rendered by the Party requesting assistance, including, where necessary, the facilitation of border-crossing formalities;

(c) Arrangements for holding harmless, indemnifying and/or compensating the assisting Party and/or its personnel, as well as for transit through territories of third Parties, where necessary;

(d) Methods of reimbursing assistance services.

Article 16 - Public information

1. The Riparian Parties shall ensure that information on the conditions of transboundary waters, measures taken or planned to be taken to prevent, control and reduce transboundary impact, and the

effectiveness of those measures, is made available to the public. For this purpose, the Riparian Parties shall ensure that the following information is made available to the public:

(a) Water-quality objectives;

(b) Permits issued and the conditions required to be met;

(c) Results of water and effluent sampling carried out for the purposes of monitoring and assessment, as well as results of checking compliance with the water-quality objectives or the permit conditions.

2. The Riparian Parties shall ensure that this information shall be available to the public at all reasonable times for inspection free of charge, and shall provide members of the public with reasonable facilities for obtaining from the Riparian Parties, on payment of reasonable charges, copies of such information.

Part III - Institutional and final provisions

[Omitted: Article 17 - Meeting of Parties, Article 18 - Right to vote, Article 19 - Secretariat]

Article 20 - Annexes

Annexes to this Convention shall constitute an integral part thereof.

[Omitted: Article 21 - Amendments to the Convention, Article 22 - Settlement of disputes, Article 23 - Signature, Article 24 - Depositary, Article 25 - Ratification, acceptance, approval and accession, Article 26 - Entry into force, Article 27 - Withdrawal, Article 28 - Authentic texts]

...

Annex I - Definition of the term "best available technology"

1. The term "best available technology" is taken to mean the latest stage of development of processes, facilities or methods of operation which indicate the practical suitability of a particular measure for limiting discharges, emissions and waste. In determining whether a set of processes, facilities and methods of operation constitute the best

available technology in general or specific cases, special consideration is given to:

(a)   Comparable processes, facilities or methods of operation which have recently been successfully tried out;

(b)   Technological advances and changes in scientific knowledge and understanding;

(c)   The economic feasibility of such technology;

(d)   Time limits for installation in both new and existing plants;

(e)   The nature and volume of the discharges and effluents concerned;

(f)   Low- and non-waste technology.

2.   It therefore follows that what is "best available technology" for a particular process will change with time in the light of technological advances, economic and social factors, as well as in the light of changes in scientific knowledge and understanding.

Annex II - Guidelines for developing best environmental practices

1.   In selecting for individual cases the most appropriate combination of measures which may constitute the best environmental practice, the following graduated range of measures should be considered:

(a)   Provision of information and education to the public and to users about the environmental consequences of the choice of particular activities and products, their use and ultimate disposal;

(b)   The development and application of codes of good environmental practice which cover all aspects of the product's life;

(c)   Labels informing users of environmental risks related to a product, its use and ultimate disposal;

(d)   Collection and disposal systems available to the public;

(e)   Recycling, recovery and reuse;

(f)   Application of economic instruments to activities, products or groups of products;

(g)   A system of licensing, which involves a range of restrictions or a ban.

2.   In determining what combination of measures constitute best environmental practices, in general or in individual cases, particular consideration should be given to:

(a)   The environmental hazard of:

(i)   The product;

(ii)   The product's production;

(iii) The product's use;

(iv)   The product's ultimate disposal;

(b)   Substitution by less polluting processes or substances;

(c)   Scale of use;

(d)   Potential environmental benefit or penalty of substitute materials or activities;

(e)   Advances and changes in scientific knowledge and understanding;

(f)   Time limits for implementation;

(g)   Social and economic implications.

3.   It therefore follows that best environmental practices for a particular source will change with time in the light of technological advances, economic and social factors, as well as in the light of changes in scientific knowledge and understanding.

Annex III - Guidelines for developing water-quality objectives and criteria

Water-quality objectives and criteria shall:

(a) Take into account the aim of maintaining and, where necessary, improving the existing water quality;

(b) Aim at the reduction of average pollution loads (in particular hazardous substances) to a certain degree within a certain period of time;

(c) Take into account specific water-quality requirements (raw water for drinking-water purposes, irrigation, etc.)

(d) Take into account specific requirements regarding sensitive and specially protected waters and their environment, e.g. lakes and groundwater resources;

(e) Be based on the application of ecological classification methods and chemical indices for the medium- and long-term review of water-quality maintenance and improvement;

(f) Take into account the degree to which objectives are reached and the additional protective measures, based on emission limits, which may be required in individual cases.

[Omitted: Annex IV - Arbitration]

8. Convention on Access to Information, Public Participation in Decision-Making and Access to Justice in Environmental Matters [Aarhus, 25 June 1998]*

The Parties to this Convention,

Recalling principle 1 of the Stockholm Declaration on the Human Environment,

Recalling also principle 10 of the Rio Declaration on Environment and Development,

Recalling further General Assembly resolutions 37/7 of 28 October 1982 on the World Charter for Nature and 45/94 of 14 December 1990 on the need to ensure a healthy environment for the well-being of individuals,

Recalling the European Charter on Environment and Health adopted at the First European Conference on Environment and Health of the World Health Organization in Frankfurt-am-Main, Germany, on 8 December 1989,

Affirming the need to protect, preserve and improve the state of the environment and to ensure sustainable and environmentally sound development,

Recognizing that adequate protection of the environment is essential to human well-being and the enjoyment of basic human rights, including the right to life itself,

Recognizing also that every person has the right to live in an environment adequate to his or her health and well-being, and the duty, both individually and in association with others, to protect and improve the environment for the benefit of present and future generations,

---

* 38 ILM 517 (1999). Entry into force: 30 October 2001. Parties and signatories (s): Albania, Armenia, Austria (s), Azerbaijan, Belarus, Belgium, Bulgaria, Croatia (s), Cyprus, Czech Republic, Denmark, Estonia, European Community (s), Finland (s), France, Georgia, Germany (s), Greece (s), Hungary, Iceland (s), Ireland (s), Italy , Kazakhstan, Kyrgyzstan, Latvia, Liechtenstein (s), Lithuania, Luxembourg (s), Malta, Monaco (s), Netherlands (s), Norway, Poland, Portugal, Republic of Moldova, Romania, Slovenia (s), Spain (s), Sweden (s), Switzerland (s), Tajikistan, The Former Yugoslav Republic of Macedonia, Turkmenistan, Ukraine, United Kingdom of Great Britain and Northern Ireland (s), as at 31 July 2004.

Considering that, to be able to assert this right and observe this duty, citizens must have access to information, be entitled to participate in decision-making and have access to justice in environmental matters, and acknowledging in this regard that citizens may need assistance in order to exercise their rights,

Recognizing that, in the field of the environment, improved access to information and public participation in decision-making enhance the quality and the implementation of decisions, contribute to public awareness of environmental issues, give the public the opportunity to express its concerns and enable public authorities to take due account of such concerns,

...

Have agreed as follows:

Article 1 - Objective

In order to contribute to the protection of the right of every person of present and future generations to live in an environment adequate to his or her health and well-being, each Party shall guarantee the rights of access to information, public participation in decision-making, and access to justice in environmental matters in accordance with the provisions of this Convention.

Article 2 - Definitions

For the purposes of this Convention,

1. "Party" means, unless the text otherwise indicates, a Contracting Party to this Convention;

2. "Public authority" means:

(a) Government at national, regional and other level;

(b) Natural or legal persons performing public administrative functions under national law, including specific duties, activities or services in relation to the environment;

(c) Any other natural or legal persons having public responsibilities or functions, or providing public services, in relation to the environment, under the control of a body or person falling within subparagraphs (a) or (b) above;

(d) The institutions of any regional economic integration organization referred to in article 17 which is a Party to this Convention.

This definition does not include bodies or institutions acting in a judicial or legislative capacity;

3. "Environmental information" means any information in written, visual, aural, electronic or any other material form on:

(a) The state of elements of the environment, such as air and atmosphere, water, soil, land, landscape and natural sites, biological diversity and its components, including genetically modified organisms, and the interaction among these elements;

(b) Factors, such as substances, energy, noise and radiation, and activities or measures, including administrative measures, environmental agreements, policies, legislation, plans and programmes, affecting or likely to affect the elements of the environment within the scope of subparagraph (a) above, and cost-benefit and other economic analyses and assumptions used in environmental decision-making;

(c) The state of human health and safety, conditions of human life, cultural sites and built structures, inasmuch as they are or may be affected by the state of the elements of the environment or, through these elements, by the factors, activities or measures referred to in subparagraph (b) above;

4. "The public" means one or more natural or legal persons, and, in accordance with national legislation or practice, their associations, organizations or groups;

5. "The public concerned" means the public affected or likely to be affected by, or having an interest in, the environmental decision-making; for the purposes of this definition, non-governmental organizations promoting environmental protection and meeting any requirements under national law shall be deemed to have an interest.

Article 3 - General provisions

1.   Each Party shall take the necessary legislative, regulatory and other measures, including measures to achieve compatibility between the provisions implementing the information, public participation and access-to-justice provisions in this Convention, as well as proper enforcement measures, to establish and maintain a clear, transparent and consistent framework to implement the provisions of this Convention.

2.   Each Party shall endeavour to ensure that officials and authorities assist and provide guidance to the public in seeking access to information, in facilitating participation in decision-making and in seeking access to justice in environmental matters.

3.   Each Party shall promote environmental education and environmental awareness among the public, especially on how to obtain access to information, to participate in decision-making and to obtain access to justice in environmental matters.

4.   Each Party shall provide for appropriate recognition of and support to associations, organizations or groups promoting environmental protection and ensure that its national legal system is consistent with this obligation.

5.   The provisions of this Convention shall not affect the right of a Party to maintain or introduce measures providing for broader access to information, more extensive public participation in decision-making and wider access to justice in environmental matters than required by this Convention.

6.   This Convention shall not require any derogation from existing rights of access to information, public participation in decision-making and access to justice in environmental matters.

7.   Each Party shall promote the application of the principles of this Convention in international environmental decision-making processes and within the framework of international organizations in matters relating to the environment.

8.   Each Party shall ensure that persons exercising their rights in conformity with the provisions of this Convention shall not be penalized, persecuted or harassed in any way for their involvement. This provision shall not affect the powers of national courts to award reasonable costs in judicial proceedings.

9.   Within the scope of the relevant provisions of this Convention, the public shall have access to information, have the possibility to participate in decision-making and have access to justice in environmental matters without discrimination as to citizenship, nationality or domicile and, in the case of a legal person, without discrimination as to where it has its registered seat or an effective centre of its activities.

Article 4 - Access to environmental information

1.   Each Party shall ensure that, subject to the following paragraphs of this article, public authorities, in response to a request for environmental information, make such information available to the public, within the framework of national legislation, including, where requested and subject to subparagraph (b) below, copies of the actual documentation containing or comprising such information:

(a)   Without an interest having to be stated;

(b)   In the form requested unless:

  (i)   It is reasonable for the public authority to make it available in another form, in which case reasons shall be given for making it available in that form; or

  (ii)   The information is already publicly available in another form.

2.   The environmental information referred to in paragraph 1 above shall be made available as soon as possible and at the latest within one month after the request has been submitted, unless the volume and the complexity of the information justify an extension of this period up to two months after the request. The applicant shall be informed of any extension and of the reasons justifying it.

3.   A request for environmental information may be refused if:

(a)   The public authority to which the request is addressed does not hold the environmental information requested;

(b)   The request is manifestly unreasonable or formulated in too general a manner; or

(c)   The request concerns material in the course of completion or concerns internal communications of public authorities where such an exemption is provided for in national law or customary practice, taking into account the public interest served by disclosure.

4.   A request for environmental information may be refused if the disclosure would adversely affect::

(a)   The confidentiality of the proceedings of public authorities, where such confidentiality is provided for under national law;

(b)   International relations, national defence or public security;

(c)   The course of justice, the ability of a person to receive a fair trial or the ability of a public authority to conduct an enquiry of a criminal or disciplinary nature;

(d)   The confidentiality of commercial and industrial information, where such confidentiality is protected by law in order to protect a legitimate economic interest. Within this framework, information on emissions which is relevant for the protection of the environment shall be disclosed;

(e)   Intellectual property rights;

(f)   The confidentiality of personal data and/or files relating to a natural person where that person has not consented to the disclosure of the information to the public, where such confidentiality is provided for in national law;

(g)   The interests of a third party which has supplied the information requested without that party being under or capable of being put under a legal obligation to do so, and where that party does not consent to the release of the material; or

(h)   The environment to which the information relates, such as the breeding sites of rare species.

The aforementioned grounds for refusal shall be interpreted in a restrictive way, taking into account the public interest served by disclosure and taking into account whether the information requested relates to emissions into the environment.

5.   Where a public authority does not hold the environmental information requested, this public authority shall, as promptly as possible, inform the applicant of the public authority to which it believes it is possible to apply for the information requested or transfer the request to that authority and inform the applicant accordingly.

6.   Each Party shall ensure that, if information exempted from disclosure under paragraphs 3(c) and 4 above can be separated out without prejudice to the confidentiality of the information exempted, public authorities make available the remainder of the environmental information that has been requested.

7.   A refusal of a request shall be in writing if the request was in writing or the applicant so requests. A refusal shall state the reasons for the refusal and give information on access to the review procedure provided for in accordance with article 9. The refusal shall be made as soon as possible and at the latest within one month, unless the complexity of the information justifies an extension of this period up to two months after the request. The applicant shall be informed of any extension and of the reasons justifying it.

8.   Each Party may allow its public authorities to make a charge for supplying information, but such charge shall not exceed a reasonable amount. Public authorities intending to make such a charge for supplying information shall make available to applicants a schedule of charges which may be levied, indicating the circumstances in which they may be levied or waived and when the supply of information is conditional on the advance payment of such a charge.

[Omitted: Article 5 - Collection and dissemination of environmental information]

<u>Article 6 - Public participation in decisions on specific activities</u>

1.   Each Party:

(a)   Shall apply the provisions of this article with respect to decisions on whether to permit proposed activities listed in annex I;

(b)   Shall, in accordance with its national law, also apply the provisions of this article to decisions on proposed activities not listed in annex I which may have a significant effect on the environment. To this end, Parties shall determine whether such a proposed activity is subject to these provisions; and

(c)   May decide, on a case-by-case basis if so provided under national law, not to apply the provisions of this article to proposed activities serving national defence purposes, if that Party deems that such application would have an adverse effect on these purposes.

2.   The public concerned shall be informed, either by public notice or individually as appropriate, early in an environmental decision-making procedure, and in an adequate, timely and effective manner, <u>inter alia</u>, of:

(a)   The proposed activity and the application on which a decision will be taken;

(b)   The nature of possible decisions or the draft decision;

(c)   The public authority responsible for making the decision;

(d)   The envisaged procedure, including, as and when this information can be provided:

      (i)   The commencement of the procedure;

      (ii)   The opportunities for the public to participate;

      (iii) The time and venue of any envisaged public hearing;

      (iv)   An indication of the public authority from which relevant information can be obtained and where the relevant information has been deposited for examination by the public;

(v) An indication of the relevant public authority or any other official body to which comments or questions can be submitted and of the time schedule for transmittal of comments or questions; and

(vi) An indication of what environmental information relevant to the proposed activity is available; and

(e) The fact that the activity is subject to a national or transboundary environmental impact assessment procedure.

3. The public participation procedures shall include reasonable time-frames for the different phases, allowing sufficient time for informing the public in accordance with paragraph 2 above and for the public to prepare and participate effectively during the environmental decision-making.

4. Each Party shall provide for early public participation, when all options are open and effective public participation can take place.

5. Each Party should, where appropriate, encourage prospective applicants to identify the public concerned, to enter into discussions, and to provide information regarding the objectives of their application before applying for a permit.

6. Each Party shall require the competent public authorities to give the public concerned access for examination, upon request where so required under national law, free of charge and as soon as it becomes available, to all information relevant to the decision-making referred to in this article that is available at the time of the public participation procedure, without prejudice to the right of Parties to refuse to disclose certain information in accordance with article 4, paragraphs 3 and 4. The relevant information shall include at least, and without prejudice to the provisions of article 4:

(a) A description of the site and the physical and technical characteristics of the proposed activity, including an estimate of the expected residues and emissions;

(b) A description of the significant effects of the proposed activity on the environment;

(c) A description of the measures envisaged to prevent and/or reduce the effects, including emissions;

(d) A non-technical summary of the above;

(e) An outline of the main alternatives studied by the applicant; and

(f) In accordance with national legislation, the main reports and advice issued to the public authority at the time when the public concerned shall be informed in accordance with paragraph 2 above.

7. Procedures for public participation shall allow the public to submit, in writing or, as appropriate, at a public hearing or enquiry with the applicant, any comments, information, analyses or opinions that it considers relevant to the proposed activity.

8. Each Party shall ensure that in the decision due account is taken of the outcome of the public participation.

9. Each Party shall ensure that, when the decision has been taken by the public authority, the public is promptly informed of the decision in accordance with the appropriate procedures. Each Party shall make accessible to the public the text of the decision along with the reasons and considerations on which the decision is based.

10. Each Party shall ensure that, when a public authority reconsiders or updates the operating conditions for an activity referred to in paragraph 1, the provisions of paragraphs 2 to 9 of this article are applied mutatis mutandis, and where appropriate.

11. Each Party shall, within the framework of its national law, apply, to the extent feasible and appropriate, provisions of this article to decisions on whether to permit the deliberate release of genetically modified organisms into the environment.

[Omitted: Article 7 - Public participation concerning plans, programmes and policies relating to the environment, Article 8 - Public participation during the preparation of executive regulations and/or generally applicable legally binding normative instruments]

Article 9 - Access to justice

1. Each Party shall, within the framework of its national legislation, ensure that any person who considers that his or her request for information under article 4 has been ignored, wrongfully refused, whether in part or in full, inadequately answered, or otherwise not dealt with in accordance with the provisions of that article, has access to a review procedure before a court of law or another independent and impartial body established by law.

   In the circumstances where a Party provides for such a review by a court of law, it shall ensure that such a person also has access to an expeditious procedure established by law that is free of charge or inexpensive for reconsideration by a public authority or review by an independent and impartial body other than a court of law.

   Final decisions under this paragraph 1 shall be binding on the public authority holding the information. Reasons shall be stated in writing, at least where access to information is refused under this paragraph.

2. Each Party shall, within the framework of its national legislation, ensure that members of the public concerned

(a) Having a sufficient interest

   or, alternatively,

(b) Maintaining impairment of a right, where the administrative procedural law of a Party requires this as a precondition,

   have access to a review procedure before a court of law and/or another independent and impartial body established by law, to challenge the substantive and procedural legality of any decision, act or omission subject to the provisions of article 6 and, where so provided for under national law and without prejudice to paragraph 3 below, of other relevant provisions of this Convention.

   What constitutes a sufficient interest and impairment of a right shall be determined in accordance with the requirements of national law and consistently with the objective of giving the public concerned wide access to justice within the scope of this Convention. To this end, the interest of any non-governmental organization meeting the requirements referred to in article 2, paragraph 5, shall be deemed sufficient for the purpose of subparagraph (a) above. Such organizations shall also be deemed to have rights capable of being impaired for the purpose of subparagraph (b) above.

The provisions of this paragraph 2 shall not exclude the possibility of a preliminary review procedure before an administrative authority and shall not affect the requirement of exhaustion of administrative review procedures prior to recourse to judicial review procedures, where such a requirement exists under national law.

3.   In addition and without prejudice to the review procedures referred to in paragraphs 1 and 2 above, each Party shall ensure that, where they meet the criteria, if any, laid down in its national law, members of the public have access to administrative or judicial procedures to challenge acts and omissions by private persons and public authorities which contravene provisions of its national law relating to the environment.

4.   In addition and without prejudice to paragraph 1 above, the procedures referred to in paragraphs 1, 2 and 3 above shall provide adequate and effective remedies, including injunctive relief as appropriate, and be fair, equitable, timely and not prohibitively expensive. Decisions under this article shall be given or recorded in writing. Decisions of courts, and whenever possible of other bodies, shall be publicly accessible.

5.   In order to further the effectiveness of the provisions of this article, each Party shall ensure that information is provided to the public on access to administrative and judicial review procedures and shall consider the establishment of appropriate assistance mechanisms to remove or reduce financial and other barriers to access to justice.

[Omitted: Article 10 - Meeting of the Parties, Article 11 - Right to vote, Article 12 - Secretariat, Article 13 - Annexes, Article 14 - Amendments to the Convention, Article 15 - Review of compliance, Article 16 - Settlement of disputes, Article 17 - Signature, Article 18 - Depositary, Article 19 - Ratification, acceptance, approval and accession, Article 20 - Entry into force, Article 21 - Withdrawal, Article 22 - Authentic texts]

...

Annex I - List of activities referred to in article 6, paragraph 1 (a)

...

5.   Waste management:

-    Installations for the incineration, recovery, chemical treatment or landfill of hazardous waste;

-    Installations for the incineration of municipal waste with a capacity exceeding 3 tons per hour;

-    Installations for the disposal of non-hazardous waste with a capacity exceeding 50 tons per day;

-    Landfills receiving more than 10 tons per day or with a total capacity exceeding 25,000 tons, excluding landfills of inert waste.

...

10.   Groundwater abstraction or artificial groundwater recharge schemes where the annual volume of water abstracted or recharged is equivalent to or exceeds 10 million cubic metres.

11.   (a)   Works for the transfer of water resources between river basins where this transfer aims at preventing possible shortages of water and where the amount of water transferred exceeds 100 million cubic metres/year;

       (b)   In all other cases, works for the transfer of water resource between river basins where the multiannual average flow of the basin of abstraction exceeds 2,000 million cubic metres/year and where the amount of water transferred exceeds 5 per cent of this flow.

       In both cases transfers of piped drinking water are excluded.

...

[Omitted: Annex II - Arbitration]

9.   **Protocol on Water and Health to the 1992 Convention on the Protection and Use of Transboundary Watercourses and International Lakes [London, 17 June 1999]***

The Parties to this Protocol,

Mindful that water is essential to sustain life and that the availability of water in quantities, and of a quality, sufficient to meet basic human needs is a prerequisite both for improved health and for sustainable development,

Acknowledging the benefits to human health and well-being that accrue from wholesome and clean water and a harmonious and properly functioning water environment,

Aware that surface waters and groundwater are renewable resources with a limited capacity to recover from adverse impacts from human activities on their quantity and quality, that any failure to respect those limits may result in adverse effects, in both the short and long terms, on the health and well-being of those who rely on those resources and their quality, and that in consequence sustainable management of the hydrological cycle is essential for both meeting human needs and protecting the environment,

Aware also of the consequences for public health of shortfalls of water in the quantities, and of the quality, sufficient to meet basic human needs, and of the serious effects of such shortfalls, in particular on the vulnerable, the disadvantaged and the socially excluded,

...

Basing themselves upon the conclusions of the United Nations Conference on Environment and Development (Rio de Janeiro, 1992), in particular the Rio Declaration on Environment and Development and Agenda 21, as well as upon the programme for the further implementation of Agenda 21 (New York, 1997) and the consequent decision of the Commission on Sustainable

---

* UN Doc. MP.WAT/2000/1. Not yet in force. Parties and signatories (s): Albania, Armenia (s), Azerbaijan, Belgium, Bulgaria (s), Croatia (s), Cyprus (s), Czech Republic, Denmark (s), Estonia, Finland (s), France (s), Georgia (s), Germany (s), Greece (s), Hungary, Iceland (s), Italy (s), Latvia (s), Lithuania, Luxembourg, Malta (s), Monaco (s), Netherlands (s), Norway, Poland (s), Portugal (s), Republic of Moldova (s), Romania, Russian Federation, Slovakia, Slovenia (s), Spain (s), Sweden (s), Switzerland (s), Ukraine, United Kingdom of Great Britain and Northern Ireland (s), as at 31 July 2004.

Development on the sustainable management of freshwater (New York, 1998),

...

Have agreed as follows:

Article 1 - Objective

The objective of this Protocol is to promote at all appropriate levels, nationally as well as in transboundary and international contexts, the protection of human health and well-being, both individual and collective, within a framework of sustainable development, through improving water management, including the protection of water ecosystems, and through preventing, controlling and reducing water-related disease.

Article 2 - Definitions

For the purposes of this Protocol,

1. "Water-related disease" means any significant adverse effects on human health, such as death, disability, illness or disorders, caused directly or indirectly by the condition, or changes in the quantity or quality, of any waters;

2. "Drinking water" means water which is used, or intended to be available for use, by humans for drinking, cooking, food preparation, personal hygiene or similar purposes;

3. "Groundwater" means all water which is below the surface of the ground in the saturation zone and in direct contact with the ground or subsoil;

...

5. "Transboundary waters" means any surface or groundwaters which mark, cross or are located on boundaries between two or more States;

6. "Transboundary effects of water-related disease" means any significant adverse effects on human health, such as death, disability, illness or disorders, in an area under the jurisdiction of one Party, caused directly

or indirectly by the condition, or changes in the quantity or quality, of waters in an area under the jurisdiction of another Party, whether or not such effects constitute a transboundary impact;

7.   "Transboundary impact" means any significant adverse effect on the environment resulting from a change in the conditions of transboundary waters caused by a human activity, the physical origin of which is situated wholly or in part within an area under the jurisdiction of a Party to the Convention, within an area under the jurisdiction of another Party to the Convention. Such effects on the environment include effects on human health and safety, flora, fauna, soil, air, water, climate, landscape, and historical monuments or other physical structures or the interaction among these factors;

...

10.   "Water-management plan" means a plan for the development, management, protection and/or use of the water within a territorial area or groundwater aquifer, including the protection of the associated ecosystems;

11.   "The public" means one or more natural or legal persons, and, in accordance with national legislation or practice, their associations, organizations or groups;

12.   "Public authority" means:

(a)   Government at national, regional and other levels;

(b)   Natural or legal persons performing public administrative functions under national law, including specific duties, activities or services in relation to the environment, public health, sanitation, water management or water supply;

(c)   Any other natural or legal persons having public responsibilities or functions, or providing public services, under the control of a body or person falling within subparagraphs (a) or (b) above;

(d)   The institutions of any regional economic integration organization referred to in article 21 which is a Party.

This definition does not include bodies or institutions acting in a judicial or legislative capacity;

13. "Local" refers to all relevant levels of territorial unit below the level of the State;

14. "Convention" means the Convention on the Protection and Use of Transboundary Watercourses and International Lakes, done at Helsinki on 17 March 1992;

15. "Meeting of the Parties to the Convention" means the body established by the Parties to the Convention in accordance with its article 17;

16. "Party" means, unless the text otherwise indicates, a State or a regional economic integration organization referred to in article 21 which has consented to be bound by this Protocol and for which this Protocol is in force;

17. "Meeting of the Parties" means the body established by the Parties in accordance with article 16.

Article 3 - Scope

The provisions of this Protocol shall apply to:

(a)   Surface freshwater;

(b)   Groundwater;

(c)   Estuaries;

(d)   Coastal waters which are used for recreation or for the production of fish by aquaculture or for the production or harvesting of shellfish;

(e)   Enclosed waters generally available for bathing;

(f)   Water in the course of abstraction, transport, treatment or supply;

(g)   Waste water throughout the course of collection, transport, treatment and discharge or reuse.

Article 4 - General provisions

1.   The Parties shall take all appropriate measures to prevent, control and reduce water-related disease within a framework of integrated water-management systems aimed at sustainable use of water resources, ambient water quality which does not endanger human health, and protection of water ecosystems.

2.   The Parties shall, in particular, take all appropriate measures for the purpose of ensuring:

(a) Adequate supplies of wholesome drinking water which is free from any micro-organisms, parasites and substances which, owing to their numbers or concentration, constitute a potential danger to human health. This shall include the protection of water resources which are used as sources of drinking water, treatment of water and the establishment, improvement and maintenance of collective systems;

...

(c) Effective protection of water resources used as sources of drinking water, and their related water ecosystems, from pollution from other causes, including agriculture, industry and other discharges and emissions of hazardous substances. This shall aim at the effective reduction and elimination of discharges and emissions of substances judged to be hazardous to human health and water ecosystems;

...

3.   Subsequent references in this Protocol to "drinking water" and "sanitation" are to drinking water and sanitation that are required to meet the requirements of paragraph 2 of this article.

4.   The Parties shall base all such measures upon an assessment of any proposed measure in respect of all its implications, including the benefits, disadvantages and costs, for:

(a) Human health;

(b) Water resources; and

(c)   Sustainable development, which takes account of the differing new impacts of any proposed measure on the different environmental mediums.

5.   The Parties shall take all appropriate action to create legal, administrative and economic frameworks which are stable and enabling and within which the public, private and voluntary sectors can each make its contribution to improving water management for the purpose of preventing, controlling and reducing water-related disease.

6.   The Parties shall require public authorities which are considering taking action, or approving the taking by others of action, that may have a significant impact on the environment of any waters within the scope of this Protocol to take due account of any potential impact of that action on public health.

7.   Where a Party is a Party to the Convention on Environmental Impact Assessment in a Transboundary Context, compliance by public authorities of that Party with the requirements of that Convention in relation to a proposed action shall satisfy the requirement under paragraph 6 of this article in respect of that action.

...

Article 5 - Principles and approaches

In taking measures to implement this Protocol, the Parties shall be guided in particular by the following principles and approaches:

(a)   The precautionary principle, by virtue of which action to prevent, control or reduce water-related disease shall not be postponed on the ground that scientific research has not fully proved a causal link between the factor at which such action is aimed, on the one hand, and the potential contribution of that factor to the prevalence of water-related disease and/or transboundary impacts, on the other hand;

(b)   The polluter-pays principle, by virtue of which costs of pollution prevention, control and reduction shall be borne by the polluter;

(c)   States have, in accordance with the Charter of the United Nations and the principles of international law, the sovereign right to exploit their own resources pursuant to their own environmental and developmental policies, and the responsibility to ensure that activities within their jurisdiction or control do not cause damage to the environment of other States or of areas beyond the limits of national jurisdiction;

(d)   Water resources shall be managed so that the needs of the present generation are met without compromising the ability of future generations to meet their own needs;

(e)   Preventive action should be taken to avoid outbreaks and incidents of water-related disease and to protect water resources used as sources of drinking water because such action addresses the harm more efficiently and can be more cost-effective than remedial action;

(f)   Action to manage water resources should be taken at the lowest appropriate administrative level;

(g)   Water has social, economic and environmental values and should therefore be managed so as to realize the most acceptable and sustainable combination of those values;

(h)   Efficient use of water should be promoted through economic instruments and awareness-building;

(i)   Access to information and public participation in decision-making concerning water and health are needed, inter alia, in order to enhance the quality and the implementation of the decisions, to build public awareness of issues, to give the public the opportunity to express its concerns and to enable public authorities to take due account of such concerns. Such access and participation should be supplemented by appropriate access to judicial and administrative review of relevant decisions;

(j)   Water resources should, as far as possible, be managed in an integrated manner on the basis of catchment areas, with the aims of linking social and economic development to the protection of natural ecosystems and of relating water-resource management to regulatory measures concerning other environmental mediums. Such an integrated approach should apply across the whole of a catchment area, whether transboundary or not, including its associated coastal waters, the whole of a groundwater aquifer or the relevant parts of such a catchment area or groundwater aquifer;

(k) Special consideration should be given to the protection of people who are particularly vulnerable to water-related disease;

(l) Equitable access to water, adequate in terms both of quantity and of quality, should be provided for all members of the population, especially those who suffer a disadvantage or social exclusion;

(m) As a counterpart to their rights and entitlements to water under private law and public law, natural and legal persons and institutions, whether in the public sector or the private sector, should contribute to the protection of the water environment and the conservation of water resources; and

(n) In implementing this Protocol, due account should be given to local problems, needs and knowledge.

Article 6 - Targets and target dates

1. In order to achieve the objective of this Protocol, the Parties shall pursue the aims of:

(a) Access to drinking water for everyone;

(b) Provision of sanitation for everyone within a framework of integrated water-management systems aimed at sustainable use of water resources, ambient water quality which does not endanger human health, and protection of water ecosystems.

2. For these purposes, the Parties shall each establish and publish national and/or local targets for the standards and levels of performance that need to be achieved or maintained for a high level of protection against water-related disease. These targets shall be periodically revised. In doing all this, they shall make appropriate practical and/or other provisions for public participation, within a transparent and fair framework, and shall ensure that due account is taken of the outcome of the public participation. Except where national or local circumstances make them irrelevant for preventing, controlling and reducing water-related disease, the targets shall cover, inter alia:

...

(f) The application of recognized good practice to the management of water supply and sanitation, including the protection of waters used as sources for drinking water;

(g) The occurrence of discharges of:

    (i) Untreated waste water; and

    (ii) Untreated storm water overflows

from waste-water collection systems to waters within the scope of this Protocol;

(h) The quality of discharges of waste water from waste-water treatment installations to waters within the scope of this Protocol;

...

(j) The quality of waters which are used as sources for drinking water, which are generally used for bathing or which are used for aquaculture or for the production or harvesting of shellfish;

...

(l) The identification and remediation of particularly contaminated sites which adversely affect waters within the scope of this Protocol or are likely to do so and which thus threaten to give rise to water-related disease;

(m) The effectiveness of systems for the management, development, protection and use of water resources, including the application of recognized good practice to the control of pollution from sources of all kinds;

(n) The frequency of the publication of information on the quality of the drinking water supplied and of other waters relevant to the targets in this paragraph in the intervals between the publication of information under article 7, paragraph 2.

3.   Within two years of becoming a Party, each Party shall establish and publish targets referred to in paragraph 2 of this article, and target dates for achieving them.

4.   Where a long process of implementation is foreseen for the achievement of a target, intermediate or phased targets shall be set.

5.   In order to promote the achievement of the targets referred to in paragraph 2 of this article, the Parties shall each:

(a) Establish national or local arrangements for coordination between their competent authorities;

(b) Develop water-management plans in transboundary, national and/or local contexts, preferably on the basis of catchment areas or groundwater aquifers. In doing so, they shall make appropriate practical and/or other provisions for public participation, within a transparent and fair framework, and shall ensure that due account is taken of the outcome of the public participation. Such plans may be incorporated in other relevant plans, programmes or documents which are being drawn up for other purposes, provided that they enable the public to see clearly the proposals for achieving the targets referred to in this article and the respective target dates;

...

Article 7 - Review and assessment of progress

1.   The Parties shall each collect and evaluate data on:

(a) Their progress towards the achievement of the targets referred to in article 6, paragraph 2;

...

[Omitted: Article 8 - Response systems]

Article 9 - Public awareness, education, training, research and development and information

1. The Parties shall take steps designed to enhance the awareness of all sectors of the public regarding:

(a) The importance of, and the relationship between, water management and public health;

(b) The rights and entitlements to water and corresponding obligations under private and public law of natural and legal persons and institutions, whether in the public sector or the private sector, as well as their moral obligations to contribute to the protection of the water environment and the conservation of water resources.

2. The Parties shall promote:

(a) Understanding of the public-health aspects of their work by those responsible for water management, water supply and sanitation; and

(b) Understanding of the basic principles of water management, water supply and sanitation by those responsible for public health.

3. The Parties shall encourage the education and training of the professional and technical staff who are needed for managing water resources and for operating systems of water supply and sanitation, and encourage the updating and improvement of their knowledge and skills. This education and training shall include relevant aspects of public health.

...

Article 10 - Public information

1. As a complement to the requirements of this Protocol for Parties to publish specific information or documents, each Party shall take steps within the framework of its legislation to make available to the public such information as is held by public authorities and is reasonably needed to inform public discussion of:

(a) The establishment of targets and of target dates for their achievement and the development of water-management plans in accordance with article 6;

...

(c) The promotion of public awareness, education, training, research, development and information in accordance with article 9.

2. Each Party shall ensure that public authorities, in response to a request for other information relevant to the implementation of this Protocol, make such information available within a reasonable time to the public, within the framework of national legislation.

3. The Parties shall ensure that information referred to in article 7, paragraph 4, and paragraph 1 of this article shall be available to the public at all reasonable times for inspection free of charge, and shall provide members of the public with reasonable facilities for obtaining from the Parties, on payment of reasonable charges, copies of such information.

4. Nothing in this Protocol shall require a public authority to publish information or make information available to the public if:

...

5. Nothing in this Protocol shall require a public authority to publish information or make information available to the public if disclosure of the information would adversely affect:

...

Article 11 - International cooperation

The Parties shall cooperate and, as appropriate, assist each other:

(a) In international actions in support of the objectives of this Protocol;

(b) On request, in implementing national and local plans in pursuance of this Protocol.

Article 12 - Joint and coordinated international action

In pursuance of article 11, subparagraph (a), the Parties shall promote cooperation in international action relating to:

(a)   The development of commonly agreed targets for matters referred to in article 6, paragraph 2;

...

Article 13 - Cooperation in relation to transboundary waters

1.   Where any Parties border the same transboundary waters, as a complement to their other obligations under articles 11 and 12, they shall cooperate and, as appropriate, assist each other to prevent, control and reduce transboundary effects of water-related disease. In particular, they shall:

(a)   Exchange information and share knowledge about the transboundary waters and the problems and risks which they present with the other Parties bordering the same waters;

(b)   Endeavour to establish with the other Parties bordering the same transboundary waters joint or coordinated water-management plans in accordance with article 6, paragraph 5 (b), and surveillance and early-warning systems and contingency plans in accordance with article 8, paragraph 1, for the purpose of responding to outbreaks and incidents of water-related disease and significant threats of such outbreaks and incidents, especially from water-pollution incidents or extreme weather events;

(c)   On the basis of equality and reciprocity, adapt their agreements and other arrangements regarding their transboundary waters in order to eliminate any contradictions with the basic principles of this Protocol and to define their mutual relations and conduct regarding the aims of this Protocol;

(d)   Consult each other, at the request of any one of them, on the significance of any adverse effect on human health which may constitute a water-related disease.

2. Where the Parties concerned are Parties to the Convention, the cooperation and assistance in respect of any transboundary effects of water-related disease which are transboundary impacts shall take place in accordance with the provisions of the Convention.

Article 14 - International support for national action

When cooperating and assisting each other in the implementation of national and local plans in pursuance of article 11, subparagraph (b), the Parties shall, in particular, consider how they can best help to promote:

(a) Preparation of water-management plans in transboundary, national and/or local contexts and of schemes for improving water supply and sanitation;

(b) Improved formulation of projects, especially infrastructure projects, in pursuance of such plans and schemes, in order to facilitate access to sources of finance;

(c) Effective execution of such projects;

(d) Establishment of systems for surveillance and early-warning systems, contingency plans and response capacities in relation to water-related disease;

(e) Preparation of legislation needed to support the implementation of this Protocol;

(f) Education and training of key professional and technical staff;

(g) Research into, and development of, cost-effective means and techniques for preventing, controlling and reducing water-related disease;

(h) Operation of effective networks to monitor and assess the provision and quality of water-related services, and development of integrated information systems and databases;

(i) Achievement of quality assurance for monitoring activities, including inter-laboratory comparability.

[Omitted: Article 15 - Review of compliance, Article 16 - Meeting of the Parties, Article 17 - Secretariat, Article 18 - Amendments to the Protocol, Article 19 - Right to vote, Article 20 - Settlement of disputes, Article 21 - Signature, Article 22 - Ratification, acceptance, approval and accession, Article 23 - Entry into force, Article 24 - Withdrawal, Article 25 - Depositary, Article 26 - Authentic texts]

. . .

10.   Revised Protocol on Shared Watercourses in the Southern African Development Community (SADC) [Windhoek, 7 August 2000]*

Preamble

[The Parties]

Bearing in mind the progress with the development and codification of international water law initiated by the Helsinki Rules and that the United Nations subsequently adopted the United Nations Convention on the Law of the Non-Navigational Uses of International Watercourses;

Recognising the relevant provisions of Agenda 21 of the United Nations Conference on Environment and Development, the concepts of environmentally sound management, sustainable development and equitable utilisation of shared watercourses in the SADC Region;
Considering the existing and emerging socio-economic development programmes in the SADC Region and their impact on the environment;

Desirous of developing close co-operation for judicious, sustainable and co-ordinated utilisation of the resources of the shared watercourses in the SADC Region;

Convinced of the need for co-ordinated and environmentally sound development of the resources of shared watercourses in the SADC Region in order to support sustainable socio-economic development;

---

* 40 ILM 321 (2001). Entry into force: 22 September 2003. Parties and/or signatories: Angola, Botswana, Congo, Lesotho, Malawi, Mauritius, Mozambique, Namibia, Seychelles, South Africa, Swaziland, United Republic of Tanzania, Zambia, Zimbabwe.

Recognising that there are as yet no regional conventions regulating common utilisation and management of the resources of shared watercourses in the SADC Region;

Mindful of the existence of other Agreements in the SADC Region regarding the common utilisation of certain watercourses; and

In accordance with Article 22 of the Treaty, have agreed as follows:

Article 1 - Definitions

1. For the purposes of this Protocol the following terms shall have the meanings ascribed to them hereunder:

"Agricultural use" means use of water for irrigation purposes;

"Domestic use" means use of water for drinking, washing, cooking, bathing, sanitation and stock watering purposes;

"Emergency situation" means a situation that causes or poses an imminent threat of causing serious harm to Watercourse States and which results suddenly from natural causes, such as torrential rains, floods, landslides or earthquakes or from human conduct;

"Environmental use" means the use of water for the preservation and maintenance of ecosystems;

"Industrial use" means use of water for commercial, electrical power generation, industrial, manufacturing and mining purposes;

"Management of a shared watercourse" means

(i)   planning the sustainable development of a shared watercourse and providing for the implementation of any plans adopted; and

(ii) otherwise promoting the rational, equitable and optimal utilisation, protection, and control of the watercourse;

"Navigational use" means use of water for sailing whether it be for transport, fishing, recreation or tourism;

"Pollution of a shared watercourse" means any detrimental alteration in the composition or quality of the waters of a shared watercourse which results directly or indirectly from human conduct;

"Regulation of the flow of the waters of a shared watercourse" means the use of hydraulic works or any other continuing measure to alter, vary or otherwise control the flow of waters of a shared watercourse;

"Shared watercourse" means a watercourse passing through or forming the border between two or more Watercourse States;

"Significant Harm" means non-trivial harm capable of being established by objective evidence without necessarily rising to the level of being substantial;

"State Party" means a member of SADC that ratifies or accedes to this Protocol;

"Watercourse" means a system of surface and groundwaters consisting by virtue of their physical relationship a unitary whole normally flowing into a common terminus such as the sea, lake or aquifer;

"Watercourse State" means a State Party in whose territory part of a watercourse is situated.

2.   Any other term defined in the Treaty and used in this Protocol shall have the same meaning as ascribed to it in the Treaty.

Article 2 - Objective

The overall objective of this Protocol is to foster closer cooperation for judicious, sustainable and co-ordinated management, protection and utilisation of shared watercourses and advance the SADC agenda of regional integration and poverty alleviation. In order to achieve this objective, this Protocol seeks to:

(a)   promote and facilitate the establishment of shared watercourse agreements and Shared Watercourse Institutions for the management of shared watercourses;

(b)   advance the sustainable, equitable and reasonable utilisation of the shared watercourses;

(c)   promote a co-ordinated and integrated environmentally sound development and management of shared watercourses;

(d)   promote the harmonisation and monitoring of legislation and policies for planning, development, conservation, protection of shared watercourses, and allocation of the resources thereof; and

(e)   promote research and technology development, information exchange, capacity building, and the application of appropriate technologies in shared watercourses management.

Article 3 - General principles

For the purposes of this Protocol the following general principles shall apply:

1.   The State Parties recognise the principle of the unity and coherence of each shared watercourse and in accordance with this principle, undertake to harmonise the water uses in the shared watercourses and to ensure that all necessary interventions are consistent with the sustainable development of all Watercourse States and observe the objectives of regional integration and harmonisation of their socio-economic policies and plans.

2.   The utilisation of shared watercourses within the SADC Region shall be open to each Watercourse State, in respect of the watercourses within its territory and without prejudice to its sovereign rights, in accordance with the principles contained in this Protocol. The utilisation of the resources of the watercourses shall include agricultural, domestic, industrial, navigational and environmental uses.

3.   State Parties undertake to respect the existing rules of customary or general international law relating to the utilisation and management of the resources of shared watercourses.

4.   State Parties shall maintain a proper balance between resource development for a higher standard of living for their people and conservation and enhancement of the environment to promote sustainable development.

5.   State Parties undertake to pursue and establish close co-operation with regard to the study and execution of all projects likely to have an effect on the regime of the shared watercourse.

6.   State Parties shall exchange available information and data regarding the hydrological, hydrogeological, water quality, meteorological and environmental condition of shared watercourses.

7.   (a)   Watercourse States shall in their respective territories utilise a shared watercourse in an equitable and reasonable manner. In particular, shared watercourse shall be used and developed by Watercourse States with a view to attain optimal and sustainable utilisation thereof and benefits therefrom, taking into account the interests of the Watercourse States concerned, consistent with adequate protection of the watercourse for the benefit of current and future generations.

     (b)   Watercourse States shall participate in the use, development and protection of a shared watercourse in an equitable and reasonable manner. Such participation, includes both the right to utilise the watercourse and the duty to co-operate in the protection and development thereof, as provided in this Protocol.

8.   (a)   Utilisation of a shared watercourse in an equitable and reasonable manner within the meaning of Article 7(a) and (b) requires taking into account all relevant factors and circumstances including:

          (i)   geographical, hydrographical, hydrological, climatical, ecological and other factors of a natural character;

          (ii)   the social, economic and environmental needs of the Watercourse States concerned;

          (iii) the population dependent on the shared watercourse in each Watercourse State;

          (iv)   the effects of the use or uses of a shared watercourse in one Watercourse State on other Watercourse States;

          (v)   existing and potential uses of the watercourse;

(vi) conservation, protection, development and economy of use of the water resources of the shared watercourse and the costs of measures taken to that effect; and

(vii) the availability of alternatives, of comparable value, to a particular planned or existing use.

(b) The weight to be given to each factor is to be determined by its importance in comparison with that of other relevant factors. In determining what is an equitable and reasonable use, all relevant factors are to be considered together and a conclusion reached on the basis of the whole.

9. State Parties shall deal with planned measures in conformity with the procedure set out in Article 4 (1).

10. (a) State Parties shall, in utilising a shared watercourse in their territories, take all appropriate measures to prevent the causing of significant harm to other Watercourse States.

(b) Where significant harm is nevertheless caused to another Watercourse State, the State whose use causes such harm shall, in the absence of agreement to such use, take all appropriate measures, having due regard for the provisions of paragraph (a) above in consultation with the affected States, to eliminate or mitigate such harm and, where appropriate, to discuss the question of compensation.

(c) Unless the Watercourse States concerned have agreed otherwise for the protection of the interests of persons, natural or juridical, who have suffered or are under a serious threat of suffering significant transboundary harm as a result of activities related to a shared watercourse, a Watercourse State shall not discriminate on the basis of nationality or residence or place where the injury occurred, in granting to such persons, in accordance with its legal system, access to judicial or other procedures, or a right to claim compensation or other relief in respect of significant harm caused by such activities carried on in its territory.

Article 4 - Specific provisions

1.   Planned Measures

(a)   Information concerning planned measures

State Parties shall exchange information and consult each other and, if necessary, negotiate the possible effects of planned measures on the condition of a shared watercourse.

(b)   Notification concerning planned measures with possible adverse effects

Before a State Party implements or permits the implementation of planned measures which may have a significant adverse effect upon other Watercourse States, it shall provide those States with timely notification thereof. Such notification shall be accompanied by available technical data and information, including the results of any environmental impact assessment, in order to enable the notified States to evaluate the possible effects of the planned measures.

(c)   Period for reply to notification

    (i)   Unless otherwise agreed, a State Party providing a notification under paragraph (b) shall allow the notified States a period of six months within which to study and evaluate the possible effects of the planned measures and to communicate the findings to it;

    (ii)   This period shall, at the request of a notified State for which the evaluation of the planned measures poses difficulty, be extended for a period of six months.

(d)   Obligations of the notifying State during the period for reply

During the period referred to in paragraph (c), the notifying State:

    (i)   shall co-operate with the notified States by providing them, on request, with any additional data and information that is available and necessary   for an accurate evaluation; and

    (ii)   shall not implement or permit the implementation of the planned measures without the consent of the notified States.

(e)   Reply to Notification

The notified States shall communicate their findings to the notifying State as early as possible within the period applicable pursuant to paragraph (c). If a notified State finds that implementation of the planned measures would be inconsistent with the provisions of Article 3 (7) or (10), it shall attach to its finding a documented explanation setting the reasons for the findings.

(f)   Absence of reply to notification

    (i)   If, within the period applicable pursuant to paragraph (c), the notifying State receives no communication under (e), it may, subject to its obligations under Article 3 (7) and (10), proceed with the implementation of the planned measures, in accordance with the notification and any other data and information provided to the notified States.

    (ii)   Any claim to compensation by a notified State which has failed to reply within the period applicable pursuant to paragraph (c) may be offset by the costs incurred by the notifying State for action undertaken after the expiration of the time for a reply which would not have been undertaken if the notified State had objected within that period.

(g)   Consultations and negotiations concerning planned measures

    (i)   If a communication is made under paragraph (e) that implementation of the planned measures would be inconsistent with the provisions of Article 3 (7) or (10), the notifying State and the State making the communication shall enter into consultations and, if necessary, negotiations with a view to arriving at an equitable resolution of the situation.

    (ii)   The consultations and negotiations shall be conducted on the basis that each State must in good faith pay reasonable regard to the rights and legitimate interests of the other States.

    (iii)   During the course of the consultations and negotiations, the notifying State shall, if so requested by the notified State at the time it makes the communication, refrain from implementing or permitting the implementation of the planned measures for a period of six months unless otherwise agreed.

(h) Procedures in the absence of notification

(i) If a State Party has reasonable grounds to believe that another Watercourse State is planning measures that may have a significant adverse effect upon it, the former State may request the latter to apply the provisions of paragraph (b). The request shall be accompanied by a documented explanation setting forth its grounds.

(ii) If the State planning the measures finds that it is not under an obligation to provide a notification under paragraph (b), it shall so inform the other State, providing a documented explanation setting forth the reasons for such finding. If this finding does not satisfy the other State, the two States shall, at the request of that other State, promptly enter into consultations and negotiations in the manner provided in sub-paragraphs (i) and (ii) of paragraph (g).

(iii) During the course of the consultations and negotiations, the State planning the measures shall, if so requested by the other State at the time it requests the initiation of consultations and negotiations, refrain from implementing or permitting the implementation of those measures for a period of six months unless otherwise agreed.

(i) Urgent implementation of planned measures

(i) In the event that the implementation of planned measures is of the utmost urgency in order to protect public health, public safety or other equally important interests, the State planning the measures may, subject to paragraphs 7 and 10 of Article 3, immediately proceed to implementation, notwithstanding the provisions of paragraph (d) and sub-paragraph (iii) of paragraph (g).

(ii) In such case, a formal declaration of the urgency of the measures shall be communicated without delay to the other Watercourse States referred to in paragraph (b) together with the relevant data and information.

(iii) The State planning the measures shall, at the request of any of the States referred to in paragraph (ii), promptly enter into consultations and negotiations with it in the manner indicated in sub-paragraphs (i) and (ii) of paragraph (g).

2. Environmental Protection and Preservation

(a) Protection and preservation of ecosystems

State Parties shall, individually and, where appropriate, jointly, protect and preserve the ecosystems of a shared watercourse.

(b) Prevention, reduction and control of pollution

(i) State Parties shall, individually and, where appropriate, jointly, prevent, reduce and control the pollution and environmental degradation of a shared watercourse that may cause significant harm to other Watercourse States or to their environment, including harm to human health or safety, to the use of the waters for any beneficial purpose or to the living resources of the watercourse.

(ii) Watercourse States shall take steps to harmonise their policies and legislation in this connection.

(iii) State Parties shall, at the request of any one or more of them, consult with a view to arriving at mutually agreeable measures and methods to prevent, reduce and control pollution of a shared watercourse, such as:

(aa) setting joint water quality objectives and criteria;

(bb) establishing techniques and practices to address pollution from point and non-point sources;

(cc) establishing lists of substances the introduction of which, into the waters of a shared watercourse, is to be prohibited, limited, investigated or monitored.

(c)   Introduction of alien or new species

State Parties shall take all measures necessary to prevent the introduction of species, alien or new, into a shared watercourse which may have effects detrimental to the ecosystems of the watercourse resulting in significant harm to other Watercourse States.

(d)   Protection and preservation of the aquatic environment

State Parties shall individually and, where appropriate, in co-operation with other States, take all measures with respect to a shared watercourse that are necessary to protect and preserve the aquatic environment, including estuaries, taking into account generally accepted international rules and standards.

3.   Management of Shared Watercourses

(a)   Management

Watercourse States shall, at the request of any of them, enter into consultations concerning the management of a shared watercourse, which may include the establishment of a joint management mechanism.

(b)   Regulation

(i)   Watercourse States shall co-operate, where appropriate, to respond to needs or opportunities for regulation of the flow of the waters of a shared watercourse.

(ii)   Unless otherwise agreed, Watercourse States shall participate on an equitable and reasonable basis in the construction and maintenance or defrayal of the costs of such regulation works as they may have agreed to undertake.

(c)   Installations

(i)   Watercourse States shall, within their respective territories, employ their best efforts to maintain and protect installations, facilities and other works related to a shared watercourse.

(ii) Watercourse States shall, at the request of any of them which has reasonable grounds to believe that it may suffer significant adverse effects, enter into consultations with regards to:

    (aa) the safe operation and maintenance of installations, facilities, or other works related to a shared watercourse; and

    (bb) the protection of installations, facilities or other works from willful or negligent acts or the forces of nature.

(iii) Shared watercourses and related installations, facilities and other works shall enjoy the protection accorded by the principles and rules of international law applicable in international and non-international armed conflict and shall not be used in violation of those principles and rules.

4. Prevention and mitigation of harmful conditions

(a) State Parties shall individually and, where appropriate, jointly take all appropriate measures to prevent or mitigate conditions related to a shared watercourse that may be harmful to other Watercourse States, whether resulting from natural causes or human conduct, such as floods, water-borne diseases, siltation, erosion, salt-water intrusion, drought or desertification.

(b) State Parties shall require any person intending to use the waters of a shared watercourse within their respective territories for purposes other than domestic or environmental use or who intends to discharge any type of waste into such waters, to first obtain a permit, licence or other similar authorisation from the relevant authority within the State concerned. The permit or other similar authorisation shall be granted only after such State has determined that the intended use or discharge will not cause significant harm on the regime of the watercourse.

5. Emergency situations

State Parties shall, without delay, notify other potentially affected States, the SADC Water Sector Co-ordinating Unit and competent international organisations of any emergency situation originating within their respective territories and promptly supply the necessary information to such affected

States and competent organisations with a view to co-operate in the prevention, mitigation, and elimination, of harmful effects of the emergency.

Article 5 - Institutional framework for implementation

1.   The following institutional mechanisms responsible for the implementation of this Protocol are hereby established -

(a)   SADC Water Sector Organs

    (i)   the Committee of Water Ministers;

    (ii)   the Committee of Water Senior Officials;

    (iii)   the Water Sector Co-ordinating Unit; and

    (iv)   the Water Resources Technical Committee and sub-Committees.

(b)   Shared Watercourse Institutions

(c)   The Committee of Water Ministers shall consist of Ministers responsible for water.

(d)   The Committee of Water Senior Officials shall consist of the Permanent Secretaries or officials of equivalent rank responsible for water.

(e)   The Water Sector Coordinating Unit which shall be the executing agency of the Water Sector shall be headed by a Co-ordinator appointed by the State Party responsible for coordinating the Water Sector, and he or she shall be assisted by such supporting staff of professional, administrative and secretarial personnel as the Coordinator may deem necessary.

2.   The SADC Water Sector Organs shall have the following functions:

(a)   The Committee of Water Ministers

    (i)   Oversee and monitor the implementation of the Protocol and assist in resolving potential conflicts on shared watercourses.

(ii) Guide and co-ordinate cooperation and harmonisation of legislation, policies, strategies, programmes and projects.

(iii) Advise the Council on policies to be pursued.

(iv) Recommend to Council the creation of such other organs as may be necessary for the implementation of this Protocol.

(v) Provide regular updates to the Council on the status of the implementation of this Protocol.

(b) The Committee of Water Senior Officials

(i) Examine all reports and documents put before them by the Water Resources Technical Committee and the Water Sector Co-ordinating Unit.

(ii) Initiate and advise the Committee of Water Ministers on policies, strategies, programmes and projects to be presented to the Council for approval.

(iii) Recommend to the Committee of Water Ministers the creation of such other organs as may be necessary for the implementation of this Protocol.

(iv) Provide regular updates to the Committee of Water Ministers on the status of the implementation of this Protocol.

(c) The Water Sector Co-ordinating Unit

(i) Monitor the implementation of this Protocol.

(ii) Liase with other SADC organs and Shared Watercourse Institutions on matters pertaining to the implementation of this Protocol.

(iii) Provide guidance on the interpretation of this Protocol.

(iv) Advise State Parties on matters pertaining to this Protocol.

(v) Organise and manage all technical and policy meetings.

(vi) Draft terms of reference for consultancies and manage the execution of those assignments.

(vii) Mobilise or facilitate the mobilisation of financial and technical resources for the implementation of this Protocol.

(viii) Annually submit a status report on the implementation of the Protocol to the Council through the Committee of Water Ministers.

(ix) Keep an inventory of all shared watercourse management institutions and their agreements on shared watercourses within the SADC Region.

(d) The Water Resources Technical Committee

(i) Provide technical support and advice to the Committee of Water Senior Officials through the Water Sector Co-ordinating Unit with respect to the implementation of this Protocol.

(ii) Discuss issues tabled by the Water Sector Co-ordinating Unit and prepare for the Committee of Water Senior Officials.

(iii) Consider and approve terms of reference for consultancies, including the appointment of consultants.

(iv) Recommend to the Committee of Water Senior Officials any matter of interest to it on which agreement has not been reached.

(v) Appoint working groups for short-term tasks and standing sub-committees for longer term tasks.

(vi) Address any other issues that may have implications on the implementation of this Protocol.

3. Shared watercourse institutions

(a) Watercourse States undertake to establish appropriate institutions such as watercourse commissions, water authorities or boards as may be determined.

(b) The responsibilities of such institutions shall be determined by the nature of their objectives which must be in conformity with the principles set out in this Protocol.

(c) Shared Watercourse Institutions shall provide on a regular basis or as required by the Water Sector Co-ordinating Unit, all the information necessary to assess progress on the implementation of the provisions of this Protocol, including the development of their respective agreements.

4. State Parties undertake to adopt appropriate measures to give effect to the institutional framework referred to in this Article for the implementation of this Protocol.

Article 6 - Shared watercourse agreements

1. In the absence of any agreement to the contrary, nothing in this Protocol shall affect the rights or obligations of a Watercourse State arising from agreements in force for it on the date on which it became a party to the Protocol.

2. Notwithstanding the provisions of paragraph 1, parties to agreements referred to in paragraph 1 may harmonise such agreements with this Protocol.

3. Watercourse States may enter into agreements, which apply the provision of this Protocol to the characteristics and uses of a particular shared watercourse or part thereof.

4. Where a watercourse agreement is concluded between two or more Watercourse States, it shall define the waters to which it applies. Such an agreement may be entered into with respect to an entire shared watercourse or any part thereof or a particular project, programme or use except insofar as the agreement adversely affects, to a significant extent, the use by one or more other Watercourse States of the waters of the watercourse, without their express consent.

5. Where some but not all Watercourse States to a particular shared watercourse are parties to an agreement, nothing contained in such agreement shall affect the rights or obligations under this Protocol of Watercourse States that are not parties to such an agreement.

6.   Every Watercourse State is entitled to participate in the negotiation of and to become a party to any watercourse agreement that applies to the entire shared watercourse, as well as to participate in any relevant consultations.

7.   A Watercourse State whose use of a shared watercourse may be affected to a significant extent by the implementation of a proposed watercourse agreement that applies only to a part of the watercourse or to a particular project, programme or use is entitled to participate in consultations on such an agreement and, where appropriate, in the negotiation thereof in good faith with a view to becoming a party thereto, to the extent that its use is thereby affected.

Article 7 - Settlement of disputes

1.   State Parties shall strive to resolve all disputes regarding the implementation, interpretation or application of the provisions of this Protocol amicably in accordance with the principles enshrined in Article 4 of the Treaty.

2.   Disputes between State Parties regarding the interpretation or application of the provisions of this Protocol which are not settled amicably, shall be referred to the Tribunal.

3.   If a dispute arises between SADC on the one hand and a State Party on the other, a request shall be made for an advisory opinion in accordance with article 16(4) of the Treaty.

[Omitted: Article 8 - Signature, Article 9 - Ratification, Article 10 - Entry into force, Article 11 - Accession, Article 12 - Amendment, Article 13 - Withdrawal, Article 14 - Termination, Article 15 - Depositary]

Article 16 - Protocol on shared watercourse systems in the SADC region

1.   Upon entry into force of this Protocol, the Protocol on Shared Watercourse Systems in the Southern African Development Community (SADC) Region, which entered into force on 29th September 1998, shall be repealed and replaced by this Protocol.

...

11. Framework Convention on the Protection and Sustainable Development of the Carpathians [Kiev, 22 May 2003]*

"The Parties",

Acknowledging that the Carpathians are a unique natural treasure of great beauty and ecological value, an important reservoir of biodiversity, the headwaters of major rivers, an essential habitat and refuge for many endangered species of plants and animals and Europe's largest area of virgin forests, and aware that the Carpathians constitute a major ecological, economic, cultural, recreational and living environment in the heart of Europe, shared by numerous peoples and countries;

...

Being aware of the fact that efforts to protect, maintain and sustainably manage the natural resources of the Carpathians cannot be achieved by one country alone and require regional cooperation, and of the added value of transboundary cooperation in achieving ecological coherence;

Have agreed as follows:

Article 1 - Geographical scope

1. The Convention applies to the Carpathian region (hereinafter referred to as the "Carpathians"), to be defined by the Conference of the Parties.

2. Each Party may extend the application of this Convention and its Protocols to additional parts of its national territory by making a declaration to the Depositary, provided that this is necessary to implement the provisions of the Convention.

Article 2 - General objectives and principles

1. The Parties shall pursue a comprehensive policy and cooperate for the protection and sustainable development of the Carpathians with a view

---

* FAOLEX (FAO legal database online). UN Doc. ECE/CEP/104. Parties and/or signatories: Czech Republic, Hungary, Poland, Romania, Serbia and Montenegro, Slovakia, Ukraine.

to inter alia improving quality of life, strengthening local economies and communities, and conservation of natural values and cultural heritage.

2.   In order to achieve the objectives referred to in paragraph 1, the Parties shall take appropriate measures, in the areas covered by Articles 4 to 13 of this Convention by promoting:

(a)   the precaution and prevention principles,

(b)   the "polluter pays" principle,

(c)   public participation and stakeholder involvement,

(d)   transboundary cooperation,

(e)   integrated planning and management of land and water resources,

(f)   a programmatic approach, and

(g)   the ecosystem approach.

3.   To achieve the objectives set forth in this Convention and to ensure its implementation, the Parties may, as appropriate, develop and adopt Protocols.

Article 3 - Integrated approach to the land resources management

The Parties shall apply the approach of the integrated land resources management as defined in Chapter 10 of the Agenda 21, by developing and implementing appropriate tools, such as integrated management plans, relating to the areas of this Convention.

[Omitted: Article 4 - Conservation and sustainable use of biological and landscape diversity, Article 5 - Spatial planning]

Article 6 - Sustainable and integrated water/river basin management

Taking into account the hydrological, biological and ecological, and other specificities of mountain river basins, the Parties shall:

(a) take appropriate measures to promote policies integrating sustainable use of water resources, with land-use planning, and aim at pursuing policies and plans based on an integrated river basin management approach, recognizing the importance of pollution and flood management, prevention and control, and reducing water habitats fragmentation,

(b) pursue policies aiming at sustainable management of surface and groundwater resources, ensuring adequate supply of good quality surface and groundwater as needed for sustainable, balanced and equitable water use, and adequate sanitation and treatment of waste water,

(c) pursue policies aiming at conserving natural watercourses, springs, lakes and groundwater resources as well as preserving and protecting of wetlands and wetland ecosystems, and protecting against natural and anthropogenic detrimental effects such as flooding and accidental water pollution,

(d) further develop a coordinated or joint system of measures, activities and early warning for transboundary impacts on the water regime of flooding and accidental water pollution, as well as co-operate in preventing and reducing the damages and giving assistance in restoration works.

[Omitted: Article 7 - Sustainable agriculture and forestry, Article 8 - Sustainable transport and infrastructure, Article 9 - Sustainable tourism, Article 10 - Industry and energy, Article 11 - Cultural heritage and traditional knowledge]

Article 12 - Environmental assessment/information system, monitoring and early warning

1. The Parties shall apply, where necessary, risk assessments, environmental impact assessments, and strategic environmental assessments, taking into account the specificities of the Carpathian mountain ecosystems, and shall consult on projects of transboundary character in the Carpathians, and assess their environmental impact, in order to avoid transboundary harmful effects.

2.   The Parties shall pursue policies, using existing methods of monitoring and assessment, aiming at promoting:

(a)   cooperation in the carrying out of research activities and scientific assessments in the Carpathians,

(b)   joint or complementary monitoring programmes, including the systematic monitoring of the state of the environment,

(c)   comparability, complementarity and standardization of research methods and related data-acquisition activities,

(d)   harmonization of existing and development of new environmental, social and economic indicators,

(e)   a system of early warning, monitoring and assessment of natural and man-made environmental risks and hazards, and

(f)   an information system, accessible to all Parties.

[Omitted: Article 13 - Awareness raising, education and public participation, Article 14 - Conference of the Parties, Article 15 - Secretariat, Article 16 - Subsidiary bodies, Article 17 - Financial contributions, Article 18 - Protocols, Article 19 - Amendments to the Convention, Article 20 - Settlement of disputes, Article 21 - Entry into force, Article 22 - Withdrawal, Article 23 - Depositary]

...

12. African Convention on the Conservation of Nature and Natural Resources [Maputo, 11 July 2003]*

Preamble

We, the Heads of State and Government of the Member States of the African Union (AU),

Conscious that the natural environment of Africa and the natural resources with which Africa is endowed are an irreplaceable part of the African heritage and constitute a capital of vital importance to the continent and humankind as a whole;

...

Conscious of the ever-growing importance of natural resources from economic, social, cultural and environmental points of view;

...

Re-affirming that States have, in accordance with the Charter of the United Nations and the principles of international law, a sovereign right to exploit their own resources pursuant to their environmental and developmental policies, and the responsibility to ensure that activities within their jurisdiction or control do not cause damage to the environment of other States or of areas beyond the limits of national jurisdiction;

Re-affirming further that States are responsible for protecting and conserving their environment and natural resources and for using them in a sustainable manner with the aim to satisfy human needs according to the carrying capacity of the environment;

Conscious of the dangers which threaten some of these irreplaceable assets;

Desirous of undertaking individual and joint action for the conservation, utilization and development of these assets by establishing and maintaining their sustainable use;

---

* FAOLEX (FAO legal database online). Parties and/or signatories: Benin, Burundi, Djibouti, Gambia, Ghana, Guinea, Kenya, Liberia, Mali, Mozambique, Namibia, Nigeria, Rwanda, Senegal, Sierra Leone, Tanzania, Togo, Uganda, Zimbabwe.

...

Conscious of the need to continue furthering the principles of the Stockholm Declaration, to contribute to the implementation of the Rio Declaration and of Agenda 21, and to work closely together towards the implementation of global and regional instruments supporting their goals;

...

Convinced that the above objectives would be better achieved by amending the 1968 Algiers Convention on the Conservation of Nature and Natural Resources by expanding elements related to sustainable development;

Have agreed as follows:

Article I - Scope

This Convention shall apply

1. to all areas which are within the limits of national jurisdiction of any Party; and

2. to the activities carried out under the jurisdiction or control of any Party within the area of its national jurisdiction or beyond the limits of its national jurisdiction.

Article II - Objectives

The objectives of this Convention are:

1. to enhance environmental protection;

2. to foster the conservation and sustainable use of natural resources; and

3. to harmonize and coordinate policies in these fields with a view to achieving ecologically rational, economically sound and socially acceptable development policies and programmes.

Article III - Principles

In taking action to achieve the objectives of this Convention and implement its provisions, the Parties shall be guided by the following:

1.   the right of all peoples to a satisfactory environment favourable to their development;

2.   the duty of States, individually and collectively to ensure the enjoyment of the right to development;

3.   the duty of States to ensure that developmental and environmental needs are met in a sustainable, fair and equitable manner.

Article IV - Fundamental obligation

The Parties shall adopt and implement all measures necessary to achieve the objectives of this Convention, in particular through preventive measures and the application of the precautionary principle, and with due regard to ethical and traditional values as well as scientific knowledge in the interest of present and future generations.

Article V - Use of terms

For purposes of this Convention:

1.   "Natural Resources" means renewable resources, tangible and non tangible, including soil, water, flora and fauna and non renewable resources. Whenever the text of the Convention refers to non renewable resources this will be specified.

...

6.   "Conservation area" means

...

(b)   other areas designated and/or managed primarily for the conservation and sustainable use of natural resources, for which criteria may be adopted and from time to time reviewed by the Conference of the Parties.

...

Article VI - Land and soil

1.   The Parties shall take effective measures to prevent land degradation, and to that effect shall develop long-term integrated strategies for the conservation and sustainable management of land resources, including soil, vegetation and related hydrological processes.

2.   They shall in particular adopt measures for the conservation and improvement of the soil, to, inter alia, combat its erosion and misuse as well as the deterioration of its physical, chemical and biological or economic properties.

3.   To this end:

(a)   they shall establish land-use plans based on scientific investigations as well as local knowledge and experience and, in particular, classification and land-use capability;

(b)   they shall, when implementing agricultural practices and agrarian reforms,

  (i)   improve soil conservation and introduce sustainable farming and forestry practices, which ensure long-term productivity of the land,

  (ii) control erosion caused by land misuse and mismanagement which may lead to long-term loss of surface soils and vegetation cover,

  (iii) control pollution caused by agricultural activities, including aquaculture and animal husbandry;

(c)   they shall ensure that non-agricultural forms of land use, including but not limited to public works, mining and the disposal of wastes, do not result in erosion, pollution, or any other form of land degradation;

(d)   they shall, in areas affected by land degradation, plan and implement mitigation and rehabilitation measures.

4. Parties shall develop and implement land tenure policies able to facilitate the above measures, inter alia by taking into account the rights of local communities.

Article VII - Water

1. The Parties shall manage their water resources so as to maintain them at the highest possible quantitative and qualitative levels. They shall, to that effect, take measures designed to:

(a) maintain water-based essential ecological processes as well as to protect human health against pollutants and water-borne diseases,

(b) prevent damage that could affect human health or natural resource in another State by the discharge of pollutants, and

(c) prevent excessive abstraction, to the benefit of downstream communities and States.

2. The Parties shall establish and implement policies for the planning, conservation, management, utilization and development of underground and surface water, as well as the harvesting and use of rain water, and shall endeavour to guarantee for their populations a sufficient and continuous supply of suitable water, taking appropriate measures with due regard to:

(a) the study of water cycles and the investigation of each catchment area,

(b) the integrated management of water resources,

(c) the conservation of forested and other catchment areas and the co-ordination and planning of water resources development projects,

(d) the inventory and management of all water resources, including the administration and control of all water utilization, and

(e) the prevention and control of water pollution through, inter alia, the establishment of effluent and water quality standards.

3. Where surface or underground water resources and related ecosystems, including wetlands, are transboundary to two or more of the Parties,

the latter shall act in consultation, and if the need arises, set up inter-State Commissions for their rational management and equitable utilization and to resolve disputes arising from the use of these resources, and for the cooperative development, management and conservation thereof.

4.   The Parties undertake, individually or within sub-regional arrangements, to cooperate in rational water husbandry and conservation in irrigated agriculture for improved food security and sustainable agro-based industrialization.

Article VIII - Vegetation cover

1.   The Parties shall take all necessary measures for the protection, conservation, sustainable use and rehabilitation of vegetation cover. To this end they shall:

(a)   adopt scientifically-based and sound traditional conservation, utilization and management plans for forests, woodlands, rangelands, wetlands and other areas with vegetation cover, taking into account the social and economic needs of the peoples concerned, the importance of the vegetation cover for the maintenance of the water balance of an area, the productivity of soils and the habitat requirements of species;

...

[Omitted: Article IX - Species and genetic diversity, Article X - Protected species, Article XI - Trade in specimens and products thereof]

Article XII - Conservation areas

1.   The Parties shall establish, maintain and extend, as appropriate, conservation areas. They shall, preferably within the framework of environmental and natural resources policies, legislation and programmes, also assess the potential impacts and necessity of establishing additional conservation areas and wherever possible designate such areas, in order to ensure the long term conservation of biological diversity, in particular to:

(a) conserve those ecosystems which are most representative of and peculiar to areas under their jurisdiction, or are characterized by a high degree of biological diversity;

(b) ensure the conservation of all species;

...

and of the habitats that are critical for the survival of such species.

2. The Parties shall seek to identify areas critically important to the goals referred to in sub paragraph 1(a) and 1(b) above which are not yet included in conservation areas, taking into consideration the work of competent international organisations in this field.

3. The Parties shall promote the establishment by local communities of areas managed by them primarily for the conservation and sustainable use of natural resources.

4. The Parties shall, where necessary and if possible, control activities outside conservation areas which are detrimental to the achievement of the purpose for which the conservation areas were created, and establish for that purpose buffer zones around their borders.

Article XIII - Processes and activities affecting the environment and natural resources

1. The Parties shall, individually or jointly, and in collaboration with the competent international organizations concerned, take all appropriate measures to prevent, mitigate and eliminate to the maximum extent possible, detrimental effects on the environment, in particular from radioactive, toxic, and other hazardous substances and wastes. For this purpose, they shall use the best practicable means and shall endeavour to harmonize their policies, in particular within the framework of relevant conventions to which they are Parties.

2. To that effect, Parties shall

(a) establish, strengthen and implement specific national standards, including for ambient environmental quality, emission and discharge limits as well as process and production methods and product quality;

(b)   provide for economic incentives and disincentives, with a view to preventing or abating harm to the environment, restoring or enhancing environmental quality, and implementing international obligations in these regards; and

(c)   adopt measures necessary to ensure that raw materials, non-renewable resources, and energy, are conserved and used as efficiently as possible, and that used materials are reused and recycled to the maximum extent possible while nondegradable materials are disposed of in the most effective and safe way.

Article XIV - Sustainable development and natural resources

1.   The Parties shall ensure that

(a)   conservation and management of natural resources are treated as an integral part of national and/or local development plans;

(b)   in the formulation of all development plans, full consideration is given to ecological, as well as to economic, cultural and social factors in order to promote sustainable development.

2.   To this end, the Parties shall:

(a)   to the maximum extent possible, take all necessary measures to ensure that development activities and projects are based on sound environmental policies and do not have adverse effects on natural resources and the environment in general;

(b)   ensure that policies, plans, programmes, strategies, projects and activities likely to affect natural resources, ecosystems and the environment in general are the subject of adequate impact assessment at the earliest possible stage and that regular environmental monitoring and audit are conducted;

(c)   monitor the state of their natural resources as well as the impact of development activities and projects upon such resources.

[Omitted: Article XV - Military and hostile activities]

Article XVI - Procedural rights

1. The Parties shall adopt legislative and regulatory measures necessary to ensure timely and appropriate

(a) dissemination of environmental information;

(b) access of the public to environmental information;

(c) participation of the public in decision-making with a potentially significant environmental impact; and

(d) access to justice in matters related to protection of environment and natural resources.

2. Each Party from which a transboundary environmental harm originates shall ensure that any person in another Party affected by such harm has a right of access to administrative and judicial procedures equal to that afforded to nationals or residents of the Party of origin in cases of domestic environmental harm.

Article XVII - Traditional rights of local communities and indigenous knowledge

1. The Parties shall take legislative and other measures to ensure that traditional rights and intellectual property rights of local communities including farmers' rights are respected in accordance with the provisions of this Convention.

2. The Parties shall require that access to indigenous knowledge and its use be subject to the prior informed consent of the concerned communities and to specific regulations recognizing their rights to, and appropriate economic value of, such knowledge.

3. The Parties shall take the measures necessary to enable active participation by the local communities in the process of planning and management of natural resources upon which such communities depend with a view to creating local incentives for the conservation and sustainable use of such resources.

Article XVIII - Research

1. The Parties shall strengthen their capabilities to carry out scientific and technological research in conservation, sustainable utilization and management of natural resources paying particular attention to ecological and socio-economic factors as well as their integration, and shall ensure the application of research results to the development and implementation of their environmental conservation policies.

2. The Parties shall promote cooperation in scientific and technological research, as well as in economic and marketing systems, between themselves and with third parties in the field of environmental conservation and sustainable use of natural resources.

    To that end, they shall in particular:

(a) coordinate their research programmes with a view to achieving maximum synergy and complementarity;

(b) promote the exchange of research results; and

(c) promote the development of joint research activities and programmes in the fields covered by this Convention.

Article XIX - Development and transfer of technology

1. The Parties shall encourage and strengthen cooperation for the development and use, as well as access to and transfer of, environmentally sound technologies on mutually agreed terms, with a view to accelerating the transition to sustainable development, in particular by establishing joint research programmes and ventures.

2. To that effect the Parties shall adopt legislative and regulatory measures which provide for inter alia, economic incentives for the development, importation, transfer and utilization of environmentally sound technologies in the private and public sectors.

    In implementing paragraphs 1. and 2. above, attention shall be paid to technologies which can be used locally by individuals, local communities and small/medium enterprises.

Article XX - Capacity building, education and training

1. (a) The Parties shall promote environmental education, training and awareness creation at all levels in order to enhance their peoples' appreciation of their close dependence on natural resources and their understanding of the reasons and rules for the sustainable use of these resources.

   (b) For this purpose they shall ensure that environmental matters:

...

Article XXI - National authorities

Each Party shall establish or designate, if it has not already done so, a national authority empowered to deal with all matters covered by this Convention, and/or, where appropriate, establish a co-ordinating machinery between existing national institutions.

Article XXII - Co-operation

1. The Parties shall co-operate between themselves and, where appropriate and possible, with other States:

(a) to give effect to the provisions of this Convention;

(b) whenever any national measure is likely to affect the environment or natural resources of any other State or areas beyond national jurisdiction;

(c) in order to enhance the individual and combined effectiveness of their policies and legislations, as well as measures adopted under this Convention and under other international conventions in the fields of environmental protection and natural resources conservation and use; and

(d) in order to harmonize their policies and laws at the continental or regional levels, as appropriate.

2.   In particular:

(a)   whenever an environmental emergency or natural disaster occurring in a Party is likely to affect the natural resources of another State, the latter shall be provided with all relevant available data by the former as early as practicable;

(b)   when a Party has reasons to believe that a programme, activity or project to be carried out in areas under its jurisdiction may have adverse effects on the natural resources of another State, it shall provide that other State with relevant information on the proposed measures and their possible effects, and shall consult with that State;

(c)   whenever a Party objects to an activity referred to in sub-paragraph b) above, they shall enter into negotiations;

(d)   Parties shall develop disaster preparedness, prevention and management programmes, and as the need arises hold consultations towards mutual assistance initiatives;

(e)   whenever a natural resource or an ecosystem is transboundary, the Parties concerned shall undertake to cooperate in the conservation, development and management of such resource or ecosystem and if the need arises, set up interstate commissions for their conservation and sustainable use;

...

(h)   the Parties shall exchange information bilaterally or through competent international agencies on activities and events likely to affect the natural resources and the environment of areas beyond national jurisdiction.

[Omitted: Article XXIII - Compliance]

Article XXIV - Liability

The Parties shall, as soon as possible, adopt rules and procedures concerning liability and compensation of damage related to matters covered by this Convention.

[Omitted: Article XXV - Exceptions, Article XXVI - Conference of the Parties, Article XXVII - The Secretariat, Article XXVIII - Financial resources]

Article XXIX - Reports and information

1. The Parties shall present, through the Secretariat, to the Conference of the Parties reports on the measures adopted by them in the implementation of this Convention and the results thereof in applying its provisions in such form and at such intervals as the Conference of the Parties may determine. This presentation shall be accompanied by the comments of the Secretariat, in particular regarding failure to report, adequacy of the report and of the measures described therein.

2. The Parties shall supply the Secretariat with:

(a) the texts of laws, decrees, regulations and instructions in force which are intended to ensure the implementation of this Convention;

(b) any other information that may be necessary to provide complete documentation on matters dealt with by this Convention;

(c) the names of the agencies or coordinating institutions empowered to be focal points in matters under this Convention; and

(d) information on bilateral or multilateral agreements relating to the environment and natural resources to which they are parties.

[Omitted: Article XXX - Settlement of disputes, Article XXXI - Amendments of the Convention, Article XXXII - Adoption and amendments of Annexes, Article XXXIII - Right to vote, Article XXXIV - Relationship between Parties to the revised Convention and Parties bound by the 1968 Algiers Convention, Article XXXV - Relationship with other international Conventions, Article XXXVI - Signature and ratification, Article XXXVII - Accession, Article XXXVIII - Entry into force, Article XXXIX - Reservations, Article XL - Withdrawal, Article XLI - Secretariat interim arrangements, Article XLII - Depositary, Article XLIII - Authentic texts]

...

[Omitted: Annex 1 - Threatened species definition, Annex 2 - Conservation areas, Annex 3 - Prohibited means of taking]

b.   Treaties Concerning Specific River/Lake Basins

13.   Convention on Cooperation for the Protection and Sustainable Use of the River Danube [Sofia, 29 June 1994]*

The Contracting Parties,

...

Determined by the strong intention to intensify their water management cooperation in the field of water protection and water use;

Concerned over the occurrence and threats of adverse effects, in the short or long term, of changes in conditions of watercourses within the Danube River Basin on the environment, economics and well-being of the Danubian States;

Emphasizing the urgent need for strengthened domestic and international measures to prevent, control and reduce significant adverse transboundary impact from the release of hazardous substances and of nutrients into the aquatic environment within the Danube Basin with due attention also given to the Black Sea;

Commending the measures already taken on the domestic initiative of Danubian Countries and on the bilateral and multilateral level of their cooperation as well as the efforts already undertaken within the CSCE-process, by the United Nations Economic Commission for Europe and by the European Community to promote the cooperation, on bilateral and multilateral levels, for the prevention and control of transboundary pollution, sustainable water management, rational use and conservation of water resources;

---

* Official Journal of the European Union L 342, 12.12.1997, p. 19. Entry into force 22 October 1998. Parties and/or signatories: Austria, Bosnia-Herzegovina, Bulgaria, Croatia, Czech Republic, European Community, Germany, Hungary, Republic of Moldova, Romania, Slovenia, Slovakia, Ukraine, Yugoslavia.

Referring in particular to the Convention on the protection and use of transboundary watercourses and international lakes of 17 March 1992 as well as the existing bi- and multilateral cooperation among Danubian States, which will be continued and duly taken into account by the cooperation of all Danubian States, as well as pointing to the Convention on the protection of the Black Sea against pollution of 21 April 1992;

Striving at a lasting improvement and protection of Danube River and of the waters within its catchment area in particular in the transboundary context and at sustainable water management taking duly into account the interests of the Danubian States in the field of water use and at the same time contributing to the protection of the marine environment of the Black Sea;

Have agreed as follows

Part I - General provisions

Article 1 - Definitions

For the purposes of this Convention:

(a)   "Danubian States" mean sovereign States sharing a considerable part of the hydrological catchment area of the Danube River. As considerable part there is assumed a share exceeding 2000 km2 of the total hydrological catchment area.

(b)   "Catchment area" of the Danube River means the hydrological river basin as far as it is shared by the Contracting Parties.

(c)   "Transboundary impact" means any significant adverse effect on the riverine environment resulting from a change in the conditions of waters caused by human activity and stretching out beyond an area under the jurisdiction of a Contracting Party. Such changes may affect life and property, safety of facilities and the aquatic ecosystems concerned.

(d)   "Hazardous substances" means substances which have toxic, cancerogenic, mutagenic, teratogenic or bioaccumulative effects, in particular those being persistent and having significant adverse impact on living organisms.

(e)   "Substances hazardous to water" means substances the hazard potential of which to water resources is extraordinarily high so that their handling requires special preventive and protective measures;

(f)   "Point and non-point sources of water pollution" means the sources of pollutants and nutrients the input of which to waters is caused either by locally determined discharges (point source) or by diffuse effects being wide spread over the catchment areas (non-point sources);

(g)   "Water balance" means the relationship characterising the natural water household of an entire river basin as to its components (precipitation, evaporation, surface and underground run-off). In addition a component of current man-made effects originating from water use and influencing water quantity is included.

(h)   "Connecting data" means summarised data derived from upstream water balances as far as being relevant as an input necessary for the elaboration of downstream water balances and of a general water balance for the Danube River. To this extent connecting data cover the components of the water balance for all significant transboundary waters within the catchment area of the Danube River. Connecting data refer to cross sections of transboundary waters where they mark, cross or are located on boundaries between the Contracting Parties.

(i)   "International Commission" means the organisation established by Article 18 of this Convention.

Article 2 - Objectives and principles of cooperation

1.   The Contracting Parties shall strive at achieving the goals of a sustainable and equitable water management, including the conservation, improvement and the rational use of surface waters and groundwater in the catchment area as far as possible. Moreover the Contracting Parties shall make all efforts to control the hazards originating from accidents involving substances hazardous to water, floods and ice-hazards of the Danube River. Moreover they shall endeavour to contribute to reducing the pollution loads of the Black Sea from sources in the catchment area.

2.   The Contracting Parties pursuant to the provisions of this Convention shall cooperate on fundamental water management issues and take all

appropriate legal, administrative and technical measures, to at least maintain and improve the current environmental and water quality conditions of the Danube River and of the waters in its catchment area and to prevent and reduce as far as possible adverse impacts and changes occurring or likely to be caused.

3. To this end the Contracting Parties, taking into account the urgency of water pollution abatement measures and of rational, sustainable water use, shall set priorities as appropriate and shall strengthen, harmonise and coordinate measures taken and planned to be taken at the domestic and international level throughout the Danube Basin aiming at sustainable development and environmental protection of the Danube River. This objective in particular is directed to ensure the sustainable use of water resources for municipal, industrial and agricultural purposes as well as the conservation and restauration of ecosystems and to cover also other requirements occurring as to public health.

4. The Polluter pays principle and the Precautionary principle constitute a basis for all measures aiming at the protection of the Danube River and of the waters within its catchment area.

5. Water management cooperation shall be oriented on sustainable water management, that means on the criteria of a stable, environmentally sound development, which are at the same time directed to:

   - maintain the overall quality of life;

   - maintain continuing access to natural resources;

   - avoid lasting environmental damage and protect ecosystems;

   - exercise preventive approach.

6. The application of this Convention by no means shall cause any significant direct or indirect increase of impacts to the riverine environment.

7. Each Contracting Party has the right to adopt and implement measures being more stringent than those resulting from the provisions of this Convention.

Article 3 - Scope

1.   This Convention applies to the catchment area of the Danube River as defined under Article 1, paragraph (b).

2.   Subject to this Convention in particular shall be the following planned activities and ongoing measures as far as they cause or are likely to cause transboundary impacts:

(a)   the discharge of waste water, the input of nutrients and hazardous substances both from point and non-point sources as well as heat discharge;

(b)   planned activities and measures in the field of water construction works, in particular regulation as well as run-off and storage level control of water courses, flood control and ice-hazards abatement, as well as the effect of facilities situated in or aside the watercourse on its hydraulic regime;

(c)   other planned activities and measures for the purposes of water use, such as water power utilization, water transfer and withdrawal;

(d)   the operation of the existing hydrotechnical constructions e.g. reservoirs, water power plants; measures to prevent environmental impact including: deterioration in the hydrological conditions, erosion, abrasion, inundation and sediment flow; measures to protect the ecosystems;

(e)   the handling of substances hazardous to water and the precautionary prevention of accidents.

3.   This Convention is applicable to issues of fishery and inland navigation as far as problems of water protection against pollution caused by these activities are concerned.

Article 4 - Forms of cooperation

The forms of cooperation under this Convention as a rule are the following:

(a) consultations and joint activities in the framework of the InternationalCommission pursuant to the provisions of this Convention;

(b) exchange of information on bi- and multilateral agreements, legal regulations and on measures in the field of water management; exchange of legal documents and directives and of other publications; other forms for the exchange of information and experiences.

Part II - Multilateral cooperation

Article 5 - Prevention, control and reduction of transboundary impact

1. The Contracting Parties shall develop, adopt and implement relevant legal, administrative and technical measures as well as provide for the domestic preconditions and basis required in order to ensure efficient water quality protection and sustainable water use and thereby also to prevent, control and reduce transboundary impact.

2. To this end the Contracting Parties shall separately or jointly take in particular the measures indicated below:

(a) Record conditions of natural water resources within the Danube River catchment area applying agreed quantity and quality parameters including the methodology concerned.

(b) Adopt legal provisions providing for requirements including time limits to be met by waste water discharges.

(c) Adopt legal provisions for the handling of substances hazardous to water.

(d) Adopt legal provisions for reducing inputs of nutrients or hazardous substances from non-point sources, especially for the application of nutrients as well as of plant protection agents and pesticides in agriculture.

(e) With the aim of harmonising these regulations at a high level of protection as well as for the harmonised implementation of corresponding measures the Contracting Parties shall take into account results and proposals put forward by the International Commission.

(f)   The Contracting Parties shall cooperate and take appropriate measures to avoid the transboundary impacts of wastes and hazardous substances in particular originating from transport.

Article 6 - Specific water resources protection measures

The Contracting Parties shall take appropriate measures aiming at the prevention or reduction of transboundary impacts and at a sustainable and equitable use of water resources as well as at the conservation of ecological resources, especially:

(a)   enumerate groundwater resources subject to a long-term protection as well as protection zones valuable for existing or future drinking water supply purposes;

(b)   prevent the pollution of groundwater resources, especially those in a long-term perspective reserved for drinking water supply, in particular caused by nitrates, plant protection agents and pesticides as well as other hazardous substances;

(c)   minimise by preventive and control measures the risks of accidental pollution;

(d)   take into account possible influences on the water quality resulting from planned activities and ongoing measures pursuant to Article 3 paragraph 2;

(e)   evaluate the importance of different biotope elements for the riverine ecology and propose measures for improving the aquatic and litoral ecological conditions.

Article 7 - Emission limitation: water quality objectives and criteria

1.   The Contracting Parties taking into account the proposals from the International Commission shall set emission limits applicable to individual industrial sectors or industries in terms of pollution loads and concentrations and based in the best possible way on low-and non-waste technologies at source. Where hazardous substances are discharged, the emission limits shall be based on the best available techniques for the abatement at source and/or for waste water purification. For municipal waste water, emission limits shall be based

on the application of at least biological or an equivalent level of treatment.

2. Supplementary provisions for preventing or reducing the release of hazardous substances and nutrients shall be developed by the Contracting Parties for non-point sources, in particular where the main sources are originating from agriculture, taking into account the best environmental practice.

3. For the purpose of paragraphs 1 and 2 Annex II to this Convention contains a list of industrial sectors and industries as well as an additional list of hazardous substances and groups of substances, the discharge of which from point and non-point sources shall be prevented or considerably reduced. The updating of Annex II lies with the International Commission.

4. The Contracting Parties in addition shall, where appropriate, define water quality objectives and apply water quality criteria for the purpose of preventing, controlling and reducing transboundary impact. General guidance for this is given in Annex III, which shall be applied and specified by the Contracting Parties both, at the domestic level and jointly, where appropriate.

5. Aiming at an efficient limitation of the emissions in areas under their jurisdiction the Contracting Parties shall ensure necessary preconditions and implementation.

They shall ensure that:

(a) the domestic regulations for emission limitation and their level of standards imposed are harmonised step by step with the emission limitation pursuant to this Convention;

(b) waste water discharges without exception are based on a permit imposed by the competent authorities in advance and for a limited period of validity;

(c) regulations and permits for prevention and control measures in case of new or modernised industrial facilities, in particular where hazardous substances are involved, are oriented on the best available techniques and are implemented with high priority;

(d)   more stringent provisions than the standards - in individual case even prohibition - are imposed, where the character of the receiving water and of its ecosystem so requires in connection with paragraph 4;

(e)   competent authorities surveille, that activities likely to cause transboundary impacts are carried out in compliance with the permits and provisions imposed;

(f)   environmental impact assessment in line with supranational and international regulations or other procedures for evaluation and assessment of environmental effects are applied;

(g)   when planning, licensing and implementing activities and measures as referred to in Article 3, paragraph 2 and in Article 16, paragraph 2 the competent authorities take into account risks of accidents involving substances hazardous to water by imposing preventive measures and by ordering rules of conduct for post accident response measures.

Article 8 - Emission inventories, action programmes and progress reviews

1.   The Contracting Parties shall undertake periodically inventories of the relevant point and non-point sources of pollution within the catchment area of Danube River including the prevention and abatement measures already taken for the respective discharges as well as on the actual efficiency of these measures, taking duly into account Article 5, paragraph 2, subpara a.

2.   Based on that the Contracting Parties shall in stages establish a list of further prevention and abatement measures to be taken step by step as far as this is necessary for reaching the objectives of this Convention.

3.   The inventory of emissions and the list of measures to be taken from the basis for developing joint action programmes to be developed by the Contracting Parties taking into account priorities set in terms of urgency and efficiency. These action programmes in particular shall be aimed at the reduction of pollution loads and concentrations both from industrial and municipal point sources as well as from non-point sources. They shall inter alia contain the prevention and abatement measures including the timing and cost estimates.

4. In addition the Contracting Parties shall monitor the progress made in the implementation of the joint action programmes by establishing periodical progress reviews. These reviews shall contain both, the protection measures implemented and the progress made as to the riverine conditions in the light of the actual assessment.

Article 9 - Monitoring programmes

On the basis of their domestic activities, the Contracting Parties shall cooperate in the field of monitoring and assessment.

1. For this aim, they shall:

   - harmonise or make comparable their monitoring and assessment methods as applied on their domestic levels, in particular in the field of river quality, emission control, flood forecast and water balance, with a view to achieving comparable results to be introduced into the joint monitoring and assessment activities;

   - develop concerted or joint monitoring systems applying stationary or mobile measurement devices, communication and data processing facilities;

   - elaborate and implement joint programmes for monitoring the riverine conditions in the Danube catchment area concerning both water quality and quantity, sediments and riverine ecosystems, as a basis for the assessment of transboundary impacts such as transboundary pollution and changes of the riverine regimes as well as of water balances, floods and ice-hazards;

   - develop joint or harmonised methods for monitoring and assessment of waste water discharges including processing, evaluation and documentation of data taking into account the branch-specific approach of emission limitation (Annex II, Part 1);

   - elaborate inventories on relevant point sources including the pollutants discharged (emission inventories) and estimate the water pollution from non-point sources taking into account Annex II, Part 2; review these documents according to the actual state.

2.   In particular they shall agree upon monitoring points, river quality characteristics and pollution parameters regularly to be evaluated for the Danube River with a sufficient frequency taking into account the ecological and hydrological character of the watercourse concerned as well as typical emissions of pollutants discharged within the respective catchment area.

3.   The Contracting Parties shall establish, on the basis of a harmonised methodology, domestic water balances, as well as the general water balance of the Danube River Basin. As an input for this purpose the Contracting Parties to the extent necessary shall provide connecting data which are sufficiently comparable through the application of the harmonised methodology. On the same data base water balances can also be compiled for the main tributaries of Danube River.

4.   They shall periodically assess the quality conditions of Danube River and the progress made by their measures taken aiming at the prevention, control and reduction of transboundary impacts. The results will be presented to the public by appropriate publications.

Article 10 - Obligations of reporting

The Contracting Parties shall report to the International Commission on basic issues required for the Commission to comply with its tasks. These reports shall in particular involve:

...

(f)   communication on planned activities, which for reason of their character are likely to cause transboundary impacts.

Article 11 - Consultations

1.   Having had a prior exchange of information the Contracting Parties involved shall at the request of one or several Contracting Parties concerned enter into consultations on planned activities as referred to in Article 3, paragraph 2, which are likely to cause transboundary impacts, as far as this exchange of information and these consultations are not yet covered by bilateral or other international cooperation. The consultations are carried out as a rule in the framework of the International Commission, with the aim to achieve a solution.

2.   Prior to a decision on planned activities the competent authorities - with the exception of pending danger - shall wait for the results of the consultations except the case, that they are not finalised one year after their commencement at the latest.

Article 12 - Exchange of information

1.   As determined by the International Commission the Contracting Parties shall exchange reasonably available data, inter alia, on:

(a)   the general conditions of the riverine environment within the catchment area of the Danube River;

(b)   Experience gained in the application and operating of best available techniques and results of research and development;

(c)   Emission and monitoring data;

(d)   Measures taken and planned to be taken to prevent, control and reduce transboundary impact;

(e)   Regulations for waste water discharges;

(f)   Accidents involving substances hazardous to water.

2.   In order to harmonise emission limits, the Contracting Parties shall undertake the exchange of information on their regulations.

3.   If a Contracting Party is requested by any other Contracting Party to provide data or information that is not available, the former shall endeavour to comply with the request but may condition its compliance upon the payment, by the requesting Party, of reasonable charges for collecting and, where appropriate, processing such data or information.

4.   For the purposes of the implementation of this Convention, the Contracting Parties shall facilitate the exchange of best available techniques, particularly through the promotion of: the commercial exchange of available techniques, direct industrial contacts and cooperation, including joint ventures; the exchange of information and experience; and the provision of technical assistance. The Contracting

Parties shall also undertake joint training programmes and the organisation of relevant seminars and meetings.

...

[Omitted: Article 13 - Protection of information supplied, Article 14 - Information to the public, Article 15 - Research and development]

Article 16 - Communication, warning and alarm systems, emergency plans

1. The contracting Parties shall provide for coordinated or joint communication, warning and alarm systems in the basin-wide context to the extent this is necessary to supplement the systems established and operated at a bilateral level. They shall consult on ways and means of harmonising domestic communication, warning and alarm systems and emergency plans.

2. The Contracting Parties shall in the framework of the International Commission inform each about competent authorities or points of contact designated for this purpose in case of emergency events such as accidental pollution, other critical water conditions, floods and ice-hazards. Accordingly the competent authorities shall cooperate to establish joint emergency plans, where necessary, supplementary to existing plans on the bilateral level.

3. If a competent authority identifies a sudden increase of hazardous substances in the Danube River or in waters within its catchment area or receives note of a disaster or of an accident likely to cause serious impact on the water quality of Danube River and to affect downstream Danubian States this authority shall immediately inform the contact points designated and the International Commission according to the way of procedure introduced by the Commission.

4. In order to control and reduce the risks originating from floods including ice-hazards, the competent authorities shall immediately inform the downstream Danubian States likely to be affected and the International Commission on the occurrence and run-off of floods as well as on forecasts of icehazards.

[Omitted: Article 17 - Mutual assistance]

Part III - International Commission

Article 18 - Establishment, tasks and competences

1.   With a view to implementing the objectives and provisions of this Convention the International Commission for the Protection of the Danube River, referred to in this Convention as International Commission, shall be established. The Contracting Parties shall cooperate in the framework of the International Commission. For implementing the obligations of the Contracting Parties pursuant to Articles 1 to 18 the International Commission elaborates proposals and recommendations addressed to the Contracting Parties.

2.   The structure and the procedures of the International Commission as well as its competences are stipulated in detail in Annex IV to this Convention constituting the Statute of the Commission.

3.   In addition to affairs explicitly entrusted the International Commission is competent to deal with all other affairs the Commission is entrusted with by mandate from the Contracting Parties in the framework of Article 3 of this Convention.

...

[Omitted: Article 19 - Transition concerning the Bucharest Declaration]

Part IV - Procedural and final clauses

Article 20 - Validity of the Annexes

Subject to Article 23, the Annexes I to V form integral parts of this Convention.

[Omitted: Article 21 - Existing and supplementary agreements, Article 22 - Conference of the Parties, Article 23 - Amendments to the Convention, Article 24 - Settlement of disputes, Article 25 - Signature, Article 26 - Ratification, acceptance or approval, Article 27 - Entry into force, Article 28 - Accession, participation, Article 29 - Withdrawal, Article 30 - Function of the depositary, Article 31 - Authentic texts, depositary]

...

Annex I

Part 1 - Best available techniques

1. The use of the best available techniques shall emphasize the use of non-waste technology, if available.

2. The term "best available techniques" means the latest stage of development (state of the art) of processes, of facilities or of methods of operation which indicate the practical suitability of a particular measure for limiting discharges, emissions and waste. In determining whether a set of processes, facilities and methods of operation constitute the best available techniques in general or individual cases, special consideration shall be given to:

(a) comparable processes, facilities or methods of operation which have recently been successfully tried out;

(b) technological advances and changes in scientific knowledge and understanding;

(c) the economic feasibility of such techniques;

(d) time limits for installation in both new and existing plants;

(e) the nature and volume of the discharges and emissions concerned.

3. It therefore follows that what is "best available techniques" for a particular process will change with time in the light of technological advances, economic and social factors, as well as changes in scientific knowledge and understanding.

4. If the reduction of discharges and emissions resulting from the use of best available techniques does not lead to environmentally acceptable results, additional measures have to be applied.

5. The term "techniques" includes both the technology used and the way the installation is designed, built, maintained, operated and dismantled.

Part 2 - Best environmental practice

1. Best environmental practice means the application of the most appropriate combination of sectoral environmental control strategies and measures.

2. In determining what combination of measures constitute best environmental practice, in general or individual cases, particular consideration should be given to:

    -   the precautionary principle;

    -   the environmental hazard of the product and its production, use and ultimate disposal (principle of responsibility);

    -   the substitution by less polluting activities or substances and saving resources including energy (principle of minimising);

    -   the scale of use;

    -   the potential environmental benefit or penalty of substitute materials or activities;

    -   advances and changes in scientific knowledge and understanding;

    -   time limits for implementation;

    -   social and economic implication.

3. It therefore follows that best environmental practice for a particular source of impacts will change with time in the light of technological advances, economic and social factors, as well as changes in scientific knowledge and understanding.

4. If the reduction of impacts resulting from the use of best environmental practice does not lead to environmentally acceptable results, additional measures have to be applied and best environmental practice redefined.

[Omitted: Annex II - Industrial sectors and hazardous substances, Annex III - General guidance on water quality objectives and criteria, Annex IV - Statute of the International Commission for the Protection of the River Danube, Annex V - Arbitration]

14.   Convention on the Protection of the Rhine [Berne, 12 April 1999]*

[The Contracting Parties]

...

Desiring to work towards the sustainable development of the Rhine ecosystem on the basis of a comprehensive approach, taking into consideration the natural wealth of the river, its banks and alluvial areas,

Desiring to step up their cooperation on conserving and improving the Rhine ecosystem,

Referring to the Convention of 17 March 1992 on the protection and use of transboundary watercourses and international lakes and the Convention of 22 September 1992 on the protection of the marine environment of the north-east Atlantic,

Have agreed as follows:

Article 1 - Definitions

For the purposes of this Convention:

(a)   "Rhine" means the Rhine from the outlet of Lake Untersee and, in the Netherlands, the branches Bovenrijn, Bijlands Kanaal, Pannerdensch Kanaal, Ijssel, Nederrijn, Lek, Waal, Boven-Merwede, Beneden-Merwede, Noord, Oude Maas, Nieuwe Maas and Scheur and the Nieuwe Waterweg as far as the base line as specified in Article 5 in connection with Article 11 of the United Nations Convention on the Law of the Sea, the Ketelmeer and the Ijsselmeer;

---

* Official Journal of the European Union L 289, 16.11.2000, p. 31. Parties and/or signatories: European Community, France, Germany, Luxembourg, Netherlands, Switzerland.

(b) "Commission" means the International Commission for the Protection of the Rhine (ICPR).

Article 2 - Scope

This Convention applies to:

(a)   the Rhine;

(b)   groundwater interacting with the Rhine;

(c)   aquatic and terrestrial ecosystems which interact or could again interact with the Rhine;

(d)   the Rhine catchment area, insofar as its pollution by noxious substances adversely affects the Rhine;

(e)   the Rhine catchment area, insofar as it is of importance for flood prevention and protection along the Rhine.

Article 3 - Aims

The Contracting Parties shall pursue the following aims through this Convention:

1.   sustainable development of the Rhine ecosystem, in particular through:

(a)   maintaining and improving the quality of the Rhine's waters, including the quality of suspended matter, sediments and groundwater, notably by

-   preventing, reducing or eliminating as far as possible pollution caused by noxious substances and by nutrients from point sources (e.g. industry and municipalities) and diffuse sources (e.g. agriculture and traffic) - including that from groundwater - and pollution from shipping,

-   ensuring and improving the safety of installations and preventing incidents and accidents;

...

(c)   maintaining, improving and restoring the natural function of the waters; ensuring that flow management takes account of the natural flow of solid matter and promotes interactions between river, groundwater and alluvial areas; conserving, protecting and reactivating alluvial areas as natural floodplains;

(d)   conserving, improving and restoring the most natural habitats possible for wild fauna and flora in the water, on the river bed and banks and in adjacent areas, and improving living conditions for fish and restoring their free migration;

(e)   ensuring environmentally sound and rational management of water resources;

(f)   taking ecological requirements into account when implementing technical measures to develop the waterway, e.g. for flood protection, shipping or the use of hydroelectric power;

2.   the production of drinking water from the waters of the Rhine;

3.   improvement of sediment quality in order that dredged material may be deposited or spread without adversely affecting the environment;

4.   general flood prevention and protection, taking account of ecological requirements;

...

Article 4 - Principles

To this end, the Contracting Parties shall be guided by the following principles:

(a)   precautionary principle;

(b)   principle of preventive action;

(c)   principle of rectification, as a priority at source;

(d)   polluter pays principle;

(e)   principle of not increasing damage;

(f)   principle of compensation in the event of major technical measures;

(g)   principle of sustainable development;

(h)   application and development of the state of the art and best environmental practice;

(i)   principle of not transferring environmental pollution from one environment to another.

Article 5 - Undertakings by the Contracting Parties

To achieve the aims set out in Article 3, and in the light of the principles set out in Article 4, the Contracting Parties undertake:

1.   to step up their cooperation and to inform one another, particularly regarding actions taken in their territory to protect the Rhine;

2.   to implement in their territory the international measuring programmes and the studies of the Rhine ecosystem agreed upon by the Commission and to inform the Commission of the results;

3.   to carry out analyses with a view to identifying the causes of and parties responsible for pollution;

4.   to initiate the autonomous actions they deem necessary in their territory, and in any event ensure that

(a)   discharging of waste water liable to affect water quality is subject to prior authorisation or to general rules laying down emission limits;

(b)   discharges of hazardous substances are gradually reduced with a view to complete elimination;

(c)   compliance with authorisations and general rules is monitored, as are discharges;

(d) authorisations and general rules are periodically examined and adjusted where substantial improvements in the state of the art so permit or where the state of the receiving medium so necessitates;

(e) the risk of pollution from incidents or accidents is reduced as far as possible by regulations, and the requisite measures are taken in the event of an emergency;

(f) technical measures liable to have a serious effect on the ecosystem are subject to prior authorisation, along with the necessary conditions, or to general regulations;

5. to initiate the necessary actions in their territory to implement decisions taken by the Commission in accordance with Article 11;

6. in the event of incidents or accidents that might threaten the quality of the water of the Rhine or in the event of imminent flooding, immediately to inform the Commission and the Contracting Parties liable to be affected, in accordance with the warning and alert plans coordinated by the Commission.

Article 6 - Commission

1. To implement this Convention, the Contracting Parties shall pursue their cooperation within the Commission.

2. The Commission shall have legal personality. In the territory of the Contracting Parties it shall, in particular, enjoy the legal capacity conferred on legal persons by domestic law. It shall be represented by its Chairman.

3. Questions of labour legislation and social matters shall be governed by the law of the country in which the Commission has its seat.

[Omitted: Article 7 - Organisation of the Commission]

Article 8 - Tasks of the Commission

1. To achieve the aims set out in Article 3 the Commission shall accomplish the following tasks:

(a) prepare international measuring programmes and studies of the Rhine ecosystem and make use of their results, in cooperation with scientific institutions if necessary;

(b) make proposals for individual measures and programmes of measures, where appropriate including economic instruments and taking into account the expected costs;

(c) coordinate the Contracting States' warning and alert plans for the Rhine;

(d) evaluate the effectiveness of the actions decided upon, notably on the basis of the reports of the Contracting Parties and the results of the measuring programmes and studies of the Rhine ecosystem;

(e) carry out any other tasks entrusted to it by the Contracting Parties.

2. To this end, the Commission shall take decisions in accordance with Articles 10 and 11.

3. The Commission shall submit an annual activity report to the Contracting Parties.

4. The Commission shall inform the public as to the state of the Rhine and the results of its work. It may draft and publish reports.

[Omitted: Article 9 - Plenary sessions of the Commission, Article 10 - Decision-making in the Commission, Article 11 - Implementation of Commission decisions, Article 12 - Secretariat of the Commission, Article 13 - Distribution of costs, Article 14 - Cooperation with the other States, other organisations and external experts, Article 15 - Working languages, Article 16 - Settlement of disputes, Article 17 - Entry into force, Article 18 - Withdrawal, Article 19 - Repeal and continued application of current law, Article 20 - Original and deposit]

…

Annex

[Omitted: Arbitration]

Protocol of signature

In signing the Convention for the Protection of the Rhine, the heads of delegation in the ICPR agree upon the following points.

...

2. "State of the art" and "best available techniques" are synonymous expressions and, like the expression "best environmental practice", must be understood as defined in the Convention of 17 March 1992 on the protection and use of transboundary watercourses and international lakes (Annexes I and II) and the Convention of 22 September 1992 for the protection of the marine environment of the north-east Atlantic (Appendix I).

...

15. **Tripartite Interim Agreement Between the Republic of Mozambique, the Republic of South Africa and the Kingdom of Swaziland for Co-operation on the Protection and Sustainable Utilisation of the Water Resources of the Incomati and Maputo Watercourses [Johannesburg, 29 August 2002]***

Preamble

[The Parties]

...

Bearing in mind the principles advocated in the Declaration by the Heads of State or Government of Southern African States "Towards the Southern African Development Community" and the Treaty of the Southern African Development Community signed on 17 August 1992 and the Revised Protocol on Shared Watercourses in the Southern African Development Community signed on 7 August 2000;

...

---

* FAOLEX (FAO legal database online). Parties and/or signatories: Mozambique, South Africa, Swaziland.

Taking into account the modern principles and norms of International Law as reflected in the Convention on the Law of the Non-Navigational Uses of International Watercourses adopted by the General Assembly of the United Nations on 21 May 1997;

Conscious of the mutual advantages of concluding agreements on co-operation on shared watercourses;

Determined to co-operate and seek mutually satisfactory solutions for the needs of the Parties towards water protection and to the sustainable utilization and development of the water resources with a view to improving the standard of living of their populations;

Expressing the common desire to proceed with sustainable development on the basis of Chapter 18 of Agenda 21, adopted by the United Nations Conference on Environment and Development on 14 June 1992;

Recognising that the Parties need to agree on water use in the shared watercourses to enable sustainable development;

Mindful of the fact that good relationships between the people and the governments of the Parties, good neighbourliness and mutual respect, will contribute to the improvement of co-operation on the protection and utilization of waters for the benefit and the welfare of their populations;

Taking into consideration the interim nature of this Agreement;

Hereby agree as follows:

Article 1 - Definitions

For the purposes of this Agreement the following terms shall have the meanings ascribed to them hereunder:

"catchment" means an area through which any rainfall will drain into the watercourse through surface flow to a common point;

"emergency situation" means a situation that causes or poses an imminent threat of causing serious harm to the Parties and which results suddenly from natural causes, such as torrential rains, floods, landslides or earthquakes, or from human conduct;

"environmental impact assessment" means a national procedure for evaluating the likely impact of a planned measure on the environment;

"impact" means any effect on the environment caused by an activity; such effects on the environment include effects on human health and safety, flora, fauna, soil, air, water, climate, landscape, socio-economic environment or the interaction among these factors and cultural heritage or socio-economic conditions resulting from alterations to these factors;

"Incomati watercourse" means the system of the Incomati River, which includes the tributaries Mazimechopes, Uanetze, Massintonto, Sabie, Crocodile, Komati Rivers and the estuary;

"Maputo watercourse" means the system of the Maputo River, which includes the tributaries Pongola and Usuthu Rivers and the estuary;

"ministers" means Ministers responsible for the water affairs of the Parties;

"ongoing activity" means any activity that would have been subjected to a decision of a competent authority in accordance with an applicable national procedure if it had been a planned measure;

"Piggs Peak Agreement" means the agreement reached at the Tripartite Ministerial Meeting of Ministers Responsible for Water Affairs, signed in Piggs Peak on 15 February 1991;

"planned measure" means any activity or a major change to an ongoing activity subject to a decision of a competent authority in accordance with applicable national procedures;

"pollution" means any detrimental alteration in the composition or quality of the waters of a shared watercourse, which results directly or indirectly from human conduct;

"Protocol" means the Revised Protocol on Shared Watercourses in the Southern African Development Community signed on 7 August 2000 in Windhoek;

"sustainable development" is development which meets the needs of present generations without compromising future generations to meet their own needs;

"TPTC" means the Tripartite Permanent Technical Committee established by the Agreement between the Government of the Republic of South Africa, the Government of the Kingdom of Swaziland and the Government of the People's Republic of Mozambique relative to the establishment of the Tripartite Permanent Technical Committee, signed in Pretoria on 17 February 1983;

"transboundary impact" means any adverse effect, caused by human conduct, within an area under the jurisdiction of a Party caused by a proposed activity, the physical origin of which is situated wholly or in part within the area under the jurisdiction of another Party;

"watercourse" means a system of surface and groundwaters constituting by virtue of their physical relationship a unitary whole normally flowing into a common terminus such as the sea, lake or aquifer.

Article 2 - General objective

This Agreement aims to promote co-operation among the Parties to ensure the protection and sustainable utilisation of the water resources of the Incomati and Maputo watercourses.

Article 3 - General principles

For purposes of this Agreement, the general principles of the Protocol shall apply, especially-

(a)   sustainable utilization principle;

(b)   equitable and reasonable utilisation and participation principle;

(c)   prevention principle; and

(d)   co-operation principle.

Article 4 - Responsibilities of the Parties

The Parties shall, individually and, where appropriate, jointly, develop and adopt technical, legal, administrative and other reasonable measures in order to-

(a)   prevent, reduce and control pollution of surface and groundwaters, and protect and enhance the quality status of the waters and associated ecosystems for the benefit of present and future generations;

(b)   prevent, eliminate, mitigate and control transboundary impacts;

(c)   co-ordinate management plans and planned measures;

(d)   promote partnership in effective and efficient water use;

(e)   promote the security of relevant water related infrastructures and prevent accidents;

(f)   monitor and mitigate the effects of floods and droughts;

(g)   provide warning of possible floods and implement agreed upon urgent measures during flood situations;

(h)   establish comparable monitoring systems, methods and procedures;

(i)   exchange information on the water resources quality and quantity, and the uses of water;

(j)   promote the implementation of this Agreement according to its objectives and defined principles;

(k)   implement capacity building programmes in accordance with Article 14; and

(l)   co-operate with the SADC organs and other shared watercourse institutions.

Article 5 - Shared watercourses institution

1.   The joint body for co-operation between the Parties shall be the TPTC.

...

Article 6 - Protection of the environment

1. The Parties shall, individually and, where appropriate, jointly, protect and preserve the aquatic environment of the Incomati and Maputo watercourses, taking into account generally accepted international rules and standards.

2. The Parties shall, individually and, where appropriate, jointly, take all measures to protect and preserve the ecosystems of the Incomati and Maputo watercourses.

3. The Parties shall take all measures necessary to prevent the introduction of species, alien or new, into the Incomati and Maputo watercourses, which may have effects detrimental to the ecosystems of the watercourses resulting in significant harm to other Parties.

Article 7 - Sustainable utilisation

1. The Parties shall be entitled, in their respective territories, to optimal and sustainable utilisation of and benefits from the water resources of the Incomati and Maputo watercourses, taking into account the interests of the other Parties concerned, consistent with adequate protection of the watercourses for the benefit of present and future generations.

2. The Parties shall co-ordinate their management activities by-

(a) the exchange of information on their respective experiences and perspectives; and

(b) the co-ordination of management plans, programmes and measures.

3. In pursuing the objective of this Article, the Parties shall follow the flow regimes stipulated in Annex I as determined according to Article 9.

4. In further pursuance of the objective of this Article the Parties disclose in Annex II their intentions of developing new projects that fall outside the scope of Annex I during the period of validity of this Agreement.

5.   The Parties are committed to develop measures towards improvement of efficiency and rational use of water and its conservation and to promote more efficient water use through adopting better available technology.

Article 8 - Water quality and prevention of pollution

1.   In order to protect and conserve the water resources of the Incomati and Maputo watercourses, the Parties shall, through resolutions adopted by the TPTC, and, when appropriate, through the co-ordination of management plans, programmes and measures, proceed to-

(a)   endeavour to develop an evolving classification system for the water resources of the Incomati and Maputo watercourses;

(b)   classify and state the objectives and criteria in respect of water quality variables to be achieved through the agreed classification system for the water resources;

(c)   adopt a list of substances the introduction of which, into the water resources of the Incomati and Maputo watercourses, is to be prohibited or limited, investigated or monitored;

(d)   adopt techniques and practices to prevent, reduce and control the pollution and environmental degradation of the Incomati and Maputo watercourses that may cause significant harm to the other Parties or to their environment, including human health and safety, or to the use of the waters for any beneficial purpose, or to the living resources of the watercourses; and

(e)   implement a regular monitoring programme, including biological and chemical aspects for the Incomati and Maputo watercourses and report, at the intervals established by the TPTC, on the status and trends of the associated aquatic, marine and riparian ecosystems in relation to the water quality of the said watercourses.

2.   Until such time that water quality objectives and criteria are determined, the Parties shall comply with the provisions of the Resolution of the TPTC on Exchange of Information and Water Quality. The Resolution may be reviewed by the TPTC from time to time.

Article 9 - Flow regimes

1. The agreed flow regime of the Incomati watercourse is contained in Annex I, which complements the flow regime as determined in the Piggs Peak Agreement, and the agreed flow regime of the Maputo watercourse is contained in the same Annex.

2. Any abstraction of waters from the Incomati or Maputo watercourses, regardless of the use or geographic destination of such waters, shall be in conformity with the flow regimes of Annex I and relevant provisions of this Agreement and its Annexes.

3. The Parties have considered the following criteria in establishing the flow regimes contained in Annex I:

(a) The geographic, hydrological, climatic and other natural characteristics of each watercourse;

(b) the need to ensure water of sufficient quantity with acceptable quality to sustain the watercourses and their associated ecosystems;

(c) any present and reasonably foreseeable water requirements, including afforestation;

(d) existing infrastructure which has the capacity to regulate streamflow of the watercourses; and

(e) agreements in force among the Parties.

4. The following short to medium term water requirements of each of the Parties are recognised in particular:

(a) The strategic importance to Mozambique of augmenting the water supplies to the city of Maputo and its metropolitan area from one or both of the Incomati and Maputo watercourses;

(b) the importance to Swaziland of developing the Lower Usuthu Smallholder Irrigation Project in the Usuthu River catchment; and

(c) the importance to South Africa of establishing and developing emerging irrigation farmers in the Incomati River catchment.

5.   The additional water requirements of the city of Maputo, for which additional water must be secured, have been reserved in Annex I.

[Omitted: Article 10 - Droughts and floods]

Article 11 - Incidents of accidental pollution and other emergency situations

1.   The Parties shall, without delay and by the most expeditious means available, notify other potentially affected Parties, the SADC organs or any other authorized institutions and competent international organisations of any incidents of accidental pollution and other emergency situations originating within their respective territories and shall promptly supply the necessary information to such affected Parties and competent organisations with a view to co-operate in the prevention, mitigation and elimination of the harmful effects of the emergency.

2.   The Parties shall, individually and, where appropriate, jointly, develop contingency plans for responding to any incidents of accidental pollution and other emergency situations in co-operation, where appropriate, with other potentially affected Parties and competent international organisations, to take immediately all practicable measures necessitated by the circumstances to prevent, mitigate and eliminate the harmful effects of the emergency.

Article 12 - Exchange of and access to information

1.   The Parties shall, within the TPTC, exchange available information and data regarding the hydrological, geohydrological, water quality, meteorological and environmental condition of the Incomati and Maputo watercourses to enable planning, development and management of these shared watercourses.

2.   The Parties shall exchange data, information and study reports on the activities that are likely to cause significant transboundary impacts.

3.   To enable compliance with subArticle (2), the polluting substances subject to special attention shall be as agreed in the Resolution and regularly reviewed by the TPTC.

4. The Parties shall exchange information and consult each other and if necessary, negotiate the possible effects of planned measures on the condition of the Incomati and Maputo watercourses. The Parties shall employ their best efforts to collect and where appropriate, to process data and information in a manner, which facilitates its utilisation by the other Party to which it is communicated.

5. If a Party is requested by another Party to provide data or any information in subArticles (1) and (2), and that information is not readily available, it shall employ its best efforts to comply with the request but may condition its compliance upon payment by the requesting Party of the reasonable costs of collecting and where appropriate processing such data or information.

6. The Parties shall provide one another, at intervals agreed to by the TPTC, information on the use, quantity and quality of the water resources and the ecological state of the Incomati and Maputo watercourses necessary for the implementation of this Agreement.

7. The Parties shall develop the appropriate measures to ensure that the information is homogeneous, compatible and comparable, as agreed by the TPTC.

8. The Parties shall create the necessary conditions to ensure that, in conformity with applicable domestic law or International Law, information on matters covered by this Agreement is available to whoever makes a reasonable request.

Article 13 - Transboundary impacts

1. Planned measures listed in Annex II [sic], regardless of their location, that by themselves or by accumulation with the existing ones, have the potential of a significant transboundary impact on the watercourse, shall not commence before the provisions of Article 4(1) of the Protocol are complied with.

2. Whenever, a planned measure, not listed in Annex II [sic], is likely to cause a significant transboundary impact or any of the Parties expresses concern that such may occur, it shall not commence before the provisions of Article 4(1) of the Protocol are complied with.

3. In case of a planned measure involving significant transboundary impact of substantial magnitude the Parties shall conduct an environmental impact assessment, which takes transboundary impact into account in accordance with procedures determined by the TPTC.

4. Whenever an ongoing activity causes or is likely to cause a significant transboundary impact, which will lead the Party to fail to comply with an obligation under Articles 4, 8 or 9, the national procedures on the subject shall apply and the Parties concerned shall endeavour to address the matter through the co-ordination of management plans, programmes or measures.

[Omitted: Article 14 - Capacity building, Article 15 - Settlement of disputes, Article 16 - Annexes, Article 17 - Existing watercourse agreements, Article 18 - Entry into force, termination and amendments, Article 19 - Depositary of the agreement]

...

Annex I - Flow regime

Article 1 - Determining criteria

1. Determination of the flow regime is based on the criteria in Article 9(3) of the Agreement.

2. The Parties accord a first priority to supply water for domestic, livestock and industrial use, as well as ecological water requirements as recognised by the TPTC.

3. If, upon review of the hydrology of the system, more water is found to be available in the Incomati or Maputo watercourses than that contemplated in this Annex, the Parties shall give priority to the water uses referred to in subArticle (2), when considering the allocation of the water.

4. Monitoring of the flow regime will be carried out at appropriate hydrometrical stations. The TPTC will determine their location and the conditions of installation and operation.

[Omitted: Article 2 - Incomati watercourse, Article 3 - Maputo watercourse, Article 4 - Utilisation of the Incomati watercourse]

Article 5 - Water requirements of the ecosystems of the Incomati watercourse

1. The Parties acknowledge the need to maintain interim instream flows at various key points in the Incomati watercourse to sustain the ecology of the watercourse including the estuary of the Incomati River.

    . . .

[Omitted: Article 6 - Utilisation of the Maputo watercourse, Article 7 - Water requirements of the ecosystems of the Maputo watercourse, Article 8 - Water conservation, Article 9 - Generation of hydropower, Article 10 - Concluding provisions, Annex II - Reference projects]

Annex III - Transboundary impact

The projects and activities referred to in Article 13(1) of the Agreement are the following:

(a) Industrial installation for energy production or mining activities which can impact significantly on water quality and quantity;

(b) pipelines carrying oil or chemical products;

(c) installations (facilities) for storage of dangerous products;

. . .

(g) groundwater abstraction facilities, regardless of the use or destination of the water, above 3,5 million m^3 per year;

(h) artificial recharging of aquifers with volumes above 3,5 million m^3 per year;

. . .

(j) waste water discharges, of urban, industrial, cattle raising or other origin, in which the polluting charge is above 1000 equivalent inhabitants;

...

(l)   deforestation and reforestation works, affecting an area above 500 hectares and that have the potential to increase the sediment production or to increase flood peaks or to decrease the river flow.

[Omitted: Annex IV - Bilateral and trilateral agreements, Annex V - Time frame for the establishment of comprehensive water resource development and water use agreements]

16.   Framework Agreement on the Sava River Basin [Kranjska Gora, 3 December 2002]*

[The Parties]

Recognizing the vital importance of trans-boundary co-operation for the Parties aimed towards sustainable development of the Sava River Basin;

...

Being aware of the need to promote sustainable water management by regulating utilization, protection of the waters and aquatic eco-system and protection against the detrimental effects of the waters in the Sava River Basin, taking into consideration the Convention on Cooperation for the Protection and Sustainable Use of the Danube River (Sofia 1994);

Taking into account the great political, economic and social changes that have taken place in the region of the Sava River Basin;

Confirming our commitment to a sustainable development of the region that should be brought about in co-operation with the countries in the region, and with the view to ensure that this Agreement fits, in a coherent way, in accordance with the European Union integration process;

Desiring to develop mutual co-operation on the basis of principles of equal rights, State sovereignty and territorial integrity, good faith and good neighborliness;

---

* FAOLEX (FAO legal database online). Parties and/or signatories: Bosnia and Herzegovina, Croatia, Slovenia, Yugoslavia.

Aware of the ever increasing importance attached to the protection of the environment and natural resources, as well as the need for enhanced co-operation for an effective protection of the Sava River Basin;

Recognizing the great value of the Sava River Basin and its environment and natural assets, for the economic and social well-being and living standards of the citizens;

...

Having in mind that the Sava River Basin is part of the Danube Basin and that several international law regimes established by multilateral instruments of international water law, international environmental law and European Union legislation are applied to water resources of the Danube River Basin;

Wishing to join their efforts on sustainable management of water resources of the Sava River Basin with the efforts of other countries and international institutions and arrangements present in the Danube Basin;

...

Have agreed as follows:

Part 1 - General provisions

Article 1 - Definitions

For the purposes of this Agreement:

1. "Transboundary Impact" means any adverse effect on the river environment resulting from a change in water regime, caused by human activity and stretching out beyond an area under the jurisdiction of a Party, and which change may affect life and property, safety of facilities, and the aquatic ecosystem concerned.

2. "The Sava River Basin" is the geographical area extended over the territories of the Parties, determined by the watershed limits of the Sava River and its tributaries, which comprises surface and groundwaters, flowing into a common terminus.

3. "Water Regime" comprises quantity and quality conditions of the waters of the Sava River Basin in space and time influenced by human activities or natural changes.

Article 2 - Objective of the agreement

1. The Parties shall cooperate in order to achieve the following goals:

...

(b) Establishment of sustainable water management; and

(c) Undertaking of measures to prevent or limit hazards, and reduce and eliminate adverse consequences, including those from floods, ice hazards, droughts and incidents involving substances hazardous to water.

2. For the purpose of carrying out the goals stated in Paragraph 1 of this Article, the Parties shall cooperate in the process of the creation and realization of joint plans and development programs of the Sava River Basin and harmonization of their legislation with EU legislation.

Part Two - General principles of cooperation

Article 3 - General obligation to cooperate

1. The Parties shall cooperate on the basis of sovereign equality, territorial integrity, mutual benefit, and good faith in order to attain the goals of the present agreement.

2. The Parties shall cooperate on the basis of, and in accordance with, Directive 2000/60/EC of the EU Parliament and Council of October 23, 2000, Establishing a Framework for Community Activities in the Field of Water Policy (hereinafter: EU Water Framework Directive).

Article 4 - Exchange of data and information

Pursuant to Article 3 of this Agreement, the Parties shall, on a regular basis, exchange information on the water regime of the Sava River Basin, the regime of navigation, legislation, organizational structures, and administrative and technical practices.

Article 5 - Cooperation with international organizations

In realization of this Agreement, the Parties shall especially cooperate with:

(a) The International Commission for Protection of Danube River (hereinafter: ICPDR);

(b) The Danube Commission;

(c) The United Nations Economic Commission for Europe (hereinafter: UN/ECE), and

(d) Institutions of the European Union.

Article 6 - Cooperation with national organizations (authorities or bodies)

1. The Parties agree to nominate organizations (authorities or bodies) competent for realization of this Agreement on the part of the Sava River Basin within their territories.

2. The Parties agree to inform the Chairman of the International Sava River Basin Commission (as established in Article 15 of this Agreement) of the nomination of the organizations (authorities or bodies) stated in paragraph 1 of this Article.

Article 7 - Principle of reasonable and equitable utilization of the waters

1. The Parties are entitled, within their territories, to a reasonable and equitable share of the beneficial uses of the Sava River Basin water resources.

2. Reasonable and equitable share within the meaning of Paragraph 1 of this Article is to be determined in any particular case in light of the relevant factors according to international law.

Article 8 - Transboundary impact

1. The Parties shall agree on how to regulate all issues concerning measures aimed at securing integrity of the water regime in the Sava River Basin and the elimination or reduction of transboundary impacts

on the waters of the other parties caused by economic or other activities.

2.   For that purpose, the Parties shall, by separate protocol, regulate the procedures for the issuance of water law acts (licenses, permits and confirmations) for installations and activities that may have a transboundary impact on the integrity of the water regime.

Article 9 - No harm rule

The Parties shall, in utilizing waters of the Sava River Basin in their territories, cooperate and take all appropriate measures to prevent causing significant harm to other Party(ies).

Part Three - Areas of co-operation

[Omitted: Article 10 - Regime of navigation]

Article 11 - Sustainable water management

The Parties agree to cooperate on management of the waters of the Sava River Basin in a sustainable manner, which includes integrated management of surface and groundwater resources, in a manner that shall provide for:

(a)   Water in sufficient quantity and of appropriate quality for the preservation, protection and improvement of aquatic eco-systems (including flora and fauna and eco-systems of natural ponds and wetlands);

(b)   Waters in sufficient quantity and of appropriate quality for navigation and other kinds of use/utilization;

(c)   Protection against detrimental effects of water (flooding, excessive groundwater, erosion and ice hazards);

(d)   Resolution of conflicts of interest caused by different uses and utilizations; and

(e)   Effective control of the water regime.

Article 12 - The Sava River Basin Management Plan

1. The Parties agree to develop joint and/or integrated Plan on the management of the water resources of the Sava River Basin and to cooperate on its preparatory activities.

2. The Sava River Basin Management Plan shall be adopted by the Parties on the proposal of the International Sava River Basin Commission.

3. Cooperation stated in Paragraph 1of this Article shall be coordinated with activities of the ICPDR.

4. All issues concerning the preparation and realization of the Sava River Basin Management Plan may be regulated with separate protocols.

Article 13 - Extraordinary impacts on the water regime

1. The Parties shall establish a coordinated or joint system of measures, activities, warnings and alarms in the Sava River Basin for extraordinary impacts on the water regime, such as sudden and accidental pollution, discharge of artificial accumulations and retentions caused by collapsing or inappropriate handling, flood, ice, drought, water shortage, and obstruction of navigation.

2. In realization of the obligation in paragraph 1 of this Article, the Parties shall act in accordance with activities undertaken in the framework of The Convention for Protection and Sustainable Use of Danube River and in the scope of the procedures agreed within the ICPDR.

Part Four - Mechanisms of co-operation

Article 14 - Meeting of the Parties

1. The first Meeting of the Parties shall be convened no later than one year after the date of entry into force of this Agreement. Thereafter, an ordinary Meeting of the Parties shall be held at least once every two years, unless otherwise decided by the Parties, or at the written request of any Party.

2. At their Meetings, the Parties shall keep under continuous review the implementation of this Agreement on the basis of reports of the International Sava River Basin Commission, and shall:

(a)   Review the work and operations of the International Sava River Basin
      Commission and make decisions based on its recommendations;

(b)   Consider and adopt proposals for protocols and amendments to this
      agreement; and

(c)   Consider and undertake any additional action that may be required for
      the achievement of the purposes of this Agreement.

3.   All decisions of the Meeting of the Parties shall be made by consensus.

Article 15 - International Sava River Basin Commission

1.   For the implementation of this Agreement, the Parties shall establish
      the International Sava River Basin Commission (hereinafter: Sava
      Commission).

2.   The Sava Commission shall have the international legal capacity
      necessary for the exercise of its functions.

[Omitted: Article 16 - Functions of the Sava Commission, Article 17 -
Financing the Sava Commission, Article 18 - Secretariat, Article 19 - Seat of
the Sava Commission, Article 20 - Statute]

Article 21 - Monitoring implementation of the Agreement

1.   The Parties agree to establish a methodology of permanent monitoring
      of implementation of the Agreement and activities based upon it.

2.   The implementation monitoring methodology will include timely
      provision of information to stakeholders and the general public by the
      authorities responsible for implementation of the Agreement.

3.   The Parties shall establish an implementation monitoring methodology
      within two years after the Agreement has entered into force.

Part Five - Dispute settlement

Article 22 - General provisions

1. If a dispute arises between two or more Parties about the interpretation or implementation of this Agreement, they shall seek a solution by negotiation.

2. If the concerned parties are unable to resolve the dispute through negotiation, upon the request of one of the concerned parties, they may jointly seek good services, mediation or conciliation from a third party, or they may agree to refer the dispute to arbitrage in accordance with Annex II of this Agreement, or to the International Court of Justice.

3. If, within six months from submitting a request as stated in Paragraph 2 of this Article, the concerned parties are unable to resolve the dispute through negotiation, good services, mediation or conciliation, any Party concerned may request that an independent fact-finding expert committee be established.

[Omitted: Article 23 - Fact-finding expert committee, Article 24 - Role of the Fact-finding expert committee]

Part Six - Final Provisions

[Omitted: Article 25 - Annexes, Article 26 - Amendments to the Agreement, Article 27 - Reservation, Article 28 - Duration and entering into force, Article 29 - Other agreements]

Article 30 - Protocols

1. In implementing this Agreement, the Parties shall, in addition to the protocols referred to in other provisions of this Agreement, conclude other protocols for regulating:

...

(a) Protection against flood, excessive groundwater, erosion, ice hazards, drought and water shortages;

(b) Water use/utilization;

(c)   Exploitation of stone, sand, gravel and clay;

(d)   Protection and improvement of water quality and quantity;

(e)   Protection of aquatic eco-systems;

...

(g)   Emergency situations.

2.   The Parties may agree to conclude other protocols necessary for the implementation of this Agreement.

[Omitted: Article 31 - Termination and withdrawal, Article 32 - International borders, Article 33 - Depositary]

...

[Omitted: Annex I - Statute of the International Sava River Basin Commission, Annex II - Dispute settlement by arbitrage]

17.   The Convention on the Sustainable Development of Lake Tanganyika [Dar es Salaam, 12 June 2003]*

Preamble

...

The "Contracting States";

Conscious of Lake Tanganyika's unique aquatic and other biological diversity and of the Lake's significance for the development of the riparian States;

Recognizing that Lake Tanganyika is a shared heritage of the riparian States;

---

* FAOLEX (FAO legal database online). Parties and/or signatories: Burundi, Congo, Tanzania, Zambia.

Conscious of the threats to the Lake Basin as a result of pollution, sedimentation, over-fishing and other adverse impacts of human activities within the territories of the Contracting States;

Reaffirming that in accordance with principles of international law States have the sovereign right to exploit their own resources pursuant to their own environmental and developmental policies and the responsibility to ensure that activities within their jurisdictions or control do not cause damage to the environment of other States;

Reaffirming further that the conservation of biological diversity is a common concern of humankind and that States are responsible for conserving their biological diversity and for using their biological resources in a sustainable manner;

Recognizing that the riparian States share a common interest in the conservation and equitable utilization of the resources of Lake Tanganyika;

Recognizing that integrated management of the Lake Basin by the Contracting States is essential to ensure its conservation and the sustainable use of its natural resources and to optimize the benefits derived from it by the Contracting States;

Recognizing the necessity of establishing a sustainable legal and institutional framework for co-operative management of the Lake by the Contracting States and the contribution that this would make to strengthening relations between them and to promoting development in the region;

Recalling the principles enunciated in the Declaration on Environment and Development adopted by the United Nations Conference on Environment and Development in 1992, the 1992 Convention on Biological Diversity, and international and regional agreements and instruments relating to shared watercourses;

Have agreed as follows:

Article 1 - Use of terms

For the purposes of the present Convention:

...

"Adverse impact" means any actual or potential detrimental effect on the Lake's environment and any actual or potential consequential detrimental effect on legitimate uses of the Lake, on the health of the people of a Contracting State or on their ability to provide for their health, safety and cultural and economic well-being, that results directly or indirectly from human conduct originating wholly or partly within the territory of a Contracting State or from a vessel or aircraft under its jurisdiction or control, beyond that which is negligible or which has been assessed and determined to be acceptable under this Convention and under any subsequent protocols;

"Authority" means the Lake Tanganyika Authority established under Article 23;

"Basin" means the geographical area bounded by the watershed limits of Lake Tanganyika.

"Bio-chemicals" means unimproved or unmodified chemical compounds, other than deoxyribonucleic acids or ribonucleic acids, formed by the metabolic processes of a living organism.

"Biological diversity" means the variability among living organisms from all sources, including, inter alia, terrestrial, marine and other aquatic ecosystems and the ecological complexes of which they are part; this includes diversity within species, between species and of ecosystems;

"Conference of Ministers" means the Conference of Ministers established by Article 24;

"Ecosystem" means a dynamic complex of plant, animal and micro-organism communities and their non-living environment interacting as a functional unit;

"Environment" includes, but is not limited to, the whole or any component of:

(a) nature, which includes air, water, land, including soils and minerals, energy and living organisms;

(b) the interaction between the components of nature and between those components and humans; and

(c) physical, esthetic and cultural qualities or conditions that affect the health and well-being of people;

"Executive Director" means the chief executive and legal representative of the Authority appointed according to Article 26.

...

"Lake Basin" means the whole or any component of the aquatic environment of Lake Tanganyika and those ecosystems and aspects of the environment that are associated with, affect or are dependent on, the aquatic environment of Lake Tanganyika, including the system of surface waters and groundwaters that flow into the Lake from the Contracting States and the land submerged by these waters.

"Lake Tanganyika" means the water-body known as Lake Tanganyika.

"Management Committee" means the Management Committee of the Authority described in Article 25;

"Natural resources" mean any naturally occurring living or non-living component of the environment of actual or potential use or value to humanity, including: air, land, water, soils, minerals, energy, genetic resources, bio-chemicals, organisms or parts of organisms, populations and other biotic components of an ecosystem;

"Operator" means any person, association, public or private body, whether corporate or not, including the State and any of its entities which exercises control over dangerous activities; and "dangerous activity" means any activity listed in Annex II.

"Pollution" means the introduction by humans, directly or indirectly, of substances or energy into the Lake Basin, which results or is likely to result, in hazards to human health, harm to living organisms and ecosystems, damage to amenities or interference with legitimate uses of the Lake, including fishing and navigation;

"Secretariat" means the Secretariat of the Authority described in Article 26;

"Trans-boundary adverse impact" means any adverse impact that extends beyond the territory of the Contracting State in which the physical origin of the adverse impact is situated.

Article 2 - Objective

1. The objective of the present Convention is to ensure the protection and conservation of the biological diversity and the sustainable use of the natural resources of Lake Tanganyika and its Basin by the Contracting States on the basis of integrated and co-operative management.

2. In order to achieve this objective, the Contracting States:

(a) co-operate in the development and implementation of harmonized laws and standards concerning the management of Lake Tanganyika and its Basin; and

(b) accord particular attention to ensuring that present and future communities living near the Lake benefit from the sustainable use of the Lake's natural resources and amenities.

Article 3 - Jurisdictional scope

The present Convention applies to Lake Tanganyika and to its Basin in the Contracting States as well as to all human activities, aircraft and vessels under the control of a Contracting State to the extent that these activities or the operation of such aircraft or vessels result or are likely to result in an adverse impact.

Article 4 - Co-operation

1. The Contracting States shall co-operate in good faith in the management of Lake Tanganyika and its Basin in a manner that most effectively promotes the attainment of the objective referred to in Article 2 paragraph 1, and that gives effect to the general principles set out in Article 5.

2. Such co-operation shall include:

(a) planning and managing activities under the jurisdiction or control of a Contracting State which have an adverse impact or which may have an adverse impact on the Lake and its Basin;

(b) supporting the activities and building the capacity of the institutions established under this Convention;

(c) formulating and adopting protocols to this Convention as stipulated in Article 34;

(d) exchanging information concerning the state of the Lake Basin, the results of the monitoring of activities in the Lake Basin that may affect its environment, and experience concerning the protection, sustainable use and management of Lake Tanganyika;

(e) the other Contracting States informed of planned and on-going activities that have or are likely to have an adverse impact on the Lake and its Basin;

(f) engaging in joint research; and

(g) implementing this Convention.

Article 5 - General principles

1. Lake Tanganyika and any related installations, facilities and works shall be used exclusively for peaceful purposes in accordance with the Charter of the United Nations and shall not be violated even in time of international or internal armed conflicts.

2. The natural resources of Lake Tanganyika shall be protected, conserved, managed, and used for sustainable development to meet the needs of present and future generations in an equitable manner.

   To this end the following principles shall be applied.

(a) The precautionary principle, by virtue of which preventive measures are to be taken when there are reasonable grounds for concern that an actual or planned activity within the territory or under the jurisdiction and control of a Contracting State may bring about an adverse impact, even if there is no conclusive scientific evidence of a causal relationship between the activity and the adverse impact.

(b)   The polluter pays principle, by virtue of which the costs of pollution prevention, control and reduction measures are to be borne by the polluter.

(c)   The principle of preventive action, by virtue of which action shall be taken to prevent adverse impacts arising by taking timely action to address the actual or potential causes of the adverse impacts.

(d)   The principle of participation by virtue of which concerned and affected natural and legal persons and Lake Basin communities must be given the opportunity to participate, at the appropriate level, in decision-making and management processes that affect the Lake Basin and are given appropriate access to information concerning the environment that is held by public authorities and effective access to judicial and administrative proceedings to enable them to exercise their rights effectively.

(e)   The principle of fair and equitable benefit sharing by virtue of which local communities are entitled to share in the benefits derived from local natural resources.

Article 6 - Prevention and minimisation of transboundary adverse impacts

1.   The Contracting States shall ensure that activities within their jurisdiction or control do not cause trans-boundary adverse impacts.

2.   The Contracting States shall take appropriate measures to address the causes or potential causes of adverse impacts within their jurisdiction or control, to prevent adverse impacts and to mitigate those adverse impacts that cannot be prevented, and thereby reduce the risk and magnitude of trans-boundary adverse impacts.

[Omitted: Article 7 - Fisheries management]

Article 8 - Prevention and control of pollution

1.   The Contracting States shall, as a matter of priority, take appropriate measures to prevent and reduce pollution of Lake Tanganyika and its environment arising from activities within their jurisdiction or control.

2.   In particular, each Contracting State shall:

(a)   to the extent possible, construct and maintain installations within their territory to reduce the risk of pollution of the Lake and its environment;

...

(c)   develop, adopt, implement and enforce appropriate legal, administrative and technical measures to prevent, control, monitor and reduce pollution:

   (i)   from both point and non-point sources;

   ...

   (iii) from the manufacture, handling, transportation, use and disposal of toxic or hazardous materials in the Lake Basin.

3.   The Contracting States shall develop and adopt a protocol to this Convention specifying the minimum measures and standards to be adopted by each Contracting State in order to ensure the harmonized implementation of pollution prevention and mitigation measures to protect human health and achieve a high level of protection for the Lake Basin.

[Omitted: Article 9 - Prevention of sedimentation, Article 10 - Conservation of biological diversity, Article 11 - Access to genetic resources, Article 12 - Navigation]

Article 13 - Strategic action program

1.   The Contracting States shall collaborate in the preparation and implementation of a strategic action program to give effect to the measures set out in this Convention.

2.   The strategic action program shall include specific aims directed at achieving the objective of this Convention, strategies for achieving these aims, specific measures to be taken by the Contracting States separately or jointly to achieve these aims and details of the means to be used to monitor progress toward the achievement of these aims.

3.   The Contracting States shall monitor the effectiveness of the strategic action program and shall revise it as necessary.

4.   The Contracting States shall ensure that the measures contained in the strategic action program are integrated into relevant national policies, strategies, programs and plans.

Article 14 - Prior notification

1.   The Contracting State or States under whose jurisdiction or control a proposed activity listed in Part A of Annex I is planned to take place or a public policy, plan or program that is likely to give rise to trans-boundary adverse impacts has been prepared, shall notify the Secretariat as early as possible which shall notify the other Contracting States without delay.

2.   The notification shall contain information on the proposed activity, program or policy, including any available information on its possible trans-boundary adverse impacts and effects.

3.   Any Contracting State that considers that it should have received prior notification under this article of a proposed activity, public policy, plan or program under the jurisdiction of another Contracting State, shall request the Secretariat to intercede on its behalf with that Contracting State.

4.   The Contracting States undertake to define activities that shall require simple notification and activities that shall require prior informed consent and the modalities of notification in a Protocol to the present Convention.

Article 15 - Environmental impact assessment

1.   Each Contracting State, in order to avoid and minimize adverse impacts, shall:

(a)   adopt and implement appropriate legal, administrative and other measures requiring an assessment to be conducted of the environmental impacts of proposed projects and of activities within its jurisdiction or control, that are likely to give rise to adverse impacts;

(b) adopt and implement appropriate legal and administrative procedures and institutional arrangements to ensure that when public policies, plans and programs are being developed and implemented, the consequences for the Lake Basin are taken into account including any comments received from other Contracting States;

(c) monitor compliance with and enforce any conditions in development consents or other authorizations that were imposed for the purpose of protecting the Lake Basin.

2. The Contracting State within whose jurisdiction a proposed activity listed in Part A of Annex I is planned to take place, shall ensure that the environmental impact assessment procedure results in the production of documentation conforming with Part B of Annex I.

3. A Contracting State that may be affected by a proposed activity listed in Part A of Annex I shall, at the request of a Contracting State under whose jurisdiction the proposed activity is planned to take place, promptly provide the latter through the Secretariat, with all information relevant to the assessment of the potential trans-boundary adverse impacts within the jurisdiction of the affected Contracting State as is reasonably obtainable.

4. The Contracting State or States under whose jurisdiction a proposed activity is planned to take place shall, after completion of the environmental impact assessment documentation, consult with the other Contracting States and the Secretariat on measures to prevent, reduce or eliminate trans-boundary and other impacts including any post-project monitoring and analysis that may be required. At the commencement of the consultation the Contracting States shall agree a reasonable time-table for the duration of the consultation period.

5. The Contracting States shall ensure that in reaching the final decision on the proposed activity, due account is taken of the outcome of the environmental impact assessment procedure, including the environmental impact assessment documentation, comments on it and objections to it and the consultations under this article. The Contracting State under whose jurisdiction the final decision is made shall provide the Secretariat with a copy of the final decision.

6.   If after an activity has been authorized in accordance with this article, the Secretariat or a Contracting State obtains additional information on the trans-boundary adverse impact of the activity which was not available at the time the decision was made and which could have materially affected the decision, this information shall be communicated immediately to the other Contracting States through the Secretariat and the Contracting States shall consult to decide whether or not the decision should be reviewed or additional measures taken to reduce or eliminate the impact.

7.   The Contracting States shall co-operate in the development of technical, legal and other measures concerning joint trans-boundary environmental impact procedures.

Article 16 - Education and public awareness

Each Contracting State shall:

(a)   promote and encourage public awareness of the importance of the ecosystem of Lake Tanganyika and its environment;

(b)   elaborate and implement a program of education and public awareness of the lake Basin population through all possible means in respect of the importance of the biological diversity of the Lake Basin and its management for sustainable development;

(c)   develop a sense of awareness in the Lake Basin population that they are an integral part of the Lake Basin.

Article 17 - Public participation in decision making processes

1.   Each Contracting State shall adopt and implement legal, administrative and other appropriate measures to ensure that the public, and in particular those individuals and communities living within the Lake Basin:

(a)   have the right to participate at the appropriate level, in decision-making processes that affect the Lake Basin or their livelihoods, including participation in the procedure for assessing the environmental impacts of projects or activities that are likely to result in adverse impacts; and

(b)   are given the opportunity to make oral or written representations before a final decision is taken.

2.   Each Contracting State shall ensure that appeal or review procedures exist in respect of any decision by a public body to authorize an activity that is likely to give rise to an adverse impact.

Article 18 - Accidents and emergencies

1.   If an accident or emergency arises within the territory of a Contracting State that causes or is likely to cause an adverse impact, the Contracting State concerned shall take necessary measures to control or reduce the negative impact and immediately notify the Secretariat that shall in turn notify the other Contracting States as soon as possible.

2.   The Contracting States shall establish coordinated or joint warning and emergency response plans to reduce the risk of adverse impacts and to deal effectively with potential accidents and emergencies that are likely to cause adverse impacts, including humanitarian emergencies, major pollution incidents and shipping accidents.

Article 19 - Public access to information

1.   The Contracting States shall ensure that, subject to Article 20, adequate information is made available to the public concerning the state of the Lake Basin, planned development activities, measures taken or planned to be taken to prevent, control and reduce adverse impacts, and the effectiveness of those measures. For this purpose each Contracting State shall ensure that information is made available to the public on the following:

...

(b)   the results of monitoring compliance with permits and the attainment of water and environmental quality objectives;

(c)   any notifications received by that Contracting State under Article 14 concerning proposed activities listed in Part A of Annex I;

(d)   reports on the environmental impact assessment of any of the proposed activities listed in Part A of Annex I.

2.   The Contracting States shall ensure that any information referred to in paragraph 1 that is held by a public body is available to the public for inspection at all reasonable times free of charge and shall provide members of the public with facilities for obtaining, on payment of reasonable charges, copies of such information.

Article 20 - Exchange of information

1.   The Contracting States shall exchange through the Secretariat data and information concerning the sustainable management of the Lake Basin and the implementation of this Convention, as is available including inter alia data and information on:

(a)   the state of the Lake Basin and its biological diversity, in particular monitoring data and information of a hydrological, hydro-geological, meteorological and ecological nature and related to water quality, as well as related forecasts;

(b)   the results of research relevant to the management of the Lake Basin;

(c)   legal, administrative and other measures taken and planned to be taken to prevent, control and reduce adverse impacts;

(d)   accidents and emergencies that have given or are likely to give rise to adverse impacts;

(e)   actions taken to monitor, control and enforce legal provisions or administrative measures used to give effect to this Convention, including any conditions imposed on activities listed in Part A of Annex I that were imposed for the purpose of protecting the Lake Basin, and any fisheries conservation and management measures.

2.   If a Contracting State is requested by any other Contracting State or by the Secretariat to provide data or information that is not readily available, the former shall employ its best efforts to comply with the request.

[Omitted: Article 21 - Protection of confidential information]

Article 22 - Reporting

1. Each Contracting State shall report periodically to the Authority on measures that it has taken to implement this Convention and on the effectiveness of these measures in meeting the objective of this Convention and on any other matters determined by a decision of the Conference of Ministers. These reports shall include in particular:

(a) information on the laws and administrative procedures of the Contracting State regulating, or relevant to the prevention, control and reduction of adverse impacts;

(b) legal, administrative and other measures taken relating to the assessment of the environmental impact of proposed activities and measures to give effect to the obligations envisaged in Article 15;

(c) information on the state of the Lake Basin within the territory of the Contracting State; and

(d) measures taken to implement the provisions of this Convention or to further the attainment of its objective.

2. The Secretariat shall submit recommendations to the Contracting States regarding the reports that are required for the effective implementation of this Convention, the information to be included in the reports, the frequency with which they should be submitted and how reporting should be done, for consideration by the Contracting States at the second meeting of the Conference of Ministers and at subsequent meetings.

Article 23 - Lake Tanganyika Authority

1. The Contracting States hereby establish the Lake Tanganyika Authority, hereinafter referred to as "the Authority".

2. The organs of the Authority are: the Conference of Ministers, the Management Committee and the Secretariat.

3. The function of the Authority is to co-ordinate the implementation of the present Convention by the Contracting States and, in accordance with this Convention and the decisions of the Conference of Ministers,

to advance and represent the common interests of the Contracting States in matters concerning the management of Lake Tanganyika and its Basin.

4.   The Authority shall have international legal personality and such legal capacity as may be necessary to perform its functions and mission.

5.   The Headquarters of the Authority shall be at the place, within the territory of any of the Contracting States, designated by the Conference of Ministers. The Authority shall enter into a headquarters agreement approved by the Conference of Ministers with the Host State.

6.   The Authority may with the approval of the Conference of Ministers establish regional offices within the territory of any of the Contracting States.

7.   Each Contracting State shall, having regard to the diplomatic rules governing international organizations, grant to the Authority and its property, funds and assets, the privileges, immunities and facilities that it needs to carry out its activities; and the members of the Management Committee and of the Secretariat the privileges, immunities and facilities that they need to perform their official functions.

Article 24 - The Conference of Ministers

1.   The Conference of Ministers is the supreme body of the Authority.

...

[Omitted: Article 25 - The Management Committee, Article 26 - The Secretariat, Article 27 - Technical Committees, Article 28 - Financial resources, Article 29 - Settlement of disputes]

Article 30 - Liability of Operators of dangerous activities

1.   Each Contracting State shall ensure that each Operator that undertakes on its territory one or more of the activities listed in Annex II:

(a)   is regularly monitored to ensure that such activities comply with applicable laws and administrative requirements concerning the protection of the Lake environment;

(b)　is required to participate in a financial security scheme or to have and maintain a financial guarantee up to a certain limit, of a type and on terms specified by the domestic laws of that State, to cover liability under this Convention;

(c)　is bound by the provisions of this article.

2.　An Operator undertaking a dangerous activity shall take necessary and timely response action, including prevention, containment, clean up and removal measures, if the activity results in or threatens to result in an adverse impact. The Operator shall notify the Secretariat of action taken pursuant to this paragraph and the Secretariat shall circulate the notification to all the Contracting States.

3.　An Operator shall be strictly liable for:

(a)　any adverse impacts arising from its dangerous activities, and shall be liable to pay compensation;

(b)　loss of or impairment to any legitimate use of the Lake such as navigation, tourism, or fishing, arising directly from an adverse impact referred to in paragraph (a);

(c)　loss of or damage to the property of a third party or loss of life of or personal injury to a third party arising directly from an adverse impact referred to in paragraph (a); and

(d)　reimbursement of reasonable costs incurred by any person relating to any necessary response action, including prevention, containment, clean up, removal measures and action taken to restore the Lake's environment.

4.　An Operator shall not be liable pursuant to paragraph 4[sic] if and to the extent that it proves that the adverse impact has been caused by:

(a)　a natural disaster which could not reasonably have been foreseen; or

(b)　armed conflict or an act of terrorism directed against the activities of the Operator, against which no reasonable precautionary measures could have been effective.

5. If an Operator proves that the adverse impact has been caused wholly or in part by an intentional or grossly negligent act or omission of the party seeking redress, that Operator may be relieved wholly or in part from its obligation under paragraph 4[sic] to reimburse costs incurred by such a party or to pay compensation in respect of any loss, damage or personal injury suffered by such a party.

6. The Contracting States may elaborate in a separate protocol further rules and procedures in respect of liability under this article, which rules and procedures shall be designed to enhance the protection of the Lake Basin and to facilitate the effective implementation of this Convention.

Article 31 - Liability and compensation

1. A Contracting State shall be liable in accordance with international law for any trans-boundary adverse impacts arising from its failure to fulfill its obligations under this Convention, including any failure to fulfill its obligations under paragraph 1 of Article 30 of this Convention with respect to an Operator.

...

Article 32 - Access to courts

1. Each Contracting State shall grant any person claiming compensation or other relief arising from an adverse impact caused by activities carried out within its territory, including claims made pursuant to paragraph 4 of Article 30, access to legal remedies in accordance with its legal system.

2. In granting the rights and access referred to in paragraph 1 a Contracting State shall not discriminate on the basis of nationality, residence, or place where the injury occurred.

Article 33 - Right to vote

Each Contracting State to this Convention or to any protocol shall have one vote.

Article 34 - Protocols to this Convention

1. The Contracting States shall co-operate in the formulation and adoption of any protocols to this Convention that they consider appropriate to further the attainment of the objective of this Convention.

2. Protocols shall be adopted at a meeting of the Conference of Ministers.

Article 35 - Annexes

1. The annexes to this Convention or to any protocol form an integral part of this Convention or the protocol to which it is annexed and, unless expressly provided otherwise, a reference to this Convention or to a protocol refers also to any annexes to that instrument.

2. Except as otherwise provided in any protocol, annexes to this Convention or to any protocol shall be proposed and adopted according to the procedure laid down in Article 34.

[Omitted: Article 36 - Amendment of the Convention or Protocols, Article 37 - Relationship with other international agreements, Article 38 - Relationship with national laws, Article 39 - Signature, Article 40 - Ratification, acceptance, approval or accession, Article 41 - Entry into force, Article 42 - Reservations, Article 43 - Withdrawals, Article 44 - Depositaries]

...

Annex I - Environmental impact assessment

Part A: List of activities that will be presumed to result in adverse impacts

1. Exploration for, the extraction of, and large-scale transportation of hydrocarbons in the Lake and its Basin.

2. The construction and operation of crude oil refineries in the Lake Basin.

3. The construction and operation of major storage facilities for petroleum, petrochemical and chemical products in the Lake Basin.

...

5.   Major mining operations and the on-site extraction and processing of metal ores or coal in the Lake Basin.

...

7.   The construction and operation of waste-disposal installations for the incineration, chemical treatment or landfill of toxic and dangerous wastes within the Lake Basin.

...

10.   The opening up of large forested areas within the Lake Basin to development.

11.   The conversion or destruction of large areas of wetland forming part of the Lake Basin.

12.   The development of large-scale aquaculture or fish farming operations that use surface or groundwater from the Lake Basin, or that are situated within the Lake Basin and involve the culturing of species that are not indigenous to the Lake.

...

15.   Any activity within or outside the Lake Basin which, by virtue of its scale, location, nature, or potential effects, is likely to create a significant risk of serious adverse impacts or trans-boundary adverse impacts.

Part B: Minimum content of Environmental Impact Assessment documentation

Environmental Impact Assessment Documentation required under Article 15 paragraph 2(b) shall contain the following information as a minimum.

1.   A description of the proposed activity and its purpose.

2.   A description, where appropriate, of reasonable alternatives and also of the no-action alternative.

3.   A description of the environment likely to be significantly affected by the proposed activity and its alternatives.

4. A description of the potential environmental impacts of the proposed activity and its alternatives and an evaluation of the significance of these impacts.

5. A description of prevention and mitigation measures to keep adverse impacts to a minimum (for all alternatives).

6. An analysis of the alternatives, including a comparison of the expected environmental impacts of each option after all mitigating actions have been implemented, and a selection of the preferred alternative.

7. A comprehensive mitigation plan in relation to the preferred alternative, which should contain a description of the mitigation measures to be implemented that would prevent, reduce or otherwise manage the adverse impacts of the proposed activity including an outline of monitoring and management program, post project analysis and community liaison procedures.

8. The results of any consultations with the public, interested and affected persons, communities, organizations, and government agencies in the course of conducting the environmental impact assessment.

9. An explicit indication of the predictive methods employed and underlying assumptions made as well as the relevant environmental data used.

10. An identification of gaps in knowledge and uncertainties encountered in compiling the required information.

11. A non-technical summary with visual aids, such as maps, graphs, tables and figures, as appropriate, that is suitable for explaining the findings of the assessment to the public.

Annex II - List of activities dangerous to the lake basin

For the purposes of this Annex the term "dangerous substance" means a substance or preparation which has properties which constitute a significant risk for humans, the environment or property, including a substance or preparation which is radioactive, ionizing, explosive, oxidizing, extremely flammable, highly flammable, flammable, very toxic, toxic, harmful, corrosive, irritant, sensitizing, carcinogenic, mutagenic, toxic for human or animal reproduction or dangerous for the environment.

1.   Prospecting for, and exploiting hydrocarbons within Lake Tanganyika and its Basin.

2.   The production, handling, storage, use or discharge into the Lake Basin of a dangerous substance in such a manner, or in such quantities and/or concentrations that a significant risk of serious damage to the Lake's environment is created.

[Omitted: Annex III - Fact finding commissions, Annex IV - Arbitration, Annex V - Interim mechanisms for the management of Lake Tanganyika]

18.   Protocol for Sustainable Development of Lake Victoria Basin [Arusha, 29 November 2003]*

Preamble

Whereas the Republic of Kenya, Republic of Uganda and the United Republic of Tanzania (hereinafter referred to as the Partner States) enjoy close historical, commercial, industrial, cultural and other ties and have signed a Treaty for the Establishment of the East African Community on 30th November 1999;

Recognising the need for increased investment in the field of energy, transport, communications, infrastructure, tourism, agriculture, fisheries, livestock, forestry, mining and other areas of social and economic endeavour to spur development and eradicate poverty in the Lake Victoria Basin;

And whereas the Partner States recognise in the Treaty that development activities may have negative impacts on the environment leading to degradation of the environment and depletion of natural resources and that a clean and healthy environment is a prerequisite for sustainable development;

---

* FAOLEX (FAO legal database online). Parties and/or signatories: Kenya, Tanzania, Uganda.

Recognising that water is a finite and vulnerable resource essential to sustain life, development and the environment and must be managed in an integrated and holistic manner; linking social and economic development with protection and conservation of natural ecosystems;

Recognising that water is an economic good having social and economic value, whose utilisation should give priority to its most economic use taking cognisance of basic human needs and the safeguarding of ecosystems;

Recognising further that the Treaty obliges the Partner States to cooperate in relation to Lake Victoria Basin in a co-ordinated and sustainable manner and that the Partner States have agreed to negotiate as a bloc on issues relating to the basin;

Recognising the need to develop and implement measures to enhance safety of life, navigation and preservation of aquatic environment on the Lake Victoria Basin; and

Aware that Partner States have designated the Lake Victoria Basin as an economic growth zone, established a Sectoral Council and agreed to establish a body for the management of Lake Victoria;

...

Article 1 - Definitions

1. Unless the context otherwise requires, the terms used in this Protocol shall have the same meaning as ascribed to them in the Treaty for the Establishment of the East African Community.

2. Without prejudice to paragraph 1 of this Article:

"Basin" means the Lake Victoria Basin;

"Commission" means the Lake Victoria Basin Commission established under Article 33 of this Protocol.
"Community" means the East African Community established under the Treaty for the Establishment of the East African Community signed at Arusha on 30th November 1999;

"Council" means the Council of Ministers of the East African Community;

"Emergency" means a situation that causes or poses an imminent threat of causing serious harm to a Partner State or other States and that results suddenly from natural causes, such as floods, droughts, landslides or earthquakes, or from human conduct, such as industrial accidents or inland water transport accidents;

"Lake" means Lake Victoria;

"Lake Victoria Basin" means that geographical area extending within the territories of the Partner States determined by the watershed limits of the system of waters, including surface and underground waters flowing into Lake Victoria;

"Navigation" means a nautical art or science of conducting a vessel from one place to another;

"Nile River Basin" means that geographical area extending across the territories of various States drained by the River Nile and its tributaries and determined by the watershed limits of the system of waters, including surface and underground waters flowing into the river Nile system and eventually into the Mediterranean Sea;

"Partner States" means the parties to the Treaty for the Establishment of the East Africa Community namely, the Republic of Kenya, the Republic of Uganda and the United Republic of Tanzania;

"Partnership Agreement" means the agreement signed between the East African Community and the Development Partners interested in promoting sustainable development of Lake Victoria Basin signed on 24th April 2001;

"Secretary General" means the Secretary General of the East African Community;

"Secretariat" means the Secretariat of the East African Community;

"Stakeholder" means all persons, legal or natural and all other entities being governmental or non-governmental, residing, having interest or conducting business in the Basin;

"Sustainable Development" means development that meets the needs of the present generation without compromising the ability of future generations to meet their own needs;

"Sustainable Utilisation" means use of resources by present generation, which does not impair the right of future generations to use the same to meet their needs;

"Treaty" means the Treaty for the Establishment of the East African Community signed at Arusha on 30th November 1999;

"Water Resources" means all forms of water on the surface and in the ground including the living and non-living resources therein.

[Omitted: Article 2 - Application of the Protocol]

Article 3 - Scope of co-operation

The Partner States have agreed to cooperate in the areas as they relate to the conservation and sustainable utilisation of the resources of the Basin including the following:

(a) sustainable development, management and equitable utilisation of water resources;

...

(c) promotion of sustainable agricultural and land use practices including irrigation;

(d) promotion of sustainable development and management of forestry resources;

(e) promotion of development and management of wetlands;

...

(k) environmental protection and management of the Basin;

(l) promotion of public participation in planning and decision-making;

...

Article 4 - Principles

1. The Partner States shall manage the resources of the Basin in accordance with the principles set out in Articles, 5, 6, 7 and 8 and other provisions of the Treaty.

2. Without prejudice to the generality of paragraph 1 of this Article, the management of the resources of the Basin shall be guided by the following principles:

(a) the principle of equitable and reasonable utilisation of water resources;

(b) the principle of sustainable development;

(c) the principle of prevention to cause harm to members whereby Partner States shall individually and jointly take all appropriate measures to prevent environmental harm rather than attempting to repair it after it has occurred;

(d) the principle of prior notification concerning planned measures whereby each of the Partner States shall notify other Partner States of planned activities within it's [sic] territory that may have adverse affects upon those other States;

(e) the principle of Environmental Impact Assessment and Audit;

(f) the precautionary principle whereby each Partner State shall take the necessary measures to prevent environmental degradation from threats of serious or irreversible harm to the environment, despite lack of full scientific certainty regarding the nature and extent of the threat;

(g) the 'polluter pays' principle whereby the person that causes the pollution shall as far as possible bear any costs associated with it;

(h) the principle of public participation whereby decisions about a project or policy take into account the views of the stakeholders;

(i) the principle of prevention, minimization and control of pollution of watercourses so as to minimise adverse effects on fresh water resources and their ecosystems including fish and other aquatic species and on human health;

(j) the principle of the protection and preservation of the ecosystems of international watercourses whereby ecosystems are treated as units, all of whose components are necessary to their proper functioning and that they be protected and preserved to the extent possible;

(k) the principle of community of interests in an international watercourse whereby all States sharing an international watercourse system have an interest in the unitary whole of the system;

(l) The principle of gender equality in development and decision-making;

(m) the principle that water is a social and economic good and a finite resource; and

(n) the principle of subsidiarity.

Article 5 - Equitable and reasonable utilisation of water resources

1. The Partner States shall utilise the water resources of the Basin, their respective territories in an equitable and reasonable manner.

2. The water resources shall be used and developed by Partner States with a view to attaining optimal and sustainable utilisation thereof and benefits therefrom, taking into account the interests of the Partner States;

3. Each Partner State is entitled to an equitable and reasonable share in the beneficial uses of the water resources of the Basin consistent with the principles enumerated in Article 4 of this Protocol.

4. In ensuring that the utilisation of the Basin water resources is equitable and reasonable, the Partner States shall take into account all relevant factors and circumstances, including but not limited to the following:

(a) geographic, hydrographic, hydrological, climatic, ecological and other factors of a natural character;

(b) the social and economic needs of each Partner States;

(c)   the population dependent on the water resources in each Partner State;

(d)   the effects of the use or uses of the water resources in one Partner State on other Partner States;

(e)   existing and potential uses of the water resources;

(f)   conservation, protection, development and sustainable use of the water resources and the costs of the measures taken to that effect;

(g)   the comparative costs of alternative means of satisfying the economic and social needs of each Partner State; and

(h)   the availability of alternatives of comparable value to particular planned or existing use.

5.   In determining what is reasonable and equitable use, all relevant factors shall be considered together and a conclusion reached on the basis of the whole. The weight of each factor shall be determined by its importance in comparison with that of other relevant factors.

6.   The Partner States shall, in their respective territories, keep the status of their water utilisation under review in light of substantial changes and relevant factors and circumstances.

7.   In view of the relationship between the Lake Victoria Basin and the Nile River Basin, the Partner States shall cooperate with other interested parties, regional or international bodies and programmes and in so doing, the Partner States shall negotiate as a bloc.

Article 6 - Protection and conservation of the Basin and its ecosystems

1.   The Partner States shall take all appropriate measures, individually or jointly and where appropriate with participation of all stakeholders to protect, conserve and where necessary rehabilitate the Basin and its ecosystems in particular by;

(a)   protecting and improving water quantity and quality within the Basin;

...

(c)   identifying the components of and developing strategies for protecting and conserving biological diversity within the Basin;

...

(g)   protecting and conserving wetlands within the basin;

(h)   restoring and rehabilitating degraded natural resources; and

...

2.   The Partner States shall through the institutional framework established under this Protocol, take steps to harmonise their laws and policies in relation to paragraph 1 of this Article.

Article 7 - Sustainable development of natural resources

The Partner States shall manage, develop and utilise the natural resources of the Basin in a sustainable manner.

[Omitted: Article 8 - Sustainable development and management of fisheries resources]

Article 9 - Sustainable agriculture and land use practices

The Partner States shall promote sustainable agriculture and land use practices in order to achieve food security and rational agricultural production within the Basin in accordance with the provisions of Article 105, 106, 107, 108, 109 and 110 of the Treaty.

[Omitted: Article 10 - Tourism development, Article 11 - Promotion of trade, commerce and industry]

Article 12 - Environmental impact assessment

1.   The Partner States shall develop national laws and regulations requiring developers of projects to undertake environmental impact assessment of planned activities, which are likely to have a significant impact on the resources of the Basin.

2.   The Significance of the impact under paragraph 1 of this Article shall be determined in accordance with the procedures and guidelines developed through a process of public participation by the Secretariat, and approved by the Council.

3.   Where pursuant to an environmental impact assessment, a Partner State determines that a project is likely to have a significant transboundary effect on the resources of the Basin; such a State shall avail to other Partner States and the Secretariat, the environmental impact statement for comments.

4.   In determining whether to approve an environmental impact statement for a project with transboundary effects, the Partner State in whose jurisdiction the project is proposed, shall take into account the comments of the other Partner States.

6.[sic] A Partner State, whose views on the environmental impact statement or report are not taken into account, may invoke the dispute settlement procedure under Article 46 of this Protocol by notifying the Partner State and the Secretariat of its intention.

Article 13 - Prior notification concerning planned measures

1.   A Partner State shall notify other Partner States and the Secretariat of planned activities within its territory that may have adverse effects upon those other Partner States.

2.   The notifying Partner State shall provide technical data and information concerning the planned project to enable the notified Partner States to evaluate the effects of the planned measures.

3.   The notification shall be followed by consultation among the Partner States in respect of the planned measures.

4.   The notifying Partner State all take into account the interest of the other Partner States in developing the planned measures.

Article 14 - Environmental audits

1.   The Partner States shall adopt policies, laws and regulations within their respective jurisdiction to guide the operators of facilities likely to have a

significant impact on the environment in undertaking environmental audits of existing activities.

2. The policies, laws and regulations under Paragraph 1 of this Article shall be developed in accordance with the guidelines developed through a process of public participation by the Secretariat and adopted by the Council.

3. The Partner States shall harmonise their laws and regulations to conform to the guidelines formulated by the Community.

Article 15 - Prevention of significant harm to neighbours

1. A Partner State shall, when utilizing the resources of the Basin in its jurisdiction, take all appropriate measures to prevent significant environmental harm to other Partner States.

2. A Partner State shall, in utilizing the natural resources of the Basin take into account the vital economic, social and cultural interest of other Partner States.

Article 16 - Monitoring and precautionary measures

1. Each Partner State shall, within its jurisdiction, monitor activities and natural phenomena with a view to determining the potential risk they pose to the resources of the Basin and its people.

2. The Partner States shall adopt standardized equipment and methods of monitoring natural phenomena.

3. Where there is a threat to the environment, the Partner States shall undertake such precautionary and pre-emptive measures as may be necessary in the circumstances.

...

Article 17 - Application of the "polluter pays" principle

1. The Partner States shall take necessary legal, social and economic measures to ensure that a polluter pays as near as possible the cost of the pollution resulting from their activities.

2.   The costs recovered from the polluter shall be used for clean up operations and restoration by that Partner State.

Article 18 - Application of the "user pays" principle

1.   The Partner States shall, jointly or individually, put in place measures for recovery of costs for the large-scale uses of the water resources of the Basin.

2.   The costs recovered from the user by each Partner State shall be used by that Partner State in meeting costs of management, operations and restoration in the Basin.

Article 19 - Preventing pollution at source

1.   The Partner States shall:

(a)   require developers of planned activities to put in place measures which prevent pollution, and where prevention is not possible, minimize pollution;

(b)   put in place measures that conduce operators of existing facilities to avoid, reduce, minimize and control pollution from such facilities

(c)   to develop sustainable mining and mineral and processing methods

2.   The Partner States shall adopt those measures to economic realities of the Basin, including the ability of the owners of the regulated entities to afford remedial measures provided that those realities are compatible with the long-term need of sustainable development.

3.   Partner States shall adopt measures to reduce municipal waste input into the Lake.

Article 20 - Prevention of pollution from non-point sources

The Partner States shall take all appropriate legal, economic and social measures to control pollution from non-point sources including promoting:

(a) sustainable forestry practices, agro-forestry, afforestation, reforestation and good pasture husbandry;

(b) appropriate agricultural land use methods, soil conservation, control and minimization of the use of agricultural chemical inputs;

(a)[sic] general land use planning and enforcement of urban planning laws;

(c)[sic] sanitation and hygiene in the Basin.

Article 21 - Public education and awareness

The Partner States shall:

(a) promote and encourage awareness of the importance of, and the measures required for, the sustainable development of the Basin; and

(b) co-operate, as appropriate, with other States and international organisations in developing educational and public awareness programmes, with respect to conservation and sustainable use of the resources of Basin.

2. To achieve the objectives set out in paragraph 1 of this Article, the Partner States shall employ various strategies including the use of the media, and the inclusion of these topics in educational programmes.

Article 22 - Public participation

The Partner States shall create an environment conducive for stakeholders' views to influence governmental decisions on project formulation and implementation.

Article 23 - Mainstreaming of gender concerns

The Partner States shall promote community involvement and mainstreaming of gender concerns at all levels of socio-economic development, especially with regard to decision-making, policy formulation and implementation of projects and programmes.

Article 24 - Exchange of data and information

1.   The Partner States shall, on a regular basis, exchange readily available
      and relevant data and information on existing measures on the
      condition of the natural resources of the Basin, where possible in a
      form that facilitates its utilization by the Partner States to which it is
      communicated.

2.   A Partner State that is requested by another Partner State to provide
      data or information which is not readily available, shall employ its best
      efforts to comply with the request but may condition its compliance
      upon payment by the requesting Partner State of the reasonable costs
      of collecting and, where appropriate, processing such data or
      information.

3.   The Partner States shall also provide an environment that is conducive
      for facilitating collaboration in research and the exchange of data,
      reports and information among stakeholders belonging to Partner
      States in the Basin through the Commission.

4.   The exchange of information and data shall not extend to information
      protected under any law of a Partner State or an international treaty to
      which the Partner State is a party.

Article 25 - Water resources monitoring, surveillance and standard setting

1.   The Partner States shall establish and harmonise their water quality
      standards.

2.   The Partner States shall, in their respective territories, establish water
      quality and quantity monitoring and surveillance stations and water
      quality and quantity control laboratories.

3.   The Partner States shall exchange water quality and quantity data in
      accordance with guidelines to be established by the Partner States.

Article 26 - Emergencies and disaster preparedness

1.   A Partner State shall, without delay and by the most expeditious means
      available, notify other potentially affected Partner States, the

Commission and competent international organizations of any emergency originating within is territory.

2. A Partner State within whose territory an emergency originates shall, in co-operation with potentially affected Partner States and, where appropriate, competent international organizations, immediately take all practicable measures necessitated by the circumstances to prevent, mitigate and eliminate harmful effects of the emergency.

...

Article 27 - Management Plans

1. Each Partner State shall;

(a) develop national strategies, plans or programmes for conservation and sustainable use of the resources of the Basin or adapt for this purpose existing strategies, plans or programmes which shall reflect, inter alia, the measures set out in this Protocol; including the development of infrastructure, commerce and trade, tourism, research and development; and

(b) integrate, as far as possible and as appropriate, the conservation and sustainable use of the resources of the Basin into relevant sectoral or cross-sectoral plans, programmes and policies.

2. The Commission shall develop a management plan for the conservation and the sustainable utilisation of the resources of the Basin. The management plan shall be harmonised with National Plans developed under paragraph 1 of this Article and approved by the Council.

[Omitted: Article 28 - Improvement of security, Article 29 - Infrastructure and services, Article 30 - Energy, Article 31 - Safety of navigation]

Article 32 - Prohibition of dumping of waste

The Partner States shall enact and harmonise laws and policies for:

...

(b)   regulating the movement of hazardous wastes in the Basin.

Article 33 - Institutional framework

1.   The Council of Ministers hereby establishes a body for the sustainable development and management of the Lake Victoria Basin to be known as the Lake Victoria Basin Commission.

2.   The objectives of the Commission shall be to:

(a)   promote equitable economic growth;

(b)   promote measures aimed at eradicating poverty;

(c)   promote sustainable utilisation and management of natural resources;

(d)   promote the protection of the environment within the Lake Victoria Basin: and

(e)   promote compliance on safety of navigation.

3.   The broad functions of the Commission shall be to promote, facilitate and coordinate activities of different actors towards sustainable development and poverty eradication of the Lake Victoria Basin in the following manner;

(a)   harmonisation of policies, laws, regulation and standards;

(b)   promotion of stakeholders participation in sustainable development of natural resources;

(c)   guidance on implementation of sectoral projects and programmes;

(d)   promotion of capacity building and institutional development;

(e)   promotion of security and safety on the Lake;

(f)   promotion of research development and demonstration;

(g)   monitoring, evaluation and compliance with policies and agreed actions;

(h)   prepare and harmonise negotiating positions for the Partner States against any other State on matters concerning the Lake Victoria Basin;

(i)   receive and consider reports from Partner States' institutions on their activities relating to the management of the Basin under this Protocol;

(j)   initiation and promotion of programmes that target poverty eradication; and

(k)   perform any other functions that may be conferred upon it under this Protocol.

Article 34 - Organizational structure

The Lake Victoria Basin Commission shall be an institution of the East African Community as provided for in the Treaty and shall operate within the following organizational structure:

(a)   The Sectoral Council;

(b)   The Coordination Committee;

(c)   The Sectoral Committees;

(d)   The Secretariat of the Commission

[Omitted: Article 35 - The Sectoral Council, Article 36 - Co-ordination Committee, Article 37 - Establishment and composition of Sectoral Committees, Article 38 - Functions of the Sectoral Committees, Article 39 - The Secretariat of the Commission, Article 40 - The functions of the Executive Secretary, Article 41 - Other officers of the Commission, Article 42 - Functions of the Secretariat, Article 43 - Funding of the Commission, Article 44 - Co-operation with development partners, Article 45 - Reporting by Partner States]

Article 46 - Dispute settlement

1.   In the event of a dispute between Partner States concerning the interpretation or application of this Protocol, the Partner States concerned shall seek solution by negotiation.

2.   If the Partner States do not resolve the dispute by negotiating, either Partner State or the Secretary General may refer such dispute to the East African Court of Justice in accordance with Articles 28 and 29 of the Treaty.

3.   The decision of the East African Court of Justice on any dispute referred to it under this Protocol shall be final.

Article 47 - Relationship between this Protocol and the Treaty

This protocol shall upon entry into force be an integral part of the Treaty and in case of an inconsistency between this Protocol and the Treaty, the Treaty shall prevail.

[Omitted: Article 48 - Relationship with other Agreements on Lake Victoria, Article 49 - Entry into force, Article 50 - Accession, Article 51 - Amendment, Article 52 - Saving provisions]

...

iii.   **Bilateral Treaties**

19.   *Austria - Germany, EEC*

Agreement Between the Federal Republic of Germany and the EEC, on the one hand, and the Republic of Austria, on the other, on Cooperation and Management of Water Resources in the Danube Basin [Regensburg, 1 December 1987]*

The Contracting Parties,

Desirous of increasing cooperation on management of water resources, in particular the protection of the aquatic environment and the regulation of discharges,

Anxious to take adequate account of the Contracting Parties' mutual interest concerning the management of water resources,

---

*   Official Journal of the European Union L 90, 5.4.1990, p. 20.

Concerned to improve as far as possible the quality of the waters in the Danube Basin forming a common frontier between the Republic of Austria and the Federal Republic of Germany,

Have agreed as follows:

Article 1

1. The Contracting Parties shall cooperate on water management, in particular, in carrying out water management tasks and implementing the water laws in the German and Austrian Danube Basin.

2. Such cooperation shall take the form in particular of,

(a) exchange of experience,

(b) exchange of information on water management regulations and measures,

(c) exchange of experts,

(d) exchange of publications, regulations and guidelines,

(e) participation in scientific and specialist meetings,

(f) consideration of projects on the territory of the Federal Republic of Germany or the Republic of Austria which might substantially influence the proper management of water resources on the territory of the other State,

(g) consultations in the Standing Committee on Management of Water Resources (Article 7).

3. The Agreement shall not apply to questions concerning fisheries and shipping; the treatment of questions concerning the protection of the aquatic environment against pollution shall not, however, be thereby excluded.

Article 2

1.   The Contracting Parties shall notify each other in good time of major projects on the territory of the Federal Republic of Germany or the Republic of Austria or where such projects might substantially influence the proper management of water resources on the territory of the other State.

2.   The maintenance and achievement of proper management of water resources within the meaning of this Agreement shall cover projects relating to:

(a)   protection of the aquatic environment including the groundwater, in particular the prevention of pollution, and the discharge of waste water and heat;

...

(c)   the utilization of the aquatic environment including the groundwaters, in particular the use of water power and the diversion and abstraction of water;

...

3.   Notification pursuant to paragraph 1 shall be made directly between the relevant authorities and departments insofar as the effects remain restricted to their area of competence, or through the Standing Committee on Management of Water Resources.

4.   The Contracting Parties shall inform each other of the bodies responsible for notifying the Standing Committee on Management of Water Resources and of the relevant authorities and departments.

Article 3

1.   The Contracting Parties shall take the necessary measures within their respective legal systems to ensure that projects on stretches of water forming the frontier shall not have a substantial adverse effect on the condition of water resources on the territory of the Federal Republic of Germany or the Republic of Austria. They shall hold consultations with the aim of reaching mutual agreement, insofar as one party invokes

these effects within a period of three months of notification by adducing serious grounds.

2. In the case of projects on all other waters which might have a substantial adverse effect on the condition of water resources on the territory of the other State, the Contracting Parties shall, at the request of the party concerned, discuss the possibilities of preventing such effects before the projects are carried out.

Article 4

1. In the case of projects on stretches of water forming the frontier which are carried out on the territories of the Federal Republic of Germany and the Republic of Austria, the competent authorities in each case shall decide on that part of the work to be carried out on their territory; in this connection they shall coordinate the timing of the necessary procedures and the substance of the decisions to be adopted.

2. In the case of projects on stretches of water forming the frontier which are to be carried out on the territory of only the Federal Republic of Germany or the Republic of Austria but which could have an adverse effect on the rights and interests of the other State, for example with regard to the water system and condition of the water, the competent authorities of the other State shall be given the opportunity in good time to submit their opinion, in particular on the substance and on the conditions and obligations laid down in the public interest.

3. Where a matter within paragraph 1 or 2 is communicated by one of the Contracting Parties to the Standing Committee on Management of Water Resources, the competent authorities may not take their decision until the matter has been dealt with by that Committee, unless a delay would lead to a dangerous situation.

Article 5

The competent authorities shall carry out control measurements of the quality of the waters, jointly where this is expedient, in areas where the waters form or cross the frontier between the Federal Republic of Germany and the Republic of Austria.

Article 6

The competent authorities shall coordinate their alarm, intervention and notification plans for averting dangers from high water and ice, for measures following accidents with harmful substances and in the event of critical conditions of the aquatic environment and shall, where necessary, draw up harmonized guidelines.

Article 7

1. A Standing Committee on Management of Water Resources shall be set up. Its duty shall be to contribute to the solution of questions arising from the application of this Agreement through joint consultations. For this purpose it may address to the Contracting Parties recommendations drawn up by agreement.

2. The composition, procedures and specific powers of the aforementioned Standing Committee shall be governed by the Statute in Annex 1, which is an integral part of this Agreement.

3. Recommendations pursuant to the third sentence of paragraph 1 may relate in particular to:

(a) minimum requirements in respect of discharges to the aquatic environment,

(b) measures to improve a critical condition of the aquatic environment which is due to influences from the territory of the Federal Republic of Germany or the Republic of Austria, insofar as these influences extend to the territory of the other State,

(c) other appropriate measures to protect the aquatic environment, including water quality objectives,

(d) analyses and methods to establish the type and extent of pollution of the aquatic environment and the evaluation of the analysis results.

[Omitted: Articles 8–11]

...

[Omitted: Annex I - Statute of the Standing Committee on Management of Water Resources, Annex II - Final Protocol]

Canada - United States of America

20. Protocol Amending the 1978 Agreement Between the United States of America and Canada on Great Lakes Water Quality, as Amended on October 16, 1983 [Toledo, 18 November 1987]*

The Government of the United States of America and the Government of Canada,

Reaffirming their commitment to achieving the purpose and objectives of the 1978 Agreement between the United States of America and Canada on Great Lakes Water Quality, as amended on October 16, 1983;

Having developed and implemented cooperative programs and measures to achieve such purpose and objectives;

Recognizing the need for strengthened efforts to address the continuing contamination of the Great Lakes Basin Ecosystem, particularly by persistent toxic substances;

Acknowledging that many of these toxic substances enter the Great Lakes System from air, from groundwater infiltration, from sediments in the Lakes and from the runoff of non-point sources;

Aware that further research and program development is now required to enable effective actions to be taken to address the continuing contamination of the Great Lakes;

Determined to improve management processes for achieving Agreement objectives and to demonstrate firm leadership in the implementation of control measures;

---

* TIAS No. 11551. Entry into force 18 November 1987. The text reproduced here consists of two parts. The Preamble is the Preamble of the 1987 Protocol. The balance of the text is the 1978 Agreement as amended in 1983 and by the 1987 Protocol.

Have agreed as follows:

Agreement between Canada and the United States of America on Great Lakes Water Quality, 1978

The Government of Canada and the Government of the United States of America,

Having in 1972 and 1978 entered into Agreements on Great Lakes Water Quality;

Reaffirming their determination to restore and enhance water quality in the Great Lakes System;

Continuing to be concerned about the impairment of water quality on each side of the boundary to an extent that is causing injury to health and property on the other side, as described by the International Joint Commission;

Reaffirming their intent to prevent further pollution of the Great Lakes Basin Ecosystem owing to continuing population growth, resource development and increasing use of water;

Reaffirming in a spirit of friendship and cooperation the rights and obligations of both countries under the Boundary Waters Treaty, signed on January 11, 1909, and in particular their obligation not to pollute boundary waters;

Continuing to recognize that right of each country in the use of the Great Lakes waters;

Having decided that the Great Lakes Water Quality Agreements of 1972 and 1978 and subsequent reports of the International Joint Commission provide a sound basis for new and more effective cooperative actions to restore and enhance water quality in the Great Lakes Basin Ecosystem;

Recognizing that restoration and enhancement of the boundary waters cannot be achieved independently of other parts of the Great Lakes Basin Ecosystem with which these waters interact;

Concluding that the best means to preserve the aquatic ecosystem and achieve improved water quality throughout the Great Lakes System is by adopting common objectives, developing and implementing cooperative programs and other measures, and assigning special responsibilities and functions to the International Joint Commission;

Have agreed as follows:

Article I - Definitions

As used in this Agreement:

(a) "Agreement" means the present Agreement as distinguished from the Great Lakes Water Quality Agreement of April 15, 1972;

(b) "Annex" means any of the Annexes to this Agreement, each of which is attached to and forms and integral part of this Agreement;

(c) "Boundary waters of the Great Lakes System" or "boundary waters" means boundary waters, as defined in the Boundary Waters Treaty, that are within the Great Lakes System;

(d) "Boundary Waters Treaty" means the Treaty between the United States and Great Britain Relating to Boundary Waters, and Questions Arising Between the United States and Canada, signed at Washington on January 11, 1909;

...

(f) "General Objectives" are broad descriptions of water quality conditions consistent with the protection of the beneficial uses and the level of environmental quality which the Parties desire to secure and which will provide overall water management guidance;

(g) "Great Lakes Basin Ecosystem" means the interacting components of air, land, water and living organisms, including humans, within the drainage basin of the St. Lawrence River at or upstream from the point at which this river becomes the international boundary between Canada and the United States;

(h) "Great Lakes System" means all of the streams river[sic], lakes and other bodies of water that are within the drainage basin on the St.

Lawrence River at or upstream from the point at which this river becomes the international boundary between Canada and the United States;

...

(k) "International Joint Commission" or "Commission" means the International Joint Commission established by the Boundary Waters Treaty;

(l) "Monitoring" means a scientifically designed system of continuing standardized measurements and observations and the evaluation thereof;

(m) "Objectives" means the General Objectives adopted pursuant to Article III and the Specific Objectives adopted pursuant to Article IV of this Agreement;

(n) "Parties" means the Government of Canada and the Government of the United States of America;

(o) "Phosphorus" means the element phosphorus present as a constituent of various organic and inorganic complexes and compounds;

(p) "Research" means development, interpretation and demonstration of advanced scientific knowledge for the resolution of issues but does not include monitoring and surveillance of water or air quality;

(q) "Science Advisory Board" means the Great Lakes Science Advisory Board of the International Joint Commission established pursuant to Article VIII of this Agreement;

(r) "Specific Objectives" means the concentration or quantity of a substance or level of effect that the Parties agree, after investigation, to recognize as a maximum or minimum desired limit for a defined body of water or portion thereof, taking into account the beneficial uses or level of environmental quality which the Parties desire to secure and protect;

(s) "State and Provincial Governments" means the Governments of the States of Illinois, Indiana, Michigan, Minnesota, New York, Ohio,

Wisconsin, and the Commonwealth of Pennsylvania, and the Government of the Province of Ontario;

(t) "Surveillance" means specific observations and measurements relative to control or management;

...

(v) "Toxic substance" means a substance which can cause death, disease, behavioural abnormalities, cancer, genetic mutations, physiological or reproductive malfunctions or physical deformities in any organism or its offspring, or which can become poisonous after concentration in the food chain or in combination with other substances;

...

(x) "Water Quality Board" means the Great Lakes Water Quality Board of the International Joint Commission established pursuant to Article VIII of this Agreement.

Article II - Purpose

The purpose of the Parties is to restore and maintain the chemical, physical, and biological integrity of the waters of the Great Lakes Basin Ecosystem. In order to achieve this purpose, the Parties agree to make a maximum effort to develop programs, practices and technology necessary for a better understanding of the Great Lakes Basin Ecosystem and to eliminate or reduce to the maximum extent practicable the discharge of pollutants into the Great Lakes System.

Consistent with the provisions of this Agreement, it is the policy of the Parties that:

(a) The discharge of toxic substances in toxic amounts be prohibited and the discharge of any or all persistent toxic substances be virtually eliminated;

(b) Financial assistance to construct publicly owned waste treatment works be provided by a combination of local, state, provincial, and federal participation; and

(c)   Coordinated planning processes and best management practices be developed and implemented by the respective jurisdictions to ensure adequate control of all sources of pollutants.

Article III - General objectives

The Parties adopt the following General Objectives for the Great Lakes System. These waters should be:

(a)   Free from substances that directly or indirectly enter the waters as a result of human activity and that will settle to form putrescent or otherwise objectionable sludge deposits, or that will adversely affect aquatic life or waterfowl;

(b)   Free from floating materials such as debris, oil, scum, and other immiscible substances resulting from human activities in amounts that are unsightly or deleterious;

(c)   Free from materials and heat directly or indirectly entering the water as a result of human activity that alone, or in combination with other materials, will produce colour, odour, taste, or other conditions in such a degree as to interfere with beneficial uses;

(d)   Free from materials and heat directly or indirectly entering the water as a result of human activity that alone, or in combination with other materials, will produce conditions that are toxic or harmful to human, animal, or aquatic life; and

(e)   Free from nutrients directly or indirectly entering the waters as a result of human activity in amounts that create growths of aquatic life that interfere with beneficial uses.

[Omitted: Article IV - Specific objectives, Article V - Standards, other regulatory requirements, and research]

Article VI - Programs and other measures

1.   The Parties, in cooperation with State and Provincial Governments, shall continue to develop and implement programs and other measures to fulfil the purpose of this Agreement and to meet the General and Specific Objectives. Where present treatment is inadequate to meet the

General and Specific Objectives, additional treatment shall be required. The programs and measures shall include the following:

...

(q)   Pollution from contaminated groundwater and subsurface sources.

Programs for the assessment and control of contaminated groundwater and subsurface sources entering the boundary waters of the Great Lakes System pursuant to Annex 16.

...

[Omitted: Article VII - Powers, responsibilities and functions of the International Joint Commission]

Article VIII - Joint institutions and regional office

1.   To assist the International Joint Commission in the exercise of the powers and responsibilities assigned to it under this Agreement, there shall be two Boards:

(a)   A Great Lakes Water Quality Board which shall be the principal advisor to the Commission. The Board shall be composed of an equal number of members from Canada and the United States, including representatives from the Parties and each of the State and Provincial Governments; and

(b)   A Great Lakes Science Advisory Board shall provide advice on research to the Commission and to the Water Quality Board. The Board shall further provide advice on scientific matters referred to it by the Commission, or by the Water Quality Board in consultation with the Commission. The Science Advisory Board shall consist of managers of Great Lakes research programs and recognized experts on Great Lakes water quality problems and related fields.

...

Article IX - Submission and exchange of information

1. The International Joint Commission shall be given at its request any data or other information relating to water quality in the Great Lakes System in accordance with procedures established by the Commission.

2. The Commission shall make available to the Parties and to the State and Provincial Governments upon request all data or other information furnished to it in accordance with the Article.

3. Each Party shall make available to the other at its request any data or other information in its control relating to water quality in the Great Lakes System.

4. Notwithstanding any other provision of this Agreement, the Commission shall not release without the consent of the owner any information identified as proprietary information under the law of the place where such information has been acquired.

Article X - Consultation and review

...

2. When a Party becomes aware of a special pollution problem that is of joint concern and requires an immediate response, it shall notify and consult the other Party forthwith about appropriate remedial action.

...

Article XI - Implementation

...

2. The Parties commit themselves to seek:

(a) The appropriation of funds required to implement this Agreement, including the funds needed to develop and implement the programs and other measures provided for in Article VI of this Agreement, and the funds required by the International Joint Commission to carry out its responsibilities effectively;

(b)   The enactment of any additional legislation that may be necessary in order to implement the programs and other measures provided for in Article VI of this Agreement; and

(c)   The cooperation of the State and Provincial Governments in all matters relating to this Agreement.

[Omitted: Article XII - Existing rights and obligations, Article XIII - Amendment, Article XIV - Entry into force and termination, Article XV - Supersession]

...

[Omitted: Annex 1 - Specific objectives, Annex 2 - Remedial action plans and lakewide management plans, Annex 3 - Control of phosphorus, Annex 4 - Discharges of oil and hazardous polluting substances from vessels, Annex 5 - Discharges of vessel wastes, Annex 6 - Review of pollution from shipping sources, Annex 7 - Dredging, Annex 8 - Discharges from onshore and offshore facilities, Annex 9 - Joint contingency plan, Annex 10 - Hazardous polluting substances, Annex 11 - Surveillance and monitoring, Annex 12 - Persistent toxic substances]

Annex 13 - Pollution from non-point sources

1.   Purpose.

This Annex further delineates programs and measures for the abatement and reduction on non-point sources of pollution from land-use activities. These include efforts to further reduce non-point source inputs of phosphorus, sediments, toxic substances and microbiological contaminants contained in drainage from urban and rural land, including waste disposal sites, in the Great Lakes System.

2.   Implementation.

The Parties, in conjunction with State and Provincial Governments, shall:

(a)   identify land-based activities contribution to water quality problems described in Remedial Action Plans for Areas of Concern, or in

Lakewide Management Plans including, but not limited to, phosphorus and Critical Pollutants; and

(b)   develop and implement watershed management plans, consistent with the objectives and schedules for individual Remedial Action Plans or Lakewide Management Plans, on priority hydrologic units to reduce non-point source inputs. Such watershed plans shall include a description of priority areas, intergovernmental agreements, implementation schedules, and programs and other measures to fulfill the purpose of this Annex and the General and Specific Objectives of this Agreement. Such measures shall include provisions for regulation of non-point sources of pollution.

3.   Wetlands and their Preservation. Significant wetland areas in the Great Lakes System that are threatened by urban and agricultural development and waste disposal activities should be identified, preserved and, where necessary, rehabilitated.

4.   Surveillance, Surveys and Demonstration Projects. Programs and projects shall be implemented in order to determine:

(a)   non-point source pollutants inputs to and outputs from rivers and shoreline areas sufficient to estimate loadings to the boundary waters of the Great Lakes System; and

(b)   the extent of change in land-use and land management practices that significantly affect water quality for the purpose of tracking implementation of remedial measures and estimating associated changes in loadings to the Lakes.

Demonstration projects of remedial programs on pilot urban and rural watersheds shall be encouraged to advance knowledge and enhance information and education services, including extension services, where applicable.

5.   The Parties shall report by December 31, 1988 and biennially thereafter, to the Commission on progress in developing specific watershed management plans and implementing programs and measures to control non-point sources of pollution.

[Omitted: Annex 14 - Contaminated sediment, Annex 15 - Airborne toxic substances]

Annex 16 - Pollution from contaminated groundwater

The Parties, in cooperation with State and Provincial Governments, shall coordinate existing program[sic] to control contaminated groundwater affecting the boundary waters of the Great Lakes System. For this purpose, the Parties shall;

(i)   identify existing and potential sources of contaminated groundwater affecting the Great Lakes;

(ii)   map hydrogeological conditions in the vicinity of existing and potential sources of contaminated groundwater;

    (iv)   develop a standard approach and agreed procedures for sampling and analysis of contaminants in groundwater in order to: (1) assess and characterize the degree and extent of contamination; and (2) estimate the loadings of contaminants from groundwater to the Lakes to support the development of Remedial Action Plans and Lakewide Management Plans pursuant to Annex 2;

    (v)

(iv)   control the sources of contamination of groundwater and the contaminated groundwater itself, when the problem has been identified; and

(v)   report progress on implementing this Annex to the Commission biennially, commencing with a report no later than December 31, 1988.

[Omitted: Annex 17 - Research and development.]

21. Memorandum of Agreement Related to Referral of Water Right Applications (10 October 1996) - Appendix to British Columbia/ Washington Memorandum of Understanding [12 April 1996]*

Between the State of Washington as represented by the Department of Ecology, herein called "Ecology" and the Province of British Columbia as represented by the Minister of Environment, Lands and Parks, herein called "the Ministry"

Recitals

Whereas the Environmental Cooperation Agreement of May 7, 1992, between the Province of British Columbia and the State of Washington, proposed consultation and information sharing between the State and the Province on environmental matters of mutual concern, including water resource management issues such as water resource allocation;

Whereas, the Memorandum of Understanding of April 12, 1996 between Ecology and the Ministry provides for the development of subject-specific Memoranda as Appendices to the Memorandum of Understanding.

Whereas, jurisdiction over water resource allocation of waters of the Province and the State rests, respectively, with the Province and the State, subject to the exercise of any existing applicable aboriginal and treaty rights, in the case of the Province with First Nations as recognized and affirmed in Section 35 of the Canadian Constitution Act of 1982, and in the case of the State with Native Tribes as recognized by the Congress of the United States and by the State of Washington;

Whereas, in the exercise of that jurisdiction particular regulatory schemes have been put in place in the Province and the State, and these schemes are administered by provincial and state agencies, the Ministry and Ecology respectively;

---

* FAOLEX (FAO legal database online). The Memorandum of Agreement specifically concerns the Abbotsford/Sumas Aquifer. It is an appendix to the Memorandum of Understanding between the State of Washington Department of Ecology and the British Columbia Ministry of Environment, Land & Parks (12 April 1996). The Memorandum of Agreement is not intended to constitute a contractually binding relationship between the parties, see 4.01.

Whereas, a Memorandum of Agreement was considered to be the most effective means to provide for consultation and information sharing between the Ministry and Ecology on water resource allocation by officials of those agencies, where such allocation has the potential for significantly impacting water quantity across the border.

Therefore, the Ministry and Ecology enter into this Memorandum of Agreement, hereafter called the MOA.

It is the purpose of this MOA to:

1. Define the respective roles and responsibilities of the Ministry and Ecology to provide for timely prior consultation on water quantity allocation permits, and

2. Specify procedures, schedules, and appropriate contacts within each agency to facilitate the timely sharing of the above information.

It is mutually agreed that:

1. Statement of work

1.01 The Ministry and Ecology agree, in order to provide for timely consultation between them prior to water resource allocation by officials of those agencies where, in the judgement of the administrating agency, such allocation may have the potential for significantly impacting water quantity on the other side of the border, to:

(a) provide information to the other party in accordance with the Scope of Work, which is attached to this MOA and forms part of it, and

(b) consult with the other party: on any licence or permit application for water quantity allocation which if granted, could potentially significantly impact water quantity on the other side of the border.

2. Term

2.01 This MOA will take effect commencing on the date this MOA is signed by both parties and will remain in effect for a period of three years, when it shall be subject to review and renegotiation, unless it is terminated earlier by either of the parties.

3. Termination

3.01 Either party may terminate this MOA by giving 30 days written notice of termination to the other party.

4. General

4.01 This MOA is not intended to constitute a contractually binding relationship between the parties.

...

Scope of work

Prior consultation and information sharing regarding water rights allocation

I. Coordination and cooperation

Water quantity allocation is a cross-border issue. Because water resource development on either side of the border can have a significant impact on water availability on the other side, it is imperative that the Ministry and Ecology:

(a) coordinate reviews to facilitate decision-making on applications involving water rights allocation, where the water allocation applied for has the potential for significantly impacting water quantity across the border, and

(b) cooperate in sharing relevant water quantity information necessary to provide management of those water resources.

II. Elements of consultation

In addition to the referral procedures normally followed, Ecology's Shorelands and Water Resources Program, Northwest Regional Office Section, will send all surface water, groundwater, and reservoir applications for permit and applications for change of water right to the Ministry when the point of withdrawal, point of diversion, or place of use specified in the application is within or on the exterior boundaries of the Abbotsford/Sumas

Aquifer as outlined in the attached plan (1:82,500 scale)*. Ecology will provide the Ministry a copy of the application form and a copy of the appropriate USGS quadrangle sheet or Metsker map, indicating the location of major project features such as points of diversion, nature of the works proposed, and other information normally submitted with the application. All applications will be sent to the Regional Water Manager, Lower Mainland Regional Headquarters, Ministry of Environment, Lands & Parks. In addition to the referral procedures normally followed, the Ministry will send to Ecology all surface water licence applications and water licence amendment applications when the point of withdrawal, point of diversion, or place of use identified in the application is within or on the exterior boundaries of the Abbotsford/Sumas Aquifer as outlined in the attached plan (1:82,500 scale)†.

The Ministry will provide Ecology a copy of the application form and a copy of the appropriate NTS, BCGS or cadastral map, indicating the location of major project features such as points of diversion, nature of the works proposed, and other information normally submitted with the application. All applications will be sent to the Supervisor, Shorelands and Water Resources Program, Northwest Regional Office, Department of Ecology.

Applications which meet the requirements identified above will be transmitted by the Ministry or Ecology to its counterpart at the same time that notice for comment is provided to other interested parties. Upon receipt of the application, the Ministry and Ecology will have 30 days for review and comment. If necessary, the Ministry and Ecology may request additional time for review and comment on any application.

Comments from the Ministry and Ecology should be substantive in nature; i.e., they should relate specifically to impairment of the aquifer's safe sustaining yield, impairment of existing rights, or to fish and wildlife biology or habitat impacts. Current information, based on a field investigation, is preferred. Projected effects should be quantified to the extent possible. If either agencies' staff does not fully understand the reviewer's comments, he or she should contact the reviewing agency for clarification. When findings significantly deviate from the substantive comments provided by the reviewing agency, a copy of the findings will be provided to the reviewing agency.

---

* Not available to the editors.
† Not available to the editors.

III.   Information Sharing

Subject to applicable public disclosure, freedom of information, and protection of privacy laws, the Ministry and Ecology commit to freely sharing and exchanging information on water licences/permits and water licence/permit applications under consideration.

Subject to applicable public disclosure, freedom of information, and protection of privacy laws, the Ministry and Ecology commit to freely sharing and exchanging information on regional studies pertaining to water availability and development of water resources within or on the boundaries of the aquifer.

Israel - Jordan

22.   **Treaty of Peace Between the State of Israel and the Hashemite Kingdom of Jordan [Arava/Araba Crossing Point, 26 October 1994]***

...

Article 1 - Establishment of peace

Peace is hereby established between the State of Israel and the Hashemite Kingdom of Jordan (the "Parties") effective from the exchange of the instruments of ratification of this Treaty.

[Omitted: Article 2 - General principles, Article 3 - International boundary, Article 4 - Security, Article 5 - Diplomatic and other bilateral relations]
Article 6 - Water

With the view to achieving a comprehensive and lasting settlement of all the water problems between them:

1.   The Parties agree mutually to recognise the rightful allocations of both of them in Jordan River and Yarmouk River waters and Araba/Arava groundwater in accordance with the agreed acceptable principles, quantities and quality as set out in Annex II, which shall be fully respected and complied with.

---

*   34 ILM 43 (1995).

2. The Parties, recognising the necessity to find a practical, just and agreed solution to their water problems and with the view that the subject of water can form the basis for the advancement of co- operation between them, jointly undertake to ensure that the management and development of their water resources do not, in any way, harm the water resources of the other Party.

3. The Parties recognise that their water resources are not sufficient to meet their needs. More water should be supplied for their use through various methods, including projects of regional and international co-operation.

4. In light of paragraph 3 of this Article, with the understanding that co-operation in water-related subjects would be to the benefit of both Parties, and will help alleviate their water shortages, and that water issues along their entire boundary must be dealt with in their totality, including the possibility of trans-boundary water transfers, the Parties agree to search for ways to alleviate water shortage and to co- operate in the following fields:

(a) development of existing and new water resources, increasing the water availability including co- operation on a regional basis as appropriate, and minimising wastage of water resources through the chain of their uses;

(b) prevention of contamination of water resources;

(c) mutual assistance in the alleviation of water shortages;

(d) transfer of information and joint research and development in water-related subjects, and review of the potentials for enhancement of water resources development and use.

5. The implementation of both Parties' undertakings under this Article is detailed in Annex II.

[Omitted: Article 7 - Economic relations, Article 8 - Refugees and displaced persons, Article 9 - Places of historical and religious significance, Article 10 - Cultural and scientific exchanges, Article 11 - Mutual understanding and good neighbourly relations, Article 12 - Combating crime and drugs, Article 13 - Transportation and roads, Article 14 - Freedom of navigation and access to ports, Article 15 - Civil aviation, Article 16 - Posts and telecommunications, Article 17 - Tourism]

Article 18 - Environment

The Parties will co-operate in matters relating to the environment, a sphere to which they attach great importance, including conservation of nature and prevention of pollution, as set forth in Annex IV. They will negotiate an agreement on the above, to be concluded not later than 6 months from the exchange of the instruments of ratification of this Treaty.

[Omitted: Article 19 - Energy, Article 20 - Rift Valley development, Article 21 - Health, Article 22 - Agriculture, Article 23 - Aqaba and Eilat, Article 24 - Claims, Article 25 - Rights and obligations, Article 26 - Legislation, Article 27 - Ratification, Article 28 - Interim measures, Article 29 - Settlement of disputes, Article 30 - Registration]

...

[Omitted: Annex I (a) Israel-Jordan international boundary delimitation and demarcation, (b) The Naharayim/Baqura area, (c) The Zofar/Al-Ghamr area, Appendices]

Annex II - Water and related matters

[Omitted: Article I - Allocation, Article II - Storage]

Article III - Water quality and protection

1.   Israel and Jordan each undertake to protect, within their own jurisdiction, the shared waters of the Jordan and Yarmouk Rivers, and Arava/Araba groundwater, against any pollution, contamination, harm or unauthorized withdrawals of each other's allocations.

2.   For this purpose, Israel and Jordan will jointly monitor the quality of water along their boundary, by use of jointly established monitoring stations to be operated under the guidance of the Joint Water Committee.

...

4.   The quality of water supplied from one country to the other at any given location shall be equivalent to the quality of the water used from the same location by the supplying country.

5.   Saline springs currently diverted to the Jordan River are earmarked for desalination within four years. Both countries shall cooperate to ensure that the resulting brine will not be disposed of in the Jordan River or in any of its tributaries.

6.   Israel and Jordan will each protect water systems in its own territory, supplying water to the other, against any pollution, contamination, harm or unauthorised withdrawal of each other's allocations.

Article IV - Groundwater in Emek Ha'arava/Wadi Araba

1.   In accordance with the provisions of this Treaty, some wells drilled and used by Israel along with their associated systems fall on the Jordanian side of the borders. These wells and systems are under Jordan's sovereignty. Israel shall retain the use of these wells and systems in the quantity and quality detailed an Appendix[*] to this Annex, that shall be jointly prepared by 31st December, 1994. Neither country shall take, nor cause to be taken, any measure that may appreciably reduce the yields of quality of these wells and systems.

2.   Throughout the period of Israel's use of these wells and systems, replacement of any well that may fail among them shall be licensed by Jordan in accordance with the laws and regulations then in effect. For this purpose, the failed well shall be treated as though it was drilled under license from the competent Jordanian authority at the time of its drilling. Israel shall supply Jordan with the log of each of the wells and the technical information about it to be kept on record. The replacement well shall be connected to the Israeli electricity and water systems.

3.   Israel may increase the abstraction rate from wells and systems in Jordan by up to (10) MCM/year above the yields referred to in paragraph 1 above, subject to a determination by the Joint Water Committee that this undertaking is hydrogeologically feasible and does

---

[*]   Not available to the editors.

not harm existing Jordanian uses. Such increase is to be carried out within five years from the entry into force of the Treaty.

4. Operation and maintenance

(a) Operation and maintenance of the wells and systems on Jordanian territory that supply Israel with water, and their electricity supply shall be Jordan's responsibility. The operation and maintenance of these wells and systems will be contracted at Israel's expense to authorities or companies selected by Israel.

(b) Jordan will guarantee easy unhindered access of personnel and equipment to such wells and systems for operation and maintenance. This subject will be further detailed in the agreements to be signed between Jordan and the authorities or companies selected by Israel.

[Omitted: Article V - Notification and agreement]

Article VI - Co-operation

1. Israel and Jordan undertake to exchange relevant data on water resources through the Joint Water Committee.

2. Israel and Jordan shall co-operate in developing plans for purposes of increasing water supplies and improving water use efficiency, within the context of bilateral, regional or international cooperation.

Article VII - Joint Water Committee

1. For the purpose of the implementation of this Annex, the Parties will establish a Joint Water Committee comprised of three members from each country.

2. The Joint Water Committee will, with the approval of the respective governments, specify its work procedures, the frequency of its meetings, and the details of its scope of work. The Committee may invite experts and/or advisors as may be required.

3. The Committee may form, as it deems necessary, a number of specialized sub-committees and assign them technical tasks. In this context, it is agreed that these sub-committees will include a northern

sub- committee and a southern sub-committee, for the management on the ground of the mutual water resources in these sectors.

[Omitted: Annex III - Combatting crime and drugs]

Annex IV - Environment

Israel and Jordan acknowledge the importance of the ecology of the region, its high environmental sensitivity and the need to protect the environment and prevent danger and risks for the health and well-being of the region's population. They both recognise the need for conservation of natural resources, protection of biodiversity and the imperative of attaining economic growth based on sustainable development principles.

In light of the above, both Parties agree to co-operate in matters relating to environmental protection in general and to those that may mutually effect them. Areas of such co-operation are detailed as follows:

A. Taking the necessary steps both jointly and individually to prevent damage and risks to the environment in general, and in particular those that may affect people, natural resources and environmental assets in the two countries respectively.

B. Taking the necessary steps by both countries to co-operate in the following areas:

    Environmental planning and management including conducting Environmental Impact Assessment (EIA) and exchanging of data on projects possessing potential impact on their respective environments.

    Environmental legislation, regulations, standards and enforcement thereof.

    Research and applied technology.

    Emergency response, monitoring, related notification procedures and control of damages.

    Code of conduct through regional charters.

This may be achieved through the establishment of joint modalities and mechanisms of cooperation to ensure exchange of information, communication and coordination regarding matters and activities of mutual environmental concern between their environmental administrations and experts.

C.   Environmental subjects to be addressed:

1.   Protection of nature, natural resources and biodiversity, including cooperation in planning and management of adjacent protected areas along the common border, and protection of endangered species and migratory birds.

...

4.   Waste management including hazardous wastes.

...

6.   Abatement and control of pollution, contamination and other manmade hazards to the environment.

7.   Desertification: combatting desertification, exchange of information and research knowledge, and the implementation of suitable technologies.

8.   Public awareness and environmental education, encouraging the exchange of knowledge, information, study materials, education programmes and training through public actions and awareness campaigns.

...

D.   In accordance with the above, the two Parties agree to co-operate in activities and projects in the following geographical areas:

I.   The Gulf of Aqaba

[Omitted: I.1 - The Marine Environment]

I.2   Coastal zone management - the Littoral

...

Environmental protection of water resources.

...

II.   The Rift Valley

[Omitted: II.1 The Jordan River, II.2 The Dead Sea]

II.3   Emek Ha'arava/Wadi Araba

Environmental protection of water resources.
Nature reserves and protected areas.
Pest control.
Tourism and historical heritage.
Agricultural pollution control.

[Omitted: Annex V - Interim measures, Border crossing points procedures between Israel and Jordan; Agreed Minutes]

Israel - PLO

23.   Israeli-Palestinian Interim Agreement on the West Bank and the Gaza Strip: Annex III - Protocol Concerning Civil Affairs [Washington D.C., 28 September 1995]*

The Government of the State of Israel and the Palestine Liberation Organization (hereinafter "the PLO"), the representative of the Palestinian people;

...

Hereby agree as follows:

---

* 36 ILM 551 (1997).

Chapter I - The Council

Article I - Transfer of authority

1. Israel shall transfer powers and responsibilities as specified in this
    Agreement from the Israeli military government and its Civil
    Administration to the Council in accordance with this Agreement.
    Israel shall continue to exercise powers and responsibilities not so
    transferred.

...

4. As regards the transfer and assumption of authority in civil spheres,
    powers and responsibilities shall be transferred and assumed as set out
    in the Protocol Concerning Civil Affairs attached as Annex III to this
    Agreement (hereinafter "Annex III").

...

6. A Joint Civil Affairs Coordination and Cooperation Committee
    (hereinafter "the CAC"), Joint Regional Civil Affairs Subcommittees,
    one for the Gaza Strip and the other for the West Bank, and District
    Civil Liaison Offices in the West Bank shall be established in order to
    provide for coordination and cooperation in civil affairs between the
    Council and Israel, as detailed in Annex III.

...

Annex III - Protocol concerning civil affairs

[Omitted: Article I - Liaison and coordination in civil affairs, Article II -
Transfer of civil powers and responsibilities, Article III - Modalities of
transfer, Article IV - Special provisions concerning Area C]

Appendix 1 - Powers and responsibilities for civil affairs

Article 1 - Agriculture

1. This sphere includes, inter alia, veterinary services, animal husbandry,
    all existing experimental stations, irrigation water (i.e. usage of irrigation
    water which has been allocated for this purpose), scientific data,
    forestry, pasture and grazing, licensing and supervision of agriculture,

the farming and marketing (including export and import) of crops, fruit and vegetables, nurseries, forestry products, and animal produce.

2. Irrigation water, as well as facilities, water resources, installations and networks used in agriculture are dealt with in Article 40 (Water and Sewage).

...

4. The two sides will cooperate in training and research, and shall undertake joint studies on the development of all aspects of agriculture, irrigation and veterinary services.

...

[Omitted: Article 2 - Archaeology, Article 3 - Assessments, Article 4 - Banking and monetary issues, Article 5 - Civil administration employees, Article 6 - Commerce and industry, Article 7 - Comptrol, Article 8 - Direct taxation, Article 9 - Education and culture, Article 10 - Electricity, Article 11 - Employment]

Article 12 - Environmental protection

A.   Transfer of authority

The Palestinian side and Israel, recognizing the need to protect the environment and to utilize natural resources on a sustainable basis, agreed upon the following:

1. This sphere includes, inter alia, licensing for crafts and industry, and environmental aspects of the following: sewage, solid waste, water, pest control (including anti-malaria activities), pesticides and hazardous substances, planning and zoning, noise control, air pollution, public health, mining and quarrying, landscape preservation and food production.

2. The Israeli side shall transfer to the Palestinian side, and the Palestinian side shall assume, powers and responsibilities in this sphere, in the West Bank and the Gaza Strip that are presently held by the Israeli side, including powers and responsibilities in Area C which are not related to territory.

...

B.   Cooperation and understandings

3.   Both sides will strive to utilize and exploit the natural resources, pursuant to their own environmental and developmental policies, in a manner which shall prevent damage to the environment, and shall take all necessary measures to ensure that activities in their respective areas do not cause damage to the environment of the other side.

4.   Each side shall act for the protection of the environment and the prevention of environmental risks, hazards and nuisances including all kinds of soil, water and air pollution.

5.   Both sides shall respectively adopt, apply and ensure compliance with internationally recognized standards concerning the following: levels of pollutants discharged through emissions and effluents; acceptable levels of treatment of solid and liquid wastes, and agreed ways and means for disposal of such wastes; the use, handling and transportation (in accordance with the provisions of Article 38 (Transportation)) and storage of hazardous substances and wastes (including pesticides, insecticides and herbicides); and standards for the prevention and abatement of noise, odor, pests and other nuisances, which may affect the other side.

6.   Each side shall take the necessary and appropriate measures to prevent the uncontrolled discharge of wastewater and/or effluents to water sources, water systems and water bodies, including groundwater, surface water and rivers, which may affect the other side, and to promote the proper treatment of domestic and industrial wastewater, as well as solid and hazardous wastes.

7.   Both sides shall ensure that a comprehensive Environmental Impact Assessment (EIA) shall be conducted for major development programs, including those related to industrial parks and other programs detailed in Schedule 2.

...

9.   Both sides recognize the importance of taking all necessary precautions to prevent water and soil pollution, as well as other safety hazards in

their respective areas, as a result of the storage and use of gas and petroleum products, and shall endeavor to ensure compliance with the above.

...

15. Israel and the Palestinian side shall respectively operate an emergency warning system in order to respond to events or accidents which may generate environmental pollution, damage or hazards. A mechanism for mutual notification and coordination in cases of such events or accidents will be established.

16. Recognizing the unsatisfactory situation of the environment in the West Bank, and further recognizing the mutual interest in improving this situation, Israel shall actively assist the Palestinian side, on an ongoing basis, in attaining this goal.

17. Each side shall promote public awareness on environmental issues.

18. Both sides shall work on appropriate measures to combat desertification.

19. Each side shall control and monitor the transfer of pesticides and any internationally banned and restricted chemicals in their respective areas.

20. Each side shall reimburse the other for environmental services granted in the framework of mutually agreed programs.

21. Both sides shall cooperate in the carrying out of environmental studies, including a profile, in the West Bank.

22. For the mutual benefit of both sides, the relevant Israeli authorities and the Palestinian Environmental Protection Authority and/or other relevant Palestinian authorities shall cooperate in different fields in the future. Both sides will establish an Environmental Experts Committee for environmental cooperation and understandings.

[Omitted: Article 13 - Fisheries, Article 14 - Forests, Article 15 - Gas, fuel and petroleum, Article 16 - Government and absentee land and immovables, Article 17 - Health, Article 18 - Indirect taxation, Article 19 - Insurance, Article 20 - Interior affairs, Article 21 - Labor, Article 22 - Land registration,

Article 23 - Legal administration, Article 24 - Local government, Article 25 - Nature reserves, Article 26 - Parks, Article 27 - Planning and zoning, Article 28 - Population registry and documentation, Article 29 - Postal services, Article 30 - Public works and housing, Article 31 - Quarries and mines, Article 32 - Religious sites, Article 33 - Social welfare, Article 34 - Statistics, Article 35 - Surveying, Article 36 - Telecommunications, Article 37 - Tourism, Article 38 - Transportation, Article 39 - Treasury]

Article 40 - Water and sewage

On the basis of good-will, both sides have reached the following agreement in the sphere of Water and Sewage:

Principles

1. Israel recognizes the Palestinian water rights in the West Bank. These will be negotiated in the permanent status negotiations and settled in the Permanent Status Agreement relating to the various water resources.

2. Both sides recognize the necessity to develop additional water for various uses.

3. While respecting each side's powers and responsibilities in the sphere of water and sewage in their respective areas, both sides agree to coordinate the management of water and sewage resources and systems in the West Bank during the interim period, in accordance with the following principles:

(a) Maintaining existing quantities of utilization from the resources, taking into consideration the quantities of additional water for the Palestinians from the Eastern Aquifer and other agreed sources in the West Bank as detailed in this Article.

(b) Preventing the deterioration of water quality in water resources.

(c) Using the water resources in a manner which will ensure sustainable use in the future, in quantity and quality.

(d) Adjusting the utilization of the resources according to variable climatological and hydrological conditions.

(e)   Taking all necessary measures to prevent any harm to water resources, including those utilized by the other side.

(f)   Treating, reusing or properly disposing of all domestic, urban, industrial, and agricultural sewage.

(g)   Existing water and sewage systems shall be operated, maintained and developed in a coordinated manner, as set out in this Article.

(h)   Each side shall take all necessary measures to prevent any harm to the water and sewage systems in their respective areas.

(i)   Each side shall ensure that the provisions of this Article are applied to all resources and systems, including those privately owned or operated, in their respective areas.

Transfer of authority

4.   The Israeli side shall transfer to the Palestinian side, and the Palestinian side shall assume, powers and responsibilities in the sphere of water and sewage in the West Bank related solely to Palestinians, that are currently held by the military government and its Civil Administration, except for the issues that will be negotiated in the permanent status negotiations, in accordance with the provisions of this Article.

5.   The issue of ownership of water and sewage related infrastructure in the West Bank will be addressed in the permanent status negotiations.

Additional water

6.   Both sides have agreed that the future needs of the Palestinians in the West Bank are estimated to be between 70 - 80 mcm/year.

7.   In this framework, and in order to meet the immediate needs of the Palestinians in fresh water for domestic use, both sides recognize the necessity to make available to the Palestinians during the interim period a total quantity of 28.6 mcm/year, as detailed below:

(a)   Israeli commitment:

    (1)   Additional supply to Hebron and the Bethlehem area, including the construction of the required pipeline - 1 mcm/year.

    (2)   Additional supply to Ramallah area - 0.5 mcm/year.

    (3)   Additional supply to an agreed take-off point in the Salfit area - 0.6 mcm/year.

    (4)   Additional supply to the Nablus area - 1 mcm/year.

    (5)   The drilling of an additional well in the Jenin area - 1.4 mcm/year.

    (6)   Additional supply to the Gaza Strip - 5 mcm/year.

    (7)   The capital cost of items (1) and (5) above shall be borne by Israel.

(b)   Palestinian responsibility:

    (1)   An additional well in the Nablus area - 2.1 mcm/year.

    (2)   Additional supply to the Hebron, Bethlehem and Ramallah areas from the Eastern Aquifer or other agreed sources in the West Bank - 17 mcm/year.

    (3)   A new pipeline to convey the 5 mcm/year from the existing Israeli water system to the Gaza Strip. In the future, this quantity will come from desalination in Israel.

    (4)   The connecting pipeline from the Salfit take-off point to Salfit.

    (5)   The connection of the additional well in the Jenin area to the consumers.

    (6)   The remainder of the estimated quantity of the Palestinian needs mentioned in paragraph 6 above, over the quantities mentioned in this paragraph (41.4 - 51.4 mcm/year), shall be developed by the Palestinians from the Eastern Aquifer and other agreed

sources in the West Bank. The Palestinians will have the right to utilize this amount for their needs (domestic and agricultural).

...

9. Israel shall assist the Council in the implementation of the provisions of paragraph 7 above, including the following:

(a) Making available all relevant data.

(b) Determining the appropriate locations for drilling of wells.

10. In order to enable the implementation of paragraph 7 above, both sides shall negotiate and finalize as soon as possible a Protocol concerning the above projects, in accordance with paragraphs 18 - 19 below.

The Joint Water Committee

11. In order to implement their undertakings under this Article, the two sides will establish, upon the signing of this Agreement, a permanent Joint Water Committee (JWC) for the interim period, under the auspices of the CAC.

12. The function of the JWC shall be to deal with all water and sewage related issues in the West Bank including, inter alia:

(a) Coordinated management of water resources.

(b) Coordinated management of water and sewage systems.

(c) Protection of water resources and water and sewage systems.

(d) Exchange of information relating to water and sewage laws and regulations.

(e) Overseeing the operation of the joint supervision and enforcement mechanism.

(f) Resolution of water and sewage related disputes.

(g) Cooperation in the field of water and sewage, as detailed in this Article.

(h)   Arrangements for water supply from one side to the other.

(i)   Monitoring systems. The existing regulations concerning measurement and monitoring shall remain in force until the JWC decides otherwise.

(j)   Other issues of mutual interest in the sphere of water and sewage.

13.   The JWC shall be comprised of an equal number of representatives from each side.

14.   All decisions of the JWC shall be reached by consensus, including the agenda, its procedures and other matters.

15.   Detailed responsibilities and obligations of the JWC for the implementation of its functions are set out in Schedule 8.

Supervision and enforcement mechanism

16.   Both sides recognize the necessity to establish a joint mechanism for supervision over and enforcement of their agreements in the field of water and sewage, in the West Bank.

17.   For this purpose, both sides shall establish, upon the signing of this Agreement, Joint Supervision and Enforcement Teams (JSET), whose structure, role, and mode of operation is detailed in Schedule 9.

Water purchases

18.   Both sides have agreed that in the case of purchase of water by one side from the other, the purchaser shall pay the full real cost incurred by the supplier, including the cost of production at the source and the conveyance all the way to the point of delivery. Relevant provisions will be included in the Protocol referred to in paragraph 19 below.

19.   The JWC will develop a Protocol relating to all aspects of the supply of water from one side to the other, including, inter alia, reliability of supply, quality of supplied water, schedule of delivery and off-set of debts.

Mutual cooperation

20. Both sides will cooperate in the field of water and sewage, including, inter alia:

...

(g) Cooperation in the exchange of available relevant water and sewage data, including:

(1) Measurements and maps related to water resources and uses.

(2) Reports, plans, studies, researches and project documents related to water and sewage.

(3) Data concerning the existing extractions, utilization and estimated potential of the Eastern, North-Eastern and Western Aquifers (attached as Schedule 10).

Protection of water resources and water and sewage systems

21. Each side shall take all necessary measures to prevent any harm, pollution, or deterioration of water quality of the water resources.

22. Each side shall take all necessary measures for the physical protection of the water and sewage systems in their respective areas.

23. Each side shall take all necessary measures to prevent any pollution or contamination of the water and sewage systems, including those of the other side.

24. Each side shall reimburse the other for any unauthorized use of or sabotage to water and sewage systems situated in the areas under its responsibility which serve the other side.

The Gaza Strip

25. The existing agreements and arrangements between the sides concerning water resources and water and sewage systems in the Gaza Strip shall remain unchanged, as detailed in Schedule 11.

[Omitted: Schedule 1 - Archaeological sites of importance to the Israeli side]

Schedule 2 - Environmental protection

Pursuant to Article 12, paragraph 7 of this Appendix:

...

2.   Quarries and mines (including expansion of existing quarries and mines).

...

4.   Solid waste disposal sites.

5.   Hazardous waste disposal sites.

...

[Omitted: Schedule 3 - Health, Schedule 4 - Religious sites, Schedule 5 - Telecommunications - List of approved frequencies, Schedule 6 - Telecommunications - List of approved TV channels and the locations of transmitters, Schedule 7 - Transportation arrangements]

Schedule 8 - Joint Water Committee

Pursuant to Article 40, paragraph 15 of this Appendix, the obligations and responsibilities of the JWC shall include:

1.   Coordinated management of the water resources as detailed hereunder, while maintaining the existing utilization from the aquifers as detailed in Schedule 10, and taking into consideration the quantities of additional water for the Palestinians as detailed in Article 40. It is understood that the above-mentioned Schedule 10 contains average annual quantities, which shall constitute the basis and guidelines for the operation and decisions of the JWC:

(a)   All licensing and drilling of new wells and the increase of extraction from any water source, by either side, shall require the prior approval of the JWC.

(b) All development of water resources and systems, by either side, shall require the prior approval of the JWC.

(c) Notwithstanding the provisions of (a) and (b) above, it is understood that the projects for additional water detailed in paragraph 7 of Article 40, are agreed in principle between the two sides. Accordingly, only the geo-hydrological and technical details and specifications of these projects shall be brought before the JWC for approval prior to the commencement of the final design and implementation process.

(d) When conditions, such as climatological or hydrological variability, dictate a reduction or enable an increase in the extraction from a resource, the JWC shall determine the changes in the extractions and in the resultant supply. These changes will be allocated between the two sides by the JWC in accordance with methods and procedures determined by it.

(e) The JWC shall prepare, within three months of the signing of this Agreement, a Schedule to be attached to this Agreement, of extraction quotas from the water resources, based on the existing licenses and permits. The JWC shall update this Schedule on a yearly basis and as otherwise required.

...

Schedule 9 - Supervision and enforcement mechanism

Pursuant to Article 40, Paragraph 17 of this Appendix:

1. Both sides shall establish, upon the signing of this Agreement, no less than five Joint Supervision and Enforcement Teams (JSETs) for the West Bank, under the control and supervision of the JWC, which shall commence operation immediately.

2. Each JSET shall be comprised of no less than two representatives from each side, each side in its own vehicle, unless otherwise agreed. The JWC may agree on changes in the number of JSETs and their structure.

3. Each side will pay its own costs, as required to carry out all tasks detailed in this Schedule. Common costs will be shared equally.

4. The JSETs shall operate, in the field, to monitor, supervise and enforce the implementation of Article 40 and this Schedule, and to rectify the situation whenever an infringement has been detected, concerning the following:

(a) Extraction from water resources in accordance with the decisions of the JWC, and the Schedule to be prepared by it in accordance with sub-paragraph 1.e of Schedule 8.

(b) Unauthorized connections to the supply systems and unauthorized water uses;

(c) Drilling of wells and development of new projects for water supply from all sources;

(d) Prevention of contamination and pollution of water resources and systems;

(e) Ensuring the execution of the instructions of the JWC on the operation of monitoring and measurement systems;

(f) Operation and maintenance of systems for collection, treatment, disposal and reuse, of domestic and industrial sewage, of urban and agricultural runoff, and of urban and agricultural drainage systems;

(g) The electric and energy systems which provide power to all the above systems;

(h) The Supervisory Control and Data Acquisition (SCADA) systems for all the above systems;

(i) Water and sewage quality analyses carried out in approved laboratories, to ascertain that these laboratories operate according to accepted standards and practices, as agreed by the JWC. A list of the approved laboratories will be developed by the JWC;

(j) Any other task, as instructed by the JWC.

5.   Activities of the JSETs shall be in accordance with the following:

(a)   The JSETs shall be entitled, upon coordination with the relevant DCO, to free, unrestricted and secure access to all water and sewage facilities and systems, including those privately owned or operated, as required for the fulfillment of their function.

(b)   All members of the JSET shall be issued identification cards, in Arabic, Hebrew and English containing their full names and a photograph.

(c)   Each JSET will operate in accordance with a regular schedule of site visits, to wells, springs and other water sources, water works, and sewage systems, as developed by the JWC.

(d)   In addition, either side may require that a JSET visit a particular water or sewage facility or system, in order to ensure that no infringements have occurred. When such a requirement has been issued, the JSET shall visit the site in question as soon as possible, and no later than within 24 hours.

(e)   Upon arrival at a water or sewage facility or system, the JSET shall collect and record all relevant data, including photographs as required, and ascertain whether an infringement has occurred. In such cases, the JSET shall take all necessary measures to rectify it, and reinstate the status quo ante, in accordance with the provisions of this Agreement. If the JSET cannot agree on the actions to be taken, the matter will be referred immediately to the two Chairmen of the JWC for decision.

(f)   The JSET shall be assisted by the DCOs and other security mechanisms established under this Agreement, to enable the JSET to implement its functions.

(g)   The JSET shall report its findings and operations to the JWC, using forms which will be developed by the JWC.

Schedule 10 - Data concerning aquifers

Pursuant to Article 40, paragraph 20 and Schedule 8 paragraph 1 of this Appendix:

The existing extractions, utilization and estimated potential of the Eastern, North-Eastern, and Western Aquifers are as follows:

Eastern Aquifer:

-   In the Jordan Valley, 40 mcm to Israeli users, from wells;
-   24 mcm to Palestinians, from wells;
-   30 mcm to Palestinians, from springs;
-   78 mcm remaining quantities to be developed from the Eastern Aquifer;
-   Total = 172 mcm.

North-Eastern Aquifer:

-   103 mcm to Israeli users, from the Gilboa and Beisan springs, including from wells;
-   25 mcm to Palestinian users around Jenin;
-   17 mcm to Palestinian users from East Nablus springs;
-   Total = 145 mcm.

Western Aquifer:

-   340 mcm used within Israel;
-   20 mcm to Palestinians;
-   2 mcm to Palestinians, from springs near Nablus;
-   Total = 362 mcm.

All figures are average annual estimates.
The total annual recharge is 679 mcm.

Schedule 11 - The Gaza Strip

Pursuant to Article 40, Paragraph 25:

1. All water and sewage (hereinafter referred to as "water") systems and resources in the Gaza Strip shall be operated, managed and developed (including drilling) by the Council, in a manner that shall prevent any harm to the water resources.

2. As an exception to paragraph 1., the existing water systems supplying water to the Settlements and the Military Installation Area, and the

water systems and resources inside them shall continue to be operated and managed by Mekoroth Water Co.

3. All pumping from water resources in the Settlements and the Military Installation Area shall be in accordance with existing quantities of drinking water and agricultural water. Without derogating from the powers and responsibilities of the Council, the Council shall not adversely affect these quantities. Israel shall provide the Council with all data concerning the number of wells in the Settlements and the quantities and quality of the water pumped from each well, on a monthly basis.

...

7. The Council shall take the necessary measures to ensure the protection of all water systems in the Gaza Strip.

8. The two sides shall establish a subcommittee to deal with all issues of mutual interest including the exchange of all relevant data to the management and operation of the water resources and systems and mutual prevention of harm to water resources.

9. The subcommittee shall agree upon its agenda and upon the procedures and manner of its meetings, and may invite experts or advisers as it sees fit.

[Omitted: Side letter - Bezeq]

Mexico - United States of America

24. Agreement of Cooperation Between the United States of America and the United Mexican States Regarding Pollution of the Environment Along the Inland International Boundary by Discharges of Hazardous Substances [San Diego, 18 July 1985]*

The Government of the United States of America and the Government of the United Mexican States;

In recognition of Article 3 of the Agreement between the United States of America and the United Mexican States on Cooperation for the Protection and Improvement of the Environment in the Border Area;

Aware of the importance of preserving the environment along the joint inland international boundary;

Recognizing that pollution by hazardous substances causes or may cause damage to the environment along the joint inland boundary and may constitute a threat to the public health and welfare;

Have agreed as follows:

Article I

For the purpose of this Agreement:

(a) A "polluting incident" means a discharge or the threat of a discharge of any hazardous substance on one side of the inland international boundary of a magnitude which causes, or threatens to cause, imminent and substantial adverse effects on the public health, welfare, or the environment.

(b) "Environment" means the atmosphere, land, and surface and groundwater, including the natural resources therein, such as fish, wildlife forests, crop and rangeland, rivers, streams, aquifers and all other components of the ecosystem.

---

* TIAS No. 11269. This Agreement is Annex II to the Agreement between the United States of America and the United Mexican States on Cooperation for the Protection and Improvement of the Environment in the Border Area (La Paz, 14 August 1983).

(c) "Hazardous substances" means elements and compounds which if discharged present or may present an imminent and substantial danger to the public health, welfare or the environment. according to the laws of each party and the determination of the Joint Response Team (JRT). The JRT and its responsibilities are defined in Appendix II.

(d) "Border area along the joint inland international boundary" means the non-maritime area which is the area situated 100 km on either side of the inland international boundary.

Article II

The Parties agree to establish the "United States-Mexico Joint Contingency Plan" (hereafter, "The Plan" regarding polluting incidents of the border area along the joint inland international boundary by discharges of hazardous substances. The object of the Plan is to provide cooperative measures to deal effectively with polluting incidents.

Article III

The Parties, consistent with their means, commit themselves to the development of response plans designed to permit detection of the existence or the imminent possibility of the occurrence of polluting incidents, within their respective areas and to provide adequate response measures to eliminate to the extent possible the threat posed by such incidents and to minimize any adverse effects on the environment and the public health and welfare.

Article IV

The coordinating authority for the Plan for the United States of America is the United States Environmental Protection Agency. The coordinating authority for the Plan for the United Mexican States is the Secretaria de Desarrollo Urbano y Ecologia.

Article V

The Parties will consult and exchange up-to-date information under the Plan.

Article VI

A joint response with respect to a polluting incident will be implemented upon agreement of the Parties in accordance with the plan. When a joint response is implemented, the measures necessary to respond to the polluting incident will also be determined by agreement of the Parties in accordance with the Plan.

[Omitted: Articles VII - VIII]

Article IX

Pursuant to this Agreement, the Parties may conclude specific arrangements for the solution of common problems in the border area.

Article X

The National Coordinators shall be responsible for the development of an implementation schedule and putting the Plan into effect.

[Omitted: Article XI]

...

Joint contingency plan

Appendix I

1.   On-Scene Coordinator

1.1   As soon as the Agreement enters into force each party will designate, without waiting for a polluting incident to occur, officials responsible for exercising in its territory the functions and responsibilities described in Section 1.2. Said officials will have the title of "On-Scene Coordinator" (OSC). Each Party will also designate officials who will have advisory and liaison functions. Said officials will have the title of "Advisory and Liaison Coordinator" (ALC). Each Party will divide its territory into areas and will designate OSCs and ALCs for each of those areas,

1.2   The functions and responsibilities of the On-Scene Coordinator will be:

(a)   To coordinate and direct measures related to the detection of polluting incidents;

(b)   To coordinate and direct response measures;

(c)   To authorize the use of dispersants and other chemical products in accordance with their respective laws and national policy, provided that such use:

(i)   prevents or substantially reduces the risk to human life and health or the risk of fire;

(ii)   prevents or reduces a threat to the environment; or

(iii)   appears to be the most effective method to reduce the overall adverse effects of the polluting incident.

(d)   To determine the facts concerning the polluting incident, including the nature, quantity and location of the pollutant, the direction and probable time of travel of the pollutant, the available resources and those required, and the potential impacts on public health an[sic] welfare and on the environment,

(e)   To determine priorities and to decide when to initiate a joint response in accordance with this Agreement;

(f)   To notify immediately the two Chairmen of the Joint Response Team (JRT) (see Appendix II) about every polluting incident which has occurred, or which is in imminent danger of occurring, which in the judgement of the OSC may require the initiation of a joint response.

(g)   To recommend to the Chairman of the JRT of his country that he formally propose to the Chairman of the JRT of the other Party the initiation of the joint response envisaged in Article VI, for a specific pollution incident;

(h)   To make detailed situation reports to the Joint Response Team (JRT) described in Appendix II about all aspects of the polluting incident and of the response operation.

[Omitted: Appendix II]

Niger - Nigeria

25. Agreement Between the Federal Republic of Nigeria and the Republic of Niger Concerning the Equitable Sharing in the Development, Conservation and Use of Their Common Water Resources [Maiduguri, 18 July 1990]*

The Federal Republic of Nigeria and the Republic of Niger being the Contracting Parties to this Agreement.

Aware of the role which the orderly management of the scarce water resources they share along the common frontier plays in the economic and social development and well-being of their respective populations living on both sides of the frontier;

Anxious to foster sustained co-operation in the development, conservation and use of their shared water resources through the established mechanisms for bi-lateral co-operation;

Recognizing the need for the development, conservation and use of their shared water resources in an equitable manner, and the need to formulate principles therefore;

Mindful of their commitments under the Convention creating the Niger Basin Authority, concluded at Faranah on 21 November 1980, and under the Convention and Statutes relating to the Development of the Chad Basin, concluded at N'djamena on 22 May 1964;

Have agreed as follows:

Part I - Scope and purpose of these Articles

Article 1

1.   These Articles shall govern the equitable development, conservation and use of the water resources in the river basins which are bi-sected

---

* FAOLEX (FAO legal database online). Reprinted in: FAO, Treaties Concerning the Non-Navigational Uses of International Watercourses – Africa, Legislative Study No. 61, Rome, 1997, p. 219.

by, or form, the common frontier between the Contracting Parties (hereinafter referred to as shared river basins).

2. The shared river basins to which this Agreement applies are:

(a) the Maggia/Lamido River Basin;

(b) the Gada/Goulbi of Maradi River Basin;

(c) the Tagwai/El Fadama River Basin; and

(d) the lower section of the Komadougou-Yobe River Basin,
     and each River Basin shall be defined by reference to the Maps[*] annexed to, and forming an integral part of, this Agreement.

3. Subject to the provisions of Article 9, a reference to the shared river basins shall include a reference to underground waters contributing to the flow of surface waters.

Part II - Rights and duties of Contracting Parties

Article 2

Each Contracting Party is entitled, within its territory, to an equitable share in the development, conservation and use of the water resources in the shared river basins.

Article 3

1. The Contracting Parties undertake to collect, process and provide at regular intervals the Nigeria-Niger Joint Commission for Co-operation with all the data and information which, in the opinion of the Commission, are needed to arrive at equitable sharing determinations, and to monitor the continued viability thereof.

2. At the request of the Commission, the Contracting Parties shall:

(a) install in their territory the required measuring equipment, and protect such equipment from interference; and

---

[*] Not available to the editors.

(b)   permit and facilitate inspections by the Commission of such equipment.

Article 4

The Contracting Parties undertake to inform and consult with the Nigeria-Niger Joint Commission for Co-operation in advance of undertaking any project, programme or plan for the implementation of agreed upon equitable sharing determinations, or likely to have an appreciable impact on any such determination.

Part III - Equitable sharing determinations

Article 5

1.   In determining the equitable share to which each Contracting Party is entitled pursuant to Article 2, the following factors shall be taken into account:

(a)   the climate of the region, and its influence on rainfall patterns;

(b)   rainfall patterns, and their influence on surface hydrology, and related hydro-geology;

(c)   surface hydrology and related hydro-geology;

(d)   existing uses of the waters;

(e)   reasonable planned water development requirements;

(f)   the economic and social development needs of the Contracting Parties;

(g)   the dependence of local populations on the waters in question for their own livelihood and welfare;

(h)   the availability of alternative sources of water to satisfy competing water demands;

(i)   the practicability of compensations either in cash or in kind one or the other Contracting Party as a means of adjusting competing water demands;

(j)   maintaining an acceptable environmental balance in and around a particular body of water;

(k)   the avoidance of unnecessary waste in the utilization of waters, with due regard for the technological and financial capabilities of each Contracting Party;

(l)   the proportion in which each Contracting Party contributes to the water balance of the basin.

2.   Each factor is to be given the weight warranted by the circumstances peculiar to each individual river basin, or group of basins, and all factors so weighted are to be considered together and a determination arrived at on the basis of the whole.

Article 6

A water use existing at the time an equitable sharing determination is made shall take precedence over a future use, provided the existing use is beneficial to both Contracting Parties and reasonable under the circumstances.

Article 7

A water use existing at the time an equitable sharing determination is made shall take precedence over a competing existing use which came into being later in time, provided that:

(a)   the use prior in time is beneficial to both Contracting Parties and reasonable under the circumstances; and

(b)   the weighting of the factors under Article 5 does not warrant accommodation of the later use, in whole or in part.

Article 8

A water use shall be deemed an existing use within the meaning and for the purposes of Article 6 and 7 by reference to, and within the limits of, the amount of water which has been put to a beneficial use from the date of inception of construction or comparable acts of implementation to the date of entry into force of this Agreement.

Article 9

Groundwater resources shall not be accounted for the purpose of equitable sharing determination unless:

(a) such resources are part of shared river basins within the meaning of Article 1, paragraph (3); or

(b) such resources lie in whole or only in part within the shared river basins and are bi-sected by the common frontier between the Contracting Parties.

Article 10

Agreed upon equitable sharing determination shall be binding for the Contracting Parties. They may however be opened up for review by the commission at the request of either Party.

Part IV - Institutional arrangements

Article 11

The Nigeria-Niger Joint Commission for co-operation (hereinafter referred to as the Commission) shall monitor the implementation of the provisions of this Agreement.

Article 12

1. A Permanent Technical Committee of Water Experts (hereinafter referred to as the Committee) composed of an equal number of representatives from the Contracting Parties, shall be established to assist the Commission in the discharge of its responsibilities under Article 11. The Contracting Parties will endeavour to ensure that the respective members of the Committee hold office for a minimum duration of four consecutive regular sessions.

2. The Committee shall meet once every four months, and at the request of the Commission as the need arises.

3.   The Chairmanship of the Committee shall rotate between the Contracting Parties at each regular session which shall be held alternately in Nigeria and Niger.

4.   Subject to the provisions of this Article and of Article 14, the Committee shall have the power to determine its own rules of procedure after the coming into effect of this Agreement, and from time to time.

Article 13

It shall be the duty of the Committee to:

(a)   prepare for approval by the Contracting Parties through the Commission schemes for the equitable sharing in the development, conservation and use of the shared river basins;

(b)   monitor the performance of agreed upon equitable sharing schemes, and to recommend to the Commission any adjustments deemed necessary;

(c)   recommend to the Commission for the adoption by the Contracting Parties measures called for by emergency situations related to, or stemming from, agreed upon equitable sharing scheme; and

(d)   advise the Commission on any difference concerning the interpretation or implementation of equitable sharing determinations made pursuant to this Agreement.

Article 14

Recommendations by the Committee shall be adopted by consensus.

Part V - Special provisions for the Gada/Goulbi of Maradi river basin

Article 15

The Contracting Parties shall inform the Niger Basin Authority of agreed upon equitable sharing determinations concerning the Gada/Goulbi of Maradi river basin, including any subsequent adjustments thereof, and any plans, projects and programme for the implementation of such determinations.

Part VI - Special provisions for the Komadougou-Yobe river basin

Article 16

1.　The Contracting Parties shall inform the Lake Chad Basin Commission of agreed upon equitable sharing determinations concerning the lower section of the Komadougou-Yobe river basin as defined under Article 1 (hereinafter referred to as Komadougou-Yobe shared river basin), including any subsequent adjustments thereof, and any plans, projects and programmes for the implementation of such determinations.

2.　The Contracting Parties shall further inform and consult with the Lake Chad Basin Commission prior to undertaking any hydraulic works for the implementation of agreed upon equitable sharing determinations concerning the Komadougou-Yobe shared river basin, to the extent that such works are likely to have an appreciable effect on the flow of surface and underground waters in the Lake Chad Conventional Basin as delimited pursuant to Article 2 of the Statutes Relating to Development of the Chad Basin, done at N'djamena on 22 May 1964.

[Omitted: Part VII - Settlement of disputes, Part VIII - Final provisions]

...

Spain - Portugal

26.　Agreement on Cooperation for the Protection and Sustainable Use of the Waters of the Spanish-Portuguese Hydrographic Basins [Albufeira, 30 November 1998]*

Preamble

The Kingdom of Spain and the Republic of Portugal, inspired by the traditional spirit of friendship and cooperation between the two nations, desiring to extend further the close relations between the two States, strengthened in particular by European solidarity,

---

* 2099 UNTS 275, English translation, p. 347. Entry into force 17 January 2000.

Aware of the mutual benefits of the implementation of the agreements in force and resolved to improve the legal regime relating the Spanish-Portuguese hydrographic basins by establishing more intensive cooperation,

Within the framework of international and Community law on the environment and on the sustainable use of water and the Treaty of friendship and cooperation between Spain and Portugal of 22 November 1977,

Seeking a balance between the protection of the environment and the use of the water resources necessary for the sustainable development of both countries,

Intending to work together to guard against the risks that might affect the waters or be caused by them in the Spanish-Portuguese hydrographic basins,

Determined to protect the aquatic and terrestrial ecosystems under their authority,

Aware of the need to coordinate their respective efforts towards improved knowledge of and management of the waters of the Spanish-Portuguese hydrographic basins,

Have agreed as follows:

Part I - General provisions

Article 1 - Definitions

1. For the purposes of this Agreement, the Parties have adopted the following definitions:

(a) "Agreement" means the Agreement on cooperation for the protection and sustainable use of the waters of the Spanish-Portuguese hydrographic basins;

(b) "Hydrographic basin" means the land area from which all the surface runoff flows through a series of streams, rivers and, in some cases, lakes towards the sea, entering it through a single river mouth, an estuary or a delta, and also associated groundwater;

(c)   "Transborder waters" means all the surface waters and groundwater that mark, cross or are situated on the border between the two States; should they flow directly into the sea, the boundary in respect of such waters shall be that established by an agreement between the Parties;

(d)   "Transborder impact" means any significant adverse effect on the environment resulting from an alteration of the condition of the transborder waters in an area under the jurisdiction of one of the Parties as a result of human activity the physical origin of which is situated totally or partially in an area under the jurisdiction of the other Party. Effects on the environment include any that affect human health and safety or flora, fauna, ground, air, water, climate, landscape, historic monuments or other physical structures or the interaction between such factors; they also include any effects on the cultural heritage or on socio-economic conditions resulting from the alteration of such factors;

(e)   "Sustainable use" means use that allows the needs of the present generation to be satisfied without compromising the capacity of future generations to satisfy their needs;

(f)   "Conference" and "Commission" mean the joint organs for cooperation between the Parties established by article 20;

...

2.   Any other definition or element that is relevant to this Agreement and that is contained in the international law in force between the Parties or in Community law, shall be understood in accordance with such law.

Article 2 - Object

1.   The object of this Agreement is to define the framework for cooperation between the Parties for the protection of the surface waters and groundwater and the aquatic and terrestrial ecosystems that directly depend on them and for the sustainable use of the water resources of the hydrographic basins referred to in article 3, paragraph 1.

    2.   In undertaking this cooperation, the Parties shall observe the provisions of this Agreement and the principles and provisions of the applicable international and Community law.

Article 3 - Sphere of application

1. The Agreement shall apply to the hydrographic basins of the rivers Miño, Limia, Douro, Tagus and Guadiana.

2. The Agreement shall apply to activities designed to promote and protect the satisfactory condition of the waters of these hydrographic basins and current or projected activities for the use of water resources, particularly those that have or might have a transborder impact.

Article 4 - Cooperation goals and mechanism

1. The Parties shall coordinate actions to promote and protect the satisfactory condition of the surface waters and groundwater of the Spanish-Portuguese hydraulic basins, those relating to the sustainable use of such waters and those that contribute to mitigating the effects of floods and situations of drought or scarcity.

2. In order to attain the goals defined in paragraph 1, the Parties shall establish a cooperation mechanism with the following characteristics:

(a) Regular and systematic exchange of information on the matters covered by the Agreement and also related international initiatives;

(b) Consultations and activities within the bodies established by the Agreement;

(c) Individual or joint adoption of the technical, legal, administrative or other measures necessary for the application and implementation of this Agreement.

Part II - Cooperation between the Parties

Article 5 - Exchange of information

1. Through the Commission, the Parties shall proceed to exchange available information regularly and systematically on the matters covered by this Agreement and data and records relating to it, in particular on:

(a) Management of the waters of the hydrographic basins defined in article 3, paragraph 1;

(b) Activities that may have a transborder impact on them.

2. The Parties shall exchange information on legislation, organizational structures and administrative practices in order to increase the effectiveness of the Agreement.

3. Should one of the Parties request the other to provide information that it does not have, the requested Party shall endeavour to comply with the request.

4. The data and records indicated in the preceding paragraphs include those referred to in Annex I and shall be periodically reviewed and updated.

Article 6 - Information for the public

1. In accordance with Community law, the Parties shall create the conditions to make available to anyone who submits a reasonable application the requested information on matters covered by this Agreement.

2. The preceding provision shall not affect the right of the Parties to reject such application on the basis of the provisions of national law, Community law or international law, when the information requested might affect:

(a) National security;

(b) The confidentiality of procedures carried out by public authorities;

(c) The international relations of the State;

(d) The general security of the population;

(e) The confidentiality of legal proceedings;

(f) Commercial or industrial confidentiality;

(g) Protection of the environment, in view of the risk of misuse of such information.

3. The information received by the Parties under the preceding article may be transmitted to the public in accordance with the preceding paragraphs of this article.

Article 7 - Information to the Commission

1. The Parties shall provide the Commission with all the information it needs to fulfill its terms of reference and responsibilities, particularly with regard to:

(a) The identification of entities to participate in cooperation activities in the matters covered by the Agreement;

(b) How the activities provided for in the Agreement are implemented nationally;

(c) The activities provided for in article 3, paragraph 2.

2. The Parties shall prepare an annual report on developments in the situation with regard to the matters covered by the Agreement and the status of national implementation of the actions provided for by the Agreement, to be transmitted to the Commission.

Article 8 - Consultations on transborder impacts

1. Whenever a Party considers that any of the projects or activities provided for in article 3, paragraph 2, of this Agreement to be implemented in its territory has or may have a transborder impact, it shall duly notify the other Party immediately, transmitting the pertinent information.

2. If a Party considers that a project or activity established in article 3, paragraph 2 has or may have a transborder impact and it has not been duly notified, it may request the information it considers necessary from the other Party, providing supporting evidence.

3. The Parties shall proceed to hold consultations, upon notification as provided for in the preceding paragraphs, once it has been established

that there are sufficient indications that any of the projects or activities referred to in article 3, paragraph 2, has or may have a transborder impact.

4.   These consultations shall be held within the Commission within a period of six months, which may be extended for a similar period by mutual agreement, with a view to finding a solution that ensures the prevention, elimination, mitigation or control of the impact. Where appropriate, the manner of reparation for liability shall be established in accordance with the provisions of applicable international and Community law. In such circumstances, the period specified above may be extended twice.

5.   Should the Parties not reach agreement within the Commission within the period provided for in the preceding paragraph, the provisions of article 26 of this Agreement shall apply.

6.   When, during the consultation procedure referred to in the preceding paragraphs, the Parties establish the existence of a transborder impact, they shall suspend the implementation of the project, totally or partially, during a period to be mutually decided, unless agreement is reached to the contrary within a period of two months; similarly, in the case of activities that are under way, the Parties shall abstain from implementing any measures that might aggravate the situation.

7.   If the suspension of the project or abstention from implementing measures referred to in the preceding paragraph might irreparably endanger the protection of public health or safety, or any other relevant public interest, the interested Party may proceed to implement the project or to continue the activity without prejudice to possible liabilities.

Article 9 - Assessment of transborder impacts

1.   The Parties shall adopt the necessary provisions to ensure that projects and activities covered by this Agreement which, owing to their nature, size and location, must be subjected to transborder impact assessment are so assessed before they are approved. They shall also adopt adequate measures to apply the assessment principles to plans and programmes that affect the activities provided for in article 3, paragraph 2, of this Agreement.

2. Within the Commission, the Parties shall identify the projects and activities which, owing to their nature, size and location, must be subjected to transborder impact assessment and also the procedures for conducting such assessment.

3. Until such time as the agreement referred to in the preceding paragraph is adopted, the projects or activities that must be submitted to transborder impact assessment and the procedures to be followed shall be those set forth in Annex II to this Agreement.

4. Within the Commission, the Parties shall determine those projects and activities whose effects must be continually monitored, owing to the possibility that they may produce a transborder impact because of their nature, size or location, and shall also determine the conditions and scope of such monitoring.

Article 10 - Other measures of cooperation between the Parties

1. For the purposes of the provisions of Part I, the Parties shall adopt, individually or jointly, the technical, legal, administrative and other measures that are necessary to:

(a) Achieve the satisfactory condition of the waters;

(b) Prevent the degradation of the waters and control pollution;

(c) Prevent, eliminate, mitigate or control transborder impacts;

(d) Ensure that the use of the water resources of the Spanish-Portuguese hydrographic basins is sustainable;

(e) Promote rationality and economy of use through common objectives and the co-ordination of plans and programmes of action;

(f) Prevent, eliminate, mitigate or control the effects of exceptional situations of drought and flooding;

(g) Prevent, eliminate, mitigate or control effects arising from incidents involving accidental pollution;

(h) Promote the security of infrastructures;

(i) Establish systems of control and assessment that allow the condition of the waters to be monitored using equivalent and comparable methods and procedures;

(j) Promote joint technological research and development activities with regard to the matters covered by the Agreement;

(l) [sic] Promote actions to verify compliance with the Agreement;

(m) Promote actions to enhance the effectiveness of the Agreement.

2. For each hydrographic basin, the Parties shall proceed to coordinate the management plans and the programmes of special or general measures, to be drawn up according to the provisions of Community law.

3. The actions or measures for the implementation of this Agreement may not result in a lower level of protection than the current conditions of transborder waters, except in situations and under the conditions provided for by Community law.

4. Any information on matters relating to this Agreement submitted to the European Commission or to another international organization by one of the Parties shall be notified simultaneously to the other Party.

Article 11 - Communication, early warning and emergency systems

1. The Parties shall establish or improve joint or coordinated communication systems to transmit early warning or emergency information, to prevent or correct the situation in question and to take pertinent decisions.

2. The information on early warning and emergency situations shall take into consideration conditions inherent in or arising from human activity that produce or may involve particular danger for persons, social, cultural or economic property, or the environment.

3. Within the framework of the Commission, the Parties shall provide information on the respective entities and, procedures for transmitting information on early warning and emergency situations and also on plans of action for such situations.

[Omitted: Article 12 - Infrastructure security]

Part III - Protection and sustainable use

Article 13 - Water quality

1. Within the Commission, the Parties shall proceed with regard to each hydrographic basin:

(a) To inventory, assess and classify transborder waters and any others that are likely to be altered by either Party, in terms of their quality, current and potential uses and interests from the perspective of nature conservation and also to define quality targets or standards for such waters in accordance with the applicable Community directives;

(b) To attribute special protection status, when appropriate, and to define the objectives of special protection for these waters.

2. In order to attain the objectives referred to in paragraph 1, the Parties shall, when necessary and by coordinating management plans and programmes of action, adopt adequate measures to:

(a) Prevent the degradation of surface waters and improve their quality in order to attain a satisfactory condition or, in the case of waters with hydrological regimes that have been modified by human or artificial actions, a satisfactory ecological potential;

(b) Prevent the degradation of groundwater and improve its quality in order to attain a satisfactory condition;

(c) Ensure compliance with all the quality targets and standards of waters classified under Community law as sources for the production of water for human consumption, areas for the protection of aquatic species of significant economic interest, vulnerable areas, at-risk areas, areas having a protected status and recreational areas, including bathing areas.

3. The objectives laid down in this article shall be achieved in accordance with the terms and time limits established in Community law.

Article 14 - Prevention and control of pollution

1. The Parties shall coordinate procedures for the prevention and control
    of pollution produced by limited or extensive emissions and shall adopt
    in their territory all measures deemed necessary to protect the
    transborder waters in accordance with Community law, in particular by
    establishing ceilings for emissions and quality targets for the
    surrounding environment.

2. Where relevant, the Parties shall coordinate the measures necessary to
    prevent, eliminate, mitigate and control the pollution from terrestrial
    sources of estuaries and adjacent territorial and marine waters in
    accordance with the jurisdictional competence of each State.

Article 15 - Water uses

1. The Parties recognize each other's right to the sustainable use of the
    water resources of the Spanish-Portuguese hydrographic basins and
    their obligation to protect them and to implement, in their respective
    territories, measures to prevent, eliminate, mitigate and control
    transborder impacts.

2. The use of the water resources of the Spanish-Portuguese hydrographic
    basins referred to in the preceding paragraph shall be carried out in a
    manner consistent with their unity, with the exceptions laid down in
    this Agreement.

3. The Parties shall adopt measures and actions to ensure rationality and
    economy in the use of the water resources and, through the
    Commission, shall coordinate the exchange of information about their
    respective experiences and projections.

4. Through the Commission, the Parties shall proceed to exchange
    information on forecasts for new uses of the waters of the Spanish-
    Portuguese hydrographic basins that might modify significantly their
    hydrological regime, on the basis of technical assessments and studies
    prepared in the context of the respective planning processes, taking
    into consideration the coordination of activities relating to the
    sustainable use of those waters.

[Omitted: Article 16 - Flows]

Part IV - Exceptional situations

Article 17 - Accidental pollution incidents

The Parties shall adopt measures designed to prevent incidents of accidental pollution and to limit their consequences for persons and the environment, so as to ensure, coherently and effectively, high levels of protection in the Spanish-Portuguese hydrographic basins.

[Omitted: Article 18 - Flooding]

Article 19 - Droughts and scarcity of resources

1. The Parties shall coordinate their actions to prevent and control situations of drought and scarcity, shall establish exceptional mechanisms to mitigate the effects thereof and shall define the nature of the exceptions to the general regime established in this Agreement, in particular, with regard to the satisfactory condition of the waters, in accordance with the applicable Community law.

2. The exceptional measures referred to in the preceding paragraph shall include:

(a) Conditions in which exceptional measures may be applied, including the use of indicators that permit an objective classification of situations of drought and scarcity;

(b) Measures to provide incentives for controlling and economizing water consumption;

(c) Specific rules for the use of available water resources in order to ensure community water supply;

(d) Management of infrastructures, particularly those which have a significant water storage capacity;

(e) Measures to reduce consumption and for monitoring compliance with them;

(f) Rules for the disposal of residual waters, harnessed and diverted waters and water from reservoirs.

3. The declaration of an exceptional situation shall be communicated by the affected Party to the other Party once it has been confirmed that the conditions referred to in paragraph 2 (a) of this article have been fulfilled.

4. The exceptional measures adopted by each Party and also the incidents that occur while the exceptional situation lasts shall be communicated as soon as possible to the Commission, which may issue the pertinent reports.

5. Within the Commission, the Parties shall conduct joint studies on situations of drought and scarcity in order to define measures to mitigate the effects thereof and shall define the criteria and indicators for the exceptional regime and the measures to be adopted in such situations. These criteria, indicators and measures shall be defined within a period of two years, which may be extended by special agreement.

6. In the absence of the above-mentioned criteria, indicators and measures, those set forth in the Additional Protocol and its Annex shall be adopted.

Part V - Institutional Provisions

Article 20 - Cooperation bodies

For the purpose of the attainment of the objectives of this Agreement, the "Conference of the Parties" and the "Commission for the Application and Implementation of the Agreement" shall be established.

[Omitted: Article 21 - The Conference of the Parties, Article 22 - Structure, terms of reference and responsibilities of the Commission for the Application and Implementation of the Agreement, Article 23 - Operation and decisions of the Commission; Part VI - Final Provisions: Article 24 - Questions relating to rights that may be affected, Article 25 - Invitation to hold consultations, Article 26 - Settlement of disputes, Article 27 - Validity of the provisions of previous Spanish-Portuguese agreements, Article 28 - Uses not covered by the 1964 and 1968 Agreements, Article 29 - Dissolution of the International Rivers Commission, Article 30 - Annexes and Additional Protocol, Article 31 - Amendments, Article 32 - Validity, Article 33 - Denunciation, Article 34 - Authentic texts, Article 35 - Entry into force]

...

Annex I - Exchange of information

1.   In the case of each of the hydrographic basins referred to in article 3, paragraph 1, of the Agreement, the Parties shall exchange records and databases making it possible to monitor management of the transborder waters, in particular:

(a)   Data on concessions, authorizations, licences or other rights of use of a private nature of both surface waters and groundwater, in accordance with the respective national legislation;

(b)   Representative data on pluviometry, meteorology, hydrometry, piezometric and water quality levels, and also data on the status of reservoirs with a capacity in excess of 5 hm3;

...

2.   In the case of each of the hydrographic basins referred to in article 3, paragraph 1 of the Agreement, the Parties shall exchange records, databases and studies concerning activities liable to cause transborder impacts, which shall include, in particular:

(a)   Identification and calculation of discharges of an isolated nature of urban, industrial, agricultural or any other type, particularly those involving any of the substances referred to in paragraph 8 of this Annex;

(b)   Identification and calculation of direct on-site discharges of urban, industrial, agricultural or any other type which might produce widespread pollution, particularly those involving any of the substances referred to in paragraph 8 of this Annex;

(c)   Identification of waters intended for the production of drinking water, sensitive areas (in accordance with Directive 91/271/EEC), vulnerable zones (in accordance with Directive 91/676/EEC), zones for the protection of aquatic species of economic interest, areas with special protection status under Community law and recreation zones, including bathing areas;

(d) Information on programmes of measures for the implementation of water quality directives;

(e) Summary of significant pressures and impacts of human activities on the status of surface waters and groundwater.

3. The Parties shall exchange available information on methodology, studies and data on the ecological conditions of the waters and best environmental practices.

4. The procedures established in the applicable Community directives shall be followed for the purpose of obtaining the information referred to in the preceding paragraphs.

5. It shall be understood that the information referred to in the preceding paragraphs extends to all the national territory of each hydrographic basin referred to in article 3, paragraph 1, of the Agreement, without prejudice to the Commission's right to restrict this geographical scope, taking into account the modes of acquiring and the importance of such information in relation to the management objectives for transborder waters.

6. The data referred to in the preceding paragraphs shall be reviewed and, when appropriate, updated.

7. The Parties shall take the appropriate measures to ensure that the information is homogeneous and comparable within a period of five years.

8. The list of polluting substances referred to in paragraph 2 of this Annex as subject to special monitoring is as follows:

(a) Organo-halogenic compounds and substances that can give rise to compounds of this type in an aquatic environment;

(b) Organo-phosphoric compounds;

(c) Organo-stannic compounds;

(d)   Substances and preparations with demonstrated carcinogenic or mutagenic properties or properties that can demonstrably affect reproduction in or through an aquatic environment;

(e)   Persistent hydrocarbons and persistent and bioaccumulative toxic organic substances;

(f)   Cyanides;

(g)   Metals and their compounds;

(h)   Arsenic and its compounds;

(i)   Biocides and phytosanitary products;

(j)   Matter in suspension;

(l)   [sic]   Substances that contribute to eutrophication (particularly nitrates and phosphates);

(m)   Substances that have a negative influence on the oxygen balance (measurable by parameters such as BOD, COD).

Annex II - Transborder impact

1.   When assessing transborder impact, each Party shall take into consideration the provisions of Community directives relating to the assessment of environmental impact, in particular Directives 85/337/EEC and 97/11/EEC and the amendments thereto and the norms of international law in force between the Parties. The transborder impact assessment shall be conducted in accordance with national legislation on environmental impact assessment and shall be submitted to the competent authority of the Party where the project or activity that is causing or may cause an impact is located; the other Party shall be kept informed about the procedure on an ongoing basis.

2.   Within the Commission, and at the start of the transborder impact assessment procedure, the Parties shall agree on a reasonable period of no less than two months in which it is to be conducted, provided that such period is not laid down in the applicable national legislation.

3.   The projects or activities, including their respective extensions, specified in paragraph 4 of this Annex, shall be submitted to a transborder impact assessment when one of the following situations is confirmed:

(a)   Their distance from the frontier section, either upstream or downstream, is less than 100 kilometres, measured on the hydrographical network, unless there is a specific indication to the contrary;

(b)   Alone or in combination with other existing projects or activities, they result in a significant change in the flow regime;

(c)   They result in discharges that contain any of the substances referred to in Annex I, paragraph 8.

4.   The following are the projects and activities referred to in paragraph 3 of this Annex:

(a)   Installations for industrial use, the production of energy or mining liable to have an environmental impact on transborder waters;

(b)   Pipelines for transporting petroleum or chemical products, depending on their capacity and the risk of dispersion to the border;

(c)   Installations for the storage of hazardous or radioactive products or for the elimination of waste, depending on their capacity and the risk of dispersion to the border;

...

(g)   Large-scale abstractions of groundwater, whatsoever its use and destination, inside or outside the basin, which are carried out either for individual projects or for well-fields with a unit exploitation, starting at 10 hm3/year;

(h)   Artificial groundwater recharge schemes when the total recharge volume per aquifer exceeds 10 hm3/year;

...

(m)   Deforestation work that affects a surface area of 500 ha or more.

...

[Omitted: Additional Protocol - Flow regime]

IV. INTERSTATE AGREEMENTS ON GROUNDWATER OR CONTAINING PROVISIONS ON GROUNDWATER

i.   United States

Idaho - Washington

27.   **Interagency Agreement in the Matter of the Coordinated Management of the Pullman-Moscow Ground Water Aquifer [20 April 1992]***

...

Whereas the ground water resource located in the Palouse River/Hangman Creek basins of Latah County, Idaho and Whitman County, Washington is an important water source for citizens of both Washington and Idaho, and

Whereas the Pullman Moscow Water Resources Committee (PMWRC), made up of representatives from Whitman County, Latah County, City of Pullman, City of Moscow, Washington State University and University of Idaho, has been established in recognition of local concerns for the safety and reliability of the ground water resource because of continuing declines in ground water levels in the Pullman-Moscow aquifer, and

Whereas computer-simulated modeling studies sponsored by the PMWRC indicate that the ground water level declines will continue if annual rate of withdrawal from the aquifer increases, and

Whereas applications filed in both Washington and Idaho in recent years for large withdrawals of water from the aquifer indicate the potential exists for substantially increased ground water withdrawals and an associated decline in ground water pumping levels, and

---

* FAOLEX (FAO legal database online).

Whereas the PMWRC has adopted a coordinated management plan which sets goals for improved management of the Pullman Moscow aquifer and action plans aimed at achieving these goals have been adopted by each of the entities belonging to the PMWRC, and

Whereas the Director of the Department of Ecology of the State of Washington is charged with the administration of ground water resources to maintain a safe sustained yield (Revised Code of Washington 90 44 130) and is authorized by Washington law to represent the state in matters pertaining to interstate water rights and water development, and

Whereas the Director of the Department of Water Resources of the State of Idaho is charged with the administration of ground water to maintain reasonable pumping levels (Section 42 226, Idaho Code) and is authorized by Section 42 1805, Idaho Code to represent the state in matters pertaining to interstate water rights and water development, and

Whereas the responsible officials of each state desire to achieve coordinated management of the ground water resources of the Pullman Moscow aquifer in accordance with their respective state laws and in cooperation with the PMWRC and its member entities

Now therefore it is hereby agreed that administration of the ground water resources of the Pullman Moscow aquifer will be in accordance with the adopted Groundwater Management Plan of the PMWRC to the extent that such plan can be implemented and administered under the laws of each state. The following specific actions will be taken by the administrative agency of each state to implement the plan:

1.   Issuance of new permits to appropriate ground water and approval of applications to change existing ground water rights will be guided by the withdrawal limitations in the PMWRC plan. The state administrative agencies will provide copies of all such applications to the PMWRC for review and evaluation relative to compliance with the PMWRC plan. The decision making authority rests with the state agency, but the recommendations of the PMWRC will be made part of the official record for each application.

2.   Applicants proposing significant (as determined by the director of the state within which the application is filed) increases in withdrawal of

ground water from the Pullman-Moscow aquifer will be required to provide information on alternative sources of water conservation practices to be implemented to reduce the quantity of water withdrawn and similar information needed to demonstrate compliance with the PMWRC plan.

3. Applicants for transfer of ground water rights across the state line will be considered in accordance with the applicable laws of each state and will be guided by the PMWRC plan.

4. The administrative agency of each state will, within the funding available and the priorities set by the director of each state endeavour to enforce the applicable laws of each state, relative to supervision of construction and maintenance of wells, unauthorized diversion and use of water, and conservation of water to achieve the goals of the PMWRC plan.

5. Within funding specifically available for such purposes, the administrative agency of each state will cooperate in studies necessary to evaluate the ground water resource and improve management of it.

6. A representative of each agency will be designated by the director of each agency as responsible for coordination of the agency's activities with the PMWRC.

...

ii.   Australia

South Australia - Victoria

28.   Border Groundwaters Agreement [15 October 1985]*

...

Whereas it is desirable to make provision to protect the groundwater resources adjacent to the border between the State of South Australia and the State of Victoria and to provide for the co-operative management and

---

* FAOLEX (FAO legal database online).

equitable sharing of those resources and to guard against the undue depletion or degradation thereof:

Now it is hereby agreed as follows -

Part I - Interpretation

Definitions

1.   In this Agreement save where inconsistent with the context -

"aquifer" means a geological structure or formation or an artificial land fill permeated or capable of being permeated permanently or intermittently with water;

"bore" with respect to South Australia, means any well as defined by section 5 of the Water Resources Act 1976 and with respect to Victoria, means any bore as defined by section 2 of the Groundwater Act 1969, but in neither case includes any well or bore from which water is extracted or proposed to be extracted for one or more of the following purposes and for no other purposes -

(a)   household purposes;

(b)   watering animals kept for domestic and stock purposes; or

(c)   the irrigation of a garden not exceeding 0·4 hectares in extent used solely in connexion with a dwelling and from which no produce is sold;

"Committee" means the Review Committee constituted under clause 6;

"contracting Government" means the Government of the State of South Australia or the Government of the State of Victoria;

"designated area" means the area comprising part of the State of South Australia and part of the State of Victoria as specified in the First Schedule;

"extraction" in relation to any bore includes withdrawing, taking, using or permitting the withdrawing, taking or using of water from that bore;

"granting authority" means -

(a)   in the case of South Australia, the Minister administering the Water Resources Act 1976; and

(b)   in the case of Victoria -
      (i)   the Minister administering Part III of the Groundwater Act 1969;
      (ii)   the Director-General of Water Resources; or
      (iii) the Rural Water Commission of Victoria -

as the case requires;

"groundwater" with respect to South Australia means any underground waters as defined by section 5 of the Water Resources Act 1976 and with respect to Victoria means any groundwater as defined by section 2 of the Groundwater Act 1969;

"member" means a member of the Committee;

"Minister" with respect to South Australia means the Minister administering the Water Resources Act 1976 and with respect to Victoria means the Minister administering Part V of the Groundwater Act 1969;

"permissible annual volume" means the permissible annual volume of extraction specified for each zone in the Second Schedule, or in relation to a particular zone, such other volume as has been determined by the Committee under clause 28(2);

"permissible distance from the border between the State of South Australia and the State of Victoria" means a distance of one kilometre from that border, or in relation to a particular zone, such other distance as has been determined by the Committee under clause 28(2);

"permissible level of salinity" means such level of salinity as results in electro-conductivity not in excess of so many microsiemens per centimetre at twenty-five degrees Celsius as may be agreed upon by the Minister of each Contracting Government for any zone pursuant to clause 28(6), or in relation to a particular zone, such other level as has been agreed upon by the Minister of each Contracting Government under clause 28(4);

"permissible rate of potentiometric surface lowering" means an average annual rate of potentiometric surface lowering of 0·05 metres, or in relation to a particular zone, such other rate as has been agreed upon by the Minister of each Contracting Government under clause 28(4);

"permit" means –

(a)   any licence provided for in section 43 of the South Australian Water Resources Act 1976;

(b)   any permit provided for in section 49 of the South Australian Water Resources Act 1976;

(c)   any permit provided for in Part III of the Victorian Groundwater Act 1969;

(d)   any licence provided for in section 51 of the Victorian Groundwater Act 1969;

"schedule" means a schedule to this Agreement;

"zone" means any zone as specified in the First Schedule.

[Omitted: Interpretation, Part II - Approval and enforcement]

Part III - The Review Committee

Constitution

6.   There shall be a Review Committee for the purposes of this Agreement, which shall have such status and such powers and duties and enjoy such privileges and immunities as may be conferred upon it by this Agreement and any Acts approving it.

7.   The Committee shall consist of four members.

Appointment of members and deputy members

8.   Two members and one deputy member shall be appointed by the Minister of each Contracting Government.

Term of appointment

9.   Each member and deputy member shall be appointed for a term not exceeding five years but shall be eligible for re-appointment.

When deputy member may act

10.   Whenever -

(a)   a member is -

    (i)   absent from Australia or from duty;

    (ii)   unable for any reason to attend a meeting of the Committee; or

    (iii)   otherwise unable to perform the duties of that member's office; or

(b)   there is a vacancy in the office of a member for either State -

the deputy member for the same State shall act as a member for that State and while so acting, shall have all the powers and perform all the duties of a member.

Powers of members

11.   Subject to the provisions of this Agreement the members shall have equal powers.

Remuneration of members and deputy members

12.   Each member or deputy member shall be paid by the Contracting Government by whose Minister that member or deputy member has been appointed such remuneration, allowance or expenses (if any) as shall be determined by or under any applicable law or, in the absence of such law, by that Contracting Government.

Removal from office

13.   A member or deputy member may at any time be removed from office by the Minister of the State for which that member or deputy member was appointed.

Resignation

14.   A member or a deputy member may at any time tender resignation of his or her appointment by writing signed by that member or deputy member addressed to the Minister of the State for which that member or deputy member was appointed and such resignation shall take effect upon, and only upon, acceptance thereof by that Minister.

Vacancies

15.   Whenever a vacancy occurs in the office of a member or deputy member, the Minister of the State for which the member or deputy member whose office has become vacant was appointed shall appoint a person to the vacant office.

Validity of proceedings

16.   No act, proceeding or determination of the Committee shall be invalid on the ground only of any defect in the appointment of any member or deputy member.

Meetings of the Review Committee

17.   (1)   The members may meet together for the transaction of the Committee's business and may adjourn any meeting.

(2)   A member may at any time call a meeting of the Committee.

(3)   The members shall, at the first meeting in any calendar year, elect a member as President during that year who shall preside at all meetings of the Committee at which he or she is present.

(4)   At any meeting of the Committee at which the elected president is not present, the members present shall appoint a President from among their number, for the purposes of that meeting.

(5)   The four members shall be a quorum and, subject to clause 18(2), the concurrence of all of them shall be necessary for the transaction of the business of the Committee.

(6)   Subject to this Agreement, the Committee shall regulate the conduct of its own proceedings.

(7)   The Committee shall cause proper minutes of all its proceedings to be kept.

(8)   A resolution in writing, signed by all the members of the Committee shall have the same validity and effect as it would have had if it had been passed at a meeting of the Committee duly convened and held. Any such resolution may consist of several documents in like form, each signed by one or more of the members. The date and time of affixing a signature as aforesaid shall be endorsed on the document to which it is affixed and, provided that all members have signed as aforesaid, the resolution shall be deemed to have been passed at the latest time so endorsed.

Delegation

18.   (1)   The Committee may either generally or in relation to a matter or class of matters by resolution of the Committee delegate to any member any of its powers under this Agreement, other than this power of delegation.

(2)   A delegation under clause 18(1) may be revoked by a majority vote of the four members or, and in the event of an equality of votes the President shall have a second or casting vote.

(3)   A delegation of any power pursuant to this clause shall not prevent the exercise of that power by the Committee.

(4)   A power so delegated, when exercised by the delegate, shall for the purposes of this Agreement, be deemed to have been exercised by the Committee.

Liability for acts of members of Review Committee

19.   Each Contracting Government shall indemnify the members and deputy member appointed by the Minister of that Contracting Government in respect of any act or omission of those members or that deputy member, and for any losses or costs incurred by them, in the bona fide execution of the powers vested in the Committee by or under this Agreement or the Act approving the same.

Studies and investigations

20.   The Committee may from time to time co-ordinate, or cause to be carried out, surveys, investigations and studies concerning the use, control, protection, management or administration of groundwater within the Designated Area.

Recommendations to Contracting Governments

21.   The Committee may make recommendations to the Contracting Governments or to any authority, agency or tribunal of a Contracting Government concerning any matter which in the opinion of the Committee may in any way affect the investigation, use, control, protection, management or administration of groundwater within the Designated Area.

Proposals to amend Agreement

22.   The Committee shall from time to time review this Agreement and, if in its opinion amendments thereto are necessary or desirable, make recommendations to the Contracting Governments accordingly.

Furnishing information and particulars

23.   Each Contracting Government shall furnish or cause to be furnished to the Committee, at such times as the Committee may require, all the information and particulars that the Committee may require for any of the purposes of this Agreement and which that Contracting Government is able to furnish.

Part IV - Management plan

Designation of border area and potentiometric surface levels

24.   (1)   This Agreement shall apply to all lands and to all groundwater within the Designated Area.

      (2)   For the purposes of this Agreement, the potentiometric surface levels of groundwater within any zone shall be determined by reference to, and shall be deemed to be as at 1 July 1982, as indicated in the Third Schedule.

Application of legislation

25.   Subject to the provisions of this Agreement -

      (a)   the provisions of the South Australian Water Resources Act 1976 and of regulations made thereunder shall apply to such portion of the State of South Australia as is within the Designated Area;

      (b)   the provisions of the Victorian Groundwater Act 1969 and of regulation made thereunder shall continue to apply to such portion of the State of Victoria as is within the Designated Area - and the provisions of those Acts and regulations shall respectively be applied to -

            (i)   all bores existing within the Designated Area at the date of this Agreement;

            (ii)   all applications to construct, deepen, enlarge or alter bores or to extract water therefrom as are made after the date of this Agreement; and

            (iii)   any bores constructed, deepened, enlarged or altered or from which water is extracted, after the date of this Agreement.

Management prescriptions

26. Subject to clause 28 no application for a permit shall be granted and no permit renewed -

   (a) in relation to the construction, deepening, enlarging or altering of any bore which passes or will pass through two or more aquifers unless a condition is attached to such permit which requires that an impervious seal be made and maintained between such aquifers.

   (b) in relation to the construction, deepening, enlarging or altering of any bore, or the extraction of water from any bore, in any zone where the effect of extracting water from that bore would be to exceed the permissible annual volume for that zone;

   (c) in relation to the construction, deepening, enlarging or altering of any bore, or the extraction of water from any bore, in any zone if that bore is situated within, or proposed to be situated within, a distance less than the permissible distance from the border between the State of South Australia and the State of Victoria for that zone unless the Committee has first considered the matter and determined that such application may be granted or such permit may be renewed; or

   (d) in relation to the construction, deepening, enlarging or altering of any bore, or the extraction of water from any bore, where the bore is situated in, or proposed to be situated in a zone where the average annual rate of potentiometric surface lowering has exceeded the permissible rate of potentiometric surface lowering over the preceding five years.

Preparation of reports

27. (1) As soon as practicable after 30 June in each year, each Contracting Government shall in relation to the zones within its respective jurisdiction cause to be prepared a report stating -

   (a) the number of permits granted or renewed in each of those zones in the preceding year ending on 30 June;

(b)   the annual volume of extraction which has been authorised in relation to each such permit;

(c)   the total number of bores situated in each zone in the preceding year ending on 30 June;

(d)   details of the potentiometric surface levels obtained from observation bores within each zone in the preceding year ending on 30 June; and

(e)   the levels of salinity in such bores within each zone as shall be specified by the Committee in the preceding year ending on 30 June.

(2)   The report referred to in sub-clause (1) shall be considered by the Committee as soon as practicable after the report has become available.

(3)   In this clause "observation bore" with respect to South Australia, means any well as defined by section 5 of the Water Resources Act 1976 and with respect to Victoria, means any bore as defined by section 2 of the Groundwater Act 1969.

Powers of Review Committee

28. (1)   The Committee shall meet to consider the report prepared by each Contracting Government relating to the previous year.

(2)   At intervals of not more than five years, the Committee shall review -

(a)   the permissible distance from the border between the State of South Australia and the State of Victoria; and

(b)   the permissible annual volume of extraction -

in relation to each zone and shall have the power to alter either or both of the same in relation to any zone.

(3)   At intervals of not more than five years, the Committee shall review -

    (a)   the permissible rate of potentiometric surface lowering; and

    (b)   the permissible levels of salinity (if any) established pursuant to sub-clause 28(6) -

in relation to each zone and if the Committee is satisfied that any alteration to either or both of the same is desirable in relation to any zone, it may recommend any such alteration to the Minister of each Contracting Government.

(4)   Where the Minister of each Contracting Government agrees with any such recommendation, the permissible rate of potentiometric surface lowering or the permissible level of salinity, or both as the case may be, for any zone shall be deemed to have been altered in accordance with any such recommendation.

(5)   The Committee may at any time recommend to the Minister of each Contracting Government that a permissible level of salinity be declared for any zone.

(6).   Where the Minister of each Contracting Government agrees with any such recommendation, a permissible level of salinity shall be deemed to have been declared for that zone in accordance with such recommendation.

Periods of restriction

29.   (1)   Whenever in the opinion of the Committee it is necessary or desirable for the better investigation, use, control, protection, management or administration of groundwater within the Designated Area, it may by resolution declare a period of restriction in relation to any zone.

    (2)   A period of restriction may be declared for any period not exceeding five years and may be renewed from time to time for any further period not exceeding five years.

(3) A period of restriction may be declared in relation to any zone notwithstanding that the permissible annual volume or the permissible level of salinity (if any) or the permissible rate of potentiometric surface lowering for that zone, or any or all of them, has not been exceeded in any previous year.

(4) During any period of restriction no application for a permit shall be granted and no permit renewed in relation to the construction, deepening, enlarging or altering of any bore, or the extracting of water from any bore in any zone to which the period of restriction relates unless -

    (a) the details of the application or of the proposed renewal have first been considered by the Committee;

    (b) the granting authority has first considered any recommendation made by the Committee with respect to the application or the proposed renewal; and

    (c) thirty days have elapsed from the date on which the details of the application or of the proposed renewal have been considered by the Committee.

(5) Where, contrary to any recommendation made by the Committee pursuant to sub-clause (4)(b), the granting authority determines that an application for a permit shall be granted or a permit renewed, the granting authority shall forthwith notify the Minister of the other Contracting Government of that determination.

Annual report

30. (1) As soon as practicable after 30 June in each year, the Committee shall prepare a report on its activities during the year ended on the preceding 30 June.

    (2) The Committee shall give a copy of each report under sub-clause (1) to the Minister of each Contracting Government forthwith after it is prepared.

Publication of declarations etc.

31. Any alteration made under sub-clauses 28(2) or 28(4) or any declaration made under sub-clause 28(6) or 29(1) with respect to any zone shall be published in the Government Gazette of the Contracting Government within whose jurisdiction such zone is situate and in a newspaper circulating in that zone and shall take effect from the date of such publication in the Government Gazette.

[Omitted: First Schedule, Second Schedule, Third Schedule]

...

Commonwealth of Australia - New South Wales - South Australia - Victoria

29. Murray-Darling Basin Agreement [24 June 1992]*

...

Whereas the Commonwealth, New South Wales, Victorian and South Australian Governments wish to promote and co-ordinate effective planning and management for the equitable efficient and sustainable use of the water, land and environmental resources of the Murray-Darling Basin:

And whereas those Governments have agreed that this Agreement should be substituted for an Agreement made between the parties on the first day of October 1982 and amended by Agreements of the 30th day of October 1987 and the 4th day of October 1990, each of which was subsequently approved by the Parliament of each party:

Now it is hereby agreed by the parties to this Agreement as follows -

Part I - Interpretation

Purpose

---

* FAOLEX (FAO legal database online).

1. The purpose of this Agreement is to promote and co-ordinate effective planning and management for the equitable efficient and sustainable use of the water, land and other environmental resources of the Murray-Darling Basin.

Definitions

2. In this Agreement save where inconsistent with the context:

...

"Commission" means the Murray-Darling Basin Commission.

...

"Contracting Government" means any of the Governments of the Commonwealth, New South Wales, Victoria, South Australia and of any other State becoming a party pursuant to clause 134.

...

"former Agreement" means the Agreement made on 9 September 1914 between the Prime Minister of the Commonwealth of Australia and the Premiers of the States of New South Wales, Victoria and South Australia as amended by further Agreements dated 10 August 1923, 23 July 1934, 26 November 1940, 2 November 1954, 11 September 1958, 8 October 1963, 26 February 1970, 1 October 1982, 30 October 1987 and 4 October 1990.

...

"land" includes:

    (a)   Crown lands;

    (b)   buildings; and

    (c)   any interest, right or privilege in, over or affecting any land.

...

"measures" includes strategies, plans and programs.

...

"Ministerial Council" means the Ministerial Council established by Part III.

"Murray-Darling Basin" means so much of the area within the boundaries of the map shown in Schedule B as forms part of the territory of the Contracting Governments.

"officer" means a person employed by the Commission under paragraph 36(a).

...

"President" means the President of the Commission appointed under sub-clause 20(1).

"public authority" means a body, whether incorporated or not, established for a public purpose by or under a law of the Commonwealth or a State and includes any local government body.

...

"river" and "tributary" respectively include any affluent, effluent, creek, anabranch or extension of, and any lake or lagoon connected with, the river or tributary.

...

"State" means the State of New South Wales, the State of Victoria, the State of South Australia or any State becoming a party pursuant to clause 134.

...

"State Contracting Government" means any of the Governments of New South Wales, Victoria, South Australia, or of any State becoming a party pursuant to clause 134.

...

[Omitted: Interpretation, Part II - Approval and enforcement]

Part III - The Ministerial Council

Constitution of Ministerial Council

8. (1) The Ministerial Council constituted under the former Agreement is continued in existence.

   (2) The Ministerial Council shall have such status and such powers and duties and enjoy such privileges and immunities as may be conferred upon it by this Agreement and any Acts approving the same.

   (3) The Ministerial Council shall consist of up to three Ministers from each Contracting Government who have prime responsibility for matters relating to water, land and environment.

   ...

Functions of the Ministerial Council

9. The functions of the Ministerial Council are:

   (a) generally to consider and determine major policy issues of common interest to the Contracting Governments concerning effective planning and management for the equitable efficient and sustainable use of the water, land and other environmental resources of the Murray-Darling Basin;

   (b) to develop, consider and, where appropriate, to authorise measures for the equitable, efficient and sustainable use of such water, land and other environmental resources;

   (c) to authorise works as provided for in Part VI;

   (d) to agree upon amendments to this Agreement including amendments to or addition of Schedules to this Agreement as the Ministerial Council considers desirable from time to time;

(e)   to exercise such other functions as may be conferred on the
        Council by this Agreement or any amendment or any Act
        approving the same.

[Omitted: 10 - Ministerial Council may direct Commission, 11 - Ministerial
Council may require Commission to report, 12 - Proceedings of the
Ministerial Council, 13 - Resolutions other than at meetings, 14 -
Appointment of Committees, 15 - Nomination of responsible Minister]

Part IV - The Commission

Constitution

16.   (1)   The Murray-Darling Basin Commission constituted under the
               former Agreement is continued in existence.

        (2)   The Commission shall have such status and such powers and
               duties and enjoy such privileges and immunities as may be
               conferred upon it by this Agreement and any Acts approving
               the same.

Functions and powers of the Commission

17.   (1)   The functions of the Commission are:

               (a)   to advise the Ministerial Council in relation to the
                       planning, development and management of the water,
                       land and other environmental resources of the Murray-
                       Darling Basin;

               (b)   to assist the Ministerial Council in developing measures
                       for the equitable efficient and sustainable use of water,
                       land and other environmental resources of the Murray-
                       Darling Basin;

               (c)   to co-ordinate the implementation of or, where the
                       Ministerial Council so requires, to implement any
                       measures authorised by the Ministerial Council under
                       paragraph 9(b);

(d) to give effect to any policy or decision of the Ministerial Council, which the Ministerial Council requires the Commission to implement; and

(e) to exercise the powers and discharge the duties conferred on it by this Agreement, or any Act approving the same.

(2) Paragraph 17(1)(d) does not operate:

(a) to confer any powers on the Commission in addition to powers conferred by other provisions of this Agreement, or any Act approving the same;

(b) to enable the Commission to do anything for which Part V and subsequent Parts provide, otherwise than as provided for by those Parts as amended from time to time.

(3) The advice referred to in paragraph 17(1)(a) shall be determined by majority vote of the Commissioners present who, with the presiding member, constitute a quorum. In the event of a unanimous decision not being reached, the presiding member and each Commissioner may tender separate advice to the Ministerial Council.

(4) In addition to any powers conferred upon it by other provisions of this Agreement, or any Act approving the same, the Commission has power, under the name of the Commission:

(a) to contract; and

(b) to acquire, hold, deal with or dispose of property, for the purpose of performing its functions and exercising its powers.

Composition of Commission

18. The Commission shall consist of the President and the Commissioners appointed pursuant to clause 20.

[Omitted: 19 - Declaration of interests, 20 - Appointment of President, Deputy President, Commissioners and Deputy Commissioner, 21 - Terms of appointment, 22 - Continuation in office, 23 - When Deputy President or Deputy Commissioner may act, 24 - Powers and duties of the President, 25 - Powers of Commissioners, 26 - Conditions of appointment and remuneration of the President, 27 - Remuneration of Commissioners and Deputy Commissioners, 28 - Removal from office, 29 - Resignation, 30 - Vacancies, 31 - Validity of proceedings, 32 - Meetings of the Commission, 33 - Resolutions other than at meetings, 34 - Delegation, 35 - Appointment of Committees, 36 - Employees of the Commission, 37 - Employment of officers in public service or in statutory authorities, 38 - Liability for acts of the President, the Commissioners and officers]

Part V - Investigation, measurement and monitoring

Investigations and studies

39.　(1)　The Commission may co-ordinate, carry out or cause to be carried out surveys, investigations and studies regarding the desirability and practicability of works or measures for the equitable, efficient and sustainable use of water, land and other environmental resources of the Murray-Darling Basin, including but not limited to works or measures for:

　　…

　　(c)　the conservation, protection and management of aquatic and riverine environments; and

　　(d)　the control and management of groundwater which may affect the quality or quantity of river water.

　　…

　　(3)　Except as provided in sub-clause 39(2), the Commission must not carry out or cause to be carried out surveys, investigations or studies within the territory of any State without:

　　(a)　informing the Ministerial Council of the proposed surveys, investigations and studies; and

(b)   obtaining the consent of that State Contracting Government.

(4)   The Commission may initiate proposals for works or measures resulting from surveys, investigations or studies carried out under this clause.

(5)   If the implementation of any proposal is likely significantly to affect water, land or other environmental resources under the control, supervision or protection of a Contracting Government or a public authority responsible to that Contracting Government, the Commission must –

(a)   inform the Ministerial Council of the likelihood;

(b)   consider any submissions made by that or any other Contracting Government, or public authority; and

(c)   report to the Ministerial Council on any such submissions and the result of the Commission's consideration thereof.

Monitoring

40.   The Commission:

(a)   must, from time to time, advise the Ministerial Council on the adequacy and effectiveness of the arrangements for monitoring; and

(b)   subject to Clause 42, may establish, maintain and operate effective means for monitoring the quality, extent, diversity and representativeness of water, land and other environmental resources of the Murray-Darling Basin, including but not limited to -

(i)   aquatic and riverine environments, and

(ii)   the effect of groundwater on water, land and other environmental resources.

[Omitted: 41 - Measurements of water quantity and quality, 42 - Need for approval in certain cases, 43 - Power to arrange data in lieu, 44 - Water quality objectives, 45 - Recommendations re water quantity and quality, 46 - Commission to be informed of new proposals, 47 - Environmental assessment, 48 - Protection of catchment of Hume Reservoir; Part VI - Construction, operation and maintenance of works; Part VII – Finance; Part VIII – Reports; Part IX - Proceedings in default; Part X - Distribution of waters; Part XI - Menindee Lakes storage; Part XII - Effect of Snowy Mountains Agreement; Part XIII – Miscellaneous; Schedule A – Works; Schedule B - Murray-Darling Basin; Schedule C - Salinity and drainage strategy; Schedule D - Application of agreement to Queensland; Schedule E - Interstate transfer of water allocations; Schedule F - Cap on diversions, Memorandum of Understanding - Australian Capital Territory's participation in the Murray-Darling Basin Initiative]

Commonwealth of Australia - Queensland - South Australia

30. Lake Eyre Basin Intergovernmental Agreement [21 October 2000]*

Recitals:

A. The Lake Eyre Basin has within its boundaries areas of national and international ecological and environmental significance, areas of high economic worth from activities such as pastoralism, tourism, oil and gas extraction and mining, and areas of social, cultural and heritage value, the sustainability of much of which depends upon the continued health of the Thomson/Barcoo/Cooper, Georgina and Diamantina river systems within Queensland and South Australia (as defined in the Australian National Map Drainage Divisions and Basins and including their catchments, flood plains, lakes, wetlands and overflow channels).

B. Management of the Lake Eyre Basin which will best serve the object of sustainability requires a joint cooperative approach between the States of Queensland and South Australia and the Commonwealth.

...

---

* FAOLEX (FAO legal database online).

D.   This Agreement is entered into by the Parties in accordance with the Lake Eyre Basin Heads of Agreement, and is to provide for the establishment of arrangements for the management of water and related natural resources for that portion of the Lake Eyre Basin identified as the Lake Eyre Basin Agreement Area in Clause 1.1, including the development or adoption, and implementation of agreed Policies and Strategies for the avoidance of adverse cross-border impacts and the creation of a relevant institutional structure.

E.   This Agreement is also entered into in recognition of the provisions of the Intergovernmental Agreement on the Environment dated 1 May 1992 between the Commonwealth, all States and Territories, and the Australian Local Government Association, that States use their best endeavours to establish appropriate mechanisms for ensuring cooperative management where significant adverse external effects on another State are expected and identified, and that the role of government is to establish the policy, legislative and administrative framework to determine the permissibility of land use, resource use or development proposals having regard to the appropriate, efficient and ecologically sustainable use of natural resources, and to provide for the consideration of regional implications where proposals for the use of a resource affect several jurisdictions.

...

The Parties agree as follows:

Part I - Application and interpretation

Application

1.1   This Agreement applies to that area of the Lake Eyre Basin (the Agreement Area) encompassing portions of Queensland and South Australia, as depicted in Schedule 1 of this Agreement, including within that area the following river systems and associated catchments, floodplains, overflow channels, lakes, wetlands and sub-artesian waters dependent on surface flows:

...

Definitions

1.2   In this Agreement save where inconsistent with the context:

"Ecosystem" means a community of organisms, interacting with one another, and the natural resources comprising the environment in which those organisms live and with which they also interact.

"Lake Eyre Basin Agreement Area" means the area referred to in clause 1.1 to which the Agreement applies.

"Management Plan" means a plan or other document of a State that has been adopted by the Ministerial Forum.

"Ministerial Forum" means the group of Ministers of the Crown in right of the Commonwealth and the State parties constituted under Part V.

"Natural resources" means water, soil, the atmosphere, plants, animals and micro-organisms that maintain and form components of ecosystems.

"Principles" means the guiding principles referred to in Part III.

"Policy" means a document setting out a course or line of action developed or adopted and pursued by the Ministerial Forum for the purpose of implementing this Agreement.

"Related natural resources" means natural resources the use or management of which affects or might affect, or is or might be affected by the quantity or quality of water in the water systems described in clause 1.1 of this Agreement, or the ecosystems of which such water is a component part.

"Strategy" means a document setting out a course or line of action developed or adopted and pursued by the Ministerial Forum for the purpose of implementing a Policy.

[Omitted: Interpretation]

Part II - Purpose and objectives

Purpose

2.1   The purpose of this Agreement is to provide for the development or adoption, and implementation of Policies and Strategies concerning water and related natural resources in the Lake Eyre Basin Agreement Area to avoid or eliminate so far as reasonably practicable adverse cross-border impacts.

Objectives

2.2   The objectives of this Agreement are:

(a)   to provide a means for the Parties to come together in good faith to achieve the purposes of the Agreement;

(b)   to define a process and context for raising and addressing water and related natural resource management issues in the Lake Eyre Basin Agreement Area that have cross-border impacts, particularly those related to water quantity and quality, and flow regimes;

(c)   to establish institutional arrangements for the development or adoption of Policies and Strategies and for the adoption of any relevant management plans established by a State;

(d)   to provide for each of the Parties, so far as they are able within their respective jurisdictions, to progress the implementation of Policies and Strategies developed or adopted under this Agreement and to make management decisions and allocate resources accordingly;

(e)   to provide a mechanism to review Policies and Strategies;

(f)   to provide for the Parties to jointly promote and support the management of water and related natural resources through a cooperative approach between community, industry and other stakeholders, and all levels of government in the sustainable management of the Lake Eyre Basin Agreement Area;

(g)   to encourage, promote and support water and related resource management practices which are compatible with the spirit and intent of the Agreement;

(h)   to encourage and promote research and monitoring to improve understanding and support informed decision making in the Lake Eyre Basin Agreement Area;

(i)   to provide for the review and, if necessary, revision of the Agreement from time to time; and

(j)   to raise general public awareness of the special biodiversity and heritage values of the Lake Eyre Basin Agreement Area.

Part III - Guiding principles

3.1   Consideration of all issues and the making of all decisions under this Agreement will be guided by the following Principles, namely that it be acknowledged:

(a)   that the Lake Eyre Basin Agreement Area has important social, environmental, economic and cultural values which need to be conserved and promoted;

(b)   that there are landscapes and watercourses in the Lake Eyre Basin Agreement Area that are valuable for aesthetic, wilderness, cultural and tourism purposes;

(c)   that naturally variable flow regimes and the maintenance of water quality are fundamental to the health of the aquatic ecosystems in the Lake Eyre Basin Agreement Area;

(d)   that the water requirements for ecological processes, biodiversity and ecologically significant areas within the Lake Eyre Basin Agreement Area should be maintained, especially by means of flow variability and seasonality;

...

(f)   that the storage and use of water both within and away from watercourses, and the storage and use of water from associated groundwater, are all linked and should be considered together, and that water resources throughout catchments within the Lake Eyre Basin Agreement Area should be managed on an integrated basis;

(g) that precautionary approaches need to be taken so as to minimise the impact on known environmental attributes, and reduce the possibility of affecting poorly understood ecological functions;

(h) that natural resource management decisions need to be made within the context of the National Strategy for Ecologically Sustainable Development and relevant national and international obligations;

(i) that the collective local knowledge and experience of the Lake Eyre Basin Agreement Area communities are of significant value; and

(j) that decisions need to be based on the best available scientific and technical information together with the collective local knowledge and experience of communities within the Lake Eyre Basin Agreement Area.

Part IV - Roles of the Parties

Responsibilities and interests of all Parties

4.1 The following will guide the Parties in defining the roles, responsibilities and interests of the Parties in relation to the achievement of the objectives of this Agreement.

Responsibilities and interests of the Commonwealth

4.2 The responsibilities and interests of the Commonwealth in safeguarding and accommodating matters of national interest include ensuring that the policies or practices of a State that affect or might affect the water and related natural resources to which this Agreement applies, do not result in significant adverse external effects in relation to another State.

4.3 When considering its responsibilities and interests under Clause 4.2 the Commonwealth will have regard to the role of the States in dealing with significant adverse external effects in accordance with the requirements of the Intergovernmental Agreement on the Environment, and any action taken pursuant to that Agreement.

4.4   The Commonwealth will monitor the activities of the States in the Lake Eyre Basin Agreement Area to ensure Australia meets its international obligations in accordance with the Intergovernmental Agreement on the Environment.

4.5   The Commonwealth has responsibility for the management (including operational policy) of natural resources on land which the Commonwealth owns or which it occupies for its own use.

4.6   The Commonwealth will ensure that matters of national interest relating to environmental protection, sustainable agriculture and water and related natural resources management in the Lake Eyre Basin Agreement Area are appropriately addressed in consultation with the States.

4.7   The Commonwealth will consult with the States as required by the Intergovernmental Agreement on the Environment prior to entry into any international agreement which may directly impact on the Lake Eyre Basin Agreement Area.

Responsibilities and interests of the States

4.8   Each State will continue to have responsibility for the development and implementation of policy in relation to matters concerning the Lake Eyre Basin Agreement Area which have no significant effects on the water and related natural resources of the Lake Eyre Basin Agreement Area.

4.9   Each State will continue to have responsibility for its policy formulation and the administration of its legislation relevant to water and related natural resource management within the Lake Eyre Basin Agreement Area, but in so doing will, to the fullest extent that it is able, comply with this Agreement and any applicable Policies and Strategies developed or adopted under it. Further, to the extent that may be necessary, each State will use its best endeavours to secure the passage through its respective Parliament of legislation for the purpose of conforming with and implementing this Agreement and any such Policies and Strategies.

4.10 Each State will assist in the encouragement and promotion of research and monitoring to facilitate informed decision making for the Lake Eyre Basin Agreement Area, and the sharing of access to the results of such research and monitoring so far as either State may control such access.

4.11 Each State will consult with and involve Local Government (where relevant) in the implementation of this Agreement and the Policies and Strategies developed or adopted under it to the extent that State statutes and administrative arrangements authorise or delegate relevant responsibilities to Local Government, and in a manner which reflects the concept of partnership between the Commonwealth, State and Local Governments.

Part V - Institutional structure

Constitution of the Ministerial Forum

5.1 The Ministerial Forum is constituted.

5.2 The Ministerial Forum will consist of one Minister from each State and one Minister of the Commonwealth. Each Party will appoint its Minister from time to time, by notice in writing to each other Party.

...

[Omitted: Part VI - Conference, Part VII - Scientific and technical advice]

Part VIII - Policies and Strategies

8.1 The Ministerial Forum will, without unnecessary delay, develop or adopt Policies and Strategies for the management of the Lake Eyre Basin Agreement Area in accordance with the purpose, objectives and Principles set out in this Agreement.

...

Content of Policies and Strategies

8.4   The Policies and Strategies will make provision for such matters as the
        Ministerial Forum thinks fit, including but not limited to:

(a)   objectives for water quality and river flows;

(b)   objectives for water and related natural resource management in the
        Lake Eyre Basin Agreement Area for the achievement of the water
        quality and river flow objectives;

(c)   catchment management policies and strategies for the achievement, as
        far as practicable, of the water quality and river flow objectives;

(d)   policies for dealing with relevant existing entitlements under State laws
        and significant water related developments; and

(e)   research and monitoring requirements and programs to meet those
        requirements.

[Omitted: Part IX - Ratification and effective date; Part X - Review and
amendment; Part XI - Funding and accountability; Part XII - Further parties,
Part XIII - General]

...

[Omitted: Schedule 1 - The Lake Eyre Basin Agreement Area]

New South Wales - Queensland

31.   Paroo River Intergovernmental Agreement [18 July 2003]*

Recitals:

A.   The Paroo River Catchment has within its boundaries areas of national
        and international ecological and environmental significance, areas of
        high economic worth from activities such as pastoralism and tourism
        and areas of social, cultural and heritage value, the sustainable

---

* FAOLEX (FAO legal database online).

management of which depends upon the continued health of the Paroo River system within Queensland and New South Wales (as defined in the Australian National Map Drainage Divisions and Basins and including its catchment, floodplains, lakes, wetlands and overflow channels).

B.   Management of the Paroo River Agreement Area which will best serve the object of sustainable management requires a joint cooperative approach between the States of Queensland and New South Wales.

...

Part I - Application and interpretation

Application

1.1   This Agreement applies to that area of the Paroo River catchment (the Agreement Area) encompassing portions of Queensland and New South Wales, as depicted in Schedule 1 of this Agreement, including within that area the river system and associated catchments, floodplains, overflow channels, lakes, wetlands and sub-artesian waters dependent on surface flows:

Definitions

1.2   In this Agreement save where inconsistent with the context:

"Biodiversity" means the variability among living organisms from all sources including, inter alia, terrestrial, marine and other aquatic ecosystems and the ecological complexes of which they are part; this includes diversity within species, between species and of ecosystems.

"Border Catchments Ministerial Forum" means the group of Ministers of the Crown of the States constituted under the Border Catchments Memorandum of Understanding or its future replacement.

"Ecological Sustainability" means using, conserving and enhancing the community's resources so that ecological processes, on which life depends, are maintained and quality of life for both present and future generations is increased.

"Ecosystem" means a dynamic combination of plant, animal and micro-organism species and communities and their non-living environment and the ecological processes between them interacting as a functional unit.

"Paroo River Agreement Area" means the area referred to in clause 1.1 to which the Agreement applies.

"Management Plan" means a plan or other document of a State that has been adopted by the Border Catchments Ministerial Forum.

"Natural resources" means water, soil, the atmosphere, plants, animals and micro-organisms that maintain and form components of ecosystems.

"Principles" means the guiding principles referred to in Part III.

"Policy" means a course or line of action developed or adopted and pursued by the Border Catchments Ministerial Forum for the purpose of implementing this Agreement.

"Strategy" means a course or line of action developed or adopted and pursued by the Border Catchments Ministerial Forum for the purpose of implementing a Policy.

"Sustainable management" means the management of biodiversity and health of natural ecosystems, including watercourses, floodplains, lakes, springs, wetlands and sub-artesian aquifers dependent on surface flows so they are protected from degradation, according to the principles of ecologically sustainable development and in recognition of the interests of Aboriginal people and others that depend on the water for their livelihoods.

...

Part II - Purpose and objectives

Vision

2.1   By recognising the unique character of the Paroo River, its river flows, floodplains and catchment, the people of New South Wales, Queensland and Australia will ensure it continues to provide spiritual connection, ecological diversity and integrity and economic sustenance for future generations.

Purpose

2.2 The purpose of this Agreement is to provide for the development or adoption, and implementation of Policies and Strategies concerning water and related natural resources that might be affected by or might affect the management of the quantity or quality of water in the water systems described in clause 1.1 of this Agreement, or the ecosystems of which such water is a part, in the Paroo River Agreement Area to avoid or eliminate so far as reasonably practicable adverse cross-border impacts.

Objectives

2.3 The objectives of this Agreement are:

(a) to provide a means for the Parties to come together in good faith to achieve the purposes of the Agreement;

(b) to define a process and context for raising and addressing water and related natural resource management issues in the Paroo River Agreement Area that have cross-border impacts, particularly those related to water quantity and quality, and flow regimes;

(c) to provide an emphasis for this catchment under the Border Catchments Memorandum of Understanding and the Murray-Darling Basin Agreement;

(d) to provide for the Parties to jointly promote and support the management of water and related natural resources through a cooperative approach between community, industry and other stakeholders, and all levels of government in the sustainable management of the Paroo River Agreement Area;

(g)[sic]to encourage, promote and support management that reflects the vision as defined in clause 2.1.

(h) to encourage and promote research and monitoring to improve understanding and support informed decision making in the Paroo River Agreement Area;

(i)   to provide for the review and, if necessary, revision of the Agreement
         from time to time through the Border Catchments Ministerial Forum
         or the Murray-Darling Basin Ministerial Council; and

(j)   to raise general public awareness of the special biodiversity and
         heritage values of the Paroo River Agreement Area.

Part III - Guiding principles

3.1   Consideration of all issues and the making of all decisions under this
         Agreement will be guided by the following Principles, namely that it be
         acknowledged:

(a)   that the Paroo River Agreement Area has important social,
         environmental, economic and cultural values which need to be
         conserved, promoted and, where necessary, restored;

(b)   that there are landscapes and watercourses in the Paroo River
         Agreement Area that are valuable for aesthetic, wilderness, cultural
         and tourism purposes;

(c)   that naturally variable flow regimes and the maintenance of water
         quality are fundamental to the health of the aquatic ecosystems in the
         Paroo River Agreement Area;

(d)   that the water requirements for ecological processes, biodiversity and
         ecologically significant areas within the Paroo River Agreement Area
         should be maintained, especially by means of flow variability and
         seasonality;

...

(f)   that the storage and use of water both within and away from
         watercourses, and the storage and use of water from associated
         groundwater, are all linked and should be considered together, and
         that water resources throughout catchments within the Paroo River
         Agreement Area should be managed on an integrated basis;

(j)[sic] that precautionary approaches need to be taken so as to minimise the
         impact on known environmental attributes, and reduce the possibility
         of affecting poorly understood ecological functions;

(k)   that natural resource management decisions need to be made within the context of the National Strategy for Ecologically Sustainable Development and relevant national and international obligations;

(l)   that the collective local knowledge and experience of the Paroo River Agreement Area communities are of significant value;

(m)   that the interests, perspectives and knowledge systems of the Traditional Owners be formally sought on all key matters, and be fully recognised and considered; and

(n)   that decisions need to be based on the best available scientific and technical information together with the collective local knowledge and experience of the Paroo River community, including indigenous communities.

Part IV - Roles of the Parties

Responsibilities and interests of the States

4.1   The following will guide the Parties in defining the roles, responsibilities and interests of the Parties in relation to the achievement of the objectives of this Agreement. Each State will continue to have responsibility for the development and implementation of policy in relation to matters concerning the Paroo River Agreement Area which have no significant effects on the water and related natural resources of the Paroo River Agreement Area.

4.2   Each State will continue to have responsibility for its policy formulation and the administration of its legislation relevant to water and related natural resource management within the Paroo River Agreement Area, but in so doing will, comply with this Agreement.

4.3   Each State will assist in the encouragement and promotion of research and monitoring for informed decision making for the Paroo River Agreement Area, and the sharing of access to the results of such research and monitoring so far as either State may control such access.

4.4   Each State will consult with and involve Local Government and the Paroo River community (where relevant) in the implementation of this Agreement and the Policies and Strategies developed or adopted under it to the extent that State statutes and administrative arrangements authorise or delegate relevant responsibilities to Local Government, and in a manner which reflects the concept of partnership between the Commonwealth, State and Local Governments and the Paroo River community.

Part V - Institutional structure

5.1   Consideration of issues relating to this Agreement will be under the Border Catchments Ministerial Forum or the Murray-Darling Basin Ministerial Council when the former is no longer in operation.

[Omitted: Part VI - Scientific and technical advice]

Part VII - Policies and Strategies

7.1   The Border Catchments Ministerial Forum will, without unnecessary delay, develop or adopt Policies and Strategies for the management of the Paroo River Agreement Area in accordance with the purpose, objectives and Principles set out in this Agreement.

...

Content of Policies and Strategies

7.3   The Policies and Strategies will make provision for such matters as the Border Catchments Ministerial Forum thinks fit, including but not limited to:

(a)   objectives for water quality and river flows;

(b)   objectives for water and related natural resource management in the Paroo River Agreement Area for the achievement of the water quality and river flow objectives;

(c)   catchment management policies and strategies for the achievement, as far as practicable, of the water quality and river flow objectives;

(d)   policies for dealing with relevant existing entitlements under State laws and significant water related developments; and

(e)   research and monitoring requirements and programs to meet those requirements.

[Omitted: Part VIII - Ratification and effective date; Part IX - Review and amendment; Part X - Funding and accountability arrangements; Part XI - General]

...

[Omitted: Schedule 1]

Commonwealth of Australia - Australian Capital Territory - New South Wales - Northern Territory - Queensland - South Australia - Victoria

32.   Intergovernmental Agreement on a National Water Initiative [25 une 2004]*

<u>Preamble</u>

1.   Water may be viewed as part of Australia's natural capital, serving a number of important productive, environmental and social objectives. Australia's water resources are highly variable, reflecting the range of climatic conditions and terrain nationally. In addition, the level of development in Australia's water resources ranges from heavily regulated working rivers and groundwater resources, through to rivers and aquifers in almost pristine condition.

2.   In Australia, water is vested in governments that allow other parties to access and use water for a variety of purposes - whether irrigation, industrial use, mining, servicing rural and urban communities, or for amenity values. Decisions about water management involve balancing sets of economic, environmental and other interests. The framework within which water is allocated attaches both rights and responsibilities to water users - a right to a share of the water made available for extraction at any particular time, and a responsibility to use this water in accordance with usage conditions set by government. Likewise,

---

*   FAOLEX (FAO legal database online).

governments have a responsibility to ensure that water is allocated and used to achieve socially and economically beneficial outcomes in a manner that is environmentally sustainable.

3. The 1994 Council of Australian Governments' (COAG) water reform framework and subsequent initiatives recognised that better management of Australia's water resources is a national issue. As a result of these initiatives, States and Territories have made considerable progress towards more efficient and sustainable water management over the past 10 years. For example, most jurisdictions have embarked on a significant program of reforms to their water management regimes, separating water access entitlements from land titles, separating the functions of water delivery from that of regulation, and making explicit provision for environmental water.

4. At the same time, there has been an increase in demand for water, and an increased understanding of the management needs of surface and groundwater systems, including their interconnection. There has also been an enhanced understanding of the requirements for effective and efficient water markets. The current variation in progress with water reforms between regions and jurisdictions, and the expanded knowledge base, creates an opportunity to complement and extend the reform agenda to more fully realise the benefits intended by COAG in 1994.

5. The Parties agree to implement this National Water Initiative (NWI) in recognition of the continuing national imperative to increase the productivity and efficiency of Australia's water use, the need to service rural and urban communities, and to ensure the health of river and groundwater systems by establishing clear pathways to return all systems to environmentally sustainable levels of extraction. The objective of the Parties in implementing this Agreement is to provide greater certainty for investment and the environment, and underpin the capacity of Australia's water management regimes to deal with change responsively and fairly (refer paragraph 23).

6. The Parties acknowledge that the NWI builds on the 1994 strategic framework for the efficient and sustainable reform of the Australian water industry (the 1994 COAG framework), as amended in 1996 to include groundwater and stormwater management revisions and by the Tripartite agreement in January 1999. The Parties are committed to

meeting their commitments under the 1994 COAG framework and continuing to meet the objectives and policy directions of the 1994 COAG framework in a way that is consistent with the objectives and actions set out in this Agreement.

7. Other natural resource management initiatives having a significant water focus and subject of separate agreements by the Parties, particularly the National Action Plan for Salinity and Water Quality and the Natural Heritage Trust, play an important and complementary role in improving the sustainable management of water in Australia. Continued implementation of the National Water Quality Management Strategy will also complement the outcomes of this Agreement. To the extent that there is any inconsistency between the agreements, the National Water Initiative should take precedence.

Implementation

8. The Parties agree that actions under this Agreement will be implemented in accordance with the timetable at Schedule A and in accordance with implementation plans to be developed by each jurisdiction within 12 months of signing this Agreement, to reflect their particular circumstances. The Parties will make substantial progress towards implementation of this Agreement by 2010.

9. The implementation plans will:

(i) describe how the actions and timelines agreed in the IGA are to be achieved, including milestones for each key element of the Agreement (paragraph 24 refers);

(ii) describe the timing and process for making any consequential changes to water plans and the water access entitlements framework (paragraph 26 refers);

(iii) be developed cooperatively between States and Territories which share water resources to ensure appropriate co-development of those actions which are of a cross-jurisdictional nature, including registries, trading rules, water products, and environmental outcomes; and

(iv) be made publicly available.

10. The Parties agree to the establishment of a National Water Commission (NWC) to assist with the effective implementation of this Agreement. The NWC will accredit implementation plans to ensure consistency with the timetable at Schedule A.

11. The Parties agree that the scheduled 2005 assessment of States' and Territories' National Competition Policy water-related reform commitments will be undertaken by the NWC.

12. This Agreement contains a number of interrelated actions. It is recognised that some actions have already commenced in some jurisdictions. The Parties intend that where necessary to achieve the objectives of the Agreement, actions required may be modified on the basis of further information or analysis.

13. Relevant Parties will review existing cross-jurisdictional water sharing agreements to ensure their consistency with this Agreement, and identify those instances where any new cross-jurisdictional agreements may be required to give effect to this Agreement.

14. In relation to the Murray-Darling Basin (MDB):

(i) relevant Parties agree to review the 1992 Murray-Darling Basin Agreement, where necessary, to ensure that it is consistent with this Agreement; and

(ii) a separate agreement to address the overallocation of water and achievement of environmental objectives in the MDB ('the MDB Intergovernmental Agreement') will operate between the Commonwealth Government and the Governments of New South Wales, Victoria, South Australia and the Australian Capital Territory. The MDB Intergovernmental Agreement will be consistent with the objectives, principles and actions identified in this Agreement.

Commencement

15. The provisions of this Agreement will commence for each jurisdiction as it becomes a signatory to the Agreement.

Interpretation

16.   In this Agreement words and phrases that are italicised are to be interpreted by reference to the glossary at Schedule B(i).

17.   Recognising the importance of a common lexicon for water use and management, the Parties acknowledge the desirability of adopting within their respective water management frameworks, the words and phrases, and their interpretations, contained in Schedule B(ii).

Roles and responsibilities

18.   The Natural Resource Management Ministerial Council (NRMMC) will be responsible for:

(i)   overseeing implementation of this Agreement, in consultation with other Ministerial Councils as necessary and with reference to advice from COAG; and

(ii)   addressing ongoing implementation issues as they arise.

19.   The National Water Commission (NWC) will be responsible for providing advice to COAG on national water issues and to assist in the implementation of this Agreement. The NWC's institutional structure and role are set out in Schedule C.

20.   The States and Territories are responsible for implementing this Agreement within their respective jurisdictions, consistent with their implementation plans (paragraph 9 refers).

21.   The Parties are responsible for ensuring there is adequate engagement of relevant stakeholders in the implementation of this Agreement (paragraphs 95 - 97 refer).

22.   The Commonwealth Government will assist in implementation of this Agreement by working with the States and Territories.

Objectives

23.   Full implementation of this Agreement will result in a nationally-compatible, market, regulatory and planning based system of

managing surface and groundwater resources for rural and urban use that optimises economic, social and environmental outcomes by achieving the following:

(i)   clear and nationally-compatible characteristics for secure water access entitlements;

(ii)   transparent, statutory-based water planning;

(iii)   statutory provision for environmental and other public benefit outcomes, and improved environmental management practices;

(iv)   complete the return of all currently overallocated or overused systems to environmentally-sustainable levels of extraction;

(v)   progressive removal of barriers to trade in water and meeting other requirements to facilitate the broadening and deepening of the water market, with an open trading market to be in place;

(vi)   clarity around the assignment of risk arising from future changes in the availability of water for the consumptive pool;

(vii)   water accounting which is able to meet the information needs of different water systems in respect to planning, monitoring, trading, environmental management and on-farm management;

(viii) policy settings which facilitate water use efficiency and innovation in urban and rural areas;

(ix)   addressing future adjustment issues that may impact on water users and communities; and

(x)   recognition of the connectivity between surface and groundwater resources and connected systems managed as a single resource.

<u>Key elements</u>

24.   Agreed outcomes and commitments to specific actions are set out on the basis of the following key elements:

(i)   Water Access Entitlements and Planning Framework;

(ii)   Water Markets and Trading;

(iii) Best Practice Water Pricing;

(iv)   Integrated Management of Water for Environmental and Other Public Benefit Outcomes;

(v)   Water Resource Accounting;

(vi)   Urban Water Reform;

(vii) Knowledge and Capacity Building; and

(viii) Community Partnerships and Adjustment.

<u>Water access entitlements and planning framework outcomes</u>

25.   The Parties agree that, once initiated, their water access entitlements and planning frameworks will:

(i)   enhance the security and commercial certainty of water access entitlements by clearly specifying the statutory nature of those entitlements;

(ii)   provide a statutory basis for environmental and other public benefit outcomes in surface and groundwater systems to protect water sources and their dependent ecosystems;

(iii) be characterised by planning processes in which there is adequate opportunity for productive, environmental and other public benefit considerations to be identified and considered in an open and transparent way;

(iv)   provide for adaptive management of surface and groundwater systems in order to meet productive, environmental and other public benefit outcomes;

(v)   implement firm pathways and open processes for returning previously overallocated and/or overdrawn surface and groundwater systems to environmentally-sustainable levels of extraction;

(vi)   clearly assign the risks arising from future changes to the consumptive pool;

(vii)   in the case of water access entitlements, be compatible across jurisdictions to improve investment certainty, be competitively neutral and to minimise transaction costs on water trades (where relevant);

(viii)   reflect regional differences in the variability of water supply and the state of knowledge underpinning regional allocation decisions;

(ix)   recognise indigenous needs in relation to water access and management;

(x)   identify and acknowledge surface and groundwater systems of high conservation value, and manage these systems to protect and enhance those values; and

(xi)   protect the integrity of water access entitlements from unregulated growth in interception through land-use change.

Actions

26.   The Parties agree that the general approach to implementing the entitlements and allocation framework will be to:

(i)   substantially complete plans to address any existing overallocation for all river systems and groundwater resources in accordance with commitments under the 1994 COAG water reform framework by 2005;

(ii)   incorporate the elements of the entitlements and allocation framework in this Agreement that are missing or deficient in existing water entitlement frameworks, into their legislative and administrative regimes by 2006;

(iii)   review any plans developed for the 1994 COAG framework to ensure that they now meet the requirements of this Agreement in terms of transparency of process, reporting arrangements and risk assignment;

(iv)   immediately proceed on a priority basis to develop any new plans, consistent with paragraph 38; and

(v) apply the risk assignment framework (paragraphs 46-51 refer) once plans are initialised under this Agreement.

27. Recognising that States and Territories retain the vested rights to the use, flow and control of water, they agree to modify their existing legislation and administrative regimes where necessary to ensure that their water access entitlement and planning frameworks incorporate the features identified in paragraphs 28-57 below.

Water access entitlements

28. The consumptive use of water will require a water access entitlement, separate from land, to be described as a perpetual or open-ended share of the consumptive pool of a specified water resource, as determined by the relevant water plan (paragraphs 36 to 40 refer), subject to the provisions at paragraph 33.

29. The allocation of water to a water access entitlement will be made consistent with a water plan (paragraph 36 refers).

30. Regulatory approvals enabling water use at a particular site for a particular purpose will be specified separately to the water access entitlement, consistent with the principles set out in Schedule D.

31. Water access entitlements will:

(i) specify the essential characteristics of the water product;

(ii) be exclusive;

(iii) be able to be traded, given, bequeathed or leased;

(iv) be able to be subdivided or amalgamated;

(v) be mortgageable (and in this respect have similar status as freehold land when used as collateral for accessing finance);

(vi) be enforceable and enforced; and

(vii)   be recorded in publicly-accessible reliable water registers that foster public confidence and state unambiguously who owns the entitlement, and the nature of any encumbrances on it (paragraph 59 refers).

32.   Water access entitlements will also:

(i)   clearly indicate the responsibilities and obligations of the entitlement holder consistent with the water plan relevant to the source of the water;

(ii)   only be able to be cancelled at Ministerial and agency discretion where the responsibilities and obligations of the entitlement holder have clearly been breached;

(iii)   be able to be varied, for example to change extraction conditions, where mutually agreed between the government and the entitlement holder; and

(iv)   be subject to any provisions relating to access of water during emergencies, as specified by legislation in each jurisdiction.

33.   The provisions in paragraphs 28-32 are subject to the following provisions:

(i)   fixed term or other types of entitlements such as annual licences will only be issued for consumptive use where this is demonstrably necessary, such as in Western Australia with poorly understood and/or less developed water resources, and/or where the access is contingent upon opportunistic allocations, and/or where the access is provided temporarily as part of an adjustment strategy, or where trading may otherwise not be appropriate. In some cases, a statutory right to extract water may be appropriate; and

(ii)   an ongoing process will be in place to assess the risks of expected development and demand on resources in poorly understood or undeveloped areas, with a view to moving these areas to a full entitlement framework when this becomes appropriate for their efficient management (paragraph 38 refers).

34.   The Parties agree that there may be special circumstances facing the minerals and petroleum sectors that will need to be addressed by

policies and measures beyond the scope of this Agreement. In this context, the Parties note that specific project proposals will be assessed according to environmental, economic and social considerations, and that factors specific to resource development projects, such as isolation, relatively short project duration, water quality issues, and obligations to remediate and offset impacts, may require specific management arrangements outside the scope of this Agreement.

Environmental and other public benefit outcomes

35. Water that is provided by the States and Territories to meet agreed environmental and other public benefit outcomes as defined within relevant water plans (paragraphs 36 to 40 refer) is to:

(i) be given statutory recognition and have at least the same degree of security as water access entitlements for consumptive use and be fully accounted for;

(ii) be defined as the water management arrangements required to meet the outcomes sought, including water provided on a rules basis or held as a water access entitlement; and

(iii) if held as a water access entitlement, may be made available to be traded (where physically possible) on the temporary market, when not required to meet the environmental and other public benefit outcomes sought and provided such trading is not in conflict with those outcomes.

Water planning

36. Recognising that settling the trade-offs between competing outcomes for water systems will involve judgements informed by best available science, socio-economic analysis and community input, statutory water plans will be prepared for surface water and groundwater management units in which entitlements are issued (subject to paragraph 38). Water planning is an important mechanism to assist governments and the community to determine water management and allocation decisions to meet productive, environmental and social objectives.

37.   Broadly, water planning by States and Territories will provide for:

(i)   secure ecological outcomes by describing the environmental and other public benefit outcomes for water systems and defining the appropriate water management arrangements to achieve those outcomes; and

(ii)   resource security outcomes by determining the shares in the consumptive pool and the rules to allocate water during the life of the plan.

38.   The relevant State or Territory will determine whether a plan is prepared, what area it should cover, the level of detail required, its duration or frequency of review, and the amount of resources devoted to its preparation based on an assessment of the level of development of water systems, projected future consumptive demand and the risks of not having a detailed plan.

39.   States and Territories will prepare water plans along the lines of the characteristics and components at Schedule E.

40.   In the implementation of water plans, the Parties will, consistent with the nature and intensity of resource use:

(i)   monitor the performance of water plan objectives, outcomes and water management arrangements;

(ii)   factor in knowledge improvements as provided for in the plans; and

(iii) provide regular public reports. The reporting will be designed to help water users and governments to manage risk, and be timed to give early indications of possible changes to the consumptive pool.

Addressing currently overallocated and/or overused systems

41.   The Parties note that existing commitments under National Competition Policy (ref. COAG Tripartite Agreement Clause 1) arrangements require that allocations to provide a better balance in water resource use (including appropriate allocations to the environment) for all river systems and groundwater resources which have been overallocated or are deemed to be stressed and identified in

their agreed National Competition Council (NCC) endorsed individual implementation programs, must be substantially completed by 2005.

42. This Agreement will not delay nor extend timeframes for current National Competition Policy commitments.

43. The Parties further agree that with respect to surface and groundwater resources not covered by the individual NCC endorsed implementation plans, and subject to paragraph 38, States and Territories will determine in accordance with the relevant water plan, the precise pathway by which any of those systems found to be overallocated and/or overused as defined in the water planning process will be adjusted to address the overallocation or overuse, and meet the environmental and other public benefit outcomes.

44. Subject to paragraph 41, States and Territories agree that substantial progress will be made by 2010 towards adjusting all overallocated and/or overused systems in accordance with the timelines indicated in their implementation plans.

45. Parties agree to address significant adjustment issues affecting water users, in accordance with paragraph 97.

Assigning risks for changes in allocation

46. The following risk assignment framework is intended to apply to any future reductions in the availability of water for consumptive use, that are additional to those identified for the purpose of addressing known overallocation and/or overuse in accordance with pathways agreed under the provisions in paragraphs 41 to 45 above.

47. The Parties agree that an effective risk assignment framework occurs in the context that: the new share-based water access entitlements framework has been established; water plans have been transparently developed to determine water allocation for the entitlements; regular reporting of progress with implementing plans is occurring; and a pathway for dealing with known overallocation and/or overuse has been agreed.

48.   Water access entitlement holders are to bear the risks of any reduction or less reliable water allocation, under their water access entitlements, arising from reductions to the consumptive pool as a result of:

(i)   seasonal or long-term changes in climate; and

(ii) periodic natural events such as bushfires and drought.

49.   The risks of any reduction or less reliable water allocation under a water access entitlement, arising as a result of bona fide improvements in the knowledge of water systems' capacity to sustain particular extraction levels are to be borne by users up to 2014. Risks arising under comprehensive water plans commencing or renewed after 2014 are to be shared over each ten year period in the following way:

(i)   water access entitlement holders to bear the first 3% reduction in water allocation under a water access entitlement;

(ii) State/Territory governments and the Commonwealth Government to share one-third and two-thirds respectively reductions in water allocation under water access entitlements of between 3% and 6%; and

(iii) State/Territory and Commonwealth governments to equally share reductions in water allocation under water access entitlements greater than 6%.

50.   Governments are to bear the risks of any reduction or less reliable water allocation that is not previously provided for, arising from changes in government policy (for example, new environmental objectives). In such cases, governments may recover this water in accordance with the principles for assessing the most efficient and cost effective measures for water recovery (paragraph 79 (ii) (a) refers).

51.   Alternatively, the Parties agree that where affected parties, including water access entitlement holders, environmental stakeholders and the relevant government agree, on a voluntary basis, to a different risk sharing formula to that proposed in paragraphs 48 - 50 above, that this will be an acceptable approach.

Indigenous access

52. The Parties will provide for indigenous access to water resources, in accordance with relevant Commonwealth, State and Territory legislation, through planning processes that ensure:

(i) inclusion of indigenous representation in water planning wherever possible; and

(ii) water plans will incorporate indigenous social, spiritual and customary objectives and strategies for achieving these objectives wherever they can be developed.

53. Water planning processes will take account of the possible existence of native title rights to water in the catchment or aquifer area. The Parties note that plans may need to allocate water to native title holders following the recognition of native title rights in water under the Commonwealth Native Title Act 1993.

54. Water allocated to native title holders for traditional cultural purposes will be accounted for.

Interception

55. The Parties recognise that a number of land use change activities have potential to intercept significant volumes of surface and/or ground water now and in the future. Examples of such activities that are of concern, many of which are currently undertaken without a water access entitlement, include:

(i) farm dams and bores;

(ii) intercepting and storing of overland flows; and

(iii) large-scale plantation forestry.

56. The Parties also recognise that if these activities are not subject to some form of planning and regulation, they present a risk to the future integrity of water access entitlements and the achievement of environmental objectives for water systems. The intention is therefore to assess the significance of such activities on catchments and aquifers,

based on an understanding of the total water cycle, the economic and environmental costs and benefits of the activities of concern, and to apply appropriate planning, management and/or regulatory measures where necessary to protect the integrity of the water access entitlements system and the achievement of environmental objectives.

57.   Accordingly, the Parties agree to implement the following measures in relation to water interception on a priority basis in accordance with the timetable contained in their implementation plans, and no later than 2011:

(i)   in water systems that are fully allocated, overallocated, or approaching full allocation:-

    (a)   interception activities that are assessed as being significant should be recorded (for example, through a licensing system);

    (b)   any proposals for additional interception activities above an agreed threshold size, will require a *water access entitlement*:

        -    the threshold size will be determined for the entire water system covered by a water plan, having regard to regional circumstances and taking account of both the positive and negative impacts of water interception on regional (including cross-border) natural resource management outcomes (for example, the control of rising water tables by plantations); and

        -    the threshold may not apply to activities for restricted purposes, such as contaminated water from intensive livestock operations;

    (c)   a robust compliance monitoring regime will be implemented; and

(ii)   in water systems that are not yet fully allocated, or approaching full allocation:

    (a)   significant interception activities should be identified and estimates made of the amount of water likely to be intercepted by those activities over the life of the relevant water plan;

(b)   an appropriate threshold level will be calculated of water interception by the significant interception activities that is allowable without a water access entitlement across the entire water system covered by the plan:

-     this threshold level should be determined as per paragraph 57(i)b) above; and

(c)   progress of the catchment or aquifer towards either full allocation or the threshold level of interception should be regularly monitored and publicly reported:

-     once the threshold level of interception is reached, or the system is approaching full allocation, all additional proposals for significant interception activities will require a water access entitlement unless for activities for restricted purposes, such as contaminated water from intensive livestock operations.

<u>Water markets and trading</u>

<u>Outcomes</u>

58.   The States and Territories agree that their water market and trading arrangements will:

(i)   facilitate the operation of efficient water markets and the opportunities for trading, within and between States and Territories, where water systems are physically shared or hydrologic connections and water supply considerations will permit water trading;

(ii)   minimise transaction costs on water trades, including through good information flows in the market and compatible entitlement, registry, regulatory and other arrangements across jurisdictions;

(iii)   enable the appropriate mix of water products to develop based on access entitlements which can be traded either in whole or in part, and either temporarily or permanently, or through lease arrangements or other trading options that may evolve over time;

(iv)   recognise and protect the needs of the environment; and

(v)   provide appropriate protection of third-party interests.

Actions

59.   The States and Territories agree to have in place pathways by 2004, leading to full implementation by 2006, of compatible, publicly-accessible and reliable water registers of all water access entitlements and trades (both permanent and temporary) on a whole of basin or catchment basis, consistent with the principles in Schedule F. The Parties recognise that in some instances water service providers will be responsible for recording details of temporary trades.

60.   The States and Territories agree to establish by 2007 compatible institutional and regulatory arrangements that facilitate intra and interstate trade, and manage differences in entitlement reliability, supply losses, supply source constraints, trading between systems, and cap requirements, including:

(i)   principles for trading rules to address resource management and infrastructure delivery considerations, as set out in Schedule G;

(ii)   where appropriate, the use of water access entitlement exchange rates and/or water access entitlement tagging and a system of trading zones to simplify administration;

(iii)   the application of consistent pricing policies (refer paragraph 64 below);

(iv)   in respect of any existing institutional barriers to intra and interstate trade:

   (a)   immediate removal of barriers to temporary trade;

   (b)   immediate removal of barriers to permanent trade out of water irrigation areas up to an annual threshold limit of four percent of the total water entitlement of that area, subject to a review by 2009 with a move to full and open trade by 2014 at the latest, except in the southern Murray-Darling Basin where action to remove barriers to trade is agreed as set out under paragraph 63; and

(c)   jurisdictions may remove barriers earlier than those in (b) above;

(v)   subject to (i) above, no imposition of new barriers to trade, including in the form of arrangements for addressing stranded assets; and

(vi)   where appropriate, implementing measures to facilitate the rationalisation of inefficient infrastructure or unsustainable irrigation supply schemes, including consideration of the need for any structural adjustment assistance (paragraph 97 refers).

61.   To support the above actions on trading, the Parties also agree to complete the following studies and to consider implementation of any recommendations by June 2005:

(i)   a study taking into account work already underway, on effective market and regulatory mechanisms for sharing delivery capacity and extraction rates among water users, where necessary to enhance the operation of water markets and make recommendations to implement efficient ways to manage changes in water usage patterns, channel capacity constraints and water quality issues;

(ii)   a study to facilitate cross system compatibility, that analyses the existing product mix, proposes possible choices of product mix, makes recommendations on the desirable model and proposes a transition path for implementation; and

(iii)   a study to assess the feasibility of establishing market mechanisms such as tradeable salinity and pollution credits to provide incentives for investment in water-use efficiency and farm management strategies and for dealing with environmental externalities.

62.   Recognising the need to manage the impacts of assets potentially stranded by trade out of serviced areas, the Parties agree to ensure that support mechanisms used for this purpose, such as access and exit fees and retail tagging, do not become an institutional barrier to trade (paragraph 60(v) refers).

63.   In regard to the Southern Murray-Darling Basin, the relevant Parties (Commonwealth, New South Wales, Victoria and South Australia) that are members of the Murray-Darling Basin Ministerial Council agree to:

(i)   take all steps necessary, including making any corresponding legislative and administrative changes, to enable exchange rates and/or tagging of water access entitlements traded from interstate sources to buyers in their jurisdictions by June 2005;

(ii)   reduce barriers to trade in the Southern Murray-Darling Basin by taking the necessary legislative and other actions to permit open trade and ensure competitive neutrality, and to establish an interim threshold limit on the level of permanent trade out of all water irrigation areas of four per cent per annum of the total water access entitlement for the water irrigation area by June 2005, including:

   (a)   in the case of NSW, making necessary legislative changes to give effect to a Heads of Agreement between Government and major irrigation corporations to permit increased trade, including to remove barriers to trade up to the above interim threshold limit; and

   (b)   in the case of Victoria and South Australia, bringing into effect change to permit increased trade including to remove barriers to trade up to the above interim threshold level, in the respective Authorities and Trusts, at the same time that NSW amends its legislation;

(iii)   review the above actions in June 2005 to assess whether all relevant parties have met their obligations to enable achievement of the interim threshold;

(iv)   a study into the legal, commercial and technical mechanisms necessary to enable interstate trade to commence in the Southern Murray-Darling Basin by June 2005;

(v)   review the outcome of 63(ii)(a) by 2007 and, if the actions are shown to be insufficient to ensure the desired level of open trade, to take any further action, including legislation, determined necessary to achieve the desired opening of water trading markets in the Southern Murray-Darling Basin;

(vi)   the National Water Commission monitoring the impacts of interstate trade and advising the relevant Parties on any issues arising; and

(vii) review the impact of trade under the interim threshold in 2009, with a view to raising the threshold to a higher level if considered appropriate.

Best practice water pricing and institutional arrangements

Outcomes

64. The Parties agree to implement water pricing and institutional arrangements which:

(i) promote economically efficient and sustainable use of:

    (a) water resources;

    (b) water infrastructure assets; and

    (c) government resources devoted to the management of water;

(ii) ensure sufficient revenue streams to allow efficient delivery of the required services;

(iii) facilitate the efficient functioning of water markets, including inter-jurisdictional water markets, and in both rural and urban settings;

(iv) give effect to the principles of user-pays and achieve pricing transparency in respect of water storage and delivery in irrigation systems and cost recovery for water planning and management;

(v) avoid perverse or unintended pricing outcomes; and

(vi) provide appropriate mechanisms for the release of unallocated water.

Actions

Water storage and delivery pricing

65. In accordance with NCP commitments, the States and Territories agree to bring into effect pricing policies for water storage and delivery in rural and urban systems that facilitate efficient water use and trade in water entitlements, including through the use of:

(i)   consumption based pricing;

(ii)   full cost recovery for water services to ensure business viability and avoid monopoly rents, including recovery of environmental externalities, where feasible and practical; and

(iii)   consistency in pricing policies across sectors and jurisdictions where entitlements are able to be traded.

66.   In particular, States and Territories agree to the following pricing actions:

Metropolitan

(i)   continued movement towards upper bound pricing by 2008;

(ii)   development of pricing policies for recycled water and stormwater that are congruent with pricing policies for potable water, and stimulate efficient water use no matter what the source, by 2006;

(iii)   review and development of pricing policies for trade wastes that encourage the most cost effective methods of treating industrial wastes, whether at the source or at downstream plants, by 2006; and

(iv)   development of national guidelines for customers' water accounts that provide information on their water use relative to equivalent households in the community by 2006;

Rural and Regional

(v)   full cost recovery for all rural surface and groundwater based systems, recognising that there will be some small community services that will never be economically viable but need to be maintained to meet social and public health obligations:

    (a)   achievement of lower bound pricing for all rural systems in line with existing NCP commitments;

    (b)   continued movement towards upper bound pricing for all rural systems, where practicable; and

(c)   where full cost recovery is unlikely to be achieved in the long term and a Community Service Obligation (CSO) is deemed necessary, the size of the subsidy is to be reported publicly and, where practicable, jurisdictions to consider alternative management arrangements aimed at removing the need for an ongoing CSO.

Cost recovery for planning and management

67.   The States and Territories agree to bring into effect consistent approaches to pricing and attributing costs of water planning and management by 2006, involving:

(i)   the identification of all costs associated with water planning and management, including the costs of underpinning water markets such as the provision of registers, accounting and measurement frameworks and performance monitoring and benchmarking;

(ii)   the identification of the proportion of costs that can be attributed to water access entitlement holders consistent with the principles below:

    (a)   charges exclude activities undertaken for the Government (such as policy development, and Ministerial or Parliamentary services); and

    (b)   charges are linked as closely as possible to the costs of activities or products.

68.   The States and Territories agree to report publicly on cost recovery for water planning and management as part of annual reporting requirements, including:

(i)   the total cost of water planning and management; and

(ii)   the proportion of the total cost of water planning and management attributed to water access entitlement holders and the basis upon which this proportion is determined.

Investment in new or refurbished infrastructure

69.   The Parties agree to ensure that proposals for investment in new or refurbished water infrastructure continue to be assessed as economically viable and ecologically sustainable prior to the investment occurring (noting paragraph 66 (v)).

Release of unallocated water

70.   Release of unallocated water will be a matter for States and Territories to determine. Any release of unallocated water should be managed in the context of encouraging the sustainable and efficient use of scarce water resources.

71.   If a release is justified, generally, it should occur only where alternative ways of meeting water demands, such as through water trading, making use of the unused parts of existing entitlements or by increasing water use efficiency, have been fully explored.

72.   To the extent practicable, releases should occur through market-based mechanisms.

Environmental externalities

73.   The States and Territories agree to:

(i)   continue to manage environmental externalities through a range of regulatory measures (such as through setting extraction limits in water management plans and by specifying the conditions for the use of water in water use licences);

(ii)   continue to examine the feasibility of using market based mechanisms such as pricing to account for positive and negative environmental externalities associated with water use; and

(iii) implement pricing that includes externalities where found to be feasible.

Institutional reform

74. The Parties agree that as far as possible, the roles of water resource management, standard setting and regulatory enforcement and service provision continue to be separated institutionally.

Benchmarking efficient performance

75. The States and Territories will be required to report independently, publicly, and on an annual basis, benchmarking of pricing and service quality for metropolitan, nonmetropolitan and rural water delivery agencies. Such reports will be made on the basis of a nationally consistent framework to be developed by the Parties by 2005, taking account of existing information collection including:

(i) the major metropolitan inter-agency performance and benchmarking system managed by the Water Services Association of Australia;

(ii) the non-major metropolitan inter-agency performance and bench-marking system managed by the Australian Water Association; and

(iii) the irrigation industry performance monitoring and benchmarking system, currently being managed by the Australian National Committee on Irrigation and Drainage.

76. Costs of operating the above performance and benchmarking systems are to be met by jurisdictions through recovery of water management costs.

Independent pricing regulator

77. The Parties agree to use independent bodies to:

(i) set or review prices, or price setting processes, for water storage and delivery by government water service providers, on a case-by-case basis, consistent with the principles in paragraphs 65 to 68 above; and

(ii) publicly review and report on pricing in government and private water service providers to ensure that the principles in paragraphs 65 to 68 above are met.

Integrated management of environmental water

Outcome

78. The Parties agree that the outcome for integrated management of environmental water is to identify within water resource planning frameworks the environmental and other public benefit outcomes sought for water systems and to develop and implement management practices and institutional arrangements that will achieve those outcomes by:

(i)   identifying the desired environmental and other public benefit outcomes with as much specificity as possible;

(ii) establishing and equipping accountable environmental water managers with the necessary authority and resources to provide sufficient water at the right times and places to achieve the environmental and other public benefit outcomes, including across State/Territory boundaries where relevant; and

(iii) optimising the cost effectiveness of measures to provide water for these outcomes.

Actions

79. Recognising the different types of surface water and groundwater systems, in particular the varying nature and intensity of resource use, and recognising the requirements to identify *environmental and other public benefit outcomes* in water plans, and describe the water management arrangements necessary to meet those outcomes (paragraph 35.ii) refers), the States and Territories agree to:

(i)   establish effective and efficient management and institutional arrangements to ensure the achievement of the *environmental and other public benefit outcomes*, including:

(a) environmental water managers that are accountable for the management of environmental water provisions and the achievement of *environmental and other public benefit outcomes*;

(b)   joint arrangements where resources are shared between jurisdictions;

(c)   common arrangements in the case of significantly inter-connected groundwater and surface water systems;

(d)   periodic independent audit, review and public reporting of the achievement of *environmental and other public benefit outcomes* and the adequacy of the water provision and management arrangements in achieving those outcomes;

(e)   the ability for environmental water managers to trade water on temporary markets at times such water is not required to contribute towards *environmental and other public benefit outcomes* (consistent with paragraph 35(iii));

(f)   any special requirements needed for the environmental values and water management arrangements necessary to sustain high conservation value rivers, reaches and groundwater areas;

(ii)   where it is necessary to recover water to achieve modified *environmental and other public benefit outcomes*, to adopt the following principles for determining the most effective and efficient mix of water recovery measures:

(a)   consideration of all available options for water recovery, including:

-       investment in more efficient water infrastructure;

-       purchase of water on the market, by tender or other market based mechanisms;

-       investment in more efficient water management practices, including measurement; or

-       investment in behavioural change to reduce urban water consumption;

(b)   assessment of the socio-economic costs and benefits of the most prospective options, including on downstream users, and the implications for wider natural resource management outcomes (eg. impacts on water quality or salinity); and

(c)   selection of measures primarily on the basis of cost-effectiveness, and with a view to managing socio-economic impacts.

Water resource accounting

Outcome

80.   The Parties agree that the outcome of water resource accounting is to ensure that adequate measurement, monitoring and reporting systems are in place in all jurisdictions, to support public and investor confidence in the amount of water being traded, extracted for consumptive use, and recovered and managed for *environmental and other public benefit outcomes.*

Actions

Benchmarking of accounting systems

81.   Recognising that a national framework for comparison of water accounting systems can encourage continuous improvement leading to adoption of best practice, the Parties agree to benchmark jurisdictional water accounting systems on a national scale by June 2005, including:

(i)   state based water entitlement registering systems;

(ii)   water service provider water accounting systems;

(iii)   water service provider water use/delivery efficiency; and

(iv)   jurisdictional/system water and related data bases.

Consolidated water accounts

82.   Recognising that robust water accounting will protect the integrity of the access entitlement system, the Parties agree to develop and implement by 2006:

(i)   accounting system standards, particularly where jurisdictions share the resources of river systems and where water markets are operating;

(ii)   standardised reporting formats to enable ready comparison of water use, compliance against entitlements and trading information;

(iii)   water resource accounts that can be reconciled annually and aggregated to produce a national water balance, including:

     (a)   a water balance covering all significant water use, for all managed water resource systems;

     (b)   systems to integrate the accounting of groundwater and surface water use where close interaction between groundwater aquifers and streamflow exist; and

     (c)   consideration of land use change, climate change and other externalities as elements of the water balance.

83.   States and Territories agree to identify by end 2005 situations where close interaction between groundwater aquifers and streamflow exist and implement by 2008 systems to integrate the accounting of groundwater and surface water use.

Environmental water accounting

84.   The Parties agree that principles for environmental water accounting will be developed and applied in the context of consolidated water accounts in paragraph 82.

85.   The Parties further agree to develop by mid 2005 and apply by mid 2006:

(i)   a compatible register of new and existing environmental water (consistent with paragraph 35) showing all relevant details of source, location, volume, security, use, environmental outcomes sought and type; and

(ii)   annual reporting arrangements to include reporting on the environmental water rules, whether or not they were activated in a particular year, the extent to which rules were implemented and the overall effectiveness of the use of resources in the context of the environmental and other public benefit outcomes sought and achieved.

Information

86. States and Territories agree to:

(i)   improve the coordination of data collection and management systems to facilitate better sharing of this information;

(ii)   develop partnerships in data collection and storage; and

(iii) identify best practice in data management systems for broad adoption.

Metering and measuring

87. The Parties agree that generally metering should be undertaken on a consistent basis in the following circumstances:

(i)   for categories of entitlements identified in a water planning process as requiring metering;

(ii)   where water access entitlements are traded;

(iii) in an area where there are disputes over the sharing of available water;

(iv)   where new entitlements are issued; or

(v)   where there is a community demand.

88. Recognising that information available from metering needs to be practical, credible and reliable, the Parties agree to develop by 2006 and apply by 2007:

(i)   a national meter specification;

(ii)   national meter standards specifying the installation of meters in conjunction with the meter specification; and

(iii)   national standards for ancillary data collection systems associated with meters.

Reporting

89.   The Parties agree to develop by mid 2005 and apply national guidelines by 2007 covering the application, scale, detail and frequency for open reporting addressing:

(i)   metered water use and associated compliance and enforcement actions;

(ii)   trade outcomes;

(iii)   environmental water releases and management actions; and

(iv)   availability of water access entitlements against the rules for availability and use.

Urban water reform

Outcome

90.   The Parties agree that the outcome for urban water reform is to:

(i)   provide healthy, safe and reliable water supplies;

(ii)   increase water use efficiency in domestic and commercial settings;

(iii)   encourage the re-use and recycling of wastewater where cost effective;

(iv)   facilitate water trading between and within the urban and rural sectors;

(v)   encourage innovation in water supply sourcing, treatment, storage and discharge; and

(vi)   achieve improved pricing for metropolitan water (consistent with paragraph 66.i) to 66.iv)).

Actions

Demand management

91. States and Territories agree to undertake the following actions in regard to demand management by 2006:

(i) legislation to implement the Water Efficiency Labelling Scheme (WELS) to be in place in all jurisdictions and regulator undertaking compliance activity by 2005, including mandatory labelling and minimum standards for agreed appliances;

(ii) develop and implement a 'Smart Water Mark' for household gardens, including garden irrigation equipment, garden designs and plants;

(iii) review the effectiveness of temporary water restrictions and associated public education strategies, and assess the scope for extending low level restrictions as standard practice; and

(iv) prioritise and implement, where cost effective, management responses to water supply and discharge system losses including leakage, excess pressure, overflows and other maintenance needs.

Innovation and capacity building to create water sensitive Australian cities

92. The Parties agree to undertake the following actions in regard to innovation:

(i) develop national health and environmental guidelines for priority elements of water sensitive urban designs (initially recycled water and stormwater) by 2005;

(ii) develop national guidelines for evaluating options for water sensitive urban developments, both in new urban sub-divisions and high rise buildings by 2006;

(iii) evaluate existing "icon water sensitive urban developments" to identify gaps in knowledge and lessons for future strategically located developments by 2005;

(iv) review the institutional and regulatory models for achieving integrated urban water cycle planning and management, followed by preparation of best practice guidelines by 2006; and

(v) review of incentives to stimulate innovation by 2006.

<u>Community partnerships and adjustment</u>

<u>Outcome</u>

93. Parties agree that the outcome is to engage water users and other stakeholders in achieving the objectives of this Agreement by:

(i) improving certainty and building confidence in reform processes;

(ii) transparency in decision making; and

(iii) ensuring sound information is available to all sectors at key decision points.

94. Parties also agree to address adjustment issues raised by the implementation of this Agreement.

<u>Actions</u>

95. States and Territories agree to ensure open and timely consultation with all stakeholders in relation to:

(i) pathways for returning overdrawn surface and groundwater systems to environmentally sustainable extraction levels (paragraphs 41 to 45 refer);

(ii) the periodic review of water plans (paragraph 398 refers); and

(iii) other significant decisions that may affect the security of water access entitlements or the sustainability of water use.

96. States and Territories agree to provide accurate and timely information to all relevant stakeholders regarding:

(i) progress with the implementation of water plans, including the achievement of objectives and likely future trends regarding the size of the consumptive pool; and

(ii) other issues relevant to the security of water access entitlements and the sustainability of water use, including the science underpinning the identification and implementation of environmental and other public benefit outcomes.

97. The Parties agree to address significant adjustment issues affecting water access entitlement holders and communities that may arise from reductions in water availability as a result of implementing the reforms proposed in this Agreement.

(i) States and Territories will consult with affected water users, communities and associated industry on possible appropriate responses to address these impacts, taking into account factors including:

    (a) possible trade-offs between higher reliability and lower absolute amounts of water;

    (b) the fact that water users have benefited from using the resource in the past;

    (c) the scale of the changes sought and the speed with which they are to be implemented (including consideration of previous changes in water availability); and

    (d) the risk assignment framework referred to in paragraphs 46 to 51.

(ii) The Commonwealth Government commits itself to discussing with signatories to this Agreement assistance to affected regions on a case by case basis (including set up costs), noting that it reserves the right to initiate projects on its own behalf.

<u>Knowledge and capacity building</u>

98. This Agreement identifies a number of areas where there are significant knowledge and capacity building needs for its ongoing

implementation. These include: regional water accounts and assessment of availability through time and across catchments; changes to water availability from climate and land use change; interaction between surface and groundwater components of the water cycle; demonstrating ecological outcomes from environmental flow management; improvements in farm, irrigation system and catchment water use efficiency; catchment processes that impact on water quality; improvements in urban water use efficiency; and independent reviews of the knowledge base.

99. There are significant national investments in knowledge and capacity building in water, including through the Cooperative Research programme, CSIRO Water Flagship and Land and Water Australia, State agencies, local government and higher education institutions. Scientific, technical and social aspects of water management are multidisciplinary and extend beyond the capacity of any single research institution.

Outcome

100. Parties agree that the outcome of knowledge and capacity building will assist in underpinning implementation of this Agreement.

Actions

101. Parties agree to:

(i) identify the key knowledge and capacity building priorities needed to support ongoing implementation of this Agreement; and

(ii) identify and implement proposals to more effectively coordinate the national water knowledge effort.

Variation

102. This Agreement may be amended at the request of one of the Parties, subject to the agreement of all the Parties.

103. All Parties agree to notify and consult each other on matters that come to their attention that may improve the operation of the Agreement.

Monitoring and review

104. The Natural Resource Management Ministerial Council (NRMMC) will:

(i)   commencing in 2005 provide annual reports to COAG on progress with the actions being taken by jurisdictions in implementing this Agreement; and

(ii)   in consultation with the National Water Commission (NWC), develop by mid 2005, a comprehensive national set of performance indicators for this Agreement. The indicators should, where possible, draw on existing indicators and include initialisation of water access entitlements, environmental water, water use efficiency, water pricing and water trading.

105. The NWC will:

(i)   undertake a baseline assessment of the water resource and governance arrangements, based on existing work by the Parties and undertaking further work only where required;

(ii)   accredit implementation plans to be developed by each jurisdiction, in accordance with paragraph 9, by mid-2005;

(iii) assess the implementation plans towards achieving the objectives and outcomes of this Agreement within agreed timeframes on the basis of its baseline assessment above and jurisdictions' self assessment of their respective implementation plans;

(iv)   report to COAG on accreditation of the implementation plans by 2006; and

(v)   report to the Commonwealth Government on compliance with any outstanding commitments under the 1994 COAG framework.

106. The NWC will, commencing in 2006-07, undertake:

(a)   biennial assessments of progress with the NWI Agreement and State and Territory implementation plans, and advice on actions required to better realise the objectives and outcomes of the Agreement;

(b)   a third biennial assessment in 2010-11 in the form of a comprehensive review of the Agreement against the indicators developed by the NRMMC referred to in paragraph 104(ii) above, and an assessment of the extent to which actions undertaken in this Agreement contribute to the national interest and the impacts of implementing this Agreement on regional, rural and urban communities; and

(c)   biennial assessments of the performance of the water industry against national benchmarks, in areas such as irrigation efficiency, water management costs and water pricing.

107.   The NWC reports to COAG will be publicly available.

108.   Drawing on the NWC assessment in 2010-11, COAG will review the objectives and operation of the NWC in 2011.

...

Schedule A - Timeline for implementation of key actions

Key Actions	Date	IGA Paragraphs	Responsibility
Implementation			
▪ Establish a National Water Commission	end 2004	10	All Parties
▪ Jurisdictions to develop implementation plans	June 2005	8	States[1]
▪ Substantial progress towards implementation of this Agreement	2010	8	All Parties
Water access entitlements and planning framework			
▪ Implementation of the framework:			
– substantial completion of plans to address any existing overallocation for all river systems and groundwater resources in accordance with commitments under the 1994 COAG water reform framework	end 2005	26(i)	States
– Legislative and administrative regimes amended to incorporate the elements of the entitlements and allocation framework in this Agreement	end 2006	26(ii)	States
▪ Water access entitlements to be defined and implemented	immediate	28-34	States
▪ Water to meet environmental and other public benefit outcomes identified in water plans to be defined, provided and managed.	immediate	35	States

[1] For purposes of this Schedule "States" is an abbreviation for "States and Territories".

Key Actions	Date	IGA Paragraphs	Responsibility
▪ Water plans to be prepared along the lines of the characteristics and components at Schedule D based on the following priorities:			
– plans for systems that are overallocated, fully allocated or approaching full allocation;	end 2007	39-40	States
– plans for systems that are not yet approaching full allocation	end 2009	39-40	States
▪ Substantially complete addressing overallocation as per NCC commitments.	2005	41	States
▪ substantial progress toward adjusting all *overallocated* and/or *overused* systems	end 2010	43-45	All Parties
▪ Risk assignment framework to be implemented immediately for all changes in allocation not provided for in overallocation pathways in water plans	immediate	46-50	States
▪ Water plans to address indigenous water issues	immediate	52-54	States
▪ Implementation of measures to address water interception by land use change activities on a priority basis in accordance with water plans	no later than 2011	55-57	States

Key Actions	Date	IGA Paragraphs	Responsibility
Water markets and trading			
▪ Adoption of publicly accessible, compatible systems for registering water access entitlements and trades consistent with Schedule F:			
– pathways leading to full implementation; and	end 2004	59	States
– full implementation	end 2006	59	States
▪ Establish compatible institutional and regulatory arrangements that facilitate trade, including arrangements consistent with principles in Schedule G	end 2007	60	States
– re institutional barriers to trade			
– remove barriers to temporary trade	immediate	60(iv)(a)	States
– remove barriers to permanent trade up to an annual threshold of 4 percent	immediate (except for southern MDB)	60(iv)(b)	States
– review impact on trade of interim threshold	2009	60(iv)(b)	States
– full removal of barriers to trade	end 2014		
▪ Complete the following studies and consider implementation of any recommendations:			
– review of water products	June 2005	61(i)	All Parties
– new approach to sharing delivery capacity and extraction rates among users	June 2005	61(ii)	All Parties

Key Actions	Date	IGA Paragraphs	Responsibility
– feasibility of establishing market mechanisms such as tradeable salinity and pollution credits to provide incentives for investment in water-use efficiency and farm management strategies and for dealing with environmental externalities	June 2005	61(iii)	All Parties
▪ Relevant Parties (Commonwealth, NSW, Victoria and SA) agree to:			
– take necessary steps to enable the use of exchange rates and/ or tagging for interstate trade;	June 2005	63(i)	relevant Parties
– reduce barriers to trade in southern MDB and establish an interim limit on permanent trade out of water irrigation areas of 4 percent per annum	June 2005	63(ii)	relevant Parties
– NSW make legislative changes to remove barriers and permit increased trade up to the interim limit;	June 2005	63(ii)(a)	NSW
– Vic and SA make change to remove barriers and permit increased trade up to the interim limit	June 2005	63(ii)(b)	Victoria and SA
– review actions to assess whether relevant parties have removed barriers to achieve interim limit	June 2005	63(iii)	relevant Parties
– study into mechanisms necessary to enable interstate trade	June 2005	63(iv)	relevant Parties

Key Actions	Date	IGA Paragraphs	Responsibility
– review outcome of actions by NSW	end 2007	63(v)	relevant Parties
– NWC monitor impacts of interstate trade	ongoing	63(vi)	NWC
– review the impact on trade under the interim threshold.	end 2009	63(vii)	relevant Parties
Best practice water pricing and institutional arrangements			
▪ Complete commitments under the 1994 COAG Water Reform Framework to bring into effect pricing policies for water storage and delivery in rural and urban systems	end 2004	65	States
▪ *Metropolitan*			
– Continued movement towards *upper bound pricing*;	end 2008	66(i)	States
– development of pricing policies for recycled water and stormwater;	end 2006	66(ii)	States
– review and development of pricing policies for trade wastes; and	end 2006	66(iii)	States
– development of national guidelines for water accounts.	end 2006	66(iv)	States
▪ *Rural and Regional*			
– full cost recovery for all rural surface and groundwater based systems:			
– continued movement towards *lower bound pricing* per NCC commitments; and	ongoing	66(v)(a)	States

Key Actions	Date	IGA Paragraphs	Responsibility
– achievement of *upper bound pricing* for all rural systems, where practicable.	ongoing	66(v)(b)	States
▪ Consistent approaches to pricing and attributing costs of water planning and management	end 2006	67	States
▪ Investment in new or refurbished water infrastructure to continue to be assessed as economically and ecologically sustainable before being approved	ongoing	69	States
▪ Release of unallocated water	ongoing	70-72	States
▪ Environmental externalities managed through a range of regulatory measures	ongoing	73	States
▪ *Benchmarking efficient performance* – independent, public, annual reporting of performance benchmarking for all metropolitan, non-metropolitan and rural water delivery agencies	ongoing	75	States
– develop nationally consistent report framework	2005	76	All Parties
▪ *Independent pricing regulator* – independent pricing bodies to set and review prices or pricing processes for water storage and delivery and publicly report.	ongoing	77	All Parties

Key Actions	Date	IGA Paragraphs	Responsibility
Integrated management of environmental water			
■ Recognising the different types of surface water and groundwater systems:			
– effective and efficient management and institutional arrangements to ensure the achievement of the environmental outcomes; and	immediate	79(i)	States
– where it is necessary to recover water to achieve environmental outcomes, to adopt the principles for determining the most effective and efficient mix of water recovery measures.	ongoing	79(ii)	States
Water resource accounting			
■ Benchmarking of accounting systems	mid 2005	81	All Parties
■ Consolidated water accounts			
– Develop and implement robust water accounting	end 2006	82	All Parties
– Identify situations where close interaction between surface and groundwater exist	end 2005	83	All Parties
– Implement systems to integrate the accounting of surface and groundwater	end 2008	83	All Parties
■ Environmental water accounting:			
– develop an environmental water register and annual reporting arrangements; and	mid 2005	85	All Parties

Key Actions	Date	IGA Paragraphs	Responsibility
– apply the environmental water register and annual reporting arrangements.	mid 2006	85	All Parties
▪ Implement information measures	ongoing	86	All Parties
▪ Metering and measuring actions:			
– develop metering and measuring actions; and	end 2006	88	All Parties
– implement metering and measuring actions.	end 2007	88	All Parties
▪ National guidelines on water reporting:			
– develop national guidelines on water reporting; and	mid 2005	89	All Parties
– apply national guidelines on water reporting.	end 2007	89	All Parties
Urban water reform			
▪ Implementation of demand management measures, including:			
– implementation and compliance monitoring of WELS, including mandatory labelling and minimum standards for agreed appliances;	end 2005	91(i)	States
– develop and implement 'Smart Water Mark' for garden activities;	end 2006	91(ii)	States
– review effectiveness of temporary water restricts and associated public education strategies, and consider extending low level restrictions to standard practice; and	end 2006	91(iii)	States

Key Actions	Date	IGA Paragraphs	Responsibility
– implement management responses to water supply and discharge system losses including leakage, excess pressure, overflows and other maintenance needs	end 2006	91(iv)	States
▪ Encourage further innovation in urban water use including:			
– develop and apply national health and environmental guidelines for water sensitive urban designs for recycled water and stormwater;	end 2005	92(i)	All Parties
– develop national guidelines for evaluating options for water sensitive urban developments in both new urban sub-divisions and high rise;	end 2006	92(ii)	All Parties
– evaluate existing water sensitive urban icon developments;	end 2005	92(iii)	All Parties
– review institutional and regulatory models for integrated urban water cycle planning and management and develop best practice guidelines;	end 2006	92(iv)	All Parties
– review incentives to stimulate innovation.	end 2006	92(v)	All Parties

Key Actions	Date	IGA Paragraphs	Responsibility
Community partnerships and adjustment			
Open and timely consultation with all relevant stakeholders in relation to: pathways for returning overallocated systems to sustainable extraction levels, periodic review of water plans, and other significant decisions affecting the security of water access entitlements.	ongoing	95	States
▪ Provision of accurate and timely information to all relevant stakeholders in relation to the progress of water plan implementation and other issues relevant to the security of water access entitlements.	ongoing	96	States
▪ Address significant adjustment issues affecting water access entitlement holders and communities that may arise from reductions in water availability as a result of implementing the National Water Initiative	ongoing	97	All Parties
Knowledge and capacity building			
▪ Identify the key science priorities to support implementation of the National Water Initiative and where this work is being undertaken.	ongoing	101(i)	All Parties
▪ Implement any necessary measures to ensure the research effort is well coordinated and publicised, and any gaps are addressed.	ongoing	101(ii)	All Parties

Schedule B(i) - Glossary of terms

The words and phrases that are italicised in this intergovernmental agreement are to be interpreted according to the definitions given below.

consumptive pool - the amount of water resource that can be made available for *consumptive use* in a given water system under the rules of the relevant water plan.

consumptive use - use of water for private benefit consumptive purposes including irrigation, industry, urban and stock and domestic use.

environmental and other public benefit outcomes - environmental and other public benefit outcomes are defined as part of the water planning process, are specified in water plans and may include a number of aspects, including:

-    *environmental outcomes*: maintaining ecosystem function (eg. through periodic inundation of floodplain wetlands); biodiversity, water quality; river health targets;

-    *other public benefits*: mitigating pollution, public health (eg. limiting noxious algal blooms), indigenous and cultural values, recreation, fisheries, tourism, navigation and amenity values.

environmental manager - an expertise based function with clearly identified responsibility for the management of environmental water so as to give effect to the environmental objectives of statutory water plans

-    the institutional form of the environmental manager will vary from place to place reflecting the scale at which the environmental objectives are set and the degree of active management of environmental water required

-    the environmental manager may be a separate body or an existing Basin, catchment or river manager provided that the function is assigned the necessary powers and resources, potential conflicts of interest are minimised, and lines of accountability are clear

environmentally sustainable level of extraction - the level of water extraction from a particular system which, if exceeded would compromise key environmental assets, or ecosystem functions and the productive base of the resource.

exchange rate - the rate of conversion calculated and agreed to be applied to water to be traded from one trading zone and/or jurisdiction to another.

extraction rate - the rate in terms of unit volume per unit time that water can be drawn from a surface or groundwater system. Used in the NWI in the context of a constraint that might exist due to the impact of exceeding a particular extraction rate at a particular point or within a specified system.

lower bound pricing - the level at which to be viable, a water business should recover, at least, the operational, maintenance and administrative costs, externalities, taxes or TERs (not including income tax), the interest cost on debt, dividends (if any) and make provision for future asset refurbishment/replacement. Dividends should be set at a level that reflects commercial realities and stimulates a competitive market outcome.

metropolitan - refers to water and wastewater services provided in metropolitan urban areas having in excess of 50,000 connections.

overallocation - refers to situations where with full development of water access entitlements in a particular system, the total volume of water able to be extracted by *entitlement holders* at a given time exceeds the *environmentally sustainable level of extraction* for that system.

overused - refers to situations where the total volume of water actually extracted for consumptive use in a particular system at a given time exceeds the *environmentally sustainable level of extraction* for that system. Overuse may arise in systems that are overallocated, or it may arise in systems where the planned allocation is exceeded due to inadequate monitoring and accounting.

regional natural resource management plans - plans that cover specific regions like those developed under the Natural Heritage Trust and the National Action Plan for Salinity and Water Quality.

reliability - the frequency with which water allocated under a *water access entitlement* is able to be supplied in full. Referred to in some jurisdictions as "high security" and "general security".

rural and regional - refers to water and wastewater services provided for rural irrigation and industrial users and in regional urban areas with less than 50,000 connections;

sharing delivery capacity - an approach to sharing of an irrigation supply channel capacity (supplemented systems) or a water course capacity (unsupplemented) held by an *entitlement holder* and specified as a percentage share or volumetric supply rate at a particular time.

surface water - water that flows over land and in water courses or artificial channels and is able to be captured and stored and supplemented from dams and reservoirs.

trading zones - zones established to simplify administration of a trade by setting out the known supply source or management arrangements and the physical realities of relevant supply systems within the zone. Trade can occur within and between zones without first having to investigate and establish the details and rules of the system in each zone.

upper bound pricing - the level at which, to avoid monopoly rents, a water business should not recover more than the operational, maintenance and administrative costs, externalities, taxes or tax equivalent regimes (TERs), provision for the cost of asset consumption and cost of capital, the latter being calculated using a weighted average cost of capital WACC.

water access entitlement - a perpetual or ongoing entitlement to exclusive access to a share of water from a specified *consumptive pool* as defined in the relevant *water plan*.

water allocation - the specific volume of water allocated to water access entitlements in a given season, defined according to rules established in the relevant water plan.

water irrigation area - the area under control of an individual water service provider (eg. An irrigation corporation, cooperative or trust, or water authority).

water plan - statutory plans for surface and/or ground *water systems*, consistent with the *Regional Natural Resource Management Plans,* developed in consultation with all relevant stakeholders on the basis of best scientific and socio-economic assessment, to provide secure ecological outcomes and resource security for users.

water sensitive urban design - the integration of urban planning with the management, protection and conservation of the urban water cycle, that ensures urban water management is sensitive to natural hydrological and ecological processes.

water system - a system that is hydrologically connected and described at the level desired for management purposes (eg sub-catchment, catchment, basin or drainage division and/or groundwater management unit, sub-aquifer, aquifer, groundwater basin).

water tagging - an accounting approach that allows a traded *water access entitlement* to retain its original characteristics when traded to a new jurisdiction and/or trading zone, rather than being converted into a form issued in the new jurisdiction and/or trading zone.

Schedule B (ii) - National definitions

Recognising the importance of a common lexicon for water use and management, the Parties recognise the desirability of adopting the following words and phrases, and their definitions, in their respective water management frameworks:

environmental and other public benefit outcomes - environmental and other public benefit outcomes are agreed as part of the water planning process, are specified in water plans and may include a number of aspects, including:

-   *environmental outcomes:* maintaining ecosystem function (eg. through periodic inundation of floodplain wetlands); biodiversity, water quality; river health targets;

-   *other public benefits:* mitigating pollution, public health (eg. limiting noxious algal blooms), indigenous and cultural values, recreation, fisheries, tourism, navigation and amenity values.

overallocation - refers to situations where with full development of water access entitlements in a particular system, the total volume of water able to be extracted by *entitlement holders* at a given time exceeds the *environmentally sustainable level of extraction* for that system.

overused - refers to situations where the total volume of water actually extracted for consumptive use in a particular system at a given time exceeds the *environmentally sustainable level of extraction* for that system. Overuse may arise in systems that are overallocated, or it may arise in systems where the planned allocation is exceeded due to inadequate monitoring and accounting.

reliability - the frequency with which water allocated under a *water access entitlement* is able to be supplied in full. Referred to in some jurisdictions as "high security" and "general security".

water access entitlement - a perpetual or ongoing entitlement to exclusive access to a share of water from a specified consumptive pool as defined in the relevant water plan.

water allocation - the specific volume of water allocated to water access entitlements in a given season, defined according to rules established in the relevant water plan.

Schedule C - National Water Commission

The National Water Commission (NWC) will be established as follows.

Institutional Arrangements:

The NWC will:

- be established by the Commonwealth as an independent statutory body;

- have the functions and responsibilities as set out below;

- be funded by the Commonwealth Government;

- have up to seven members including a Chair:

    - appointed for up to 3 years and eligible for re-appointment subject to agreement;

    - with expertise in the areas of: audit and evaluation, governance, resource economics, water resource management, freshwater ecology and hydrology; and

- with the Commonwealth to appoint four members (including the Chair) and States and Territories to appoint three members; and

- have an office to carry out secretariat services for the Commission and to prepare or manage the preparation of draft Commission reports as directed, including:

  - an Executive Director and a small staff appointed by the Commission at its discretion;

  - the ability to make use of staff employed by a Party with the agreement of the relevant Party; and

  - the ability to use consultants.

Role:

To provide advice on national water issues and, in particular, to assist with the effective implementation of the National Water Initiative (NWI) Agreement.

In particular, the NWC will provide advice to COAG on the following matters:

- a baseline assessment of water resources and governance arrangements nationally, based on existing work by the Parties and undertaking further work only where required;

- accreditation of State and Territory implementation plans developed for the NWI Agreement by each jurisdiction, in accordance with paragraph 9 of the Agreement;

- commencing in 2006-07, biennial assessments of progress with the NWI Agreement and State and Territory implementation plans, and advice on actions required to better realise the objectives and outcomes of the Agreement:

  - the third biennial assessment in 2010-11 will take the form of a comprehensive review of the Agreement;

- the performance of the water industry against national benchmarks, in areas such as irrigation efficiency, water management costs and water pricing; and

- compliance with any outstanding commitments under the 1994 COAG strategic framework for the efficient and sustainable reform of the Australian water industry;

The Parties agree to work cooperatively with the NWC including through providing open access to relevant officers and timely provision of information necessary to assist the NWC in carrying out its role.

In preparing its advice, the NWC will consider the views of stakeholders.

The NWC will provide annual reports of its activities.

All reports of the NWC will be publicly available.

Review of the NWC:

In 2010-11, COAG will review the ongoing role and function of the NWC following consideration of its third biennial assessment. A report on the outcome of the review is to be tabled in each House of Parliament by the end of 2011.

Schedule D - Principles for regulatory approvals for water use and works

1.   The Parties agree that regulatory approvals enabling water use at a particular site for a particular purpose will:

(i)   be consistent with water legislation and related NRM and planning legislation;

(ii) be consistent with relevant water plans;

(iii) take into account environmental, social and economic impacts of use, including on downstream users;

(iv) clearly state the conditions relating to the approval, including the circumstances and processes relating to variations or terminations of the approval;

(v) minimise application and compliance costs for applicants;

(vi) allow for applications to be assessed to a level of detail commensurate with the level of potential impact of the proposed activity;

(vii) have transparent and contestable processes in place to establish whether a proposed activity is to be approved; and

(viii) have avenues for appealing approval decisions.

2. The Parties also agree that the authority responsible for regulatory approvals needs to:

(i) be separate from water users and providers;

(ii) have the necessary legal authority and resources to monitor and enforce the conditions of a water use or works licence; and

(iii) have its practices benchmarked periodically with peer authorities in other jurisdictions.

Schedule E - Guidelines for water plans and planning processess[sic]

1. The following characteristics and components will guide States and Territories in preparing water plans: Descriptions to include:

(i) the water source or water sources covered by the plan (ie. its geographic or physical extent);

(ii) the current health and condition of the system;

(iii) the risks that could affect the size of the water resource and the allocation of water for consumptive use under the plan, in particular the impact of natural events such as climate change and land use change, or limitations to the state of knowledge underpinning estimates of the resource;

(iv)   the overall objectives of water allocation policies;

(v)   the knowledge base upon which decisions about allocations and requirements for the environment are being made, and an indication of how this base is to be improved during the course of the plan;

(vi)   the uses and users of the water including consideration of indigenous water use;

(vii) the *environmental and other public benefit outcomes* proposed during the life of the plan, and the water management arrangements required to meet those outcomes;

(viii) the estimated *reliability* of the water access entitlement and rules on how the consumptive pool is to be dispersed between the different categories of entitlements within the plan;

(ix)   the rates, times and circumstances under which water may be taken from the water sources in the area, or the quantity of water that may be taken from the water sources in the area or delivered through the area; and

(x)   conditions to which entitlements and approvals having effect within the area covered by the plan are to be subject, including monitoring and reporting requirements, minimising impacts on third parties and the environment, and complying with site-use conditions.

2.   Where systems are found to be *overallocated* or *overused*, the relevant plan should set out a pathway to correct the *overallocation* or *overuse* (paragraphs 41 to 45 refers).

3.   A plan duration should be consistent with the level of knowledge and development of the particular water source; and

4.   In the case of ongoing plans, there should be a review process that allows for changes to be made in light of improved knowledge.

5.   Further consideration to *include*:

(i)   relevant regional natural resource management plans and cross jurisdictional plans, where applicable;

(ii)   an assessment of the level of connectivity between surface (including overland flow) and groundwater systems

(iii) impacts on water users and the environment that the plan may have downstream (including estuaries) or out of its area of coverage, within or across jurisdictions;

(iv)   water interception activities as indicated in paragraphs 52-54;

6.   Water planning processes include:

(i)   consultation with stakeholders including those within or downstream of the plan area;

(ii)   the application of the best available scientific knowledge and, consistent with the level of knowledge and resource use, socio-economic analyses;

(iii) adequate opportunity for consumptive use, environmental, cultural, and other public benefit issues to be identified and considered in an open and transparent way;

(iv)   reference to broader regional natural resource management planning processes; and

(v)   consideration of, and synchronisation with, cross-jurisdictional water planning cycles.

Schedule F - Guidelines for water registries

The Parties agree that water registers will be established in each State and Territory and will:

1.   contain records of all water access entitlements in that jurisdiction, and trades of those entitlements, including their location;

2.   be of sufficient standard to achieve the characteristics of secure water access entitlements contained in the Agreement;

3.   contain protocols for the protection of third party interests that:

(i)   require the holder of a registered security interest to be notified prior to any proposed dealings in relation to the water entitlement, and requiring the consent of such interests to any proposed transfers;

(ii)   allow only authorised dealings;

(iii)   require the registration of permanent transfers of the water entitlement and encumbrances that affect the entitlement, such as mortgages and other security interests;

(iv)   enable lenders to procure the registration of their interest independently of the holder of the entitlement (to ensure the rights of the entitlement-holder are sufficiently protected);

(v)   prioritise competing dealings;

(vi)   manage time lags between date of lodgement for registration and actual registration of dealings, as such time lags may affect priorities; and

(vii)   allow for the discharge of the security interest, in conjunction with the transfer of the entitlement to a new registered holder;

(viii) ensure that lenders are only affected by a subsequently registered interest where the lender has consented to the subsequent dealing;

(ix)   assist in the process of identifying water specific or unregistered interests.

4.   be administered pursuant to certain procedures and protocols, based on land title office manuals and guidelines that exist in various States and Territories that seek to minimise transaction costs for market participants;

5.   be publicly accessible, preferably over the internet, and include information such as the prices of trades and the identity of entitlement holders; and

6.   enable resource managers to monitor and accumulate trade and water use volumes accrued under water entitlements in a separate water accounting system.

Schedule G - Principles for trading rules

The Parties agree that water trading rules will be established consistent with the principles below.

1.   Water access entitlements may be traded either permanently, through lease arrangements or through other trading options that may evolve over time where water systems are physically shared or hydrologic connections and water supply considerations would permit water trading.

2.   All trades should be recorded on a water register (Schedule E refers).

3.   Restrictions on extraction, diversion or use of water resulting from a trade can only be used to manage:

(i)   environmental impacts, including impacts on ecosystems that depend on underground water;

(ii)   hydrological, water quality and hydrogeological impacts;

(iii)   delivery constraints;

(iv)   impacts on geographical features (such as river and aquifer integrity); or

(v)   features of major indigenous, cultural heritage or spiritual significance.

4.   A trade may be refused on the basis that it is inconsistent with the relevant water plan.

5.   Trades must not generally result in sustainable yields being exceeded. That is, trades shall generally not cause an increase in commitments to take water from water sources or parts of water sources or increase seasonal reversals in flow regimes above sustainable levels identified in relevant water plans such that environmental water or water dependent ecosystems are adversely affected;

6.   Trades within overallocated water sources (including groundwater sources) may be permitted in some cases subject to conditions to manage long-term impacts on the environment and other users;

7.   Where necessary, water authorities will facilitate trade by specifying trading zones and providing related information such as the exchange rates to be applied to trades in water allocations to:

(i)   adjust for the effects of the transfer on hydrology or supply security (transmission losses) or reliability; and

(ii)   reflect transfers between different classes of water sources, unregulated streams, regulated streams, supplemented streams, groundwater systems and licensed runoff harvesting dams.

8.   Water trading zones, including groundwater trading zones, should be defined in terms of the ability to change the point of extraction of the water from one place to another, and protection of the environment. The volume of delivery losses in supplemented systems that provide opportunistic environmental flows will be estimated and taken into account when determining the maximum volume of water that may be traded out of a trading zone.

9.   Exchange rates will not be used to achieve other outcomes such as to alter the balance between economic use and environmental protection or to reduce overall water use.

10.   Trade in water allocations may occur within common aquifers or surface water flow systems consistent with water plans.

11.   Trade from a licensed runoff harvesting dam (ie. not a small farm dam) to a river may occur subject to:

(i)   a reduction in dam capacity consistent with the transferred water entitlement;

(ii)   retention of sufficient capacity to accommodate evaporative and infiltration losses; or

(iii)   conditions specified in water plans to protect the environment.

V. OTHER LEGAL INSTRUMENTS

i. European Community Law

33. Council Directive 91/676/EEC Concerning the Protection of Waters Against Pollution Caused by Nitrates from Agricultural Sources [12 December 1991]*

The Council of the European Communities,

Having regard to the Treaty establishing the European Economic Community, and in particular Article 130 thereof,

...

Whereas the nitrate content of water in some areas of Member States is increasing and is already high as compared with standards laid down in Council Directive 75/440/EEC of 16 June 1975 concerning the quality required of surface water intended for the abstraction of drinking water in the Member States[4], as amended by Directive 79/869/EEC[5], and Council Directive 80/778/EEC of 15 July 1980 relating to the quality of water intended for human consumption[6], as amended by the 1985 Act of Accession;

Whereas the fourth programme of action of the European Economic Communities on the environment[7] indicated that the Commission intended to make a proposal for a Directive on the control and reduction of water pollution resulting from the spreading or discharge of livestock effluents and the excessive use of fertilizers;

Whereas the reform of the common agricultural policy set out in the Commission's green paper 'Perspectives for the common agricultural policy` indicated that, while the use of nitrogen-containing fertilizers and manures is

---

* Official Journal of the European Union L 375, 31.12.1991, p. 1.
[4] OJ N° L 194, 25. 7. 1975, p. 26.
[5] OJ N° L 271, 29. 10. 1979, p. 44.
[6] OJ N° L 229, 30. 8. 1980, p. 11.
[7] OJ N° C 328, 7. 12. 1987, p. 1.

necessary for Community agriculture, excessive use of fertilizers constitutes an environmental risk, that common action is needed to control the problem arising from intensive livestock production and that agricultural policy must take greater account of environmental policy;

...

Whereas the main cause of pollution from diffuse sources affecting the Community's waters in nitrates from agricultural sources;

Whereas it is therefore necessary, in order to protect human health and living resources and aquatic ecosystems and to safeguard other legitimate uses of water, to reduce water pollution caused or induced by nitrates from agricultural sources and to prevent further such pollution; whereas for this purpose it is important to take measures concerning the storage and the application on land of all nitrogen compounds and concerning certain land management practices;

Whereas since pollution of water due to nitrates on one Member State can influence waters in other Member States, action at Community level in accordance with Article 130r is therefore necessary;

Whereas, by encouraging good agricultural practices, Member States can provide all waters with a general level of protection against pollution in the future;

Whereas certain zones, draining into waters vulnerable to pollution from nitrogen compounds, require special protection;

Whereas it is necessary for Member States to identify vulnerable zones and to establish and implement action programmes in order to reduce water pollution from nitrogen compounds in vulnerable zones;

Whereas such action programmes should include measures to limit the land-application of all nitrogen-containing fertilizers and in particular to set specific limits for the application of livestock manure;

Whereas it is necessary to monitor waters and to apply reference methods of measurement for nitrogen compounds to ensure that measures are effective;

Whereas it is recognized that the hydrogeology in certain Member States is such that it may be many years before protection measures lead to improvements in water quality;

Whereas a Committee should be established to assist the Commission on matters relating to the implementation of this Directive and to its adaptation to scientific and technical progress;

Whereas Member States should establish and present to the Commission reports on the implementation of this Directive;

Whereas the Commission should report regularly on the implementation of this Directive by the Member States,

Has adopted this Directive:

<u>Article 1</u>

This Directive has the objective of:

-    reducing water pollution caused or induced by nitrates from agricultural sources and

-    preventing further such pollution.

<u>Article 2</u>

For the purpose of this Directive:

(a)   "groundwater": means all water which is below the surface of the ground in the saturation zone and in direct contact with the ground or subsoil;

(b)   "freshwater": means naturally occurring water having a low concentration of salts, which is often acceptable as suitable for abstraction and treatment to produce drinking water;

(c)   "nitrogen compound": means any nitrogen-containing substance except for gaseous molecular nitrogen;

(d)   "livestock": means all animals kept for use or profit;

(e)   "fertilizer": means any substance containing a nitrogen compound or nitrogen compounds utilized on land to enhance growth of vegetation; it may include livestock manure, the residues from fish farms and sewage sludge;

(f)   "chemical fertilizer": means any fertilizer which is manufactured by an industrial process;

(g)   "livestock manure": means waste products excreted by livestock or a mixture of litter and waste products excreted by livestock, even in processed form;

(h)   "land application": means the addition of materials to land whether by spreading on the surface of the land, injection into the land, placing below the surface of the land or mixing with the surface layers of the land;

(i)   "eutrophication": means the enrichment of water by nitrogen compounds, causing an accelerated growth of algae and higher forms of plant life to produce an undesirable disturbance to the balance of organisms present in the water and to the quality of the water concerned;

(j)   "pollution": means the discharge, directly or indirectly, of nitrogen compounds from agricultural sources into the aquatic environment, the results of which are such as to cause hazards to human health, harm to living resources and to aquatic ecosystems, damage to amenities or interference with other legitimate uses of water;

(k)   "vulnerable zone": means an area of land designated according to Article 3 (2).

Article 3

1.   Waters affected by pollution and waters which could be affected by pollution if action pursuant Article 5 is not taken shall be identified by the Member States in accordance with the criteria set out in Annex I.

2.   Member States shall, within a two-year period following the notification of this Directive, designate as vulnerable zones all known areas of land in their territories which drain into the waters identified

according to paragraph 1 and which contribute to pollution. They shall notify the Commission of this initial designation within six months.

3. When any waters identified by a Member State in accordance with paragraph 1 are affected by pollution from waters from another Member State draining directly or indirectly in to them, the Member States whose waters are affected may notify the other Member States and the Commission of the relevant facts.

The Member States concerned shall organize, where appropriate with the Commission, the concertation necessary to identify the sources in question and the measures to be taken to protect the waters that are affected in order to ensure conformity with this Directive.

4. Member States shall review if necessary revise or add to the designation of vulnerable zones as appropriate, and at last [sic] every four years, to take into account changes and factors unforeseen at the time of the previous designation. They shall notify the Commission of any revision or addition to the designations within six months.

5. Member States shall be exempt from the obligation to identify specific vulnerable zones, if they establish and apply action programmes referred to in Article 5 in accordance with this Directive throughout their national territory.

Article 4

1. With the aim of providing for all waters a general level of protection against pollution, Member States shall, within a two-year period following the notification of this Directive:

(a) establish a code or codes of good agricultural practice, to be implemented by farmers on a voluntary basis, which should contain provisions covering at least the items mentioned in Annex II A;

(b) set up where necessary a programme, including the provision of training and information for farmers, promoting the application of the code(s) of good agricultural practice.

2. Member States shall submit to the Commission details of their codes of good agricultural practice and the Commission shall include information on these codes in the report referred to in Article 11. In

the light of the information received, the Commission may, if it considers it necessary, make appropriate proposals to the Council.

Article 5

1.   Within a two-year period following the initial designation referred to in Article 3 (2) or within one year of each additional designation referred to in Article 3 (4), Member States shall, for the purpose of realizing the objectives specified in Article 1, establish action programmes in respect of designated vulnerable zones.

2.   An action programme may relate to all vulnerable zones in the territory of a Member State or, where the Member State considers it appropriate, different programmes may be established for different vulnerable zones or parts of zones.

3.   Action programmes shall take into account:

(a)   available scientific and technical data, mainly with reference to respective nitrogen contributions originating from agricultural and other sources;

(b)   environmental conditions in the relevant regions of the Member State concerned.

4.   Action programmes shall be implemented within four years of their establishment and shall consist of the following mandatory measures:

(a)   the measures in Annex III;

(b)   those measures which Member States have prescribed in the code(s) of good agricultural practice established in accordance with Article 4, except those which have been superseded by the measures in Annex III.

5.   Member States shall moreover take, in the framework of the action programmes, such additional measures or reinforced actions as they consider necessary if, at the outset or in the light of experience gained in implementing the action programmes, it becomes apparent that the measures referred to in paragraph 4 will not be sufficient for achieving the objectives specified in Article 1. In selecting these measures or

actions, Member States shall take into account their effectiveness and their cost relative to other possible preventive measures.

6. Member States shall draw up and implement suitable monitoring programmes to assess the effectiveness of action programmes established pursuant to this Article.

    Member States which apply Article 5 throughout their national territory shall monitor the nitrate content of waters (surface waters and groundwater) at selected measuring points which make it possible to establish the extent of nitrate pollution in the waters from agricultural sources.

7. Member States shall review and if necessary revise their action programmes, including any additional measures taken pursuant to paragraph 5, at least every four years. They shall inform the Commission of any changes to the action programmes.

Article 6

1. For the purpose of designating and revising the designation of vulnerable zones, Member States shall:

(a) within two years of notification of the Directive, monitor the nitrate concentration in freshwaters over a period of one year:

   (i) at surface water sampling stations, laid down in Article 5 (4) of Directive 75/440/EEC and/or at other sampling stations which are representative of surface waters of Member States, at least monthly and more frequently during flood periods;

   (ii) at sampling stations which are representative of the groundwater aquifers of Member States, at regular intervals and taking into account the provisions of Directive 80/778/EEC;

(b) repeat the monitoring programme outlined in (a) at least every four years, except for those sampling stations where the nitrate concentration in all previous samples has been below 25 mg/l and no new factor likely to increase the nitrate content has appeared, in which case the monitoring programme need be repeated only every eight years;

(c)   review the eutrophic state of their fresh surface waters, estuarial and coastal waters every four years.

2.   The reference methods of measurement set out in Annex IV shall be used.

Article 7

Guidelines for the monitoring referred to in Article 5 and 6 may be drawn up in accordance with the procedure laid down in Article 9.

Article 8

The Annexes to this Directive may be adapted to scientific and technical progress in accordance with the procedure laid down in Article 9.

Article 9

1.   The Commission shall be assisted by a Committee composed of the representative of the Member States and chaired by the representative of the Commission.

2.   The representative of the Commission shall submit to the Commission a draft of the measures to be taken. The Committee shall deliver its opinion on the draft within a time limit which the chairman may lay down according to the urgency of the matter. The opinion shall be delivered by the majority laid down in Article 148 (2) of the EEC Treaty in the case of decisions which the Council is required to adopt a proposal from the Commission. The votes of the representatives of the Member States within the Committee shall be weighted in the manner set out in that Article. The chairman shall not vote.

3.   (a)   The Commission shall adopt the measures envisaged if they are in accordance with the opinion of the Committee.

   (b)   If the measures envisaged are not in accordance with the opinion of the Committee, or if no opinion is delivered, the Commission shall, without delay, submit to the Council a proposal relating to the measures to be taken. The Council shall act by a qualified majority.

(c) If, on the expiry of a period of three months from the date of referral to the Council, the Council has not acted, the proposed measures shall be adopted by the Commission, save where the Council has decided against the said measures by a simple majority.

Article 10

1. Member States shall, in respect of the four-year period following the notification of this Directive and in respect of each subsequent four-year period, submit a report to the Commission containing the information outlined in Annex V.

2. A report pursuant to this Article shall be submitted to the Commission within six months of the end of the period to which it relates.

Article 11

On the basis of the information received pursuant to Article 10, the Commission shall publish summary reports within six months of receiving the reports from Member States and shall communicate them to the European Parliament and to the Council. In the light of the implementation of the Directive, and in particular the provisions of Annex III, the Commission shall submit to the Council by 1 January 1998 a report accompanied where appropriate by proposals for revision of this Directive.

Article 12

1. The Member States shall bring into force the laws, regulations and administrative provisions necessary to comply with this Directive within two years of its notification(1). They shall forthwith inform the Commission thereof.

...

Article 13

This Directive is addressed to the Member States.

---

(1) This Directive was notified to the Member States on 19 December 1991.

...

Annex I - Criteria for identifying waters referred to in Article 3 (1)

A.   Waters referred to in Article 3 (1) shall be identified making use, inter alia, of the following criteria:

1.   whether surface freshwaters, in particular those used or intended for the abstraction of drinking water, contain or could contain, if action pursuant to Article 5 is not taken, more than the concentration of nitrates laid down in accordance with Directive 75/440/EEC;

2.   whether groundwaters contain more than 50 mg/l nitrates or could contain more than 50 mg/l nitrates if action pursuant to Article 5 is not taken;

...

B.   In applying these criteria, Member States shall also take account of:

1.   the pyhsical [sic] and environmental characteristics of the waters and land;

2.   the current understanding of the behaviour of nitrogen compounds in the environment (water and soil);

3.   the current understanding of the impact of the action taken pursuant to Article 5.

Annex II - Code(s) of good agricultural practice

A.   A code or codes of good agricultural practice with the objective of reducing pollution by nitrates and taking account of conditions in the different regions of the Community should certain provisions covering the following items, in so far as they are relevant:

1.   periods when the land application of fertilizer is inappropriate;

2.   the land application of fertilizer to steeply sloping ground;

3.   the land application of fertilizer to water-saturated, flooded, frozen or snow-covered ground;

4.   the conditions for land application of fertilizer near water courses;

5.   the capacity and construction of storage vessels for livestock manures, including measures to prevent water pollution by run-off and seepage into the groundwater and surface water of liquids containing livestock manures and effluents from stored plant materials such as silage;

6.   procedures for the land application, including rate and uniformity of spreading, of both chemical fertilizer and livestock manure, that will maintain nutrient losses to water at an acceptable level.

B.   Member States may also include in their code(s) of good agricultural practices the following items:

1.   land use management, including the use of crop rotation systems and the proportion of the land area devoted to permanent crops relative to annual tillage crops;

2.   the maintenance of a minimum quantity of vegetation cover during (rainy) periods that will take up the nitrogen from the soil that could otherwise cause nitrate pollution of water;

3.   the establishment of fertilizer plans on a farm-by-farm basis and the keeping of records on fertilizer use;

4.   the prevention of water pollution from run-off and the downward water movement beyond the reach of crop roots in irrigation systems.

<u>Annex III - Measures to be included in action programmes as referred to in Article 5(4)(a)</u>

1.   The measures shall include rules relating to:

    1.   periods when the land application of certain types of fertilizer is prohibited;

    2.   the capacity of storage vessels for livestock manure; this capacity must exceed that required for storage throughout the

longest period during which land application in the vulnerable zone is prohibited, except where it can be demonstrated to the competent authority that any quantity of manure in excess of the actual storage capacity will be disposed of in a manner which will not cause harm to the environment;

3. limitation of the land application of fertilizers, consistent with good agricultural practice and taking into account the characteristics of the vulnerable zone concerned, in particular:

(a) soil conditions, soil type and slope;

(b) climatic conditions, rainfall and irrigation;

(c) land use and agricultural practices, including crop rotation systems;

and to be based on a balance between:

(i) the foreseeable nitrogen requirements of the crops, and

(ii) the nitrogen supply to the crops from the soil and from fertilization corresponding to:

- the amount of nitrogen present in the soil at the moment when the crop starts to use it to a significant degree (outstanding amounts at the end of winter),

- the supply of nitrogen through the net mineralization of the reserves of organic nitrogen in the soil,

- additions of nitrogen compounds from livestock manure,

- additions of nitrogen compounds from chemical and other fertilizers.

2. These measures will ensure that, for each farm or livestock unit, the amount of livestock manure applied to the land each year, including by

the animals themselves, shall not exceed a specified amount per hectare.

The specified amount per hectare be the amount of manure containing 170 kg N. However:

(a)   for the first four year action programme Member States may allow an amount of manure containing up to 210 kg N;

(b)   during and after the first four-year action programme, Member States may fix different amounts from those referred to above. These amounts must be fixed so as not to prejudice the achievement of the objectives specified in Article 1 and must be justified on the basis of objectives criteria, for example:

-   long growing seasons,

-   crops with high nitrogen uptake,

-   high net precipitation in the vulnerable zone,

-   soils with exceptionally high denitrification capacity.

If a Member State allows a different amount under subparagraph (b), it shall inform the Commission which will examine the justification in accordance with the procedure laid down in Article 9.

3.   Member States may calculate the amounts referred to in paragraph 2 on the basis of animal numbers.

4.   Member States shall inform the Commission of the manner in which they are applying the provisions of paragraph 2. In the light of the information received, the Commission may, if it considers necessary, make appropriate proposals to the Council in accordance with Article 1.

Annex IV - Reference methods of measurement

Chemical fertilizer

Nitrogen compounds shall be measured using the method described in Commission Directive 77/535/EEC of 22 June 1977 on the approximation of the laws of the Member States relating to methods of sampling and analysis for fertilizers[1], as amended by Directive 89/519/EEC[2].

Freshwaters, coastal waters and marine waters

Nitrate concentration shall be measured in accordance with Article 4 a (3) of Council Decision 77/795/EEC of 12 December 1977 establishing a common procedure for the exchange of information on the quality of surface fresh water in the Community[3], as amended by Decision 86/574/EEC[4].

Annex V - Information to be contained in reports to in Article 10

1.   A statement of the preventive action taken pursuant to Article 4.

2.   A map showing the following:

(a)   waters identified in accordance with Article 3 (1) and Annex I indicating for each water which of the criteria in Annex I was used for the purpose of identification;

(b)   the location of the designed vulnerable zones, distinguishing between existing zones and zones designated since the previous report.

3.   A summary of the monitoring results obtained pursuant to Article 6, including a statement of the considerations which led to the designation of each vulnerable zone and to any revision of or addition to designations of vulnerable zones.

4.   A summary of the action programmes drawn up pursuant to Article 5 and, in particular:

(a)   the measures required by Article 5(4)(a) and (b);

(b)   the information required by Annex III (4);

---

[1] OJ N° L 213, 22. 8. 1977, p. 1.
[2] OJ N° L 265, 12. 9. 1989, p. 30.
[3] OJ N° L 334, 24. 12. 1977, p. 29.
[4] OJ N° L 335, 28. 11. 1986, p. 44.

(c)   any additional measures or reinforced actions taken pursuant to Article 5(5);

(d)   a summary of the results of the monitoring programmes implemented pursuant to Article 5 (6);

(e)   the assumptions made by the Member States about the likely timescale within which the waters identified in accordance with Article 3 (1) are expected to respond to the measure in the action programme, along with an indication of the level of uncertainty incorporated in these assumptions.

34.   Directive 2000/60/EC of the European Parliament and of the Council of 23 October 2000 Establishing a Framework for Community Action in the Field of Water Policy [23 October 2000]*

The European Parliament and the Council of the European Union,

Having regard to the Treaty establishing the European Community, and in particular Article 175(1) thereof,

. . .

Whereas:

1.   Water is not a commercial product like any other but, rather, a heritage which must be protected, defended and treated as such.

. . .

11.   As set out in Article 174 of the Treaty, the Community policy on the environment is to contribute to pursuit of the objectives of preserving, protecting and improving the quality of the environment, in prudent and rational utilisation of natural resources, and to be based on the precautionary principle and on the principles that preventive action should be taken, environmental damage should, as a priority, be rectified at source and that the polluter should pay.

. . .

---

* Official Journal of the European Union L 327, 22.12.2000, p. 1.

16. Further integration of protection and sustainable management of water into other Community policy areas such as energy, transport, agriculture, fisheries, regional policy and tourism is necessary. This Directive should provide a basis for a continued dialogue and for the development of strategies towards a further integration of policy areas. This Directive can also make an important contribution to other areas of cooperation between Member States, inter alia, the European spatial development perspective (ESDP).

...

18. Community water policy requires a transparent, effective and coherent legislative framework. The Community should provide common principles and the overall framework for action. This Directive should provide for such a framework and coordinate and integrate, and, in a longer perspective, further develop the overall principles and structures for protection and sustainable use of water in the Community in accordance with the principles of subsidiarity.

19. This Directive aims at maintaining and improving the aquatic environment in the Community. This purpose is primarily concerned with the quality of the waters concerned. Control of quantity is an ancillary element in securing good water quality and therefore measures on quantity, serving the objective of ensuring good quality, should also be established.

20. The quantitative status of a body of groundwater may have an impact on the ecological quality of surface waters and terrestrial ecosystems associated with that groundwater body.

21. The Community and Member States are party to various international agreements containing important obligations on the protection of marine waters from pollution, in particular the Convention on the Protection of the Marine Environment of the Baltic Sea Area, signed in Helsinki on 9 April 1992 and approved by Council Decision 94/157/EC[11], the Convention for the Protection of the Marine Environment of the North-East Atlantic, signed in Paris on 22 September 1992 and approved by Council Decision 98/249/EC[12],

---

[11] OJ L 73, 16.3.1994, p. 19.
[12] OJ L 104, 3.4.1998, p. 1.

and the Convention for the Protection of the Mediterranean Sea Against Pollution, signed in Barcelona on 16 February 1976 and approved by Council Decision 77/585/EEC[13], and its Protocol for the Protection of the Mediterranean Sea Against Pollution from Land-Based Sources, signed in Athens on 17 May 1980 and approved by Council Decision 83/101/EEC[14]. This Directive is to make a contribution towards enabling the Community and Member States to meet those obligations.

22. This Directive is to contribute to the progressive reduction of emissions of hazardous substances to water.

23. Common principles are needed in order to coordinate Member States' efforts to improve the protection of Community waters in terms of quantity and quality, to promote sustainable water use, to contribute to the control of transboundary water problems, to protect aquatic ecosystems, and terrestrial ecosystems and wetlands directly depending on them, and to safeguard and develop the potential uses of Community waters.

24. Good water quality will contribute to securing the drinking water supply for the population.

25. Common definitions of the status of water in terms of quality and, where relevant for the purpose of the environmental protection, quantity should be established. Environmental objectives should be set to ensure that good status of surface water and groundwater is achieved throughout the Community and that deterioration in the status of waters is prevented at Community level.

26. Member States should aim to achieve the objective of at least good water status by defining and implementing the necessary measures within integrated programmes of measures, taking into account existing Community requirements. Where good water status already exists, it should be maintained. For groundwater, in addition to the requirements of good status, any significant and sustained upward trend in the concentration of any pollutant should be identified and reversed.

---

[13] OJ L 240, 19.9.1977, p 1.
[14] OJ L 67, 12.3.1983, p. 1.

27.   The ultimate aim of this Directive is to achieve the elimination of priority hazardous substances and contribute to achieving concentrations in the marine environment near background values for naturally occurring substances.

28.   Surface waters and groundwaters are in principle renewable natural resources; in particular, the task of ensuring good status of groundwater requires early action and stable long-term planning of protective measures, owing to the natural time lag in its formation and renewal. Such time lag for improvement should be taken into account in timetables when establishing measures for the achievement of good status of groundwater and reversing any significant and sustained upward trend in the concentration of any pollutant in groundwater.

29.   In aiming to achieve the objectives set out in this Directive, and in establishing a programme of measures to that end, Member States may phase implementation of the programme of measures in order to spread the costs of implementation.

30.   In order to ensure a full and consistent implementation of this Directive any extensions of timescale should be made on the basis of appropriate, evident and transparent criteria and be justified by the Member States in the river basin management plans.

31.   In cases where a body of water is so affected by human activity or its natural condition is such that it may be unfeasible or unreasonably expensive to achieve good status, less stringent environmental objectives may be set on the basis of appropriate, evident and transparent criteria, and all practicable steps should be taken to prevent any further deterioration of the status of waters.

32.   There may be grounds for exemptions from the requirement to prevent further deterioration or to achieve good status under specific conditions, if the failure is the result of unforeseen or exceptional circumstances, in particular floods and droughts, or, for reasons of overriding public interest, of new modifications to the physical characteristics of a surface water body or alterations to the level of bodies of groundwater, provided that all practicable steps are taken to mitigate the adverse impact on the status of the body of water.

33. The objective of achieving good water status should be pursued for each river basin, so that measures in respect of surface water and groundwaters belonging to the same ecological, hydrological and hydrogeological system are coordinated.

34. For the purposes of environmental protection there is a need for a greater integration of qualitative and quantitative aspects of both surface waters and groundwaters, taking into account the natural flow conditions of water within the hydrological cycle.

35. Within a river basin where use of water may have transboundary effects, the requirements for the achievement of the environmental objectives established under this Directive, and in particular all programmes of measures, should be coordinated for the whole of the river basin district. For river basins extending beyond the boundaries of the Community, Member States should endeavour to ensure the appropriate coordination with the relevant non-member States. This Directive is to contribute to the implementation of Community obligations under international conventions on water protection and management, notably the United Nations Convention on the protection and use of transboundary water courses and international lakes, approved by Council Decision 95/308/EC[15] and any succeeding agreements on its application.

36. It is necessary to undertake analyses of the characteristics of a river basin and the impacts of human activity as well as an economic analysis of water use. The development in water status should be monitored by Member States on a systematic and comparable basis throughout the Community. This information is necessary in order to provide a sound basis for Member States to develop programmes of measures aimed at achieving the objectives established under this Directive.

37. Member States should identify waters used for the abstraction of drinking water and ensure compliance with Council Directive 80/778/EEC of 15 July 1980 relating to the quality of water intended for human consumption[16].

---

[15] OJ L 186, 5.8.1995, p. 42.
[16] OJ L 229, 30.8.1980, p. 11. Directive as last amended by Directive 98/83/EC (OJ L 330, 5.12.1998, p. 32).

38.   The use of economic instruments by Member States may be appropriate as part of a programme of measures. The principle of recovery of the costs of water services, including environmental and resource costs associated with damage or negative impact on the aquatic environment should be taken into account in accordance with, in particular, the polluter-pays principle. An economic analysis of water services based on long-term forecasts of supply and demand for water in the river basin district will be necessary for this purpose.

39.   There is a need to prevent or reduce the impact of incidents in which water is accidentally polluted. Measures with the aim of doing so should be included in the programme of measures.

40.   With regard to pollution prevention and control, Community water policy should be based on a combined approach using control of pollution at source through the setting of emission limit values and of environmental quality standards.

41.   For water quantity, overall principles should be laid down for control on abstraction and impoundment in order to ensure the environmental sustainability of the affected water systems.

42.   Common environmental quality standards and emission limit values for certain groups or families of pollutants should be laid down as minimum requirements in Community legislation. Provisions for the adoption of such standards at Community level should be ensured.

43.   Pollution through the discharge, emission or loss of priority hazardous substances must cease or be phased out. The European Parliament and the Council should, on a proposal from the Commission, agree on the substances to be considered for action as a priority and on specific measures to be taken against pollution of water by those substances, taking into account all significant sources and identifying the cost-effective and proportionate level and combination of controls.

44.   In identifying priority hazardous substances, account should be taken of the precautionary principle, relying in particular on the determination of any potentially adverse effects of the product and on a scientific assessment of the risk.

45. Member States should adopt measures to eliminate pollution of surface water by the priority substances and progressively to reduce pollution by other substances which would otherwise prevent Member States from achieving the objectives for the bodies of surface water.

46. To ensure the participation of the general public including users of water in the establishment and updating of river basin management plans, it is necessary to provide proper information of planned measures and to report on progress with their implementation with a view to the involvement of the general public before final decisions on the necessary measures are adopted.

47. This Directive should provide mechanisms to address obstacles to progress in improving water status when these fall outside the scope of Community water legislation, with a view to developing appropriate Community strategies for overcoming them.

48. The Commission should present annually an updated plan for any initiatives which it intends to propose for the water sector.

49. Technical specifications should be laid down to ensure a coherent approach in the Community as part of this Directive. Criteria for evaluation of water status are an important step forward. Adaptation of certain technical elements to technical development and the standardisation of monitoring, sampling and analysis methods should be adopted by committee procedure. To promote a thorough understanding and consistent application of the criteria for characterisation of the river basin districts and evaluation of water status, the Commission may adopt guidelines on the application of these criteria.

50. The measures necessary for the implementation of this Directive should be adopted in accordance with Council Decision 1999/468/EC of 28 June 1999 laying down the procedures for the exercise of implementing powers conferred on the Commission[17].

51. The implementation of this Directive is to achieve a level of protection of waters at least equivalent to that provided in certain

---

[17] OJ C 184, 17.7.1999, p. 23.

earlier acts, which should therefore be repealed once the relevant provisions of this Directive have been fully implemented.

52. The provisions of this Directive take over the framework for control of pollution by dangerous substances established under Directive 76/464/EEC[18]. That Directive should therefore be repealed once the relevant provisions of this Directive have been fully implemented.

53. Full implementation and enforcement of existing environmental legislation for the protection of waters should be ensured. It is necessary to ensure the proper application of the provisions implementing this Directive throughout the Community by appropriate penalties provided for in Member States' legislation. Such penalties should be effective, proportionate and dissuasive,

Have adopted this Directive:

Article 1 - Purpose

The purpose of this Directive is to establish a framework for the protection of inland surface waters, transitional waters, coastal waters and groundwater which:

(a) prevents further deterioration and protects and enhances the status of aquatic ecosystems and, with regard to their water needs, terrestrial ecosystems and wetlands directly depending on the aquatic ecosystems;

(b) promotes sustainable water use based on a long-term protection of available water resources;

(c) aims at enhanced protection and improvement of the aquatic environment, inter alia, through specific measures for the progressive reduction of discharges, emissions and losses of priority substances and the cessation or phasing-out of discharges, emissions and losses of the priority hazardous substances;

---

[18] OJ L 129, 18.5.1976, p. 23. Directive as amended by Directive 91/692/EEC (OJ L 377, 31.12.1991, p. 48).

(d) ensures the progressive reduction of pollution of groundwater and prevents its further pollution, and

(e) contributes to mitigating the effects of floods and droughts and thereby contributes to:

- the provision of the sufficient supply of good quality surface water and groundwater as needed for sustainable, balanced and equitable water use,

- a significant reduction in pollution of groundwater,

- the protection of territorial and marine waters, and

- achieving the objectives of relevant international agreements, including those which aim to prevent and eliminate pollution of the marine environment, by Community action under Article 16(3) to cease or phase out discharges, emissions and losses of priority hazardous substances, with the ultimate aim of achieving concentrations in the marine environment near background values for naturally occurring substances and close to zero for man-made synthetic substances.

Article 2 - Definitions

For the purposes of this Directive the following definitions shall apply:

1. "Surface water" means inland waters, except groundwater; transitional waters and coastal waters, except in respect of chemical status for which it shall also include territorial waters.

2. "Groundwater" means all water which is below the surface of the ground in the saturation zone and in direct contact with the ground or subsoil.

3. "Inland water" means all standing or flowing water on the surface of the land, and all groundwater on the landward side of the baseline from which the breadth of territorial waters is measured.

4.   "River" means a body of inland water flowing for the most part on the surface of the land but which may flow underground for part of its course.

5.   "Lake" means a body of standing inland surface water.

6.   "Transitional waters" are bodies of surface water in the vicinity of river mouths which are partly saline in character as a result of their proximity to coastal waters but which are substantially influenced by freshwater flows.

7.   "Coastal water" means surface water on the landward side of a line, every point of which is at a distance of one nautical mile on the seaward side from the nearest point of the baseline from which the breadth of territorial waters is measured, extending where appropriate up to the outer limit of transitional waters.

...

9.   "Heavily modified water body" means a body of surface water which as a result of physical alterations by human activity is substantially changed in character, as designated by the Member State in accordance with the provisions of Annex II.

10.   "Body of surface water" means a discrete and significant element of surface water such as a lake, a reservoir, a stream, river or canal, part of a stream, river or canal, a transitional water or a stretch of coastal water.

11.   "Aquifer" means a subsurface layer or layers of rock or other geological strata of sufficient porosity and permeability to allow either a significant flow of groundwater or the abstraction of significant quantities of groundwater.

12.   "Body of groundwater" means a distinct volume of groundwater within an aquifer or aquifers.

13.   "River basin" means the area of land from which all surface run-off flows through a sequence of streams, rivers and, possibly, lakes into the sea at a single river mouth, estuary or delta.

14.　"Sub-basin" means the area of land from which all surface run-off flows through a series of streams, rivers and, possibly, lakes to a particular point in a water course (normally a lake or a river confluence).

15.　"River basin district" means the area of land and sea, made up of one or more neighbouring river basins together with their associated groundwaters and coastal waters, which is identified under Article 3(1) as the main unit for management of river basins.

16.　"Competent Authority" means an authority or authorities identified under Article 3(2) or 3(3).

17.　"Surface water status" is the general expression of the status of a body of surface water, determined by the poorer of its ecological status and its chemical status.

18.　"Good surface water status" means the status achieved by a surface water body when both its ecological status and its chemical status are at least "good".

19.　"Groundwater status" is the general expression of the status of a body of groundwater, determined by the poorer of its quantitative status and its chemical status.

20.　"Good groundwater status" means the status achieved by a groundwater body when both its quantitative status and its chemical status are at least "good".

21.　"Ecological status" is an expression of the quality of the structure and functioning of aquatic ecosystems associated with surface waters, classified in accordance with Annex V.

22.　"Good ecological status" is the status of a body of surface water, so classified in accordance with Annex V.

23.　"Good ecological potential" is the status of a heavily modified or an artificial body of water, so classified in accordance with the relevant provisions of Annex V.

24.   "Good surface water chemical status" means the chemical status required to meet the environmental objectives for surface waters established in Article 4(1)(a), that is the chemical status achieved by a body of surface water in which concentrations of pollutants do not exceed the environmental quality standards established in Annex IX and under Article 16(7), and under other relevant Community legislation setting environmental quality standards at Community level.

25.   "Good groundwater chemical status" is the chemical status of a body of groundwater, which meets all the conditions set out in table 2.3.2 of Annex V.

26.   "Quantitative status" is an expression of the degree to which a body of groundwater is affected by direct and indirect abstractions.

27.   "Available groundwater resource" means the long-term annual average rate of overall recharge of the body of groundwater less the long-term annual rate of flow required to achieve the ecological quality objectives for associated surface waters specified under Article 4, to avoid any significant diminution in the ecological status of such waters and to avoid any significant damage to associated terrestrial ecosystems.

28.   "Good quantitative status" is the status defined in table 2.1.2 of Annex V.

29.   "Hazardous substances" means substances or groups of substances that are toxic, persistent and liable to bio-accumulate, and other substances or groups of substances which give rise to an equivalent level of concern.

30.   "Priority substances" means substances identified in accordance with Article 16(2) and listed in Annex X. Among these substances there are "priority hazardous substances" which means substances identified in accordance with Article 16(3) and (6) for which measures have to be taken in accordance with Article 16(1) and (8).

31.   "Pollutant" means any substance liable to cause pollution, in particular those listed in Annex VIII.

32.   "Direct discharge to groundwater" means discharge of pollutants into groundwater without percolation throughout the soil or subsoil.

33. "Pollution" means the direct or indirect introduction, as a result of human activity, of substances or heat into the air, water or land which may be harmful to human health or the quality of aquatic ecosystems or terrestrial ecosystems directly depending on aquatic ecosystems, which result in damage to material property, or which impair or interfere with amenities and other legitimate uses of the environment.

34. "Environmental objectives" means the objectives set out in Article 4.

35. "Environmental quality standard" means the concentration of a particular pollutant or group of pollutants in water, sediment or biota which should not be exceeded in order to protect human health and the environment.

36. "Combined approach" means the control of discharges and emissions into surface waters according to the approach set out in Article 10.

37. "Water intended for human consumption" has the same meaning as under Directive 80/778/EEC, as amended by Directive 98/83/EC.

38. "Water services" means all services which provide, for households, public institutions or any economic activity:

(a) abstraction, impoundment, storage, treatment and distribution of surface water or groundwater,

(b) waste-water collection and treatment facilities which subsequently discharge into surface water.

39. "Water use" means water services together with any other activity identified under Article 5 and Annex II having a significant impact on the status of water. This concept applies for the purposes of Article 1 and of the economic analysis carried out according to Article 5 and Annex III, point (b).

40. "Emission limit values" means the mass, expressed in terms of certain specific parameters, concentration and/or level of an emission, which may not be exceeded during any one or more periods of time. Emission limit values may also be laid down for certain groups, families or categories of substances, in particular for those identified under Article 16. The emission limit values for substances shall

normally apply at the point where the emissions leave the installation, dilution being disregarded when determining them. With regard to indirect releases into water, the effect of a waste-water treatment plant may be taken into account when determining the emission limit values of the installations involved, provided that an equivalent level is guaranteed for protection of the environment as a whole and provided that this does not lead to higher levels of pollution in the environment.

41. "Emission controls" are controls requiring a specific emission limitation, for instance an emission limit value, or otherwise specifying limits or conditions on the effects, nature or other characteristics of an emission or operating conditions which affect emissions. Use of the term "emission control" in this Directive in respect of the provisions of any other Directive shall not be held as reinterpreting those provisions in any respect.

Article 3 - Coordination of administrative arrangements within river basin districts

1. Member States shall identify the individual river basins lying within their national territory and, for the purposes of this Directive, shall assign them to individual river basin districts. Small river basins may be combined with larger river basins or joined with neighbouring small basins to form individual river basin districts where appropriate. Where groundwaters do not fully follow a particular river basin, they shall be identified and assigned to the nearest or most appropriate river basin district. Coastal waters shall be identified and assigned to the nearest or most appropriate river basin district or districts.

2. Member States shall ensure the appropriate administrative arrangements, including the identification of the appropriate competent authority, for the application of the rules of this Directive within each river basin district lying within their territory.

3. Member States shall ensure that a river basin covering the territory of more than one Member State is assigned to an international river basin district. At the request of the Member States involved, the Commission shall act to facilitate the assigning to such international river basin districts. Each Member State shall ensure the appropriate administrative arrangements, including the identification of the appropriate competent authority, for the application of the rules of

this Directive within the portion of any international river basin district lying within its territory.

4. Member States shall ensure that the requirements of this Directive for the achievement of the environmental objectives established under Article 4, and in particular all programmes of measures are coordinated for the whole of the river basin district. For international river basin districts the Member States concerned shall together ensure this coordination and may, for this purpose, use existing structures stemming from international agreements. At the request of the Member States involved, the Commission shall act to facilitate the establishment of the programmes of measures.

5. Where a river basin district extends beyond the territory of the Community, the Member State or Member States concerned shall endeavour to establish appropriate coordination with the relevant non-Member States, with the aim of achieving the objectives of this Directive throughout the river basin district. Member States shall ensure the application of the rules of this Directive within their territory.

6. Member States may identify an existing national or international body as competent authority for the purposes of this Directive.

7. Member States shall identify the competent authority by the date mentioned in Article 24.

8. Member States shall provide the Commission with a list of their competent authorities and of the competent authorities of all the international bodies in which they participate at the latest six months after the date mentioned in Article 24. For each competent authority the information set out in Annex I shall be provided.

9. Member States shall inform the Commission of any changes to the information provided according to paragraph 8 within three months of the change coming into effect.

Article 4 - Environmental objectives

1. In making operational the programmes of measures specified in the river basin management plans:

(a)   for surface waters

(i)   Member States shall implement the necessary measures to prevent deterioration of the status of all bodies of surface water, subject to the application of paragraphs 6 and 7 and without prejudice to paragraph 8;

(ii)   Member States shall protect, enhance and restore all bodies of surface water, subject to the application of subparagraph (iii) for artificial and heavily modified bodies of water, with the aim of achieving good surface water status at the latest 15 years after the date of entry into force of this Directive, in accordance with the provisions laid down in Annex V, subject to the application of extensions determined in accordance with paragraph 4 and to the application of paragraphs 5, 6 and 7 without prejudice to paragraph 8;

(iii) Member States shall protect and enhance all artificial and heavily modified bodies of water, with the aim of achieving good ecological potential and good surface water chemical status at the latest 15 years from the date of entry into force of this Directive, in accordance with the provisions laid down in Annex V, subject to the application of extensions determined in accordance with paragraph 4 and to the application of paragraphs 5, 6 and 7 without prejudice to paragraph 8;

(iv)   Member States shall implement the necessary measures in accordance with Article 16(1) and (8), with the aim of progressively reducing pollution from priority substances and ceasing or phasing out emissions, discharges and losses of priority hazardous substances without prejudice to the relevant international agreements referred to in Article 1 for the parties concerned;

(b)   for groundwater

(i)   Member States shall implement the measures necessary to prevent or limit the input of pollutants into groundwater and to prevent the deterioration of the status of all bodies of groundwater, subject to the application of paragraphs 6 and 7 and without prejudice to paragraph 8 of this Article and subject to the application of Article 11(3)(j);

(ii)   Member States shall protect, enhance and restore all bodies of groundwater, ensure a balance between abstraction and recharge of groundwater, with the aim of achieving good groundwater status at the latest 15 years after the date of entry into force of this Directive, in accordance with the provisions laid down in Annex V, subject to the application of extensions determined in accordance with paragraph 4 and to the application of paragraphs 5, 6 and 7 without prejudice to paragraph 8 of this Article and subject to the application of Article 1(3)(j);

(iii)   Member States shall implement the measures necessary to reverse any significant and sustained upward trend in the concentration of any pollutant resulting from the impact of human activity in order progressively to reduce pollution of groundwater.

Measures to achieve trend reversal shall be implemented in accordance with paragraphs 2, 4 and 5 of Article 17, taking into account the applicable standards set out in relevant Community legislation, subject to the application of paragraphs 6 and 7 and without prejudice to paragraph 8;

(c)   for protected areas

1.   Member States shall achieve compliance with any standards and objectives at the latest 15 years after the date of entry into force of this Directive, unless otherwise specified in the Community legislation under which the individual protected areas have been established.

2.   Where more than one of the objectives under paragraph 1 relates to a given body of water, the most stringent shall apply.

3.   Member States may designate a body of surface water as artificial or heavily modified, when:

(a)   the changes to the hydromorphological characteristics of that body which would be necessary for achieving good ecological status would have significant adverse effects on:

(i)   the wider environment;

(ii)   navigation, including port facilities, or recreation;

(iii) activities for the purposes of which water is stored, such as drinking-water supply, power generation or irrigation;

(iv) water regulation, flood protection, land drainage, or

(v) other equally important sustainable human development activities;

(b) the beneficial objectives served by the artificial or modified characteristics of the water body cannot, for reasons of technical feasibility or disproportionate costs, reasonably be achieved by other means, which are a significantly better environmental option.

Such designation and the reasons for it shall be specifically mentioned in the river basin management plans required under Article 13 and reviewed every six years.

4. The deadlines established under paragraph 1 may be extended for the purposes of phased achievement of the objectives for bodies of water, provided that no further deterioration occurs in the status of the affected body of water when all of the following conditions are met:

(a) Member States determine that all necessary improvements in the status of bodies of water cannot reasonably be achieved within the timescales set out in that paragraph for at least one of the following reasons:

(i) the scale of improvements required can only be achieved in phases exceeding the timescale, for reasons of technical feasibility;

(ii) completing the improvements within the timescale would be disproportionately expensive;

(iii) natural conditions do not allow timely improvement in the status of the body of water.

(b) Extension of the deadline, and the reasons for it, are specifically set out and explained in the river basin management plan required under Article 13.

(c)   Extensions shall be limited to a maximum of two further updates of the river basin management plan except in cases where the natural conditions are such that the objectives cannot be achieved within this period.

(d)   A summary of the measures required under Article 11 which are envisaged as necessary to bring the bodies of water progressively to the required status by the extended deadline, the reasons for any significant delay in making these measures operational, and the expected timetable for their implementation are set out in the river basin management plan. A review of the implementation of these measures and a summary of any additional measures shall be included in updates of the river basin management plan.

5.   Member States may aim to achieve less stringent environmental objectives than those required under paragraph 1 for specific bodies of water when they are so affected by human activity, as determined in accordance with Article 5(1), or their natural condition is such that the achievement of these objectives would be infeasible or disproportionately expensive, and all the following conditions are met:

(a)   the environmental and socioeconomic needs served by such human activity cannot be achieved by other means, which are a significantly better environmental option not entailing disproportionate costs;

(b)   Member States ensure,

-       for surface water, the highest ecological and chemical status possible is achieved, given impacts that could not reasonably have been avoided due to the nature of the human activity or pollution,

-       for groundwater, the least possible changes to good groundwater status, given impacts that could not reasonably have been avoided due to the nature of the human activity or pollution;

(c)   no further deterioration occurs in the status of the affected body of water;

(d)   the establishment of less stringent environmental objectives, and the reasons for it, are specifically mentioned in the river basin management plan required under Article 13 and those objectives are reviewed every six years.

6.   Temporary deterioration in the status of bodies of water shall not be in breach of the requirements of this Directive if this is the result of circumstances of natural cause or force majeure which are exceptional or could not reasonably have been foreseen, in particular extreme floods and prolonged droughts, or the result of circumstances due to accidents which could not reasonably have been foreseen, when all of the following conditions have been met:

(a)   all practicable steps are taken to prevent further deterioration in status and in order not to compromise the achievement of the objectives of this Directive in other bodies of water not affected by those circumstances;

(b)   the conditions under which circumstances that are exceptional or that could not reasonably have been foreseen may be declared, including the adoption of the appropriate indicators, are stated in the river basin management plan;

(c)   the measures to be taken under such exceptional circumstances are included in the programme of measures and will not compromise the recovery of the quality of the body of water once the circumstances are over;

(d)   the effects of the circumstances that are exceptional or that could not reasonably have been foreseen are reviewed annually and, subject to the reasons set out in paragraph 4(a), all practicable measures are taken with the aim of restoring the body of water to its status prior to the effects of those circumstances as soon as reasonably practicable, and

(e)   a summary of the effects of the circumstances and of such measures taken or to be taken in accordance with paragraphs (a) and (d) are included in the next update of the river basin management plan.

7.   Member States will not be in breach of this Directive when:

-      failure to achieve good groundwater status, good ecological status or, where relevant, good ecological potential or to prevent deterioration in the status of a body of surface water or groundwater is the result of new modifications to the physical characteristics of a surface water body or alterations to the level of bodies of groundwater, or

- failure to prevent deterioration from high status to good status of a body of surface water is the result of new sustainable human development activities

and all the following conditions are met:

(a) all practicable steps are taken to mitigate the adverse impact on the status of the body of water;

(b) the reasons for those modifications or alterations are specifically set out and explained in the river basin management plan required under Article 13 and the objectives are reviewed every six years;

(c) the reasons for those modifications or alterations are of overriding public interest and/or the benefits to the environment and to society of achieving the objectives set out in paragraph 1 are outweighed by the benefits of the new modifications or alterations to human health, to the maintenance of human safety or to sustainable development, and

(d) the beneficial objectives served by those modifications or alterations of the water body cannot for reasons of technical feasibility or disproportionate cost be achieved by other means, which are a significantly better environmental option.

8. When applying paragraphs 3, 4, 5, 6 and 7, a Member State shall ensure that the application does not permanently exclude or compromise the achievement of the objectives of this Directive in other bodies of water within the same river basin district and is consistent with the implementation of other Community environmental legislation.

9. Steps must be taken to ensure that the application of the new provisions, including the application of paragraphs 3, 4, 5, 6 and 7, guarantees at least the same level of protection as the existing Community legislation.

Article 5 - Characteristics of the river basin district, review of the environmental impact of human activity and economic analysis of water use

1.   Each Member State shall ensure that for each river basin district or for the portion of an international river basin district falling within its territory:

-     an analysis of its characteristics,

-     a review of the impact of human activity on the status of surface waters and on groundwater, and

-     an economic analysis of water use

      is undertaken according to the technical specifications set out in Annexes II and III and that it is completed at the latest four years after the date of entry into force of this Directive.

2.   The analyses and reviews mentioned under paragraph 1 shall be reviewed, and if necessary updated at the latest 13 years after the date of entry into force of this Directive and every six years thereafter.

Article 6 - Register of protected areas

1.   Member States shall ensure the establishment of a register or registers of all areas lying within each river basin district which have been designated as requiring special protection under specific Community legislation for the protection of their surface water and groundwater or for the conservation of habitats and species directly depending on water. They shall ensure that the register is completed at the latest four years after the date of entry into force of this Directive.

2.   The register or registers shall include all bodies of water identified under Article 7(1) and all protected areas covered by Annex IV.

3.   For each river basin district, the register or registers of protected areas shall be kept under review and up to date.

Article 7 - Waters used for the abstraction of drinking water

1.   Member States shall identify, within each river basin district:

-       all bodies of water used for the abstraction of water intended for
        human consumption providing more than 10 m3 a day as an average
        or serving more than 50 persons, and

-       those bodies of water intended for such future use.

        Member States shall monitor, in accordance with Annex V, those
        bodies of water which according to Annex V, provide more than 100
        m^3 a day as an average.

2.   For each body of water identified under paragraph 1, in addition to
        meeting the objectives of Article 4 in accordance with the
        requirements of this Directive, for surface water bodies including the
        quality standards established at Community level under Article 16,
        Member States shall ensure that under the water treatment regime
        applied, and in accordance with Community legislation, the resulting
        water will meet the requirements of Directive 80/778/EEC as
        amended by Directive 98/83/EC.

3.   Member States shall ensure the necessary protection for the bodies of
        water identified with the aim of avoiding deterioration in their quality
        in order to reduce the level of purification treatment required in the
        production of drinking water. Member States may establish safeguard
        zones for those bodies of water.

Article 8 - Monitoring of surface water status, groundwater status and
protected areas

1.   Member States shall ensure the establishment of programmes for the
        monitoring of water status in order to establish a coherent and
        comprehensive overview of water status within each river basin
        district:

-       for surface waters such programmes shall cover:

        (i)   the volume and level or rate of flow to the extent relevant for
                ecological and chemical status and ecological potential, and

        (ii)   the ecological and chemical status and ecological potential;

-          for groundwaters such programmes shall cover monitoring of the chemical and quantitative status,

-          for protected areas the above programmes shall be supplemented by those specifications contained in Community legislation under which the individual protected areas have been established.

2.   These programmes shall be operational at the latest six years after the date of entry into force of this Directive unless otherwise specified in the legislation concerned. Such monitoring shall be in accordance with the requirements of Annex V.

3.   Technical specifications and standardised methods for analysis and monitoring of water status shall be laid down in accordance with the procedure laid down in Article 21.

Article 9 - Recovery of costs for water services

1.   Member States shall take account of the principle of recovery of the costs of water services, including environmental and resource costs, having regard to the economic analysis conducted according to Annex III, and in accordance in particular with the polluter pays principle.

Member States shall ensure by 2010

-          that water-pricing policies provide adequate incentives for users to use water resources efficiently, and thereby contribute to the environmental objectives of this Directive,

-          an adequate contribution of the different water uses, disaggregated into at least industry, households and agriculture, to the recovery of the costs of water services, based on the economic analysis conducted according to Annex III and taking account of the polluter pays principle.

Member States may in so doing have regard to the social, environmental and economic effects of the recovery as well as the geographic and climatic conditions of the region or regions affected.

2.   Member States shall report in the river basin management plans on the planned steps towards implementing paragraph 1 which will

contribute to achieving the environmental objectives of this Directive and on the contribution made by the various water uses to the recovery of the costs of water services.

3.   Nothing in this Article shall prevent the funding of particular preventive or remedial measures in order to achieve the objectives of this Directive.

4.   Member States shall not be in breach of this Directive if they decide in accordance with established practices not to apply the provisions of paragraph 1, second sentence, and for that purpose the relevant provisions of paragraph 2, for a given water-use activity, where this does not compromise the purposes and the achievement of the objectives of this Directive. Member States shall report the reasons for not fully applying paragraph 1, second sentence, in the river basin management plans.

Article 10 - The combined approach for point and diffuse sources

1.   Member States shall ensure that all discharges referred to in paragraph 2 into surface waters are controlled according to the combined approach set out in this Article.

2.   Member States shall ensure the establishment and/or implementation of:

(a)   the emission controls based on best available techniques, or

(b)   the relevant emission limit values, or

(c)   in the case of diffuse impacts the controls including, as appropriate, best environmental practices set out in:

> Council Directive 96/61/EC of 24 September 1996 concerning integrated pollution prevention and control[19],

---

[19] OJ L 257, 10.10.1996, p. 26.

- Council Directive 91/271/EEC of 21 May 1991 concerning urban waste-water treatment[20],

- Council Directive 91/676/EEC of 12 December 1991 concerning the protection of waters against pollution caused by nitrates from agricultural sources[21],

- the Directives adopted pursuant to Article 16 of this Directive,

- the Directives listed in Annex IX,

- any other relevant Community legislation

at the latest 12 years after the date of entry into force of this Directive, unless otherwise specified in the legislation concerned.

3. Where a quality objective or quality standard, whether established pursuant to this Directive, in the Directives listed in Annex IX, or pursuant to any other Community legislation, requires stricter conditions than those which would result from the application of paragraph 2, more stringent emission controls shall be set accordingly.

Article 11 - Programme of measures

1. Each Member State shall ensure the establishment for each river basin district, or for the part of an international river basin district within its territory, of a programme of measures, taking account of the results of the analyses required under Article 5, in order to achieve the objectives established under Article 4. Such programmes of measures may make reference to measures following from legislation adopted at national level and covering the whole of the territory of a Member State. Where appropriate, a Member State may adopt measures applicable to all river basin districts and/or the portions of international river basin districts falling within its territory.

---

[20] OJ L 135, 30.5.1991, p. 40. Directive as amended by Commission Directive 98/15/EC (OJ L 67, 7.3.1998, p. 29).
[21] OJ L 375, 31.12.1991, p. 1.

2.   Each programme of measures shall include the "basic" measures specified in paragraph 3 and, where necessary, "supplementary" measures.

3.   "Basic measures" are the minimum requirements to be complied with and shall consist of:

(a)   those measures required to implement Community legislation for the protection of water, including measures required under the legislation specified in Article 10 and in part A of Annex VI;

(b)   measures deemed appropriate for the purposes of Article 9;

(c)   measures to promote an efficient and sustainable water use in order to avoid compromising the achievement of the objectives specified in Article 4;

(d)   measures to meet the requirements of Article 7, including measures to safeguard water quality in order to reduce the level of purification treatment required for the production of drinking water;

(e)   controls over the abstraction of fresh surface water and groundwater, and impoundment of fresh surface water, including a register or registers of water abstractions and a requirement of prior authorisation for abstraction and impoundment. These controls shall be periodically reviewed and, where necessary, updated. Member States can exempt from these controls, abstractions or impoundments which have no significant impact on water status;

(f)   controls, including a requirement for prior authorisation of artificial recharge or augmentation of groundwater bodies. The water used may be derived from any surface water or groundwater, provided that the use of the source does not compromise the achievement of the environmental objectives established for the source or the recharged or augmented body of groundwater. These controls shall be periodically reviewed and, where necessary, updated;

(g)   for point source discharges liable to cause pollution, a requirement for prior regulation, such as a prohibition on the entry of pollutants into water, or for prior authorisation, or registration based on general binding rules, laying down emission controls for the pollutants concerned, including controls in accordance with Articles 10 and 16. These controls shall be periodically reviewed and, where necessary, updated;

(h)   for diffuse sources liable to cause pollution, measures to prevent or control the input of pollutants. Controls may take the form of a requirement for prior regulation, such as a prohibition on the entry of pollutants into water, prior authorisation or registration based on general binding rules where such a requirement is not otherwise provided for under Community legislation. These controls shall be periodically reviewed and, where necessary, updated;

(i)   for any other significant adverse impacts on the status of water identified under Article 5 and Annex II, in particular measures to ensure that the hydromorphological conditions of the bodies of water are consistent with the achievement of the required ecological status or good ecological potential for bodies of water designated as artificial or heavily modified. Controls for this purpose may take the form of a requirement for prior authorisation or registration based on general binding rules where such a requirement is not otherwise provided for under Community legislation. Such controls shall be periodically reviewed and, where necessary, updated;

(j)   a prohibition of direct discharges of pollutants into groundwater subject to the following provisions:

Member States may authorise reinjection into the same aquifer of water used for geothermal purposes.

They may also authorise, specifying the conditions for:

injection of water containing substances resulting from the operations for exploration and extraction of hydrocarbons or mining activities, and injection of water for technical reasons, into geological formations from which hydrocarbons or other substances have been extracted or into geological formations which for natural reasons are permanently unsuitable for other purposes. Such injections shall not contain substances other than those resulting from the above operations,

- reinjection of pumped groundwater from mines and quarries or associated with the construction or maintenance of civil engineering works,

- injection of natural gas or liquefied petroleum gas (LPG) for storage purposes into geological formations which for natural reasons are permanently unsuitable for other purposes,

- injection of natural gas or liquefied petroleum gas (LPG) for storage purposes into other geological formations where there is an overriding need for security of gas supply, and where the injection is such as to prevent any present or future danger of deterioration in the quality of any receiving groundwater,

- construction, civil engineering and building works and similar activities on, or in the ground which come into contact with groundwater. For these purposes, Member States may determine that such activities are to be treated as having been authorised provided that they are conducted in accordance with general binding rules developed by the Member State in respect of such activities,

- discharges of small quantities of substances for scientific purposes for characterisation, protection or remediation of water bodies limited to the amount strictly necessary for the purposes concerned provided such discharges do not compromise the achievement of the environmental objectives established for that body of groundwater;

(k)   in accordance with action taken pursuant to Article 16, measures to eliminate pollution of surface waters by those substances specified in the list of priority substances agreed pursuant to Article 16(2) and to progressively reduce pollution by other substances which would otherwise prevent Member States from achieving the objectives for the bodies of surface waters as set out in Article 4;

(l)   any measures required to prevent significant losses of pollutants from technical installations, and to prevent and/or to reduce the impact of accidental pollution incidents for example as a result of floods, including through systems to detect or give warning of such events including, in the case of accidents which could not reasonably have been foreseen, all appropriate measures to reduce the risk to aquatic ecosystems.

4.   "Supplementary" measures are those measures designed and implemented in addition to the basic measures, with the aim of achieving the objectives established pursuant to Article 4. Part B of Annex VI contains a non-exclusive list of such measures.

       Member States may also adopt further supplementary measures in order to provide for additional protection or improvement of the waters covered by this Directive, including in implementation of the relevant international agreements referred to in Article 1.

5.   Where monitoring or other data indicate that the objectives set under Article 4 for the body of water are unlikely to be achieved, the Member State shall ensure that:

-      the causes of the possible failure are investigated,

-      relevant permits and authorisations are examined and reviewed as appropriate,

-      the monitoring programmes are reviewed and adjusted as appropriate, and

-      additional measures as may be necessary in order to achieve those objectives are established, including, as appropriate, the establishment of stricter environmental quality standards following the procedures laid down in Annex V.

       Where those causes are the result of circumstances of natural cause or force majeure which are exceptional and could not reasonably have been foreseen, in particular extreme floods and prolonged droughts, the Member State may determine that additional measures are not practicable, subject to Article 4(6).

6.   In implementing measures pursuant to paragraph 3, Member States shall take all appropriate steps not to increase pollution of marine waters. Without prejudice to existing legislation, the application of measures taken pursuant to paragraph 3 may on no account lead, either directly or indirectly to increased pollution of surface waters. This requirement shall not apply where it would result in increased pollution of the environment as a whole.

7.   The programmes of measures shall be established at the latest nine years after the date of entry into force of this Directive and all the measures shall be made operational at the latest 12 years after that date.

8.   The programmes of measures shall be reviewed, and if necessary updated at the latest 15 years after the date of entry into force of this Directive and every six years thereafter. Any new or revised measures established under an updated programme shall be made operational within three years of their establishment.

Article 12 - Issues which can not be dealt with at Member State level

1.   Where a Member State identifies an issue which has an impact on the management of its water but cannot be resolved by that Member State, it may report the issue to the Commission and any other Member State concerned and may make recommendations for the resolution of it.

2.   The Commission shall respond to any report or recommendations from Member States within a period of six months.

Article 13 - River basin management plans

1.   Member States shall ensure that a river basin management plan is produced for each river basin district lying entirely within their territory.

2.   In the case of an international river basin district falling entirely within the Community, Member States shall ensure coordination with the aim of producing a single international river basin management plan. Where such an international river basin management plan is not produced, Member States shall produce river basin management plans covering at least those parts of the international river basin district falling within their territory to achieve the objectives of this Directive.

3.   In the case of an international river basin district extending beyond the boundaries of the Community, Member States shall endeavour to produce a single river basin management plan, and, where this is not possible, the plan shall at least cover the portion of the international

river basin district lying within the territory of the Member State concerned.

4.   The river basin management plan shall include the information detailed in Annex VII.

5.   River basin management plans may be supplemented by the production of more detailed programmes and management plans for sub-basin, sector, issue, or water type, to deal with particular aspects of water management. Implementation of these measures shall not exempt Member States from any of their obligations under the rest of this Directive.

6.   River basin management plans shall be published at the latest nine years after the date of entry into force of this Directive.

7.   River basin management plans shall be reviewed and updated at the latest 15 years after the date of entry into force of this Directive and every six years thereafter.

Article 14 - Public information and consultation

1.   Member States shall encourage the active involvement of all interested parties in the implementation of this Directive, in particular in the production, review and updating of the river basin management plans. Member States shall ensure that, for each river basin district, they publish and make available for comments to the public, including users:

(a)   a timetable and work programme for the production of the plan, including a statement of the consultation measures to be taken, at least three years before the beginning of the period to which the plan refers;

(b)   an interim overview of the significant water management issues identified in the river basin, at least two years before the beginning of the period to which the plan refers;

(c)   draft copies of the river basin management plan, at least one year before the beginning of the period to which the plan refers.

On request, access shall be given to background documents and information used for the development of the draft river basin management plan.

2.   Member States shall allow at least six months to comment in writing on those documents in order to allow active involvement and consultation.

3.   Paragraphs 1 and 2 shall apply equally to updated river basin management plans.

Article 15 - Reporting

1.   Member States shall send copies of the river basin management plans and all subsequent updates to the Commission and to any other Member State concerned within three months of their publication:

(a)   for river basin districts falling entirely within the territory of a Member State, all river management plans covering that national territory and published pursuant to Article 13;

(b)   for international river basin districts, at least the part of the river basin management plans covering the territory of the Member State.

2.   Member States shall submit summary reports of:

-   the analyses required under Article 5, and

-   the monitoring programmes designed under Article 8 undertaken for the purposes of the first river basin management plan within three months of their completion.

3.   Member States shall, within three years of the publication of each river basin management plan or update under Article 13, submit an interim report describing progress in the implementation of the planned programme of measures.

Article 16 - Strategies against pollution of water

1.   The European Parliament and the Council shall adopt specific
      measures against pollution of water by individual pollutants or groups
      of pollutants presenting a significant risk to or via the aquatic
      environment, including such risks to waters used for the abstraction of
      drinking water. For those pollutants measures shall be aimed at the
      progressive reduction and, for priority hazardous substances, as
      defined in Article 2(30), at the cessation or phasing-out of discharges,
      emissions and losses. Such measures shall be adopted acting on the
      proposals presented by the Commission in accordance with the
      procedures laid down in the Treaty.

2.   The Commission shall submit a proposal setting out a list of priority
      substances selected amongst those which present a significant risk to
      or via the aquatic environment. Substances shall be prioritised for
      action on the basis of risk to or via the aquatic environment, identified
      by:

(a)   risk assessment carried out under Council Regulation (EEC) No
      793/93[22], Council Directive 91/414/EEC[23], and Directive 98/8/EC
      of the European Parliament and of the Council[24], or

(b)   targeted risk-based assessment (following the methodology of
      Regulation (EEC) No 793/93) focusing solely on aquatic ecotoxicity
      and on human toxicity via the aquatic environment.

      When necessary in order to meet the timetable laid down in paragraph
      4, substances shall be prioritised for action on the basis of risk to, or
      via the aquatic environment, identified by a simplified risk-based
      assessment procedure based on scientific principles taking particular
      account of:

      -      evidence regarding the intrinsic hazard of the substance
             concerned, and in particular its aquatic ecotoxicity and human
             toxicity via aquatic exposure routes, and

---

[22] OJ L 84, 5.4.1993, p. 1.
[23] OJ L 230, 19.8.1991, p. 1. Directive as last amended by Directive 98/47/EC (OJ
L 191, 7.7.1998, p. 50).
[24] OJ L 123, 24.4.1998, p. 1.

- evidence from monitoring of widespread environmental contamination, and

- other proven factors which may indicate the possibility of widespread environmental contamination, such as production or use volume of the substance concerned, and use patterns.

3. The Commission's proposal shall also identify the priority hazardous substances. In doing so, the Commission shall take into account the selection of substances of concern undertaken in the relevant Community legislation regarding hazardous substances or relevant international agreements.

4. The Commission shall review the adopted list of priority substances at the latest four years after the date of entry into force of this Directive and at least every four years thereafter, and come forward with proposals as appropriate.

5. In preparing its proposal, the Commission shall take account of recommendations from the Scientific Committee on Toxicity, Ecotoxicity and the Environment, Member States, the European Parliament, the European Environment Agency, Community research programmes, international organisations to which the Community is a party, European business organisations including those representing small and medium-sized enterprises, European environmental organisations, and of other relevant information which comes to its attention.

6. For the priority substances, the Commission shall submit proposals of controls for:

- the progressive reduction of discharges, emissions and losses of the substances concerned, and, in particular

- the cessation or phasing-out of discharges, emissions and losses of the substances as identified in accordance with paragraph 3, including an appropriate timetable for doing so. The timetable shall not exceed 20 years after the adoption of these proposals by the European Parliament and the Council in accordance with the provisions of this Article.

In doing so it shall identify the appropriate cost-effective and proportionate level and combination of product and process controls for both point and diffuse sources and take account of Community-wide uniform emission limit values for process controls. Where appropriate, action at Community level for process controls may be established on a sector-by-sector basis. Where product controls include a review of the relevant authorisations issued under Directive 91/414/EEC and Directive 98/8/EC, such reviews shall be carried out in accordance with the provisions of those Directives. Each proposal for controls shall specify arrangements for their review, updating and for assessment of their effectiveness.

7.   The Commission shall submit proposals for quality standards applicable to the concentrations of the priority substances in surface water, sediments or biota.

8.   The Commission shall submit proposals, in accordance with paragraphs 6 and 7, and at least for emission controls for point sources and environmental quality standards within two years of the inclusion of the substance concerned on the list of priority substances. For substances included in the first list of priority substances, in the absence of agreement at Community level six years after the date of entry into force of this Directive, Member States shall establish environmental quality standards for these substances for all surface waters affected by discharges of those substances, and controls on the principal sources of such discharges, based, inter alia, on consideration of all technical reduction options. For substances subsequently included in the list of priority substances, in the absence of agreement at Community level, Member States shall take such action five years after the date of inclusion in the list.

9.   The Commission may prepare strategies against pollution of water by any other pollutants or groups of pollutants, including any pollution which occurs as a result of accidents.

10. In preparing its proposals under paragraphs 6 and 7, the Commission shall also review all the Directives listed in Annex IX. It shall propose, by the deadline in paragraph 8, a revision of the controls in Annex IX for all those substances which are included in the list of priority substances and shall propose the appropriate measures including the

possible repeal of the controls under Annex IX for all other substances.

All the controls in Annex IX for which revisions are proposed shall be repealed by the date of entry into force of those revisions.

11.   The list of priority substances of substances mentioned in paragraphs 2 and 3 proposed by the Commission shall, on its adoption by the European Parliament and the Council, become Annex X to this Directive. Its revision mentioned in paragraph 4 shall follow the same procedure.

Article 17 - Strategies to prevent and control pollution of groundwater

1.   The European Parliament and the Council shall adopt specific measures to prevent and control groundwater pollution. Such measures shall be aimed at achieving the objective of good groundwater chemical status in accordance with Article 4(1)(b) and shall be adopted, acting on the proposal presented within two years after the entry into force of this Directive, by the Commission in accordance with the procedures laid down in the Treaty.

2.   In proposing measures the Commission shall have regard to the analysis carried out according to Article 5 and Annex II. Such measures shall be proposed earlier if data are available and shall include:

(a)   criteria for assessing good groundwater chemical status, in accordance with Annex II.2.2 and Annex V 2.3.2 and 2.4.5;

(b)   criteria for the identification of significant and sustained upward trends and for the definition of starting points for trend reversals to be used in accordance with Annex V 2.4.4.

3.   Measures resulting from the application of paragraph 1 shall be included in the programmes of measures required under Article 11.

4.   In the absence of criteria adopted under paragraph 2 at Community level, Member States shall establish appropriate criteria at the latest five years after the date of entry into force of this Directive.

5.   In the absence of criteria adopted under paragraph 4 at national level, trend reversal shall take as its starting point a maximum of 75 % of the level of the quality standards set out in existing Community legislation applicable to groundwater.

Article 18 - Commission report

1.   The Commission shall publish a report on the implementation of this Directive at the latest 12 years after the date of entry into force of this Directive and every six years thereafter, and shall submit it to the European Parliament and to the Council.

2.   The report shall include the following:

(a)   a review of progress in the implementation of the Directive;

(b)   a review of the status of surface water and groundwater in the Community undertaken in coordination with the European Environment Agency;

(c)   a survey of the river basin management plans submitted in accordance with Article 15, including suggestions for the improvement of future plans;

(d)   a summary of the response to each of the reports or recommendations to the Commission made by Member States pursuant to Article 12;

(e)   a summary of any proposals, control measures and strategies developed under Article 16;

(f)   a summary of the responses to comments made by the European Parliament and the Council on previous implementation reports.

3.   The Commission shall also publish a report on progress in implementation based on the summary reports that Member States submit under Article 15(2), and submit it to the European Parliament and the Member States, at the latest two years after the dates referred to in Articles 5 and 8.

4.   The Commission shall, within three years of the publication of each report under paragraph 1, publish an interim report describing

progress in implementation on the basis of the interim reports of the Member States as mentioned in Article 15(3). This shall be submitted to the European Parliament and to the Council.

5.   The Commission shall convene when appropriate, in line with the reporting cycle, a conference of interested parties on Community water policy from each of the Member States, to comment on the Commission's implementation reports and to share experiences.

Participants should include representatives from the competent authorities, the European Parliament, NGOs, the social and economic partners, consumer bodies, academics and other experts.

Article 19 - Plans for future Community measures

1.   Once a year, the Commission shall for information purposes present to the Committee referred to in Article 21 an indicative plan of measures having an impact on water legislation which it intends to propose in the near future, including any emerging from the proposals, control measures and strategies developed under Article 16. The Commission shall make the first such presentation at the latest two years after the date of entry into force of this Directive.

2.   The Commission will review this Directive at the latest 19 years after the date of its entry into force and will propose any necessary amendments to it.

Article 20 - Technical adaptations to the Directive

1.   Annexes I, III and section 1.3.6 of Annex V may be adapted to scientific and technical progress in accordance with the procedures laid down in Article 21, taking account of the periods for review and updating of the river basin management plans as referred to in Article 13. Where necessary, the Commission may adopt guidelines on the implementation of Annexes II and V in accordance with the procedures laid down in Article 21.

2.   For the purpose of transmission and processing of data, including statistical and cartographic data, technical formats for the purpose of paragraph 1 may be adopted in accordance with the procedures laid down in Article 21.

Article 21 - Regulatory committee

1.   The Commission shall be assisted by a committee (hereinafter referred to as "the Committee").

2.   Where reference is made to this Article, Articles 5 and 7 of Decision 1999/468/EC shall apply, having regard to the provisions of Article 8 thereof.

      The period laid down in Article 5(6) of Decision 1999/468/EC shall be set at three months.

3.   The Committee shall adopt its rules of procedure.

Article 22 - Repeals and transitional provisions

1.   The following shall be repealed with effect from seven years after the date of entry into force of this Directive:

-     Directive 75/440/EEC of 16 June 1975 concerning the quality required of surface water intended for the abstraction of drinking water in the Member States[25],

-     Council Decision 77/795/EEC of 12 December 1977 establishing a common procedure for the exchange of information on the quality of surface freshwater in the Community[26],

-     Council Directive 79/869/EEC of 9 October 1979 concerning the methods of measurement and frequencies of sampling and analysis of surface water intended for the abstraction of drinking waters in the Member States[27].

2.   The following shall be repealed with effect from 13 years after the date of entry into force of this Directive:

---

[25] OJ L 194, 25.7.1975, p. 26. Directive as last amended by Directive 91/692/EEC.
[26] OJ L 334, 24.12.1977, p. 29. Decision as last amended by the 1994 Act of Accession.
[27] OJ L 271, 29.10.1979, p. 44. Directive as last amended by the 1994 Act of Accession.

- Council Directive 78/659/EEC of 18 July 1978 on the quality of freshwaters needing protection or improvement in order to support fish life[28],

- Council Directive 79/923/EEC of 30 October 1979 on the quality required of shellfish waters[29],

- Council Directive 80/68/EEC of 17 December 1979 on the protection of groundwater against pollution caused by certain dangerous substances,

- Directive 76/464/EEC, with the exception of Article 6, which shall be repealed with effect from the entry into force of this Directive.

3. The following transitional provisions shall apply for Directive 76/464/EEC:

(a) the list of priority substances adopted under Article 16 of this Directive shall replace the list of substances prioritised in the Commission communication to the Council of 22 June 1982;

(b) for the purposes of Article 7 of Directive 76/464/EEC, Member States may apply the principles for the identification of pollution problems and the substances causing them, the establishment of quality standards, and the adoption of measures, laid down in this Directive.

4. The environmental objectives in Article 4 and environmental quality standards established in Annex IX and pursuant to Article 16(7), and by Member States under Annex V for substances not on the list of priority substances and under Article 16(8) in respect of priority substances for which Community standards have not been set, shall be regarded as environmental quality standards for the purposes of point 7 of Article 2 and Article 10 of Directive 96/61/EC.

5. Where a substance on the list of priority substances adopted under Article 16 is not included in Annex VIII to this Directive or in Annex III to Directive 96/61/EC, it shall be added thereto.

---

[28] OJ L 222, 14.8.1978, p. 1. Directive as last amended by the 1994 Act of Accession.
[29] OJ L 281, 10.11.1979, p. 47. Directive as amended by Directive 91/692/EEC.

6.   For bodies of surface water, environmental objectives established under the first river basin management plan required by this Directive shall, as a minimum, give effect to quality standards at least as stringent as those required to implement Directive 76/464/EEC.

Article 23 - Penalties

Member States shall determine penalties applicable to breaches of the national provisions adopted pursuant to this Directive. The penalties thus provided for shall be effective, proportionate and dissuasive.

Article 24 - Implementation

1.   Member States shall bring into force the laws, regulations and administrative provisions necessary to comply with this Directive at the latest 22 December 2003. They shall forthwith inform the Commission thereof.

When Member States adopt these measures, they shall contain a reference to this Directive or shall be accompanied by such a reference on the occasion of their official publication. The methods of making such a reference shall be laid down by the Member States.

2.   Member States shall communicate to the Commission the texts of the main provisions of national law which they adopt in the field governed by this Directive. The Commission shall inform the other Member States thereof.

Article 25 - Entry into force

This Directive shall enter into force on the day of its publication in the Official Journal of the European Communities.

Article 26 - Addressees

This Directive is addressed to the Member States.

...

[Omitted: Annex I - Information required for the list of competent authorities]

Annex II

[Omitted: 1. Surface waters]

2.   Groundwaters

2.1.   Initial characterisation

Member States shall carry out an initial characterisation of all groundwater bodies to assess their uses and the degree to which they are at risk of failing to meet the objectives for each groundwater body under Article 4. Member States may group groundwater bodies together for the purposes of this initial characterisation. This analysis may employ existing hydrological, geological, pedological, land use, discharge, abstraction and other data but shall identify:

-    the location and boundaries of the groundwater body or bodies,

-    the pressures to which the groundwater body or bodies are liable to be subject including:

-    diffuse sources of pollution

-    point sources of pollution

-    abstraction

-    artificial recharge,

-    the general character of the overlying strata in the catchment area from which the groundwater body receives its recharge,

-    those groundwater bodies for which there are directly dependent surface water ecosystems or terrestrial ecosystems.

2.2.   Further characterisation

Following this initial characterisation, Member States shall carry out further characterisation of those groundwater bodies or groups of bodies which have been identified as being at risk in order to establish a more precise assessment of the significance of such risk and identification of any measures to be required under Article 11. Accordingly, this characterisation shall include relevant information on the impact of human activity and, where relevant, information on:

- geological characteristics of the groundwater body including the extent and type of geological units,

- hydrogeological characteristics of the groundwater body including hydraulic conductivity, porosity and confinement,

- characteristics of the superficial deposits and soils in the catchment from which the groundwater body receives its recharge, including the thickness, porosity, hydraulic conductivity, and absorptive properties of the deposits and soils,

- stratification characteristics of the groundwater within the groundwater body,

- an inventory of associated surface systems, including terrestrial ecosystems and bodies of surface water, with which the groundwater body is dynamically linked,

- estimates of the directions and rates of exchange of water between the groundwater body and associated surface systems,

- sufficient data to calculate the long term annual average rate of overall recharge,

- characterisation of the chemical composition of the groundwater, including specification of the contributions from human activity. Member States may use typologies for groundwater characterisation when establishing natural background levels for these bodies of groundwater.

2.3.   Review of the impact of human activity on groundwaters

For those bodies of groundwater which cross the boundary between two or more Member States or are identified following the initial characterisation undertaken in accordance with paragraph 2.1 as being at risk of failing to meet the objectives set for each body under Article 4, the following information shall, where relevant, be collected and maintained for each groundwater body:

(a) the location of points in the groundwater body used for the abstraction of water with the exception of:

- points for the abstraction of water providing less than an average of 10 m^3 per day, or,

- points for the abstraction of water intended for human consumption providing less than an average of 10 m3 per day or serving less than 50 persons,

(b) the annual average rates of abstraction from such points,

(c) the chemical composition of water abstracted from the groundwater body,

(d) the location of points in the groundwater body into which water is directly discharged,

(e) the rates of discharge at such points,

(f) the chemical composition of discharges to the groundwater body, and

(g) land use in the catchment or catchments from which the groundwater body receives its recharge, including pollutant inputs and anthropogenic alterations to the recharge characteristics such as rainwater and run-off diversion through land sealing, artificial recharge, damming or drainage.

2.4. Review of the impact of changes in groundwater levels

Member States shall also identify those bodies of groundwater for which lower objectives are to be specified under Article 4 including as a result of consideration of the effects of the status of the body on:

(i) surface water and associated terrestrial ecosystems

(ii) water regulation, flood protection and land drainage

(iii)   human development.

2.5. Review of the impact of pollution on groundwater quality

Member States shall identify those bodies of groundwater for which lower objectives are to be specified under Article 4(5) where, as a result of the impact of human activity, as determined in accordance with Article 5(1), the body of groundwater is so polluted that achieving good groundwater chemical status is infeasible or disproportionately expensive.

Annex III - Economic analysis

The economic analysis shall contain enough information in sufficient detail (taking account of the costs associated with collection of the relevant data) in order to:

(a)   make the relevant calculations necessary for taking into account under Article 9 the principle of recovery of the costs of water services, taking account of long term forecasts of supply and demand for water in the river basin district and, where necessary:

-     estimates of the volume, prices and costs associated with water services, and

-     estimates of relevant investment including forecasts of such investments;

(b)   make judgements about the most cost-effective combination of measures in respect of water uses to be included in the programme of measures under Article 11 based on estimates of the potential costs of such measures.

Annex IV - Protected areas

1.   The register of protected areas required under Article 6 shall include the following types of protected areas:

(i)   areas designated for the abstraction of water intended for human consumption under Article 7;

(ii) areas designated for the protection of economically significant aquatic species;

(iii) bodies of water designated as recreational waters, including areas designated as bathing waters under Directive 76/160/EEC;

(iv) nutrient-sensitive areas, including areas designated as vulnerable zones under Directive 91/676/EEC and areas designated as sensitive areas under Directive 91/271/EEC; and

(v) areas designated for the protection of habitats or species where the maintenance or improvement of the status of water is an important factor in their protection, including relevant Natura 2000 sites designated under Directive 92/43/EEC[1] and Directive 79/409/EEC[2].

2. The summary of the register required as part of the river basin management plan shall include maps indicating the location of each protected area and a description of the Community, national or local legislation under which they have been designated.

---

[1] OJ L 206, 22.7.1992, p. 7. Directive as last amended by Directive 97/62/EC (OJ L 305, 8.11.1997, p. 42).
[2] OJ L 103, 25.4.1979, p. 1. Directive as last amended by Directive 97/49/EC (OJ L 223, 13.8.1997, p. 9).

Annex V

[Omitted: 1. Surface water status]

2.   Groundwater

2.1. Groundwater quantitative status

2.1.1. Parameter for the classification of quantitative status

Groundwater level regime

2.1.2. Definition of quantitative status

Elements	Good status
Groundwater level	The level of groundwater in the groundwater body is such that the available groundwater resource is not exceeded by the long-term annual average rate of abstraction. Accordingly, the level of groundwater is not subject to anthropogenic alterations such as would result in: – failure to achieve the environmental objectives specified under Article 4 for associated surface waters, – any significant diminution in the status of such waters, – any significant damage to terrestrial ecosystems which depend directly on the groundwater body. and alterations to flow direction resulting from level changes may occur temporarily, or continuously in a spatially limited area, but such reversals do not cause saltwater or other intrusion, and do not indicate a sustained and clearly identified anthropogenically induced trend in flow direction likely to result in such intrusions.

2.2. Monitoring of groundwater quantitative status

2.2.1. Groundwater level monitoring network

The groundwater monitoring network shall be established in accordance with the requirements of Articles 7 and 8. The monitoring network shall be designed so as to provide a reliable assessment of the quantitative status of all groundwater bodies or groups of bodies including assessment of the available groundwater resource. Member States shall provide a map or maps showing the groundwater monitoring network in the river basin management plan.

2.2.2. Density of monitoring sites

The network shall include sufficient representative monitoring points to estimate the groundwater level in each groundwater body or group of bodies taking into account short and long-term variations in recharge and in particular:

- for groundwater bodies identified as being at risk of failing to achieve environmental objectives under Article 4, ensure sufficient density of monitoring points to assess the impact of abstractions and discharges on the groundwater level,

- for groundwater bodies within which groundwater flows across a Member State boundary, ensure sufficient monitoring points are provided to estimate the direction and rate of groundwater flow across the Member State boundary.

2.2.3. Monitoring frequency

The frequency of observations shall be sufficient to allow assessment of the quantitative status of each groundwater body or group of bodies taking into account short and long-term variations in recharge. In particular:

- for groundwater bodies identified as being at risk of failing to achieve environmental objectives under Article 4, ensure sufficient frequency of measurement to assess the impact of abstractions and discharges on the groundwater level,

- for groundwater bodies within which groundwater flows across a Member State boundary, ensure sufficient frequency of measurement to estimate the direction and rate of groundwater flow across the Member State boundary.

2.2.4. Interpretation and presentation of groundwater quantitative status

The results obtained from the monitoring network for a groundwater body or group of bodies shall be used to assess the quantitative status of that body or those bodies. Subject to point 2.5. Member States shall provide a map of the resulting assessment of groundwater quantitative status, colour-coded in accordance with the following regime:

Good: green

Poor: red

2.3. Groundwater chemical status

2.3.1. Parameters for the determination of groundwater chemical status

Conductivity

Concentrations of pollutants

2.3.2. Definition of good groundwater chemical status

Elements	Good status
General	The chemical composition of the groundwater body is such that the concentrations of pollutants: — as specified below, do not exhibit the effects of saline or other intrusions — do not exceed the quality standards applicable under other relevant Community legislation in accordance with Article 17

Elements	Good status
	– are not such as would result in failure to achieve the environmental objectives specified under Article 4 for associated surface waters nor any significant diminution of the ecological or chemical quality of such bodies nor in any significant damage to terrestrial ecosystems which depend directly on the groundwater body
Conductivity	Changes in conductivity are not indicative of saline or other intrusion into the groundwater body

2.4.   Monitoring of groundwater chemical status

2.4.1. Groundwater monitoring network

The groundwater monitoring network shall be established in accordance with the requirements of Articles 7 and 8. The monitoring network shall be designed so as to provide a coherent and comprehensive overview of groundwater chemical status within each river basin and to detect the presence of long-term anthropogenically induced upward trends in pollutants.

On the basis of the characterisation and impact assessment carried out in accordance with Article 5 and Annex II, Member States shall for each period to which a river basin management plan applies, establish a surveillance monitoring programme. The results of this programme shall be used to establish an operational monitoring programme to be applied for the remaining period of the plan.

Estimates of the level of confidence and precision of the results provided by the monitoring programmes shall be given in the plan.

2.4.2. Surveillance monitoring

Objective

Surveillance monitoring shall be carried out in order to:

-   supplement and validate the impact assessment procedure,

-   provide information for use in the assessment of long term trends both as a result of changes in natural conditions and through anthropogenic activity.

Selection of monitoring sites

Sufficient monitoring sites shall be selected for each of the following:

-   bodies identified as being at risk following the characterisation exercise undertaken in accordance with Annex II,

-   bodies which cross a Member State boundary.

Selection of parameters

The following set of core parameters shall be monitored in all the selected groundwater bodies:

-   oxygen content
-   pH value
-   conductivity
-   nitrate
-   ammonium

Bodies which are identified in accordance with Annex II as being at significant risk of failing to achieve good status shall also be monitored for those parameters which are indicative of the impact of these pressures.

Transboundary water bodies shall also be monitored for those parameters which are relevant for the protection of all of the uses supported by the groundwater flow.

2.4.3. Operational monitoring

Objective

Operational monitoring shall be undertaken in the periods between surveillance monitoring programmes in order to:

-   establish the chemical status of all groundwater bodies or groups of bodies determined as being at risk,

-   establish the presence of any long term anthropogenically induced upward trend in the concentration of any pollutant.

Selection of monitoring sites

Operational monitoring shall be carried out for all those groundwater bodies or groups of bodies which on the basis of both the impact assessment carried out in accordance with Annex II and surveillance monitoring are identified as being at risk of failing to meet objectives under Article 4. The selection of monitoring sites shall also reflect an assessment of how representative monitoring data from that site is of the quality of the relevant groundwater body or bodies.

Frequency of monitoring

Operational monitoring shall be carried out for the periods between surveillance monitoring programmes at a frequency sufficient to detect the impacts of relevant pressures but at a minimum of once per annum.

2.4.4. Identification of trends in pollutants

Member States shall use data from both surveillance and operational monitoring in the identification of long term anthropogenically induced upward trends in pollutant concentrations and the reversal of such trends. The base year or period from which trend identification is to be calculated shall be identified. The calculation of trends shall be undertaken for a body or, where appropriate, group of bodies of groundwater. Reversal of a trend shall be demonstrated statistically and the level of confidence associated with the identification stated.

2.4.5. Interpretation and presentation of groundwater chemical status

In assessing status, the results of individual monitoring points within a groundwater body shall be aggregated for the body as a whole. Without prejudice to the Directives concerned, for good status to be achieved for a groundwater body, for those chemical parameters for which environmental quality standards have been set in Community legislation:

-        the mean value of the results of monitoring at each point in the groundwater body or group of bodies shall be calculated, and

-        in accordance with Article 17 these mean values shall be used to demonstrate compliance with good groundwater chemical status.

Subject to point 2.5, Member States shall provide a map of groundwater chemical status, colour-coded as indicated below:

Good: green

Poor: red

Member States shall also indicate by a black dot on the map, those groundwater bodies which are subject to a significant and sustained upward trend in the concentrations of any pollutant resulting from the impact of human activity. Reversal of a trend shall be indicated by a blue dot on the map.

These maps shall be included in the river basin management plan.

2.5.   Presentation of groundwater status

Member States shall provide in the river basin management plan a map showing for each groundwater body or groups of groundwater bodies both the quantitative status and the chemical status of that body or group of bodies, colour-coded in accordance with the requirements of points 2.2.4 and 2.4.5. Member States may choose not to provide separate maps under points 2.2.4 and 2.4.5 but shall in that case also provide an indication in accordance with the requirements of point 2.4.5 on the map required under this point, of those bodies which are subject to a significant and sustained upward trend in the concentration of any pollutant or any reversal in such a trend.

Annex VI - Lists of measures to be included within the programmes of measures

Part A

Measures required under the following Directives:

(i)   The Bathing Water Directive (76/160/EEC);

(ii)   The Birds Directive (79/409/EEC)(1);

(iii)   The Drinking Water Directive (80/778/EEC) as amended by Directive (98/83/EC);

(iv)   The Major Accidents (Seveso) Directive (96/82/EC)(2);

(v)   The Environmental Impact Assessment Directive (85/337/EEC)(3);

(vi)   The Sewage Sludge Directive (86/278/EEC)(4);

(vii)   The Urban Waste-water Treatment Directive (91/271/EEC);

(viii) The Plant Protection Products Directive (91/414/EEC);

(ix)   The Nitrates Directive (91/676/EEC);

(x)   The Habitats Directive (92/43/EEC)(5);

(xi)   The Integrated Pollution Prevention Control Directive (96/61/EC).

---

(1) OJ L 103, 25.4.1979, p. 1.
(2) OJ L 10, 14.1.1997, p. 13.
(3) OJ L 175, 5.7.1985, p. 40. Directive as amended by Directive 97/11/EC (OJ L 73, 14.3.1997, p. 5).
(4) OJ L 181, 8.7.1986, p. 6.
(5) OJ L 206, 22.7.1992, p. 7.

Part B
__

The following is a non-exclusive list of supplementary measures which Member States within each river basin district may choose to adopt as part of the programme of measures required under Article 11(4):

(i)   legislative instruments

(ii)   administrative instruments

(iii)   economic or fiscal instruments

(iv)   negotiated environmental agreements

(v)   emission controls

(vi)   codes of good practice

(vii)   recreation and restoration of wetlands areas

(viii) abstraction controls

(ix)   demand management measures, inter alia, promotion of adapted agricultural production such as low water requiring crops in areas affected by drought

(x)   efficiency and reuse measures, inter alia, promotion of water-efficient technologies in industry and water-saving irrigation techniques

(xi)   construction projects

(xii)   desalination plants

(xiii) rehabilitation projects

(xiv)   artificial recharge of aquifers

(xv)   educational projects

(xvi)   research, development and demonstration projects

(xvii) other relevant measures

<u>Annex VII - River basin management plans</u>

A.   River basin management plans shall cover the following elements:

1.   a general description of the characteristics of the river basin district required under Article 5 and Annex II. This shall include:

1.1.   for surface waters:

-   mapping of the location and boundaries of water bodies,

-   mapping of the ecoregions and surface water body types within the river basin,

-   identification of reference conditions for the surface water body types;

1.2.   for groundwaters:

-   mapping of the location and boundaries of groundwater bodies;

2.   a summary of significant pressures and impact of human activity on the status of surface water and groundwater, including:

-   estimation of point source pollution,

-   estimation of diffuse source pollution, including a summary of land use,

-   estimation of pressures on the quantitative status of water including abstractions,

-   analysis of other impacts of human activity on the status of water;

3.   identification and mapping of protected areas as required by Article 6 and Annex IV;

4.   a map of the monitoring networks established for the purposes of Article 8 and Annex V, and a presentation in map form of the results of the monitoring programmes carried out under those provisions for the status of:

4.1.   surface water (ecological and chemical);

4.2.   groundwater (chemical and quantitative);

4.3.   protected areas;

5.   a list of the environmental objectives established under Article 4 for surface waters, groundwaters and protected areas, including in particular identification of instances where use has been made of Article 4(4), (5), (6) and (7), and the associated information required under that Article;

6.   a summary of the economic analysis of water use as required by Article 5 and Annex III;

7.   a summary of the programme or programmes of measures adopted under Article 11, including the ways in which the objectives established under Article 4 are thereby to be achieved;

7.1.   a summary of the measures required to implement Community legislation for the protection of water;

7.2.   a report on the practical steps and measures taken to apply the principle of recovery of the costs of water use in accordance with Article 9;

7.3.   a summary of the measures taken to meet the requirements of Article 7;

7.4.   a summary of the controls on abstraction and impoundment of water, including reference to the registers and identifications of the cases where exemptions have been made under Article 11(3)(e);

7.5.   a summary of the controls adopted for point source discharges and other activities with an impact on the status of water in accordance with the provisions of Article 11(3)(g) and 11(3)(i);

7.6.   an identification of the cases where direct discharges to groundwater have been authorised in accordance with the provisions of Article 11(3)(j);

7.7. a summary of the measures taken in accordance with Article 16 on priority substances;

7.8. a summary of the measures taken to prevent or reduce the impact of accidental pollution incidents;

7.9. a summary of the measures taken under Article 11(5) for bodies of water which are unlikely to achieve the objectives set out under Article 4;

7.10. details of the supplementary measures identified as necessary in order to meet the environmental objectives established;

7.11. details of the measures taken to avoid increase in pollution of marine waters in accordance with Article 11(6);

8. a register of any more detailed programmes and management plans for the river basin district dealing with particular sub-basins, sectors, issues or water types, together with a summary of their contents;

9. a summary of the public information and consultation measures taken, their results and the changes to the plan made as a consequence;

10. a list of competent authorities in accordance with Annex I;

11. the contact points and procedures for obtaining the background documentation and information referred to in Article 14(1), and in particular details of the control measures adopted in accordance with Article 11(3)(g) and 11(3)(i) and of the actual monitoring data gathered in accordance with Article 8 and Annex V.

B. The first update of the river basin management plan and all subsequent updates shall also include:

1. a summary of any changes or updates since the publication of the previous version of the river basin management plan, including a summary of the reviews to be carried out under Article 4(4), (5), (6) and (7);

2. an assessment of the progress made towards the achievement of the environmental objectives, including presentation of the monitoring results for the period of the previous plan in map form, and an

explanation for any environmental objectives which have not been reached;

3.   a summary of, and an explanation for, any measures foreseen in the earlier version of the river basin management plan which have not been undertaken;

4.   a summary of any additional interim measures adopted under Article 11(5) since the publication of the previous version of the river basin management plan.

Annex VIII

Indicative list of the main pollutants

1.   Organohalogen compounds and substances which may form such compounds in the aquatic environment.

2.   Organophosphorous compounds.

3.   Organotin compounds.

4.   Substances and preparations, or the breakdown products of such, which have been proved to possess carcinogenic or mutagenic properties or properties which may affect steroidogenic, thyroid, reproduction or other endocrine-related functions in or via the aquatic environment.

5.   Persistent hydrocarbons and persistent and bioaccumulable organic toxic substances.

6.   Cyanides.

7.   Metals and their compounds.

8.   Arsenic and its compounds.

9.   Biocides and plant protection products.

10.   Materials in suspension.

11. Substances which contribute to eutrophication (in particular, nitrates and phosphates).

12. Substances which have an unfavourable influence on the oxygen balance (and can be measured using parameters such as BOD, COD, etc.).

Annex IX

Emission limit values and environmental quality standards

The "limit values" and "quality objectives" established under the re Directives of Directive 76/464/EEC shall be considered emission limit values and environmental quality standards, respectively, for the purposes of this Directive. They are established in the following Directives:

(i)   The Mercury Discharges Directive (82/176/EEC)[1];

(ii)   The Cadmium Discharges Directive (83/513/EEC)[2];

(iii) The Mercury Directive (84/156/EEC)[3];

(iv)   The Hexachlorocyclohexane Discharges Directive (84/491/EEC)[4]; and

(v)   The Dangerous Substance Discharges Directive (86/280/EEC)[5].

[Omitted: Annex X - Priority substances, Annex XI, Map A, Map B]

---

[1] OJ L 81, 27.3.1982, p. 29.
[2] OJ L 291, 24.10.1983, p. 1.
[3] OJ L 74, 17.3.1984, p. 49.
[4] OJ L 274, 17.10.1984, p. 11.
[5] OJ L 181, 4.7.1986, p. 16.

35. Proposal for a Directive of the European Parliament and of the Council on the Protection of Groundwater Against Pollution [19 September 2003]*

[Omitted: Explanatory memorandum]

The European Parliament and the Council of the European Union,
Having regard to the Treaty establishing the European Community, and in particular Article 175(1) thereof,

Having regard to the proposal from the Commission[13],

Having regard to the opinion of the European Economic and Social Committee[14],

Having regard to the opinion of the Committee of the Regions[15],

Acting in accordance with the procedure laid down in Article 251 of the Treaty[16],

Whereas:

1. Groundwater is a valuable natural resource which should be protected from pollution in its own right.

2. Decision No 1600/2002/EC of the European Parliament and of the Council of 22 July 2002 laying down the Sixth Community Environment Action Programme[17] includes the objective to achieve levels of water quality that do not give rise to unacceptable impacts on, and risks to, human health and the environment.

---

* COM (2003) 550 final, at the time of finalizing this publication, the proposed Groundwater Directive was still under discussion in the Council and the European Parliament.

[13] OJ C , , p. .
[14] OJ C , , p. .
[15] OJ C , , p. .
[16] OJ C , , p. .
[17] OJ L 242, 10.9.2002, p. 81

3. In order to protect the environment as a whole, and human health in particular, concentrations of harmful pollutants in groundwater should be avoided, prevented or reduced.

4. Council Directive 2000/60/EC of 23 October 2000 establishing a framework for Community action in the field of water policy[18] sets out extensive provisions for the protection and conservation of groundwater. As provided for in Article 17 of that Directive, measures to prevent and control groundwater pollution should be adopted, including criteria for assessing good chemical status and criteria for identifying significant and sustained upward trends and for defining starting points for trend reversals.

5. Quality standards, threshold values, and assessment methods should be developed in order to provide criteria for the assessment of the chemical status of bodies of groundwater.

6. Criteria need to be established for identifying any significant and sustained upward trends in pollutant concentrations and for defining the starting point for trend reversal, taking into account the likelihood of adverse effects on associated aquatic ecosystems or dependent terrestrial ecosystems.

7. By virtue of Article 22, paragraph 2, third indent, of Directive 2000/60/EC, Council Directive 80/68/EEC of 17 December 1979 on the protection of groundwater against pollution by certain dangerous substances[19] will be repealed with effect from 22 December 2013. It is necessary to ensure the continuity of the protection regime set up by Directive 80/68/EEC with regard to both direct and indirect discharge of pollutants into groundwater by also establishing a link with relevant provisions of Directive 2000/60/EC.

8. It is necessary to provide for transitional measures as regards the period between the date of implementation of this Directive and the date from which Directive 80/68/EEC is repealed.

9. The measures necessary for the implementation of this Directive should be adopted in accordance with Council Decision 1999/468/EC

---

[18] OJ L 327, 22.12.2000, p. 72.
[19] OJ L 20, 26.1.1980, p. 43.

of 28 June 1999 laying down the procedures for the exercise of implementing powers conferred on the Commission[20],

Have adopted this Directive:

Article 1 - Subject matter

This Directive establishes specific measures as set out in Article 17(1) and (2) of Directive 2000/60/EC in order to prevent and control groundwater pollution. These measures include in particular:

(a) criteria for the assessment of good groundwater chemical status; and

(b) criteria for the identification and reversal of significant and sustained upward trends and for the definition of starting points for trend reversals.

This Directive also establishes a requirement to prevent or limit indirect discharges of pollutants into groundwater.

Article 2 - Definitions

For the purposes of this Directive, the following definitions shall apply in addition to those laid down in Article 2 of Directive 2000/60/EC:

1. "threshold value" means a concentration limit for a pollutant in groundwater, exceedance of which would cause a body of groundwater or groundwater bodies to be characterised as having poor chemical status.

2. "significant and sustained upward trend" means any statistically significant increase of concentration of a pollutant as compared to concentrations measured at the start of the monitoring programme referred to in Article 8 of Directive 2000/60/EC, taking into consideration quality standards and threshold values.

3. "indirect discharges to groundwater" means discharge of pollutants into groundwater after percolation through the ground or subsoil.

---

[20] OJ C 184, 17.7.1999, p. 23.

Article 3 - Criteria for assessing good groundwater chemical status

For the purposes of the characterisation to be carried out under Article 5 of Directive 2000/60/EC and under sections 2.1 and 2.2 of Annex II thereto, a body or group of bodies of groundwater shall be considered as having good groundwater chemical status when:

(a) with regard to any of the substances referred to in column 1 of Annex I to this Directive, the measured or predicted concentration does not exceed the quality standards laid down in column 2 thereof;

(b) with regard to any other polluting substances, it can be demonstrated, in accordance with the indications given in Annex II to this Directive, that the concentration of the substance complies with indent 3 of the definition set out in section 2.3.2 of Annex V to Directive 2000/60/EC.

Article 4 - Threshold values

1. On the basis of the characterisation process to be carried out under Article 5 of Directive 2000/60/EC and under sections 2.1 and 2.2 of Annex II thereto, in accordance with the procedure described in Annex II to this Directive, and taking account of the economic and social costs, Member States shall, by 22 December 2005, establish threshold values for each of the pollutants, which within their territory have been identified as contributing to the characterisation of bodies or group of bodies of groundwater as being at risk. Member States shall as a minimum establish threshold values for the pollutants referred to in parts A.1 and A.2 of Annex III to this Directive. These threshold values shall inter alia be used for the purposes of carrying out the review of groundwater status as provided for in Article 5.2 of Directive 2000/60/EC. Those threshold values can be established at the national level, at the level of the river basin district or at the level of body or group of bodies of groundwater.

2. At the latest by 22 June 2006, Member States shall provide the Commission with a list of all pollutants for which they have established threshold values. For each pollutant on the list, Member States shall provide the information set out in part B of Annex III to this Directive.

3.   On the basis of the information provided by Member States in accordance with paragraph 2, the Commission shall publish a report, accompanied, if appropriate, by a proposal for a directive amending Annex I to this Directive. Before publishing the report and before adopting any legislative proposals amending Annex I to this Directive, the Commission shall seek the opinion of the Committee referred to in Article 16(5) of Directive 2000/60/EC.

Article 5 - Criteria for the identification of significant and sustained upward trends and the definition of starting points for trend reversals

Member States shall identify any significant and sustained upward trend of concentrations of pollutants found in bodies of groundwater, or groups of bodies, and define the starting point for reversing that trend, in accordance with Annex IV to this Directive. For those bodies of groundwater where significant and sustained upward trends in pollutant concentrations are identified, Member States shall reverse the trend through the programme of measures referred to in Article 11 of Directive 2000/60/EC, in order progressively to reduce pollution of groundwater.

Article 6 - Measures to prevent or limit indirect discharges into groundwater

In addition to the basic measures set out in Article 11(3) of Directive 2000/60/EC, Member States shall ensure that the programme of measures for each river basin district includes the prevention of indirect discharges to groundwater of any of the pollutants referred to in points 1 to 6 of Annex VIII to that Directive. Furthermore, with regard to the pollutants referred to in points 7 to 12 of Annex VIII to Directive 2000/60/EC, the programme of measures set out in Article 11(3) of that directive shall include the provision that any indirect discharges to groundwater shall only be permitted on condition that the discharges does not put at risk the achievement of good groundwater chemical status.

Article 7 - Transitional arrangements

In the period between [insert date of implementation as in Article 9(1) of this Directive] and the 22 December 2013 prior investigations and authorisations pursuant to Articles 4 and 5 of Directive 80/68/EEC shall take into account the requirements set out in Articles 3, 4 and 5 of this Directive.

Article 8 - Technical adaptations

Annexes II to IV to this Directive may be adapted to scientific and technical progress in accordance with the procedure referred to in Article 21(2) of Directive 2000/60/EC, considering the period of reviews and updating of the river basin management plan, as referred to in Article 13(7) of Directive 2000/60/EC.

Article 9 - Implementation

Member States shall bring into force the laws, regulations and administrative provisions necessary to comply with this Directive at the latest [18 months after the date of entry into force of this Directive]. They shall forthwith inform the Commission thereof. When Member States adopt those provisions, they shall contain a reference to this Directive or be accompanied by such a reference on the occasion of their official publication. Member States shall determine how such reference is to be made.

Article 10 - Entry into force

This Directive shall enter into force on the twentieth day of its publication in the Official Journal of the European Union.

Article 11 - Addressees

This Directive is addressed to the Member States.

...

Annex I - Groundwater quality standards

Pollutant	Quality standards[21], [22]	Comment
Nitrates	50 mg/1	The quality standard applies to all bodies of groundwater, with the exception of the nitrate vulnerable zones identified under Directive 91/676/EEC[23]. For these areas, Article 4(1)(c) of Directive 2000/60/EC applies.
Active ingredients in pesticides, including their relevant metabolites, degradation and reaction products[24]	0.1 μg/1 21	

---

[21] Where for a given body of groundwater, it is considered that the groundwater quality standards could result in failure to achieve the environmental objectives specified in Article 4 of Directive 2000/60/EC for associated surface waters or result in any significant diminution of the ecological or chemical quality of such bodies, or any significant damage to terrestrial ecosystems which depend directly on the body of groundwater, more stringent threshold values shall be established in accordance with Article 4 and Annex IV to this Directive.

[22] Compliance with the standards shall be based on a comparison with the arithmetic means of the monitoring values at each of the sampling points in the body or group of bodies of groundwater characterised as being at risk pursuant to the analysis to be carried out under Article 5 of Directive 2000/60/EC.

[23] OJ L 375, 31.12.1991, p. 1.

[24] Pesticides refer to plant protection products and biocidal products as defined by Article 2 of Directive 91/414/EEC and Article 2 of Directive 98/8/EC, respectively.

Annex II - Assessment of groundwater chemical status for pollutants
for which community quality standards do not exist

The assessment procedure for testing compliance to good groundwater
chemical status for pollutants for which Community quality standards do not
exist shall be carried out in relation to all bodies of groundwater
characterised as being at risk and in relation to each of the pollutants which
contribute to the body or group of bodies of groundwater being so
characterised.

The assessment procedure shall in particular address the following issues:

(a) the information collected as part of the characterisation to be carried
     out under Article 5 of Directive 2000/60/EC and under sections 2.1
     and 2.2 of Annex II thereto;

(b) environmental quality objectives and other standards for water
     protection that exist at national, Community or international level;

(c) any relevant information concerning the toxicology, ecotoxicology,
     persistence and bioaccumulation potential concerning the pollutant or
     related substances;

(d) the estimated amounts and the concentrations of the pollutants
     transferred from the body of groundwater to the associated surface
     waters and/or dependent terrestrial ecosystems;

(e) the estimated impact of the amounts and concentrations of the
     pollutants as determined in (d) on the associated surface waters and
     dependent terrestrial ecosystems;

(f) an assessment based on (d) and (e) as to whether the concentrations of
     the pollutants in the body of groundwater are such as would result in
     failure to achieve the environmental objectives specified in Article 4 of
     Directive 2000/60/EC for associated surface waters or any significant
     deterioration of the ecological or chemical quality of such bodies or any
     significant damage to terrestrial ecosystems which depend directly on
     the body of groundwater.

Annex III - Threshold values for groundwater pollutants

Part A.1 - Minimum list of substances or ions, which may both occur naturally and as a result of human activities, for which member states are required to establish threshold values in accordance with Article 4.2[25]

Substance or ion
Ammonium
Arsenic
Cadmium
Chloride
Lead
Mercury
Sulphate

Part A.2 - Minimum list of man-made synthetic substances for which member states are required to establish threshold values in accordance with Article 4.2

Substance
Trichloroethylene
Tetrachloroethylene

Part B: Information to be provided by member states with regard to the list of pollutants for which threshold values have been determined

In accordance with Article 4(2) and section 2 of Annex II to this Directive, for each of the pollutants that characterise bodies of groundwater as being at risk, Member States shall provide as a minimum the following information:

---

[25] This list should be complemented by Member States for all pollutants which have been identified to characterise bodies of groundwater at being at risk following the analysis carried out under Article 5 of Directive 2000/60/EC.

1. Information on bodies of groundwater characterised as being at risk

1.1 Information on the number of bodies of groundwater characterised as being at risk in which the selected pollutants contribute to this classification.

1.2 Information on each of the bodies of groundwater characterised as being at risk, in particular the size of the bodies, the relationship between the bodies of groundwater and the associated surface waters and dependent terrestrial ecosystems and, in case of naturally occurring substances, the background levels in the bodies of groundwater.

2. Information on the establishment of threshold values

2.1 The threshold values, whether they apply at the national level, or at the level of the river basin district, or for individual bodies or groups of bodies of groundwater.

2.2 The relationship between the threshold values and, in the case of naturally occurring substances, the observed background levels.

2.3 The manner in which economic and social costs were taken into account in establishing the threshold values.

Annex IV - Identification and reversal of significant and sustained upward trends

1. Identification of significant and sustained upward trends

Member States shall identify significant and sustained upward trends, taking into account the following requirements:

1.1 In accordance with Section 2.4 of Annex V to Directive 2000/60/EC, the monitoring programme shall be adjusted to detect any significant and sustained upward trends of concentrations of the pollutants identified pursuant to Article 4 of this Directive.

1.2 The procedure for the identification of significant and sustained upward trends shall be based on the following procedure:

(a)   the assessment shall be based on arithmetic mean values of the mean values of the individual monitoring points in each bodies or groups of bodies of groundwater bodies, as calculated on the basis of a quarterly, a half-yearly or an annual monitoring frequency.

(b)   in order to avoid bias in trend identification, all measurements below the limit of quantification shall be eliminated for the calculation.

(c)   the minimum number of data values and the minimum length of time series are laid down in the following table. The time series shall not exceed 15 years.

Monitoring frequency	Minimum number of years	Maximum number of years	Minimum number of measurements
Annual	8	15	8
Half-yearly	5	15	10
Quarterly	5	15	15

(d)   The missing of two or more subsequent data values should be avoided, and further requirements on the sampling scheme shall be considered to allow for calculations of reliable results.

1.3   The identification of significant and sustained upward trends in the concentrations of substances which occur both naturally and as a result of human activities shall consider data gathered before the start of the monitoring programme in order to report on trend identification within the first River Basin Management Plan set out in Article 13 of Directive 2000/60/EC.

1.4   Specific trend assessment shall be carried out for relevant pollutants in bodies of groundwater that are affected by point sources of pollution, including historical point sources, in order to verify that plumes from contaminated sites do not expand over a defined area and deteriorate the chemical status of the groundwater body.

1.5   Similarly, specific trend assessment shall be performed in those areas of groundwater bodies in which significant and sustained upward trends of concentrations of any pollutants identified pursuant to Article 4 of this Directive might result in adverse effects on associated aquatic ecosystems or dependent terrestrial ecosystems, or interference with existing or future uses of groundwater.

1.6   The identification of significant and sustained upward trends shall be based on the procedure for the assessment of chemical status specified in Annex II to this Directive.

2.   Starting points for trend reversals

2.1   Trend reversals shall be focused on trends which present a risk of harm to associated aquatic ecosystems, directly dependent terrestrial ecosystems, human health or legitimate uses of the water environment.

2.2   The procedure for identifying the starting point for a trend reversal shall be established on a time basis, and at the minimum on the basis of monitoring data collected in accordance with Article 8 of Directive 2000/60/EC. In this case, the reference points shall correspond to the start of the monitoring programme.

2.3   The minimum number of measurement values and the minimum length of time series for the analysis of trend reversal in years includes and depends on the selected monitoring frequency according to paragraph 1.2 item (c) of this Annex and is laid down in the following table. The time series shall not exceed 30 years.

Monitoring frequency	Minimum number of years	Maximum number of years	Minimum number of measurements
Annual	14	30	14
Half-yearly	10	30	18
Quarterly	10	30	30

2.4   There is a trend reversal if in the first section the slope of the trend line is positive, and in the second section negative. To allow for a reliable assessment of the trend reversal, it shall be ensured that the number of values before and after the break in the time series is adequate to the monitoring frequency.

2.5   The decision for reversing a trend shall also be based on the environmental significance of the upward and sustained increase in pollutant concentrations. As a recommended value, and in accordance with Article 17(4) of Directive 2000/60/EC, the starting point for trend reversal shall be at a maximum of 75% of the level of the quality standards set out in Annex I and/or of the threshold values established pursuant to Article 4.

2.6   If data obtained earlier than the start of the monitoring programme exist, they should be used for establishing the reference points for the identification of the starting point for trend reversal.

2.7   Once a reference point has been established, pursuant to paragraphs 2.1 and 2.2 above, it shall be used for the groundwater bodies characterised as being at risk and the associated substance, and shall not be changed.

ii.   **International Non-Binding Instruments**

36.   **United Nations Water Conference - Mar del Plata Action Plan [1977]***

Chapter I - Mar del Plata Action Plan

...

Recommendations

A.   Assessment of water resources

1.   In most countries there are serious inadequacies in the availability of data on water resources, particularly in relation to ground water and water quality. Hitherto, relatively little importance has been attached to its systematic measurement. The processing and compilation of data have also been seriously neglected.

2.   To improve the management of water resources, greater knowledge about their quantity and quality is needed. Regular and systematic collection of hydrometeorological, hydrological and hydrogeological data needs to be promoted and be accompanied by a system for processing quantitative and qualitative information for various types of water bodies. The data should be used to estimate available precipitation, surface-water and ground water resources and the potentials for augmenting these resources. Countries should review, strengthen and co-ordinate arrangements for the collection of basic data. Network densities should be improved; mechanisms for data collection, processing and publication and arrangement for monitoring water quality should be reinforced.

3.   To this end, it is recommended that countries should:

...

(c)   Establish observation networks and strengthen existing systems and facilities for measurements and recording fluctuations in ground-water

---

* Report of the United Nations Water Conference, Mar del Plata, 14–25 March 1977, UN Doc. E/Conf.70/29. United Nations publication Sales No. E.77.II.A.12.

quality and level; organize the collection of all existing data on ground water (borehole logs, geological structure, and hydrogeological characteristics, etc.) systematically index such data, and attempt a quantitative assessment so as to determine the present status of and gaps in knowledge; increase the search for, and determination of, the variables of aquifers, with an evaluation of their potential and the possibilities of recharge;

...

(f)   Make periodic assessments of surface- and ground-water resources, including rainfall, evaporation and run-off, lakes, lagoons, glaciers and snowfields, both for individual basins and at the national level, in order to determine a programme of investigation for the future in relation to development needs; intensify programmes already under way and formulate new programmes wherever needed;

...

(j)   Co-operate in the co-ordination, collection and exchange of relevant data in the case of shared resources;

...

(o)   Provide for the studying and analysing of hydrological data on surface and ground water by mutlidisciplinary [sic] teams so as to make adequate information available for planning purposes;

...

4.   International organizations and other supporting bodies should, as appropriate, and on request, take the following action:

...

(b)   Groundwater

(i)   Offer assistance for the establishment or strengthening of observational networks for recording quantitative and qualitative characteristics of ground-water resources;

(ii)   Offer assistance for the establishment of ground-water data banks and for reviewing the studies, locating gaps and formulating programmes of future investigations and prospection;

(iii) Offer help, including personnel and equipment, to make available the use of advanced techniques, such as geophysical methods, nuclear techniques, mathematical models, etc.

…

B.   Water use and efficiency

…

Efficiency and efficacy in regulation and distribution of the resources

9.   National mechanisms for the management of water resources should apply the best measures to improve the existing systems and the best available techniques for planning and design of conservation and distribution systems in the most efficient way and should equally attend to proper maintenance, control at the regional, national and farm level and operation of delivery systems to increase efficiency.

10.   To this end, it is recommended that:

(a)   Measures be taken to utilize ground-water aquifers in the form of collective and integrated systems, whenever possible and useful, taking into account the regulation and use of surface-water resources. This will provide an opportunity to exploit the ground-water aquifers to their physical limits, to protect spring and ground water from overdraught and salinity, as well as to ensure proper sharing of the resources;

(b)   Studies should explore the potential of ground-water basins, the use of aquifers as storage and distribution systems, and the conjunctive use of surface and subsurface resources to maximize efficacy and efficiency;

…

Community water supply and waste disposal

…

17. International organizations and other supporting bodies should, as appropriate, and on request, take the following action:

...

(v) Support research, development and demonstration in relation to predominant needs, particularly:

(a) Low-cost ground-water pumping equipment;

...

Agricultural water use

18. The increase of agricultural production and productivity should be aimed at achieving optimum yield in food production by a definite date, and at a significant improvement in total agricultural production as early as possible. Measures to attain these objectives should receive the appropriate high priority. Particular attention should be given to land and water management both under irrigated and rainfed cultivation, with due regard to long-term as well as short-term productivity. National legislation and policies should provide for the properly integrated management of land and water resources. Countries should, when reviewing national policies, institutions and legislation, ensure the co-ordination of activities and services involved in irrigation and drainage development and management. It is necessary to expand the use of water for agriculture together with an improvement in efficiency of use. This should be achieved through funding, providing the necessary infrastructure and reducing losses in transit, in distribution and on the farm, and avoiding the use of wasteful irrigation practices, to the extent possible. Each country should apply known techniques for the prevention and control of land and water degradation resulting from improper management. Countries should give early attention to the improvement of existing irrigation and drainage projects,

19. In this context, countries should:

(a) Bear in mind principles of integrated land and water management when reviewing national policies, administrative arrangements and legislation, and pay heed to the need to augment present levels of agricultural production;

(b) Undertake or continue studies on the relationship between land use and the elements of the hydrological cycle at the national and international levels;

...

(d) Plan and carry out irrigation programmes in such a way as to ensure that surface and subsurface drainage are treated as integral components and that provision of all requirements is co-ordinated with a view to optimizing the use of water and associated land resources;

(e) Provide financial resources and qualified manpower services for better water-use and management practices, proper maintenance, control and operation of distribution systems, and joint use of surface and ground water and eventually waste water, paying due attention to the needs of small-scale agriculture;

...

20. To this end it is recommended that:

(a) The institutional machinery responsible for water management should possess sufficient means and powers for the management of water for agricultural purposes, bearing in mind the physical interdependence of surface and ground water and in accordance with all its uses;

...

C.   Environment, health and pollution control

34. Large-scale water-development projects have important environmental repercussions of a physical, chemical, biological, social and economic nature, which should be evaluated and taken into consideration in the formulation and implementation of water projects. Furthermore, water-development projects may have unforeseen adverse consequences affecting human health in addition to those associated with the use of water for domestic purposes. Water pollution from sewage and industrial effluents and the use of chemical fertilizers and pesticides in agriculture is on the increase in many countries. It is also recognized that control measures regarding the discharge of urban, industrial and mining effluents are inadequate. Increased emphasis must be given to

the question of water pollution, within the over-all context of waste management.

...

Pollution control

38. Concerted and planned action is necessary to avoid and combat the effects of pollution in order to protect and improve where necessary the quality of water resources.

39. To this end it is recommended that countries should:

(a) Conduct surveys of present levels of pollution in surface-water and ground-water resources, and establish monitoring networks for the detection of pollution;

...

(f) Conduct research on and measurement of the pollution of surface and ground water by agricultural fertilizers and biocides with a view to lessening their adverse environmental impact;

...

(m) Promote the use of infiltration techniques when the nature of the effluents and the terrain makes it possible to do so without endangering surface and ground-water resources;

...

(o) Apply appropriate land-use planning as a tool for preventing water pollution, especially in the case of ground water;

...

[Omitted: D. Policy, planning and management]

E.   Natural hazards

...

Drought loss management

66.   In the recent past droughts of exceptional severity have caused major hardships in many areas of the world. Such disasters can arise again at any time. In consequence, steps to mitigate the effects of drought in such areas is a top priority. In order to remedy the situation, structural and non-structural and emergency measures should be adopted and for this purpose the development and management of water resources as well as drought forecasting on a long-term basis should be viewed as a key element,

67.   There is a need to develop improved bases for planning land and water management in order to make optimum use of land and water resources in areas subject to severe drought. Comprehensive programmes should be formulated for the progressive implementation of the development of water resources for the benefit of drought-affected areas: specific short-term and long-term objectives, as well as targets, should be outlined. There is also a need to study basic meteorological processes with a view to formulating long-term forecasts in weather behaviour in any given area.

68.   To this end, it is recommended that countries should:

...

(d)   Intensify the exploration of ground water through geophysical and hydrogeological investigations and undertake on a regional scale large-scale programmes for the development of wells and boreholes, to be explored in groups where appropriate for water for human and livestock consumption, taking into account the needs of pastures while preventing overgrazing and avoiding overexploitation of underground aquifers;

(e)   Determine the effect of drought on aquifers and in the assessment of the response of ground-water systems to drought, basing such assessment on concepts such as storage/flow ratio in order to characterize ground-water flow regions in periods of drought;

...

(n) Study the potential role of integration of surface and underground phases of water basins utilizing the stocks of water stored in ground-water formations in order to maintain a minimum supply under drought conditions.

...

F.   Public information, education, training and research

...

Research needs

...

82.   To this end it is recommended that countries should:

...

(f) Promote research into problems of methodologies for the assessment of supplies of surface and ground-water resources, and for their use, development and management.   Research organizations should use their resources first for applied research and application of research results already available to solve some of the most urgent national problems. As scientific personnel and equipment become available, more basic research may be undertaken and also research into high-technology fields;

(g) Promote research in areas related to their respective needs including where relevant:

...

Artificial recharge of aquifers

...

Contamination of groundwaters

...

[Omitted: G. Regional co-operation]

H.   International co-operation

...

Technical co-operation among developing countries

99.   The promotion of technical co-operation among developing countries
will supplement, upgrade and give a new dimension to the traditional
forms of bilateral and multilateral development co-operation to help
the developing countries achieve greater intrinsic self-reliance. The
development of water resources in developing countries provides a
promising area where technical co-operation among developing
countries can be achieved. Many developing countries have expertise
and capacity which they can share with other developing countries.
Alternate appropriate technologies have been developed and many
developing countries have reached the stage of self-reliance in water-
resource development to enable them to apply the more appropriate
techniques using the latest know-how and promote better
understanding among the countries concerned. This can be adapted to
the needs of other developing countries by means of technical co-
operation among developing countries.

...

102.   In the light of these considerations it is recommended that where
appropriate countries should at the national, regional and subregional
level:

...

(e)   Identify programmes for water resources development that can be achieved through technical co-operation among developing countries in specific sectors such as community water supply, irrigation, drainage, hydroelectric generation, the development and management of transboundary water resources, groundwater development, and means for the prevention and reduction of losses due to floods and droughts and pollution control, water legislation and training, transfer of technology suited to the requirements of the developing countries and the general development of such technology;

...

[Omitted: Annex - Specific regional recommendations]

Resolutions

[Omitted: I - Assessment of water resources, II - Community water supply, III - Agricultural water use, IV - Research and development of industrial technologies]

V.   Role of water in combating desertification

The United Nations Water Conference,

Bearing in mind the recommendations of the United Nations Conference on the Environment held in Stockholm in June 1972,

Taking into account the urgent need for concerted action to combat desertification and the forthcoming United Nations Conference on Desertification,

...

5.   Recommends further that in most countries facing problems of desertification, urgent action is necessary to:

...

(b)   Intensify and improve the arrangements existing for the assessment of water resources - surface as well as ground water;

(c) Consider, on the basis of prior environmental and health impact studies, a programme of surface and ground-water use and conservation with intensive mobilization of public participation on the basis of self-help. Such a programme should provide for the construction and maintenance of existing small dams or wells, with appropriate national and international assistance;

...

(e) Set up appropriate institutional arrangements at the national and regional levels in order that adequate attention be given to the problems of management and development of surface and ground-water resources in arid and semi-arid regions, including collation of related policies, promotion of efficient use of water by developing appropriate technologies, including the application of water-saving technologies;

...

VI. Technical co-operation among developing countries in the water sector

The United Nations Water Conference,

...

5. Recommends further that the United Nations Development Programme in co-operation with the regional commissions and the United Nations system assist in promoting programmes of technical co-operation among developing countries in the field of water-resources development, which may include such areas as surface and ground-water development, drainage and reclamation, hydropower development and inland navigation;

...

[Omitted: VII - River commissions, VIII - Institutional arrangements for international co-operation in the water sector, IX - Financing arrangements for international co-operation in the water sector, X - Water policies in the occupied territories; Chapter II - Other resolutions: XI - Question of the Panama Canal Zone, XII - Expression of thanks to the host country]

37. United Nations Economic Commission for Europe - Charter on Groundwater Management [1989]*

Foreword

Groundwater – as a natural resource with both ecological and economic value – is of vital importance for sustaining life, health and the integrity of ecosystems. This resource is, however, increasingly threatened by over-use and insidious long-term effects of pollution. Pollution comes from both point sources and diffuse sources. Potential risks or actual impacts could permanently impair underground water resources, with far-reaching and unpredictable implications for present and future generations. Action is urgently needed. The Charter on Groundwater Management provides policy measures for such action.

The adoption of the Charter by the member Governments of the Economic Commission for Europe was the culmination of intense regional co-operation aimed at reaching agreement on common policies for the protection of this vital natural resource. Prepared by the Senior Advisers to ECE Governments on Environmental and Water Problems, assisted by the Working Party on Water Problems, the Charter builds on the results of extensive experience. It reflects, in particular, the outcome of two special meetings devoted to the subject: the Seminar on Groundwater Protection Strategies and Practices, held in Athens (Greece) in 1983 and the Seminar on Protection of Soil and Aquifers against Non-point Source Pollution, held in Madrid (Spain) in 1987.

The Charter on Groundwater Management gives broad support to ECE member Governments in their common endeavours to protect groundwater by providing planners and decision-makers with appropriate policy instruments. Publication of the Charter is intended to heighten public awareness of the need for concerted action to protect groundwater. The Commission has recommended that member Governments apply the provisions of the Charter when formulating, adopting and implementing water-related policies and strategies at both national and international levels.

---

* Adopted by the Economic Commission for Europe at its Forty-Fourth Session (1989) by decision E (44), UN Doc. E/ECE/1197, ECE/ENVWA/12.

Contents

...

I. Groundwater policy

Governments should formulate and adopt a long-term policy to protect groundwater by preventing pollution and overuse. This policy should be comprehensive and implemented at all appropriate levels. It should be consistent with other water-management policies and be duly taken into account in other sectorial policies.

II. Groundwater strategies

1. As groundwater should be recognized as a natural resource with economic and ecological value, groundwater strategies should aim at the sustainable use of groundwater and preservation of its quality. These strategies should be flexible so as to respond to changing conditions and various regional and local situations.

2. Groundwater pollution is interrelated with the pollution of other environmental media (surface water, soils, atmosphere). Groundwater protection planning should be incorporated into general environmental protection planning.

3. Protection measures aimed at prevention of groundwater pollution and over-use should be the basic tools for groundwater management. Such protection measures include, *inter alia,* monitoring of groundwaters, development of aquifer vulnerability maps, regulations for industry and waste disposal sites paying due account to groundwater protection considerations, geo-ecological assessment of the impact of industrial and agricultural activities on groundwaters, and zoning of groundwater protection areas.

III. Integration of instruments

1. In formulating and implementing national groundwater policy, legal, administrative and regulatory measures should be co-ordinated with the best available technologies and economic instruments.

2.   Integrated water management should be promoted by paying equal attention to both quantity and quality aspects of groundwater. Likewise, emphasis should be placed on the co-ordinated management of groundwater and surface water, while taking into account the distinguishing features of groundwater as compared to surface water which necessitate special protective measures for aquifers.

IV.   Groundwater allocation

An appropriate policy should be adopted for preferential allocation of groundwater, giving appropriate weight to competitive uses and balancing short-term demands with long-term objectives in the interest of present and future generations. In allocating groundwater resources, account should be taken of the amount of groundwater in reserve and of the rate of its replenishment. Allocation of high-quality groundwater only to uses demanding high-quality water, in particular for human and animal consumption, should be encouraged. More emphasis should be given to the nature conservation value provided by groundwater resources, in particular where nature protection areas are vulnerable to changes in groundwater conditions.

V.   Groundwater legislation

1.   Provisions of the Charter should be applied in national groundwater legislation. Legal provisions specific to peculiarities of groundwater management should be formulated and promulgated. Legislation should contain provisions for its effective implementation including the mandate, competence and power of the relevant authorities in accordance with uniform principles, e.g. as set out in this document. Governments' rights to control groundwater abstraction and use as well as all activities with a potential impact on the quantity and quality of groundwater resources should be recognized by legislation.

2.   Adequate definitions of groundwater characteristics, use and protection should be formulated and integrated into legislation with a view to avoiding ambiguities and thus facilitate implementation of legal provisions for groundwater management.

3.   Ownership with respect to groundwater should be clearly defined in a water act or code depending on national legislation. Groundwater should be declared in the public domain or authority should be vested

in Government to restrict, in the public interest, the rights accruing from its private ownership. New legislation should strive towards changing ownership rights into groundwater use rights subject to a government-controlled permit system. To this end, it would be necessary to draw up precise rules concerning the selection of criteria applicable for the recognition of groundwater use rights and for the granting of permits taking into account orders of priority for the allocation of available water. Such rules should also determine conditions of transfer, modification or abolition of use rights. Priorities to use groundwater, however, should be kept flexible so as to satisfy present and future requirements such as socio-economic factors.

VI. Competence

1. Water authorities or co-ordinating bodies should have the competence to integrate all aspects of water management and should be rendered competent to arbitrate among the various competing demands, and diverging interests regarding groundwater abstraction and use, both short- and long-term. The authority or body should collaborate with other authorities, competent for public health, land-use planning, soils' management, waste management, etc. Legislation should provide administrative mechanisms for emergency cases and should empower the competent authorities to act immediately against damage.

2. The territorial competence of such authorities with respect to groundwater management should not necessarily be limited to either administrative boundaries or catchment areas but should allow for encompassing, as appropriate, management of aquifers in their entirety. The work of these authorities should be supp6rted and facilitated by providing them with the resources necessary for the proper discharge of their functions.

3. Regulations, within the framework of legislation mentioned above, should define the actions to be taken by competent authorities in case of accidental pollution or other emergencies impacting on groundwater.

VII. Economic measures

1. Economic measures such as fees and waste-disposal charges should be applied in co-ordination and have sufficient impact to constitute an

effective incentive to use groundwater rationally or be a disincentive to polluting aquifers.

2. The abstraction of groundwater could be subjected to differentiated fees in proportion to the volume abstracted, in relation to the available resource or according to the anticipated use of the abstracted groundwater, while complying with legal provisions and regulations governing the applied permit system.

3. Costs attributable to pollution should be borne by the polluter whenever the latter can be identified. Serious consideration should be given to all possible economic measures which could have an influence on preventing, mitigating and counteracting damage as well as those bearing on remedying critical situations caused by pollution or over-exploitation of aquifers.

VIII. Permit and penalty system

An appropriate and effective permit and penalty system should be introduced and administered by the competent authorities. The system should promote preventive approaches inducing users to control any activity affecting the quantity and quality of groundwater.

IX. Exploration and abstraction permits

Permits for groundwater exploration or prospection should be granted by the responsible authority separately from those for groundwater abstraction or use because of the functional difference between the sinking of an exploration well and the large-scale exploitation of aquifers. Exploration permits should have short-term duration.

X. Abstraction and recharge permits

1. Abstraction of water from aquifers and the artificial recharge of groundwater should be licensed and controlled by competent authorities according to specific requirements laid down in an appropriate permit system which should be flexible so as to adapt to site-specific conditions. The question of groundwater exploitability should be clarified on a case-by-case basis, taking into account all relevant aspects, including ecological ones. The relevant regulations should establish the extent to which exemptions can be allowed in cases

of, for example, groundwater abstraction for households and dystems[sic] for draining fields. Where compatible with national legislation, permits for groundwater abstraction and use as well as pollution control should not release the user of groundwater from responsibility in case of detrimental effects on groundwater quality and quantity as a result of interventions covered by the permit granted.

2. Specifications of licences should include, *inter alia,* the purpose, amount, location, duration and technical characteristics of abstraction, as well as the legal status of the groundwater user.

3. Authorization for artificially recharging the aquifer should be granted only if the hydrogeological situation, environmental conditions and the recharge-water quality permit injection, percolation or infiltration of water by artificial means into aquifers for storage and retrieval of good-quality water as well as for restoring over-exploited groundwater resources. For induced recharge from adjacent streams or lakes, appropriate security measures should be applied to forestall accidental pollution.

4. Appropriate measures should be taken to combat saltwater encroachment into coastal aquifers. In such areas special regulations for groundwater abstraction should be enforced to avoid seepage into aquifers owing to over-pumping and the resultant lowering of the groundwater table.

XI. Pollution-control permits

1. To prevent groundwater pollution, permits issued to regulate the discharge, disposal and possibly the storage of waste should specifically take into account the vulnerability of the aquifer concerned and the provisions necessary for its protection. These provisions should, in particular apply to production, handling, trading, transporting, storage and use of potentially hazardous substances especially those which are toxic, persistent and bioaccumulative and apply above all to:

-   Effluents and sludges produced by waste-water treatment plants;

-   Domestic-waste disposal sites;

-   Subsurface waste containment by deep-well injection or container storage as ultima ratio;

-   Surface storage of wastes potentially hazardous by virtue of their chemical composition.

    In permitting such activities, inter alia, the hydrogeological situation of the area should be taken into consideration. On this matter the opinion of qualified specialists should be sought in all above-mentioned cases. Continuous monitoring programmes should be set up both to control water quality in aquifers as well as for checking compliance with permits granted. The specific regulations on nuclear plants and the handling and processing of radioactive substances should include appropriate provisions for the protection of underground waters.

2. Siting of controlled waste disposal should assure that there is no immediate and/or long-term hazard to groundwater. Controlled sites should be equipped with protective installations according to the best available technology and monitored by competent authorities. Regulations or guidelines should be drawn up for the site selection of controlled waste-disposal sites, their operation, monitoring, shut-down and eventual rehabilitation, with particular emphasis on groundwater quality protection. Solid or liquid wastes which are toxic, persistent, bioaccumulative or radioactive and which put groundwater at risk should be subject to special treatment. Legislation should ban dumping of solid or liquid wastes at unauthorized sites.

3. When applying and operating pollution-control technology for cleaning gases, liquids or solids, during or after treatment processes, the pollutants concentrated in sludges, slurries, gases or solids should not be released uncontrolled into the environment and nor ultimately reach and pollute aquifers. Care should be taken so that pollutants separated from exhaust gas, flue gas and other gaseous emissions do not enter groundwater. Measures should be taken to prevent pollution by volatile organic compounds and other aerosols.

4. Pollution control at the source should cover, in particular, those pollutants which are toxic, persistent and bioaccumulative. To this end, regulatory measures and economic incentives should encourage the replacement of chemicals hazardous to groundwater by less harmful substances in industrial production processes. Similarly, regulations

governing contaminants could be enforced with regard to trade, processing and transport of hazardous substances, with a view to averting or minimizing the risks of leakage into aquifers, and preventing accidental spills of hazardous substances.

5.   Application of treated waste water and resulting sludge on land should be subject to licence and/or conform to nationally agreed codes of practice and be restricted to areas where there is no immediate or long-term hazard to groundwater quality. In this respect, particular care should be taken not to overload the self-purification capacity of the soil filter and corresponding natural processes therein. Special attention should be paid to hazardous substances, for example heavy metals.

6.   In principle, injection of liquid wastes into the ground should be prohibited. Deep-well injection of liquid wastes of industrial origin and other water of objectionable quality into the ground should be authorized only case-by-case as ultima ratio, if the necessary precautions and controls for deep-well disposal can be specified, and if injected wastes cannot harm nearby aquifers. Control methods should include proper siting, design, construction, operation, abandonment and monitoring of deep-well injection. Control measures should be taken to prevent wastes escaping into freshwater aquifers. Continuous hydrogeological surveys should be carried out in the planning stage and during construction. These should serve as a basis for authorization. Permits should specify, inter alia, restrictions on the operation programme, emergency procedures in the event of malfunction, as well as monitoring and abandonment procedures for deep wells.

XII. Wells and boreholes

Drilling and sinking of wells and boreholes should as a rule be carried out by qualified and properly skilled personnel and with appropriate equipment. Prior notice should be given to competent authorities for drilling, sinking, constructing, enlarging, altering, sealing and repairing wells or boreholes and, once work is terminated, a report on the work accomplished should be filed. Provisions might be made for exemptions following precise rules in the case of small and shallow wells. Systematic control should be carried out over the technical status of operation, exploring and monitoring wells, in order to prevent the intrusion into aquifers of polluting substances from the land surface and the mixing of various water layers through drilling of wells.

XIII. Monitoring and control

1. Monitoring programmes for groundwater protection should be set up and applied. These programmes should include monitoring at the source of potential pollution which could pose a serious or chronic threat to an aquifer. There should be regular inspections to ensure compliance with protection requirements imposed. Attention should also be paid to the monitoring of groundwater quality changes brought about by air-borne pollution.

2. Systematic monitoring should be carried out for all aquifers found to be vulnerable to pollution and/or over-use, as well as for those whose particular importance has been recognized for public water supply, mineral water supply and industry.

3. Monitoring and control should be considered a public-service activity. Facilities should be set up for co-ordinating the assessment and availability of monitoring data and information on aquifers. The resulting collections of data should be related to information on groundwater quantity and quality characteristics of aquifers as well as details of their location, use, and exposure to various impacts from land uses such as agriculture, industry and urban development. Information should be readily available to those interested.

4. The data from monitoring should make it possible, *inter alia,* to revise periodically plans and forecasts of groundwater use, taking into account actual evolution of aquifers, and to determine measures necessary to ensure the sustainable use of groundwater resources in the long term. Legislative provisions and regulations should, as appropriate, allow for the revision of protection requirements imposed depending on the measures thus determined.

5. Monitoring programmes should be periodically reviewed to ensure that they are achieving their stated aims and that the results have been used effectively.

XIV. Impact assessment

1. All projects in any economic sector expected to affect aquifers adversely should be subject to an assessment procedure aiming at evaluating the project's possible impact on the water regime and/or the

quality of groundwater resources, with particular attention to the important role groundwater plays in the ecological system. Impact assessment surveys should continue during the construction and operation phases of a project, in order to keep under review any adverse impacts on groundwater resources before, during and after human interventions.

2. Impact assessments should be undertaken at an early stage of project planning and should be systematically applied to the different alternatives considered in a project study. Results of impact assessment procedures should duly be taken into account in decision making. Systematic monitoring of project realization by competent authorities should ensure compliance with conditions of groundwater protection.

XV. Inventories

Inventories of all groundwater aquifers should be made, including data on their quantitative and qualitative characteristics, and their vulnerability to over-exploitation and pollution. The evaluation should include data on the present situation and future prospects with regard to aquifer use.

XVI. Planning and forecasting

1. Special attention should be accorded to the application of planning tools and forecasting methods when managing groundwaters and protecting aquifers against pollution and over-use. Programmes for continuous assessment of both the quality and quantity of groundwater should be implemented, particularly for those aquifers vulnerable to or threatened by pollution or over-exploitation.

2. In the planning procedures, procedures, prospective studies and forecasts - both in terms of water quantity and quality - of future groundwater demands, use, consumption, discharge and environmental stress should not only be an extrapolation of past trends but should also take into account the anticipated effect of applied or foreseen control measures, economic incentives and other managerial instruments for groundwater protection. Objectives of planning, and in particular long-term planning should not only serve the purpose of exploitation and utilization of groundwater resources but - to an increasing extent - should serve their protection. Planning should among other elements seek to include quality-forecasts of groundwater

resources for appropriate time horizons, taking into account potential pollutants already in the ground and which would eventually contaminate groundwater long after strict pollution-control measures had become effective.

3.   Groundwater models should be built so that multi-variant/multiple forecasts can be made of the groundwater regime, particularly for aquifers at risk.

XVII. Land-use policies

1.   Land-use policies should take duly into account the exigencies of natural recharge and protection of groundwater against pollution and over-exploitation. Co-ordination between the various responsible authorities should be promoted. The general application of land-use plans, where appropriate, can be an effective measure in this connection.

2.   A co-ordinated approach to groundwater management and land-use control may call for negotiation procedures. Land-use policies should be co-ordinated with other relevant policies of integrated water management such as surface-water and groundwater management policies. Water managers should be involved in land-use planning already at an early stage of development processes. In areas where aquifers are unique, endangered or already impaired, groundwater protection strategies should carry decisive weight in land-use planning and control.

3.   Aquifers should be designated critical when already heavily endangered or impaired by pollution or over-use. To avoid further degradation and to make possible their restoration, appropriate measures should be taken which could include changes in land-use patterns and related rights.

4.   Sites of waste disposal and places where activities may result in contamination of land should be appropriately restored.

5.   Increased attention should be paid to enhancing natural recharge of aquifers.

XVIII. Protection zones

1. Where compatible with national legislation, groundwater protection zones should be established over and above the general protection of groundwaters through relevant legal provisions, as a preventive measure protecting aquifers around present and future abstraction sites and in recharge areas where aquifers are vulnerable. Compliance with the prescribed restrictions should be strictly controlled.

2. Protection zones could be divided into different classes with differentiated restrictions on land-use and water-use graduated according to environmental considerations and the relative importance of the underlying aquifer. In this respect, particular consideration should be given to the establishment of well-head protection areas. Necessary measures should be taken to minimize the risks of accidental or diffuse pollution in protection zones.

3. Restrictions and/or prohibitions on land-use activities should include mining and industrial processes, manufacturing, intensive farming, including the application of fertilizers and pesticides on agricultural land, transportation, waste disposal and treatment as well as storage of dangerous substances.

XIX. Pollution from agriculture

1. Advice, recommendations, codes of good agricultural practice, legislation, regulations or economic measures should be applied to keep under control the widespread use of fertilizers and any chemicals in agriculture having potential effects on groundwater. Policies applied through such measures should take into account the general diffuse nature of such pollution as well as the often considerable time-lag in the transfer of polluting substances to aquifers. These policies should, therefore, promote the application of preventive measures. To that end, all appropriate measures mentioned above should also be implemented to encourage and to promote the rational application of industrial fertilizers, manures, crop-protection products and pesticides. Restrictive measures with penalties for non-compliance should be adopted in particular for the protection of vulnerable aquifers and for protection zones.

2.   In order to promote the rational use of agricultural inputs, appropriate measures or a combination of them should be taken, wherever deemed necessary, e.g. the establishment of contractual arrangements between professional agricultural organizations and water authorities; restrictive measures of a legal, regulatory or economic character taking into account socio-economic constraints and environmental conditions prevailing in each country or region.

3.   Appropriate measures for controlled use of manure could be, for instance: limiting the operation of intensive large-scale livestock farming to sites where sufficient land is available for correct application and use of manure and slurry; making available large tracts of arable land through co-operative agreement between crop-farmers and livestock farmers, if necessary transporting manure over longer distances to croplands. If in a particular region manure is produced in excess of that needed for plant growth, transport to regions which are deficient should be considered as a solution (manure banks). Conditioning of wastes for stabilization and sale as well as treatment of manure with recuperation of by-products (fertilizers) could also be considered. Manure-application control measures may also include: regulations including dosage and timing; volume increase of manure storage tanks; designing and using better equipment for manure spraying.

4.   Strict licensing procedures should be introduced for the manufacture and distribution of crop-protection products and pesticides. Their use and application, however, is difficult to regulate. Recommendations should nevertheless be made with regard to their dosage, conditions of use, periodicity of application, precautions to be taken, etc. This advice may be included in information campaigns for farmers.

XX. Pollution from urban and industrial sources

1.   Measures should be taken to control pollution associated with surface run-off from paved impermeable areas (e.g. streets) and with leakage from industry, transport, sewerage systems and treatment plants. Polluted surface run-off should be properly treated especially where vulnerable aquifers could be affected.

2.   Sites of unauthorized waste disposal and other contaminated areas should be identified and adequately restored.

3. Leakage and spillage of contaminants from industries, transport, sewerage systems and waste-water treatment plants should be prevented through appropriate design as well as efficient maintenance and supervision including leakage tests Detection of leakage from pipelines, storage tanks and other industrial facilities should be improved by appropriate inspection procedures.

XXI. Control of mining activities

1. Dewatering of mines should be kept under control so as to minimize the adverse effects on the water regime, prevent depletion or pollution of nearby aquifers and infiltration of low-quality water. Special attention should be paid to the disposal of mining wastes so that they do not put at risk the quality of groundwater. When mines are closed down they should be properly sealed off parallel to the abandoned wells and waste dumps. Vegetation on them should be re-established.

2. In planning and operating *in situ* conversion of coal into natural gas or fluids, strict safety measures should be designed and applied to avoid groundwater pollution induced by processing gases or liquids. This should be done in order to prevent leaching of minerals from reaction zones after mining, or to bar solvents, sulphur and phenol-rich fluids from reaching the groundwater. Sites of any kind of waste, in particular tailings ponds for wastes from oil-sand and oil-shale extraction, as well as coal and metal mining should be sealed off against their contaminating groundwater.

XXII. Heat pumps

Water authorities should specify criteria for the location, operation, maintenance and closing down of heat pumps and other installations likely to use significant quantities of substances with potential to pollute groundwater, e.g. dielectrics, and should draw up guidelines on related groundwater protection measures. Specific requirements should be set for a cooling agent and other chemicals used. Further restriction or even prohibition may be necessary in groundwater protection zones.

XXIII. Research

Research programmes should be intensified in order to improve knowledge of:

(a)   hydrodynamics in aquifers;

(b)   transportation, fixation and leaching processes of pollutants as well as cumulative phenomena of chemical compounds in the subsoil, in both saturated and unsaturated zones and even in deep-lying aquifers;

(c)   appropriate technical measures which prevent, or at least reduce substantially, the transfer of undesirable substances from human activities into groundwaters and/or related surface waters;

(d)   elaboration of guidelines and technologies with regard to the prevention of groundwater pollution from agriculture;

(e)   economical and effective clean-up methods for polluted soils arid aquifers; and

(f)   development and calibration of representative groundwater models. International co-operation aiming at the exchange of experience and views and/or joint or co-ordinated research programmes in these fields should be encouraged.

XXIV. Education and information

1.   Education and information should promote greater awareness of the inherent groundwater problems at all levels, contributing to efficient implementation of the measures taken.

2.   Every effort should be made to raise the level of knowledge of the public, in general, and of water users, in particular, as regards the nature, behaviour and vulnerability of groundwater resources. To this end, public information, education and training programmes should be encouraged.

3.   Active participation of all parties concerned with the management and use of groundwater should be promoted, with a view, inter alia, to achieving public acceptance of legal and administrative measures

which could restrict the freedom of individual water users, in order to avert possible hazards in the case of misuse. Such knowledge should forestall resistance or outright opposition to the implementation of sound policies for groundwater management.

XXV. International co-operation

1. Concerted endeavours to strengthen international co-operation for harmonious development, equitable use and joint conservation of groundwater resources located beneath national boundaries should be intensified. To this end, existing or new bilateral or multilateral agreements or other legally binding arrangements should be supplemented, if necessary, or concluded in order to place on a firmer basis co-operative efforts among countries for the protection of those groundwater resources which can be affected by neighbouring countries through exploitation or pollution. In order to implement such co-operation, joint commissions or other intergovernmental bodies should be established. The work of other international organizations, particularly on data harmonization, should be taken into account.

2. Co-operative arrangements could include: data collection, standardization and exchange; establishment of joint inventories; research and training; planning and demand-management; joint control and monitoring of activities with regard to quantitative and qualitative aspects of groundwater protection; elaboration of compatible monitoring methods, standards and permits; establishment of adjacent protection zones; establishment of commonly agreed land-use plans and practices; monitoring of surface-and groundwater resources' behaviour and interdependence; and the obligation to give notification concerning any activity which might modify the volume and/or the quality of groundwater.

38. International Conference on Water and the Environment - The Dublin Statement on Water and Sustainable Development [1992]*

Introduction

Scarcity and misuse of fresh water pose a serious and growing threat to sustainable development and protection of the environment. Human health and welfare, food security, industrial development and the ecosystems on which they depend, are all at risk, unless water and land resources are managed more effectively in the present decade and beyond than they have been in the past.

...

In commending this Dublin Statement to the world leaders assembled at the United Nations Conference on Environment and Development (UNCED) in Rio de Janeiro in June 1992, the Conference participants urge all governments to study carefully the specific activities and means of implementation recommended in the Conference Report, and to translate those recommendations into urgent action programmes for water and sustainable development.

Guiding principles

Concerted action is needed to reverse the present trends of overconsumption, pollution, and rising threats from drought and floods. The Conference Report sets out recommendations for action at local, national and international levels, based on four guiding principles.

Principle No. 1

Fresh water is a finite and vulnerable resource, essential to sustain life, development and the environment

Since water sustains life, effective management of water resources demands a holistic approach, linking social and economic development with protection of natural ecosystems. Effective management links land and water uses across the whole of a catchment area or groundwater aquifer.

---

* International Conference on Water and the Environment: Development Issues for the 21st Century, 26-31 January 1992, Dublin, Ireland.

Principle No. 2

Water development and management should be based on a participatory approach, involving users, planners and policy-makers at all levels

The participatory approach involves raising awareness of the importance of water among policy-makers and the general public. It means that decisions are taken at the lowest appropriate level, with full public consultation and involvement of users in the planning and implementation of water projects.

Principle No. 3

Women play a central part in the provision, management and safeguarding of water

This pivotal role of women as providers and users of water and guardians of the living environment has seldom been reflected in institutional arrangements for the development and management of water resources. Acceptance and implementation of this principle requires positive policies to address women's specific needs and to equip and empower women to participate at all levels in water resources programmes, including decision-making and implementation, in ways defined by them.

Principle No. 4

Water has an economic value in all its competing uses and should be recognized as an economic good

Within this principle, it is vital to recognize first the basic right of all human beings to have access to clean water and sanitation at an affordable price. Past failure to recognize the economic value of water has led to wasteful and environmentally damaging uses of the resource. Managing water as an economic good is an important way of achieving efficient and equitable use, and of encouraging conservation and protection of water resources.

...

**39.   United Nations Conference on Environment and Development -
        Agenda 21 - Chapter 18, Protection of the Quality and Supply of
        Freshwater Resources: Application of Integrated Approaches to
        the Development, Management and Use of Water Resources
        [1992]***

18.1.   Freshwater resources are an essential component of the Earth's
        hydrosphere and an indispensable part of all terrestrial ecosystems.
        The freshwater environment is characterized by the hydrological cycle,
        including floods and droughts, which in some regions have become
        more extreme and dramatic in their consequences. Global climate
        change and atmospheric pollution could also have an impact on
        freshwater resources and their availability and, through sea-level rise,
        threaten low-lying coastal areas and small island ecosystems.

18.2.   Water is needed in all aspects of life. The general objective is to make
        certain that adequate supplies of water of good quality are maintained
        for the entire population of this planet, while preserving the
        hydrological, biological and chemical functions of ecosystems,
        adapting human activities within the capacity limits of nature and
        combating vectors of water-related diseases. Innovative technologies,
        including the improvement of indigenous technologies, are needed to
        fully utilize limited water resources and to safeguard those resources
        against pollution.

18.3.   The widespread scarcity, gradual destruction and aggravated pollution
        of freshwater resources in many world regions, along with the
        progressive encroachment of incompatible activities, demand
        integrated water resources planning and management. Such integration
        must cover all types of interrelated freshwater bodies, including both
        surface water and groundwater, and duly consider water quantity and
        quality aspects. The multisectoral nature of water resources
        development in the context of socio-economic development must be
        recognized, as well as the multi-interest utilization of water resources
        for water supply and sanitation, agriculture, industry, urban
        development, hydropower generation, inland fisheries, transportation,
        recreation, low and flat lands management and other activities.
        Rational water utilization schemes for the development of surface and

---

* Report of the United Nations Conference on Environment and Development, Rio de
Janeiro, 3-14 June 1992, UN Doc. A/Conf. 151/26/Rev.1, Volume 1, Annex II.

underground water-supply sources and other potential sources have to be supported by concurrent water conservation and wastage minimization measures. Priority, however, must be accorded to flood prevention and control measures, as well as sedimentation control, where required.

18.4. Transboundary water resources and their use are of great importance to riparian States. In this connection, cooperation among those States may be desirable in conformity with existing agreements and/or other relevant arrangements, taking into account the interests of all riparian States concerned.

18.5. The following programme areas are proposed for the freshwater sector:

(a)   Integrated water resources development and management;

(b)   Water resources assessment;

(c)   Protection of water resources, water quality and aquatic ecosystems;

(d)   Drinking-water supply and sanitation;

(e)   Water and sustainable urban development;

(f)   Water for sustainable food production and rural development;

(g)   Impacts of climate change on water resources.

Programme areas

A.   Integrated water resources development and management

Basis for action

18.6. The extent to which water resources development contributes to economic productivity and social well-being is not usually appreciated, although all social and economic activities rely heavily on the supply and quality of freshwater. As populations and economic activities grow, many countries are rapidly reaching conditions of water scarcity or facing limits to economic development. Water demands are increasing rapidly, with 70-80 per cent required for irrigation, less than 20 per cent for industry and a mere 6 per cent for domestic consumption. The holistic management of freshwater as a finite and vulnerable resource, and the integration of sectoral water plans and programmes within the framework of national economic and social policy, are of paramount importance for action in the 1990s and beyond. The fragmentation of responsibilities for water resources development among sectoral agencies is proving, however, to be an even greater impediment to promoting integrated water management than had been anticipated. Effective implementation and coordination mechanisms are required.

Objectives

18.7. The overall objective is to satisfy the freshwater needs of all countries for their sustainable development.

18.8. Integrated water resources management is based on the perception of water as an integral part of the ecosystem, a natural resource and a social and economic good, whose quantity and quality determine the nature of its utilization. To this end, water resources have to be protected, taking into account the functioning of aquatic ecosystems and the perenniality of the resource, in order to satisfy and reconcile needs for water in human activities. In developing and using water resources, priority has to be given to the satisfaction of basic needs and the safeguarding of ecosystems. Beyond these requirements, however, water users should be charged appropriately.

18.9. Integrated water resources management, including the integration of land- and water-related aspects, should be carried out at the level of the catchment basin or sub-basin. Four principal objectives should be pursued, as follows:

(a) To promote a dynamic, interactive, iterative and multisectoral approach to water resources management, including the identification and protection of potential sources of freshwater supply, that integrates technological, socio-economic, environmental and human health considerations;

(b)   To plan for the sustainable and rational utilization, protection, conservation and management of water resources based on community needs and priorities within the framework of national economic development policy;

(c)   To design, implement and evaluate projects and programmes that are both economically efficient and socially appropriate within clearly defined strategies, based on an approach of full public participation, including that of women, youth, indigenous people and local communities in water management policy-making and decision-making;

(d)   To identify and strengthen or develop, as required, in particular in developing countries, the appropriate institutional, legal and financial mechanisms to ensure that water policy and its implementation are a catalyst for sustainable social progress and economic growth.

18.10. In the case of transboundary water resources, there is a need for riparian States to formulate water resources strategies, prepare water resources action programmes and consider, where appropriate, the harmonization of those strategies and action programmes.

18.11. All States, according to their capacity and available resources, and through bilateral or multilateral cooperation, including the United Nations and other relevant organizations as appropriate, could set the following targets:

A)   By the year 2000:

(i)   To have designed and initiated costed and targeted national action programmes, and to have put in place appropriate institutional structures and legal instruments;

(ii)   To have established efficient water-use programmes to attain sustainable resource utilization patterns;

B)   By the year 2025:

(i)   To have achieved subsectoral targets of all freshwater programme areas.

It is understood that the fulfilment of the targets quantified in (i) and (ii) above will depend upon new and additional financial resources that will be made available to developing countries in accordance with the relevant provisions of General Assembly resolution 44/228.

Activities

18.12. All States, according to their capacity and available resources, and through bilateral or multilateral cooperation, including the United Nations and other relevant organizations as appropriate, could implement the following activities to improve integrated water resources management:

(a) Formulation of costed and targeted national action plans and investment programmes;

(b) Integration of measures for the protection and conservation of potential sources of freshwater supply, including the inventorying of water resources, with land-use planning, forest resource utilization, protection of mountain slopes and riverbanks and other relevant development and conservation activities;

(c) Development of interactive databases, forecasting models, economic planning models and methods for water management and planning, including environmental impact assessment methods;

(d) Optimization of water resources allocation under physical and socio-economic constraints;

(e) Implementation of allocation decisions through demand management, pricing mechanisms and regulatory measures;

(f) Flood and drought management, including risk analysis and environmental and social impact assessment;

(g) Promotion of schemes for rational water use through public awareness-raising, educational programmes and levying of water tariffs and other economic instruments;

(h) Mobilization of water resources, particularly in arid and semi-arid areas;

(i)   Promotion of international scientific research cooperation on freshwater resources;

(j)   Development of new and alternative sources of water-supply such as sea-water desalination, artificial groundwater recharge, use of marginal-quality water, waste-water reuse and water recycling;

(k)   Integration of water (including surface and underground water resources) quantity and quality management;

(l)   Promotion of water conservation through improved water-use efficiency and wastage minimization schemes for all users, including the development of water-saving devices;

(m) Support to water-users groups to optimize local water resources management;

(n)   Development of public participatory techniques and their implementation in decision-making, particularly the enhancement of the role of women in water resources planning and management;

(o)   Development and strengthening, as appropriate, of cooperation, including mechanisms where appropriate, at all levels concerned, namely:

   (i)   At the lowest appropriate level, delegation of water resources management, generally, to such a level, in accordance with national legislation, including decentralization of government services to local authorities, private enterprises and communities;

   (ii) At the national level, integrated water resources planning and management in the framework of the national planning process and, where appropriate, establishment of independent regulation and monitoring of freshwater, based on national legislation and economic measures;

   (iii) At the regional level, consideration, where appropriate, of the harmonization of national strategies and action programmes;

   (iv) At the global level, improved delineation of responsibilities, division of labour and coordination of international organizations and programmes, including facilitating discussions and sharing of experiences in areas related to water resources management;

(p)   Dissemination of information, including operational guidelines, and promotion of education for water users, including the consideration by the United Nations of a World Water Day.

...

B.   Water resources assessment

Basis for action

18.23. Water resources assessment, including the identification of potential sources of freshwater supply, comprises the continuing determination of sources, extent, dependability and quality of water resources and of the human activities that affect those resources. Such assessment constitutes the practical basis for their sustainable management and a prerequisite for evaluation of the possibilities for their development. There is, however, growing concern that at a time when more precise and reliable information is needed about water resources, hydrologic services and related bodies are less able than before to provide this information, especially information on groundwater and water quality. Major impediments are the lack of financial resources for water resources assessment, the fragmented nature of hydrologic services and the insufficient numbers of qualified staff. At the same time, the advancing technology for data capture and management is increasingly difficult to access for developing countries. Establishment of national databases is, however, vital to water resources assessment and to mitigation of the effects of floods, droughts, desertification and pollution.

Objectives

18.24. Based upon the Mar del Plata Action Plan, this programme area has been extended into the 1990s and beyond with the overall objective of ensuring the assessment and forecasting of the quantity and quality of water resources, in order to estimate the total quantity of water resources available and their future supply potential, to determine their current quality status, to predict possible conflicts between supply and demand and to provide a scientific database for rational water resources utilization.

18.25. Five specific objectives have been set accordingly, as follows:

(a)   To make available to all countries water resources assessment technology that is appropriate to their needs, irrespective of their level of development, including methods for the impact assessment of climate change on freshwaters;

(b)   To have all countries, according to their financial means, allocate to water resources assessment financial resources in line with the economic and social needs for water resources data;

(c)   To ensure that the assessment information is fully utilized in the development of water management policies;

(d)   To have all countries establish the institutional arrangements needed to ensure the efficient collection, processing, storage, retrieval and dissemination to users of information about the quality and quantity of available water resources at the level of catchments and groundwater aquifers in an integrated manner;

(d)[sic]To have sufficient numbers of appropriately qualified and capable staff recruited and retained by water resources assessment agencies and provided with the training and retraining they will need to carry out their responsibilities successfully.

18.26. All States, according to their capacity and available resources, and through bilateral or multilateral cooperation, including cooperation with the United Nations and other relevant organizations, as appropriate, could set the following targets:

(a)   By the year 2000, to have studied in detail the feasibility of installing water resources assessment services;

(b)   As a long-term target, to have fully operational services available based upon high-density hydrometric networks.

Activities

18.27. All States, according to their capacity and available resources, and through bilateral or multilateral cooperation, including the United Nations and other relevant organizations as appropriate, could undertake the following activities:

A)   Institutional framework:

(i)   Establish appropriate policy frameworks and national priorities;

(ii)   Establish and strengthen the institutional capabilities of countries, including legislative and regulatory arrangements, that are required to ensure the adequate assessment of their water resources and the provision of flood and drought forecasting services;

(iii)   Establish and maintain effective cooperation at the national level between the various agencies responsible for the collection, storage and analysis of hydrologic data;

(iv)   Cooperate in the assessment of transboundary water resources, subject to the prior agreement of each riparian State concerned;

B)   Data systems:

(i)   Review existing data-collection networks and assess their adequacy, including those that provide real-time data for flood and drought forecasting;

(ii)   Improve networks to meet accepted guidelines for the provision of data on water quantity and quality for surface and groundwater, as well as relevant land-use data;

(iii)   Apply standards and other means to ensure data compatibility;

(iv)   Upgrade facilities and procedures used to store, process and analyse hydrologic data and make such data and the forecasts derived from them available to potential users;

(v)   Establish databases on the availability of all types of hydrologic data at the national level;

(vi)   Implement "data rescue" operations, for example, establishment of national archives of water resources;

(vii)   Implement appropriate well-tried techniques for the processing of hydrologic data;

(viii)   Derive area-related estimates from point hydrologic data;

(ix)   Assimilate remotely sensed data and the use, where appropriate, of geographical information systems;

C)   Data dissemination:

(i)   Identify the need for water resources data for various planning purposes;

(ii)   Analyse and present data and information on water resources in the forms required for planning and management of countries' socio-economic development and for use in environmental protection strategies and in the design and operation of specific water-related projects;

(iii)   Provide forecasts and warnings of flood and drought to the general public and civil defence;

D)   Research and development:

(i)   Establish or strengthen research and development programmes at the national, subregional, regional and international levels in support of water resources assessment activities;

(ii)   Monitor research and development activities to ensure that they make full use of local expertise and other local resources and that they are appropriate for the needs of the country or countries concerned.

...

C.   <u>Protection of water resources, water quality and aquatic ecosystems</u>

<u>Basis for action</u>

18.35. Freshwater is a unitary resource. Long-term development of global freshwater requires holistic management of resources and a recognition of the interconnectedness of the elements related to freshwater and freshwater quality. There are few regions of the world that are still exempt from problems of loss of potential sources of freshwater supply, degraded water quality and pollution of surface and groundwater sources. Major problems affecting the water quality of rivers and lakes arise, in variable order of importance according to different situations, from inadequately treated domestic sewage, inadequate controls on the discharges of industrial waste waters, loss and destruction of catchment areas, ill-considered siting of industrial plants, deforestation, uncontrolled shifting cultivation and poor agricultural practices. This gives rise to the leaching of nutrients and pesticides. Aquatic ecosystems are disturbed and living freshwater resources are threatened. Under certain circumstances, aquatic ecosystems are also affected by agricultural water resource development projects such as dams, river diversions, water installations and irrigation schemes. Erosion, sedimentation, deforestation and desertification have led to increased land degradation, and the creation of reservoirs has, in some cases, resulted in adverse effects on ecosystems. Many of these problems have arisen from a development model that is environmentally destructive and from a lack of public awareness and education about surface and groundwater resource protection. Ecological and human health effects are the measurable consequences, although the means to monitor them are inadequate or non-existent in many countries. There is a widespread lack of perception of the linkages between the development, management, use and treatment of water resources and aquatic ecosystems. A preventive approach, where appropriate, is crucial to the avoiding of costly subsequent measures to rehabilitate, treat and develop new water supplies.

<u>Objectives</u>

18.36. The complex interconnectedness of freshwater systems demands that freshwater management be holistic (taking a catchment management approach) and based on a balanced consideration of the needs of people and the environment. The Mar del Plata Action Plan has already recognized the intrinsic linkage between water resource development projects and their significant physical, chemical, biological, health and socio-economic repercussions. The overall environmental health objective was set as follows: "to evaluate the consequences which the various users of water have on the environment, to support measures aimed at controlling water-related diseases, and to protect ecosystems"[1].

18.37. The extent and severity of contamination of unsaturated zones and aquifers have long been underestimated owing to the relative inaccessibility of aquifers and the lack of reliable information on aquifer systems. The protection of groundwater is therefore an essential element of water resource management.

18.38. Three objectives will have to be pursued concurrently to integrate water-quality elements into water resource management:

(a) Maintenance of ecosystem integrity, according to a management principle of preserving aquatic ecosystems, including living resources, and of effectively protecting them from any form of degradation on a drainage basin basis;

(b) Public health protection, a task requiring not only the provision of safe drinking-water but also the control of disease vectors in the aquatic environment;

(c) Human resources development, a key to capacity-building and a prerequisite for implementing water-quality management.

18.39. All States, according to their capacity and available resources, through bilateral or multilateral cooperation, including the United Nations and other relevant organizations as appropriate, could set the following targets:

(a) To identify the surface and groundwater resources that could be developed for use on a sustainable basis and other major developable

---

[1] Report of the United Nations Water Conference, Mar del Plata, 14-25 March 1977, Part one, Chapter I, Section C, para. 35, United Nations publication, Sales No. E.77.II.A.12.

water-dependent resources and, simultaneously, to initiate programmes for the protection, conservation and rational use of these resources on a sustainable basis;

(b)   To identify all potential sources of water-supply and prepared outlines for their protection, conservation and rational use;

(c)   To initiate effective water pollution prevention and control programmes, based on an appropriate mixture of pollution reduction-at-source strategies, environmental impact assessments and enforceable standards for major point-source discharges and high-risk non-point sources, commensurate with their socio-economic development;

(d)   To participate, as far as appropriate, in international water-quality monitoring and management programmes such as the Global Water Quality Monitoring Programme (GEMS/WATER), the UNEP Environmentally Sound Management of Inland Waters (EMINWA), the FAO regional inland fishery bodies, and the Convention on Wetlands of International Importance Especially as Waterfowl Habitat (Ramsar Convention);

(e)   To reduce the prevalence of water-associated diseases, starting with the eradication of dracunculiasis (guinea worm disease) and onchocerciasis (river blindness) by the year 2000;

(f)   To establish, according to capacities and needs, biological, health, physical and chemical quality criteria for all water bodies (surface and groundwater), with a view to an ongoing improvement of water quality;

(g)   To adopt an integrated approach to environmentally sustainable management of water resources, including the protection of aquatic ecosystems and freshwater living resources;

(h)   To put in place strategies for the environmentally sound management of freshwaters and related coastal ecosystems, including consideration of fisheries, aquaculture, animal grazing, agricultural activities and biodiversity.

Activities

18.40. All States, according to their capacity and available resources, and through bilateral or multilateral cooperation, including United Nations and other relevant organizations as appropriate, could implement the following activities:

A)   Water resources protection and conservation:

(i)   Establishment and strengthening of technical and institutional capacities to identify and protect potential sources of water-supply within all sectors of society;

(ii)   Identification of potential sources of water-supply and preparation of national profiles;

(iii) Preparation of national plans for water resources protection and conservation;

(iv)   Rehabilitation of important, but degraded, catchment areas, particularly on small islands;

(v)   Strengthening of administrative and legislative measures to prevent encroachment on existing and potentially usable catchment areas;

B)   Water pollution prevention and control:

(i)   Application of the "polluter pays" principle, where appropriate, to all kinds of sources, including on-site and off-site sanitation;

(ii)   Promotion of the construction of treatment facilities for domestic sewage and industrial effluents and the development of appropriate technologies, taking into account sound traditional and indigenous practices;

(iii) Establishment of standards for the discharge of effluents and for the receiving waters;

(iv)   Introduction of the precautionary approach in water-quality management, where appropriate, with a focus on pollution minimization and prevention through use of new technologies, product and process change, pollution reduction at source and effluent reuse, recycling and recovery, treatment and environmentally safe disposal;

(v)   Mandatory environmental impact assessment of all major water resource development projects potentially impairing water quality and aquatic ecosystems, combined with the delineation of appropriate remedial measures and a strengthened control of new industrial installations, solid waste landfills and infrastructure development projects;

(vi)   Use of risk assessment and risk management in reaching decisions in this area and ensuring compliance with those decisions;

(vii)   Identification and application of best environmental practices at reasonable cost to avoid diffuse pollution, namely, through a limited, rational and planned use of nitrogenous fertilizers and other agrochemicals (pesticides, herbicides) in agricultural practices;

(viii)   Encouragement and promotion of the use of adequately treated and purified waste waters in agriculture, aquaculture, industry and other sectors;

C)   <u>Development and application of clean technology:</u>

(i)   Control of industrial waste discharges, including low-waste production technologies and water recirculation, in an integrated manner and through application of precautionary measures derived from a broad-based life-cycle analysis;

(ii)   Treatment of municipal waste water for safe reuse in agriculture and aquaculture;

(iii)   Development of biotechnology, inter alia, for waste treatment, production of biofertilizers and other activities;

(iv)   Development of appropriate methods for water pollution control, taking into account sound traditional and indigenous practices;

D) Groundwater protection:

(i) Development of agricultural practices that do not degrade groundwaters;

(ii) Application of the necessary measures to mitigate saline intrusion into aquifers of small islands and coastal plains as a consequence of sealevel rise or overexploitation of coastal aquifers;

(iii) Prevention of aquifer pollution through the regulation of toxic substances that permeate the ground and the establishment of protection zones in groundwater recharge and abstraction areas;

(iv) Design and management of landfills based upon sound hydrogeologic information and impact assessment, using the best practicable and best available technology;

(v) Promotion of measures to improve the safety and integrity of wells and well-head areas to reduce intrusion of biological pathogens and hazardous chemicals into aquifers at well sites;

(vi) Water-quality monitoring, as needed, of surface and groundwaters potentially affected by sites storing toxic and hazardous materials;

E) Protection of aquatic ecosystems:

(i) Rehabilitation of polluted and degraded water bodies to restore aquatic habitats and ecosystems;

(ii) Rehabilitation programmes for agricultural lands and for other users, taking into account equivalent action for the protection and use of groundwater resources important for agricultural productivity and for the biodiversity of the tropics;

(iii) Conservation and protection of wetlands (owing to their ecological and habitat importance for many species), taking into account social and economic factors;

(iv) Control of noxious aquatic species that may destroy some other water species;

...

G)   <u>Monitoring and surveillance of water resources and waters receiving wastes</u>:

(i)   Establishment of networks for the monitoring and continuous surveillance of waters receiving wastes and of point and diffuse sources of pollution;

(ii)   Promotion and extension of the application of environmental impact assessments of geographical information systems;

(iii) Surveillance of pollution sources to improve compliance with standards and regulations and to regulate the issue of discharge permits;

(iv)   Monitoring of the utilization of chemicals in agriculture that may have an adverse environmental effect;

(v)   Rational land use to prevent land degradation, erosion and siltation of lakes and other water bodies;

H)   <u>Development of national and international legal instruments that may be required to protect the quality of water resources, as appropriate, particularly for</u>:

(i)   Monitoring and control of pollution and its effects in national and transboundary waters;

(ii)   Control of long-range atmospheric transport of pollutants;

(iii) Control of accidental and/or deliberate spills in national and/or transboundary water bodies;

(iv)   Environmental impact assessment.

...

[Omitted: D. Drinking-water supply and sanitation]

E.   Water and sustainable urban development

...

Activities

18.59. All States, according to their capacity and available resources, and through bilateral or multilateral cooperation, including the United Nations and other relevant organizations as appropriate, could implement the following activities:

A)   Protection of water resources from depletion, pollution and degradation:

...

(vii)   Encouragement of the best management practices for the use of agrochemicals with a view to minimizing their impact on water resources;

...

F.   Water for sustainable food production and rural development

...

Activities

18.76. All States, according to their capacity and available resources, and through bilateral or multilateral cooperation, including the United Nations and other relevant organizations as appropriate, could implement the following activities:

...

C)   Waterlogging, salinity control and drainage:

...

(iii)   Encourage conjunctive use of surface and groundwaters, including monitoring and water-balance studies;

(iv)   Practise drainage in irrigated areas of arid and semi-arid regions;

...

G.   Impacts of climate change on water resources

Basis for action

18.82. There is uncertainty with respect to the prediction of climate change at the global level. Although the uncertainties increase greatly at the regional, national and local levels, it is at the national level that the most important decisions would need to be made. Higher temperatures and decreased precipitation would lead to decreased water-supplies and increased water demands; they might cause deterioration in the quality of freshwater bodies, putting strains on the already fragile balance between supply and demand in many countries. Even where precipitation might increase, there is no guarantee that it would occur at the time of year when it could be used; in addition, there might be a likelihood of increased flooding. Any rise in sealevel will often cause the intrusion of salt water into estuaries, small islands and coastal aquifers and the flooding of low-lying coastal areas; this puts low-lying countries at great risk.

18.83. The Ministerial Declaration of the Second World Climate Conference states that "the potential impact of such climate change could pose an environmental threat of an up to now unknown magnitude ... and could even threaten survival in some small island States and in low-lying coastal, arid and semi-arid areas" [3] . The Conference recognized that among the most important impacts of climate change were its effects on the hydrologic cycle and on water management systems and, through these, on socio-economic systems. Increase in incidence of extremes, such as floods and droughts, would cause increased frequency and severity of disasters. The Conference therefore called for a strengthening of the necessary research and monitoring programmes and the exchange of relevant data and information, these actions to be undertaken at the national, regional and international levels.

---

[3] A/45/696/Add. 1, Annex III, Preamble, para. 2.

Objectives

18.84. The very nature of this topic calls first and foremost for more information about and greater understanding of the threat being faced. This topic may be translated into the following objectives, consistent with the United Nations Framework Convention on Climate Change:

(a) To understand and quantify the threat of the impact of climate change on freshwater resources;

(b) To facilitate the implementation of effective national countermeasures, as and when the threatening impact is seen as sufficiently confirmed to justify such action;

(c) To study the potential impacts of climate change on areas prone to droughts and floods.

Activities

18.85. All States, according to their capacity and available resources, and through bilateral or multilateral cooperation, including the United Nations and other relevant organizations as appropriate, could implement the following activities:

(a) Monitor the hydrologic regime, including soil moisture, groundwater balance, penetration and transpiration of water-quality, and related climate factors, especially in the regions and countries most likely to suffer from the adverse effects of climate change and where the localities vulnerable to these effects should therefore be defined;

(b) Develop and apply techniques and methodologies for assessing the potential adverse effects of climate change, through changes in temperature, precipitation and sealevel rise, on freshwater resources and the flood risk;

(c) Initiate case-studies to establish whether there are linkages between climate changes and the current occurrences of droughts and floods in certain regions;

(d) Assess the resulting social, economic and environmental impacts;

(e)   Develop and initiate response strategies to counter the adverse effects that are identified, including changing groundwater levels and to mitigate saline intrusion into aquifers;

(f)   Develop agricultural activities based on brackish-water use;

(g)   Contribute to the research activities under way within the framework of current international programmes.

...

40.   United Nations International Law Commission - Resolution on Confined Transboundary Groundwater [1994]*

The International Law Commission,

Having completed its consideration of the topic "The law of the non-navigational uses of international watercourses",

Having considered in that context groundwater which is related to an international watercourse,

Recognizing that confined groundwater, that is groundwater not related to an international watercourse, is also a natural resource of vital importance for sustaining life, health and the integrity of ecosystems,

Having also the need for continuing efforts to elaborate rules pertaining to confined transboundary groundwater,

Considering its view that the principles contained in its draft articles on the law of the non-navigational uses of international watercourses may be applicable to transboundary confined groundwater,

1.   Commends States to be guided by the principles contained in the draft articles on the law of the non-navigational uses of international watercourses, where appropriate, in regulating transboundary groundwater;

---

* Yearbook of the International Law Commission, Vol. 2, Part 2, p. 135, 1994.

2.   Recommends States to consider entering into agreements with the other State or States in which the confined transboundary groundwater is located;

3.   Recommends also that, in the event of any dispute involving transboundary confined groundwater, the States concerned should consider resolving such dispute in accordance with the provisions contained in article 33 of the draft articles, or in such other manner as may be agreed upon.

41.   United Nations Economic Commission for Europe - Guidelines on Monitoring and Assessment of Transboundary Groundwaters [2000]*

1.   Introduction

1.1   Background

The Convention on the Protection and Use of Transboundary Watercourses and International Lakes (Helsinki, 1992) include important provisions on the monitoring and assessment of transboundary waters, the assessment of the effectiveness of measures taken to prevent, control and reduce transboundary impact, and the exchange of information on water and effluent monitoring. Other relevant aspects deal with the harmonisation of rules for setting up and operating monitoring programmes, which includes measurement systems and devices, analytical techniques, data processing and evaluation techniques. Further needs for monitoring arise, because the Convention aims to protect ecosystems, which may be closely connected with groundwaters and the protection of sources of drinking-water supply.

Monitoring and assessment are also part of the 1999 Protocol on Water and Health to the Convention on the Protection and Use of Transboundary Watercourses and International Lakes. This Protocol contains provisions

---

* UN ECE Task Force on Monitoring and Assessment, Guidelines on Monitoring and Assessment of Transboundary Groundwaters, Lelystad, 2000. The Guidelines were endorsed by the Parties to the Convention on the Protection and Use of Transboundary Watercourses and International Lakes (Helsinki, 17 March 1992) at their second meeting held at The Hague, 23–25 March 2000, in: UN Doc. ECE/MP.WAT/5 of 29 August 2000, p. 13.

regarding the establishment of joint or coordinated systems for surveillance and early-warning systems to identify outbreaks or incidents of water-related diseases or significant threats of such outbreaks or incidents (including those resulting from water pollution or extreme weather). It also foresees the development of integrated information systems and databases, the exchange of information and the sharing of technical and legal knowledge and experience.

1.2   About these Guidelines

These Guidelines refer to transboundary groundwaters. They form part of a series of Guidelines for the monitoring and assessment of rivers, groundwaters, lakes and estuaries.

The character of these Guidelines is strategic rather than technical[1]. They are intended to assist ECE governments and joint bodies in developing harmonised rules for the setting up and operation of systems for transboundary groundwater monitoring and assessment. The target group comprises decision makers and planners in ministries, organisations and institutions responsible for environmental, water or hydrogeological issues and all those who are also responsible for managing transboundary groundwaters. The Guidelines also aim to provide advice to those who are responsible for or involved in the development of sustainable water management schemes.

The Guidelines are intended to be concise and realistic; they are not intended to be prescriptive. They provide an approach for the identification of problems and guidance to meet information needs. The Guidelines deal mostly with monitoring and assessment needs that arise from the Convention. As far as possible, monitoring and assessment needs that arise from the Protocol on Water and Health are also considered. However, a full consideration of the latter will be possible only when more experience has been gathered on issues linked to water and human health.

---

[1] For technical details, the background reports prepared by the Core Group Groundwater, and international literature and handbooks on operational practices of monitoring and assessment (see further reading) should be consulted.

Definitions used in these Guidelines:

- Monitoring

    Monitoring is the process of repetitive observing, for defined purposes of one or more elements of the environment according to pre-arranged schedules in space and time and using comparable methodologies for environmental sensing and data collection. It provides information concerning the present state and past trends in environmental behaviour.

- Assessment

    The evaluation of the hydrological, chemical and/or micro-biological state of groundwaters in relation to the background conditions, human effects, and the actual or intended uses, which may adversely affect human health or the environment.

- Survey

    A finite duration, intensive programme to measure, evaluate and report the state of the groundwater system for a specific purpose.

The general approach of the monitoring cycle (figure 1.1), as presented in the Guidelines on monitoring and assessment of transboundary rivers[2], will be followed in these Guidelines as well.

The monitoring cycle offers a readers' guide for these Guidelines and an [sic] valuable approach when drawing up programmes for the monitoring and assessment of transboundary groundwaters.

An exchange of information (and joint assessment/modelling) between riparian parties is meaningful only if the data are comparable. This can be achieved when all components of groundwater monitoring activities on both sides of the border use similar principles or adopt an approach such as the monitoring cycle presented below.

---

[2] In these Guidelines, as much use as possible has been made of the experience with the implementation of the Guidelines on Monitoring and Assessment of Transboundary Rivers in pilot projects and their updated version.

[Omitted: Figure 1.1 - Monitoring cycle]

...

[Omitted: 2. Identification of groundwater management issues, 3. Information needs 4. Strategies for monitoring and assessment, 5. Monitoring programmes, 6. Data management, 7. Quality management]

8.   Joint or coordinated action and institutional arrangements

The successful drawing-up and implementation of policies, strategies and methodologies on groundwater management crucially depends on institutional aspects. These include the organisation, structures, arrangements for cooperation and the responsibilities of institutions and organisations involved. In transboundary groundwater management, international cooperation is governed by the provisions of the Convention, which stipulates that the socio-economic conditions in the riparian countries should be taken into account when deciding on the specific institutional arrangements.

8.1   Concerted action plans and programmes

Riparian parties should agree on quantified management targets. These targets should become part of a concerted action plan or programme. This plan or programme should also cover other measures aimed at achieving an ecologically sound and rational groundwater management, conserving groundwater resources and protecting the environment. This action plan or programme should include provisions for mutual assistance, where necessary. It should be subject to approval at ministerial or senior official level.

The action plan or programme can either be derived from existing national plans or programmes or set the preconditions for the establishment of such national plans or programmes.

The concerted action plan should at least include such items as:

(a)   Land and groundwater uses, taking into account that restrictions, and in some cases even bans, on land use should be imposed for mining and processing industries, intensive agricultural practices, including fertiliser and pesticide use, solid wastes, and hazardous chemicals.

(b) Zoning criteria, taking into account that zoning criteria depend on environmental quality and the importance of underlying aquifers.

(c) Protection zones, taking into account that these should help to prevent pollution of groundwaters in current and future groundwater abstraction areas for supplying drinking water. Necessary measures should be taken to minimise the accidental pollution from non-point sources in protection zones.

(d) Economic activities, whereby particular attention should be paid to the transboundary impact of economic activities on groundwater quality and quantity. At present there are few examples of effective coordination between transboundary land development and groundwater protection planning. An exchange of necessary information and bilateral and multilateral cooperation are needed to this end. The establishment of effective and harmonised monitoring programmes should be an effective tool to coordinate these activities.

(e) Groundwater pollution, taking into account that both pollutant discharges and concentrations in transboundary aquifers shall be regularly monitored.

(f) Groundwater abstractions, taking into account that groundwater abstractions for economic needs should be agreed upon to ensure the sustainability of groundwater use.

(g) Wetlands, taking into account that groundwater monitoring should be comprehensive and should address the qualitative as well as the quantitative characteristics of transboundary aquifers, providing reliable tools for the integrated management of groundwaters. Data collection and monitoring programmes should be tailored to the required information level, which is determined by the assessment goal.

8.2 Joint bodies and their activities

(a) General recommendations

Governments should set up joint bodies, where these do not yet exist, and include monitoring and assessment of transboundary groundwaters in the activities of these joint bodies. It is of less importance whether riparian countries set up separate joint bodies responsible for either transboundary surface waters or transboundary groundwaters, or whether they entrust one body with activities both linked with surface waters and groundwaters. However, it is of the utmost importance that, where two or more joint bodies have been set up by riparian countries in the same catchment area, these countries agree on ways and means to coordinate the activities of these joint bodies.

Riparian countries should, where appropriate:

- assign to the joint body the task of transboundary groundwater monitoring and assessment following the recommendations of these Guidelines;

- make the joint body responsible for assessing the effectiveness of the agreed measures and the resulting improvements in groundwater management.

Joint bodies

According to the Convention, a joint body means any bilateral or multilateral commission or other appropriate institutional arrangements for cooperation between the Riparian Parties. In general, the tasks of joint bodies include the following:

- collect, compile and evaluate data in order to identify pollution sources likely to cause transboundary impact;

- develop joint monitoring programmes concerning water quality and quantity;

- draw up inventories and exchange information on the pollution sources mentioned above;

- establish emission limits for waste water and evaluate the effectiveness of control programmes;

- elaborate joint water-quality objectives and criteria for the purpose of preventing, controlling and reducing transboundary impact, and propose relevant measures for maintaining and, where necessary, improving the existing water quality;

- develop concerted action programmes for the reduction of pollution loads from both point sources (e.g. municipal and industrial sources) and diffuse sources (particularly from agriculture);

- establish warning and alarm procedures;

- serve as a forum for the exchange of information on existing and planned uses of water and related installations that are likely to cause transboundary impact;

- promote cooperation and exchange of information on the best available technology in accordance with the provisions of article 13 of the Convention (exchange of information between the Riparian Parties), as well as to encourage cooperation in scientific research programmes;

- participate in the implementation of environmental impact assessments relating to transboundary water, in accordance with appropriate international regulations;

- where two or more joint bodies exist in the same catchment area, they shall endeavour to coordinate their activities in order to strengthen the prevention, control and reduction of transboundary [sic]

(b)   Drawing-up and implementation of action plans

Riparian countries should, where appropriate, entrust the joint body with the drawing-up and supervision of the concerted action plan or programme outlined in paragraph 8.1.

Where appropriate, riparian countries should also establish a technical working group under the joint body which is responsible for ongoing investigations under the action plan related to monitoring and assessment as well as for defining and implementing the monitoring and assessment strategy, including its technical, financial and organisational aspects.

Riparian countries should, through their respective joint bodies, establish close cooperation "across the border" between administrative authorities dealing with land-use planning and development, the rational use and the protection of groundwater and groundwater monitoring at the early stages of the planning process and at all levels of administration. This will help to overcome conflicting interests in sectoral planning both in the national and in the transboundary contexts.

Because of differences in the organisation of licensing procedures, riparian countries should jointly agree on a harmonised system of licensing procedures which does not conflict with the existing national legislation systems or adapt the national systems accordingly.

(c)   Access to information

Through their joint bodies, riparian countries should give each other access to relevant information on surface water and groundwater quality and quantity. This should include, for example, information on surface water quality when surface water has been used as infiltration water for drinking water purposes.

Through their joint bodies, riparian countries should make arrangements so that the public has access to relevant information, collected both by riparian countries and by joint bodies.

To be effective, arrangements for the exchange of information among riparian countries and arrangements for the provision of information to the public should be governed by rules jointly agreed by the riparian countries. These arrangements should specify the format and frequency of reporting. The creation and maintenance of a joint database could also be useful. In drawing-up these arrangements, account should be taken of obligations under other international agreements and supranational law, such as European Community directives, to monitor, assess and report on groundwater quality and quantity.

(d)   Quality systems

Riparian countries should, where appropriate, assign to their joint bodies responsibilities related to quality systems. Particular attention should be paid to the harmonisation of sampling and data-processing methodologies, as well as laboratory accreditation. Cooperation on the local level for carrying out monitoring practices should be encouraged and promoted including direct contacts between laboratories and institutions involved.

8.3   Other arrangements at the national and/or local levels

(a)   Institutional, legal or administrative arrangements

The lack of proper institutional, legal or administrative arrangements at the national and local levels may considerably hamper international cooperation. Such arrangements include the cooperation between local governments, the responsibility for and ownership of groundwater, legislation and regulations (e.g. abstraction permits, protection areas), the coordination of quality and quantity monitoring by various national institutes and the appointment of a national reference laboratory.

Riparian countries should adapt existing agreements to the obligations set out in the Convention and draw up new agreements for establishing and maintaining harmonised or joint monitoring programmes in transboundary aquifers. These programmes should use standardised sampling and laboratory procedures.

(b)   Financial arrangements

Riparian parties should provide sufficient funding for the execution of monitoring and assessment activities and joint research within the framework of the Convention. This funding could be part of the regular budget. Each country should take care of its own requirements. Funding can, for example, be based on pollution charges or fees. The establishment of an environmental fund, from which companies can take loans for investments, may accelerate improvements. Other possibilities for funding are applying for EU budgets (TACIS, PHARE) or other funds (GEF, World Bank). Generally, joint proposals are recommended because they are accepted more easily by the institutions involved.

[Omitted: Annex - Internationally used indicators]

42. **Conference of the Contracting Parties to the Convention on Wetlands - Resolution VIII.40 - Guidelines for Rendering the Use of Groundwater Compatible with the Conservation of Wetlands [2002]***

1.   Recognizing the importance of the whole water cycle and the link existing between ground and surface water for their use and management, not only in arid and semi-arid regions but also in humid regions;

2.   Taking into account the urgent need to decrease the loss and degradation of aquatic ecosystems through policies of sustainable development and conservation of biodiversity;

3.   Also taking into account that maintenance of the ecological integrity of most wetlands, especially those located in arid and semi-arid zones, is closely linked to the supply of groundwater;

4.   Aware of the importance that the use of groundwater has had for the economic development and improvement of welfare in many regions (mainly because of irrigated agriculture);

5.   Equally aware of the negative impact that can be caused to wetlands because of uncontrolled development and lack of planning for groundwater; and recognizing the value of the Guidelines for the allocation and management of water for maintaining the ecological functions of wetlands, adopted in Resolution VIII.1;

6.   Emphasizing that examples of the solution of conflicts between the use of groundwater and conservation of wetlands (for example, in the Mediterranean basin) can serve as exportable models for other areas facing the same problems;

7.   Recalling that the Strategic Plan 1997-2002 of the Convention (Operative Objective 2.2) stresses the conservation of water and the need to protect wetlands dependent upon groundwater;

---

* Adopted at the 8th Meeting of the Conference of the Contracting Parties, 18–26 November 2002, accessible at ‹http://www.ramsar.org/key_res_viii_40_e.pdf›, last accessed 31 July 2004).

8. Taking into account that on occasions some regions suffer from inefficient management and regulation in the use of groundwater;

9. Aware of the difficulties of rendering the interests of the users (primarily farmers) compatible with conservation criteria for those areas, due to the fact that environmental problems are not taken into account;

10. Recognizing that many of these conflicts may be stimulated by certain subsidies for agriculture and other types of economic incentives, including for tourism; and

11. Stressing that the analysis of these issues and the solution of conflicts require a completely transparent environment, scientific rigour and, above all, participation of all actors involved in the management and use of water resources;

The Conference of the Contracting Parties

12. Urges the Contracting Parties to study the impact of the use of groundwater on the conservation of their wetlands in those territories where these conflicts exist;

13. Recommends that this analysis be carried out from an interdisciplinary point of view and with the participation of civil society;

14. Invites Contracting Parties to review their respective programmes of subsidies in order to ensure that they do not have negative consequences for the conservation of wetlands;

15. Encourages Contracting Parties to continue their efforts aimed at implementing existing provisions in this field; requests the Ramsar Bureau to support these efforts as much as possible; and proposes that the Scientific and Technical Review Panel advance in the study of the interaction between groundwater and wetlands, as requested in Resolution VIII.1, paragraph 19, and to develop guidance on the sustainable use of groundwater resources to maintain wetland ecosystem functions for discussion at COP9, in line with Action 3.4.7 of the Convention's Strategic Plan 2003–2008;

16. Urges the promotion of initiatives, supported by both the public and private sectors, for the participation of civil society in the management of groundwater, within the framework of integrated management of water resources;

17. Also encourages recognition of the importance of the associations of users for the management of groundwater, and the creation of such associations where they do not exist, and the dedication of efforts towards the objective that these associations contribute to the sustainable development of this resource in order to make possible the efficient use of groundwater and the conservation of wetlands;

18. Urges public institutions to ensure that a more decisive effort is made, within the framework of wetland-related education, communication and public awareness (CEPA) activities, with regard to groundwater, placing emphasis on its hydro-geological, social, economic and environmental aspects; and

19. Invites Parties to give more attention to the role of groundwater in maintaining the ecological functions of wetlands, in line with Operational Objective 3.4 of the Convention's Strategic Plan 2003-2008.

43. World Summit on Sustainable Development - Plan of Implementation of the World Summit on Sustainable Development [2002]*

[Omitted: I. Introduction, II. Poverty eradication, III. Changing unsustainable patterns of consumption and production]

IV.   Protecting and managing the natural resource base of economic and social development

24. Human activities are having an increasing impact on the integrity of ecosystems that provide essential resources and services for human well-being and economic activities. Managing the natural resources base in a sustainable and integrated manner is essential for sustainable

---

* Report of the World Summit on Sustainable Development, Johannesburg, 26 August–2 September 2002, UN Doc. A/CONF.199/20.

development. In this regard, to reverse the current trend in natural resource degradation as soon as possible, it is necessary to implement strategies which should include targets adopted at the national and, where appropriate, regional levels to protect ecosystems and to achieve integrated management of land, water and living resources, while strengthening regional, national and local capacities. This would include actions at all levels as set out below.

25. Launch a programme of actions, with financial and technical assistance, to achieve the Millennium development goal on safe drinking water. In this respect, we agree to halve, by the year 2015, the proportion of people who are unable to reach or to afford safe drinking water, as outlined in the Millennium Declaration, and the proportion of people without access to basic sanitation, which would include actions at all levels to:

...

(d) Intensify water pollution prevention to reduce health hazards and protect ecosystems by introducing technologies for affordable sanitation and industrial and domestic wastewater treatment, by mitigating the effects of groundwater contamination and by establishing, at the national level, monitoring systems and effective legal frameworks;

...

26. Develop integrated water resources management and water efficiency plans by 2005, with support to developing countries, through actions at all levels to:

(a) Develop and implement national/regional strategies, plans and programmes with regard to integrated river basin, watershed and groundwater management and introduce measures to improve the efficiency of water infrastructure to reduce losses and increase recycling of water;

...

[Omitted: V. Sustainable development in a globalizing world; VI. Health and sustainable development; VII. Sustainable development of small island developing States]

VIII. Sustainable development for Africa

...

66. Promote integrated water resources development and optimize the upstream and downstream benefits therefrom, the development and effective management of water resources across all uses and the protection of water quality and aquatic ecosystems, including through initiatives at all levels, to:

...

(d) Protect water resources, including groundwater and wetland ecosystems, against pollution, and, in cases of the most acute water scarcity, support efforts for developing non-conventional water resources, including the energy-efficient, cost-effective and sustainable desalination of seawater, rainwater harvesting and recycling of water.

...

[Omitted: IX. Other regional initiatives; X. Means of implementation; XI. Institutional framework for sustainable development]

iii. **Non-Governmental Instruments**

44. **International Law Association (ILA) - The Seoul Rules on International Groundwaters [1986]***

Article I - The waters of international aquifers

The waters of an aquifer that is intersected by the boundary between two or more States are international groundwaters if such an aquifer with its waters

---

* Approved by the International Law Association (ILA) at its Sixty-Second Conference held at Seoul in 1986. ILA, Report of the Sixty-Second Conference held at Seoul, 24–30 August 1986, London, 1987, p. 251.

forms an international basin or part thereof. Those states are basin States within the meaning of the Helsinki Rules whether or not the aquifer and its waters form surface waters part of a hydraulic system flowing into a common terminus.

Article II - Hydraulic interdependence

1. An aquifer that contributes water to, or receives water from, surface waters of an international basin constitutes part of an international basin for the purposes of the Helsinki Rules.

2. An aquifer intersected by the boundary between two or more States that does not contribute water to, or receive water from, surface waters of an international drainage basin constitutes an international drainage basin for the purposes of the Helsinki Rules.

3. Basin states, in exercising their rights and performing their duties under international law, shall take into account any interdependence of the groundwater and other waters including any interconnections between aquifers, and any leaching into aquifers caused by activities and areas under their jurisdiction.

Article III - Protection of groundwater

1. Basin states shall prevent or abate the pollution of international groundwaters in accordance with international law applicable to existing, new, increased and highly dangerous pollution. Special consideration shall be given to the long-term effects of the pollution of groundwater.

2. Basin states shall consult and exchange relevant available information and data at the request of any one of them.

(a) for the purpose of preserving the groundwaters of the basin from degradation and protecting form impairment the geologic structure of the aquifers, including recharge areas;

(b) for the purpose of considering joint or parallel quality standards and environmental protection measures applicable to international groundwaters and their aquifers.

3.   Basin states shall cooperate, at the request of any one of them, for the purpose of collecting and analyzing additional needed information and data pertinent to the international groundwaters or their aquifers.

Article IV - Groundwater management and surface waters

Basin states should consider the integrated management, including conjunctive use with surface waters, of their international groundwaters at the request of any one of them.

45.   Bellagio "Model Agreement Concerning the Use of Transboundary Groundwaters" [1989]*

The High Contracting Parties,

Motivated by the spirit of cordiality and cooperation which characterizes the relations between them;

Desirous of expanding the scope of their concerted actions with respect to the problems confronting their Peoples along their common frontier;

Recognizing the critical importance of their transboundary water resources and the need to enhance the rational use and conservation of the said resources on a long-term basis;

Noting especially the present unsatisfactory state of protection and control of their transboundary groundwater as well as the prospects of crisis conditions in some areas because of increasing demands upon, and the decreasing quality of, those groundwaters;

Seeking to provide for the utilization, protection and control of those groundwaters on an equitable basis and, to that end, for the creation and maintenance of an adequate data base;

Recognizing that the optimum and efficient use of their transboundary water resources is essential to the interests of both Parties;

---

* Hayton, Robert D. and Albert E. Utton, Transboundary Groundwaters: The Bellagio Draft Treaty, 29 Natural Resources Journal (1989), pp. 663 and 676.

Resolving to protect the quality of the transboundary groundwaters for present and future generations;

Wishing to resolve amicably any difference that may arise in connection with the use, protection or control of the said transboundary groundwaters and, for that purpose, to utilize a joint agency; and

Concluding that the best means to achieve the rational management of their transboundary water resources and the protection of the underground environment is to adopt, in principle, an integrated approach including, where appropriate, the conjunctive use of surface water and groundwater in their border region,

Have agreed as follows:

[Omitted: Comment]

Article I - Definitions

As used in this agreement:

1. "Aquifer" means a subsurface waterbearing geologic formation from which significant quantities of water may be extracted.

2. "Border region" means the area within approximately kilometers from each side of the mutual boundary as set forth on the annexed map.

3. "The Commission" means the agency designated in Article m, para. 1, of this Agreement.

4. "Conjunctive Use" means the integrated development and management of surface and groundwater as a total water supply system.

5. "Contaminant" means any substance, species or energy which detrimentally affects directly, indirectly, cumulatively or in combination with other substances, human health or safety or agricultural or industrial products or processes, or flora, fauna or an ecosystem.

6.   "Contamination" means any detrimental chemical, physical, biological, or temperature change in the content or characteristics of a body of water.

7.   "Depletion" means the withdrawals of water from an aquifer at a rate faster than it is recharged, otherwise known as "mining" the water.

8.   "Drought" means a condition of abnormal water scarcity in a specific area resulting from natural conditions.

9.   "Drought Alert" means the declared condition provided for in Article XII.

10. "Drought Emergency" means the declared emergency provided for in Article XII.

11. "Drought Management Plan" means the plan provided for pursuant to Article XII.

12. "Environmental sensitivity" means vulnerability or susceptibility to changes detrimentally affecting the quality of life of one or more biological or physical systems

13. "Government(s)" means the governments of the Parties to this Agreement.

14. "Groundwater" means the water in aquifers.

15. "Impairment" means any physical change in an aquifer or its recharge area which significantly reduces or restricts the potential for use of the waters of the aquifer.

16. "Interrelated surface water" means those surface waters in the territory of either Party, the quantity or quality of which is affected by the outflows from, or the inflows to, transboundary groundwater.

17. "Pollution" means the introduction of any contaminant by man, directly or indirectly, into groundwaters or surface waters.

18. "Public Health Emergency" means the declared emergency provided for in Article IX.

19. "Recharge" means the addition of water to an aquifer by infiltration of precipitation through the soil or of water from surface streams, lakes, or reservoirs, by discharges of water to the land surface, or by injection of water into the aquifer through wells.

20. "Transboundary aquifer" means an aquifer intersected by a common boundary.

21. "Transboundary Groundwater Conservation Area" means an area declared by the Commission pursuant to Article VII.

22. "Transboundary groundwaters" means waters in transboundary aquifers.

[Omitted: Comment]

Article II - General purposes

1. The Parties recognize their common interest and responsibility in ensuring the reasonable and equitable development and management of groundwaters in the border region for the well being of their Peoples.

2. Accordingly, the Parties have entered into this Agreement in order to attain the optimum utilization and conservation of transboundary groundwaters and to protect the underground environment. It is also the purpose of the Parties to develop and maintain reliable data and information concerning transboundary aquifers and their waters in order to use and protect these waters in a rational and informed manner.

[Omitted: Comment]

Article III - The Commission responsible under this Agreement

1. The Commission is designated as the Parties' agency to carry out the functions and responsibilities provided for by this Agreement.

2. The Commission shall be authorized a technical staff, which, in collaboration with the technical staffs of the Governments, shall assist the Commission in the accomplishment of its functions and responsibilities.

3. The Commission is authorized to declare Transboundary Groundwater Conservation Areas, Drought Alerts, Drought Emergencies and Public Health Emergencies, and to promulgate the corresponding plans and Depletion Plans, in accordance with the provisions of this Agreement.

4. The Commission shall have jurisdiction over such additional matters concerning the border region as are from time to time referred to it by the Governments jointly.

5. The Commission shall prepare and propose to the Governments a budget, conforming insofar as practicable to the budget cycles and procedures of the Governments, covering the projected expenses and capital costs of the Commission's joint operations, plant and staff. The total amount of each budget shall be divided between the Governments in the proportions agreed upon by the Commission and approved by the Governments.

6. The budget for the separate operating costs of each national Section shall be the responsibility of the respective Government.

7. The Governments may jointly refer a specific matter relating to transboundary groundwater to the Commission for investigation or action. Individually Governments may request the Commission's advice relating to transboundary groundwaters on matters originating within the requesting Government's portion of the border region.

8. The Commission shall cause each such referral and request to be taken up and investigated, studied or acted upon, as appropriate. The Commission shall render a report to the Governments on every referral and request taken up.

[Omitted: Comment]

Article IV - Enforcement and oversight responsibilities

1. The enforcement of water quality and quantity measures and related land use controls within the territory of each Party shall be the responsibility of that Party or of its political subdivisions, as appropriate.

2.	The Commission shall biennially conduct a review of the water quality and quantity control measures taken within each Party's territory affecting the border region and shall issue a Report containing its assessment of the adequacy and effectiveness of programs for the protection and improvement of the transboundary aquifers and their waters and withdrawal and land use controls, including with respect to any Transboundary Groundwater Conservation Areas, Depletion Plans, Drought Emergency Plans and Health Emergencies. To that end, each Government shall furnish the Commission with the relevant data, information, and studies for use by the Commission in preparing its Report, in accordance with the reporting formats provided by the Commission.

3.	In addition to facilitating, as needed, the Commission's oversight responsibilities under paragraph 2, each Government shall make a biennial Report to the Commission specifying the water quality and conservation measures taken; quantities withdrawn, transferred and exchanged, and any problems encountered in carrying out the provisions of this Agreement or in implementation of any of the conservation, depletion and drought management plans and health emergency measures adopted.

[Omitted: Comment]

Article V - Establishment and maintenance of the database

1.	The Commission is charged with the creation and maintenance of a comprehensive and unified database pertaining to transboundary groundwaters, in the languages of the Parties. The database shall include an inventory of all transboundary groundwater resources taking into account quantity, quality, aquifer geometry, recharge rates, interaction with surface waters, and other pertinent data and shall identify all transboundary aquifers.

2.	The Commission shall carry out studies directly, or through research programs conducted by or with other bodies, public or private:

(a)	to identify inadequacies in available data and to propose remedial action;

(b) to examine present and potential future uses of said groundwaters, taking into account demographic projections and socio-economic development plans;

(c) to assess the impact of present and potential development on transboundary groundwaters and related resources;

(d) to study possible alternative sources of surface water and groundwater for use in the border region, taking into account the quantity and quality of the waters and the potential for the conjunctive use of the available waters; and

(e) to examine the potential for, and the consequences of, drought, floods, and contamination in the border region.

3. The Parties undertake to facilitate the acquisition of information and data by the Commission on a timely basis in accordance with the Commission's requirements.

4. The Commission shall compile, analyze, and disseminate the data, information and studies and provide the results to the Governments.

[Omitted: Comment]

Article VI - Water quality protection

1. The Parties undertake cooperatively to protect and to improve, insofar as practicable, the quality of transboundary aquifers and their waters in conjunction with their programs for surface water quality control, and to avoid appreciable harm in or to the territories of the Parties.

2. The Governments shall promptly inform the Commission of any actual or planned, significantly polluting discharge into transboundary groundwaters or recharge areas, or of other activity with the potential for significant leaching into transboundary groundwaters.

3. The Commission shall without delay consider the gravity of any situation indicating significant groundwater contamination, or the threat thereof, in any part of the border region in accordance with the provisions of Article VII.

[Omitted: Comment]

Article VII - Transboundary groundwater conservation areas

1. The Commission shall determine the desirability of declaring any area within the border region containing transboundary groundwaters to be a Transboundary Groundwater Conservation Area.

2. In the event that the Commission determines that a Transboundary Groundwater Conservation Area is desirable, such determination shall be reported to the Governments with a draft of the proposed declaration and justification therefore, including the delineation of the area and its aquifer(s).

3. If no Government files an objection with the Commission within one hundred eighty (180) days, the Commission shall issue the formal declaration. Any objection(s) filed shall specify, with an explanation, the objectionable Section(s) of the proposed declaration or justification or both.

4. Unless an objection requires termination of consideration, the Commission shall within ninety (90) days of receipt of objections, report to the Governments a revised proposed declaration, to be effective within ninety (90) days, unless a Government files a subsequent objection with the Commission. If no subsequent objection is filed within the said ninety (90) day period, the formal declaration shall be issued by the Commission. If a subsequent objection is filed within ninety (90) day period, the Commission shall refer the matter, together with the entire record, to the Governments for resolution by consultation.

5. In making its determination, the Commission shall consider whether:

(a) groundwater withdrawals exceed or are likely to exceed recharge so as to endanger yield or water quality or are likely to diminish the quantity or quality of interrelated surface water;

(b) recharge has been or may become impaired;

(c) the use of the included aquifer(s) as an important source of drinking water has been, or may become impaired;

(d)   the aquifer(s) have been or may become contaminated; and

(e)   recurring or persistent drought conditions necessitate management of all or some water supplies in the particular area.

6   In making its determination, the Commission shall take into account the impact of the implementation of the declaration under consideration on the sources and uses of water previously allocated by agreements between the Parties or under the Drought Management Plan.

7.   The Commission shall periodically review the appropriateness of continuing or modifying Transboundary Groundwater Conservation Areas.

[Omitted: Comment]

Article VIII - Comprehensive management plans

1.   For each declared Transboundary Groundwater Conservation Area, the Commission shall prepare a Comprehensive Management Plan for the rational development use, protection and control of the waters in the Transboundary Groundwater Conservation Area.

2.   A Comprehensive Management Plan may:

(a)   prescribe measures to prevent, eliminate or mitigate degradation of transboundary groundwater quality, and for that purpose may:

   (1)   classify transboundary groundwaters according to use and coordinate the formulation of water quality standards;

   (2)   identify toxic and hazardous contaminants in the Area and require a continuing record of such substances from origin to disposal;

   (3)   establish criteria for the safe storage of wastes and maintain an inventory of dumpsites, abandoned as well as active, that have caused or may cause transboundary aquifer pollution;

   (4)   propose a scheme for monitoring water quality conditions including the placement and operation of test wells and for

remedial actions where required, including pretreatment and effluent discharge limitations and charges; and

(5) provide for the establishment where required of protective zones in which land use must be regulated;

(b) allocate the uses of groundwaters and interrelated surface waters taking into account any other allocation(s) previously made applicable within the Transboundary Groundwater Conservation Area;

(c) prescribe measures including pumping limitations, criteria for well placement and number of new wells, retirement of existing wells, imposition of extraction fees, planned depletion regimes or reservations of groundwaters for future use;

(d) arrange, where conditions are favorable, programs of transboundary aquifer recharge;

(e) articulate programs of conjunctive use where appropriate;

(f) prescribe the integration and coordination of water quality and quantity control programs;

(g) include other measures and actions as may be deemed appropriate by the Commission.

3. In making any allocations of water uses within a Comprehensive Management Plan, the Commission shall consider all relevant factors such as:

(a) hydrogeology and meteorology;

(b) existing and planned uses;

(c) environmental sensitivity;

(d) quality control requirements;

(e) socio-economic implications (including dependency);

(f) water conservation practices (including efficiency of water use);

(g)　artificial recharge potential; and

(h)　comparative costs and implications of alternative sources of supply.

The weight to be given to each factor is to be determined by its importance in comparison with that of the other relevant factors.

4.　The Commission shall submit proposed Comprehensive Management Plans to the Governments.

(a)　If no Government files an objection with the Commission within one hundred eighty (180) days, the Commission shall adopt the Plan and monitor its implementation.

(b)　A Government's objections shall specify with an explanation the objectionable portions of the proposed Comprehensive Management Plan.

(c)　Within ninety (90) days of receipt of objections, the Commission shall submit to the Governments a revised proposed Comprehensive Management Plan to be effective within ninety (90) days unless a subsequent objection is filed. If no subsequent objection is filed within the ninety (90) day period, the proposed Comprehensive Management Plan shall be adopted and the Commission shall monitor its implementation. If subsequent objections are filed within the ninety (90) day period, the Commission shall refer the matter, together with the entire record, to the Governments for resolution by consultation.

5.　The Commission is authorized to approve advances and exchanges of water consistent with the objectives of the applicable Comprehensive Management Plan.

6.　The Commission shall monitor and evaluate the measures taken under the Comprehensive Management Plan and shall propose, as appropriate, modifications thereto.

[Omitted: Comment]

Article IX - Public health emergencies

1. Upon a determination by the Commission or any Government that there is an imminent or actual public health hazard involving the contamination of transboundary groundwaters, the Commission shall notify the respective Governments, and may declare a Public Health Emergency for a stated period.

2. In the event that the Public Health Emergency is not mitigated or abated within the initial stated period, the Commission may extend the emergency for such additional period as may be deemed necessary under the circumstances.

3. On the basis of the declaration, the Commission shall have the authority to investigate the area of imminent or actual contamination and to prescribe measures to prevent, eliminate or mitigate the public health hazard.

4. The Governments shall provide the indicated information, data, studies and reports concerning public health emergencies as set forth in Paragraphs 2 and 3 of Article IV.

[Omitted: Comment]

Article X - Planned depletion

1. The Commission, after evaluation of all relevant considerations, may prepare and, with the consent of the Governments, may approve a plan for the depletion of an aquifer over a calculated period. The plan may apportion the uses and specify the rates and means of extraction of the transboundary groundwaters, and may authorize advances, exchanges and transboundary transfers of water consistent with the objectives of the Depletion Plan.

2. The Governments shall provide the indicated information, data, studies and reports concerning depletion as set forth in Paragraphs 2 and 3 of Article IV.

[Omitted: Comment]

<u>Article XI - Transboundary transfers</u>

Nothing in this Agreement shall be so construed as to preclude either short-term or long-term transfers of waters between the Parties under terms and conditions approved by the Commission.

[Omitted: Comment]

<u>Article XII - Planning for drought</u>

1. The Commission shall, within two (2) years of the coming into force of this Agreement, complete the preparation of a Drought Management Plan applicable to the border region for activation in the region, or in parts thereof, in the event of drought. The completed Plan shall be submitted to the Governments for standby approval.

2. The Drought Management Plan shall:

(a) specify the hydrometeorological preconditions for the declaration of a Drought Alert and, thereunder, the conservation measures to be observed by all water users within the border region;

(b) specify the hydrometeorological preconditions for the declaration of a Drought Emergency and, thereunder, the specific measures to be observed by all water users within the border region;

(c) provide for the monitoring of the hydrometeorological conditions generally in the border region, and compliance with prescribed conservation or other specific measures under any Drought Alert or Drought Emergency; and

(d) provide for periodic reports to the Governments during any Drought Alert or Drought Emergency, to include any proposed modifications to the Drought Emergency Plan and any modifications made to the prescribed measures under any Drought Alert or Drought Emergency.

3. The Drought Management Plan may:

(a) Designate and reserve certain transboundary aquifers or specific well sites for use in times of drought;

(b) provide, for the duration of any declared Drought Emergency:

    (1) the conjunctive management of groundwater and surface water supplies within or made available to the border region or part(s) thereof governed by the declaration;

    (2) increases and reductions in the normal allowable withdrawals and at variance with allocations made under a Comprehensive Management Plan for a Transboundary Groundwater Conservation Area or by prior agreements between the parties, maintaining to the extent practicable the established withdrawal ratios between the Parties and an equitable balance of all emergency obligations;

    (3) authorization to use designated and reserved groundwaters within the border region;

(c) include other structural and nonstructural measures deemed likely to be needed under various drought conditions.

4. The conservation and other specific measures provided in the Plan for Drought Alert declarations or Drought Emergency declarations may be modified or suspended by the Commission to meet the specific requirements of the situation at the time of such declarations and during the time such declarations remain in force.

5. The authority to determine the existence of the preconditions specified in the approved Drought Management Plan and to declare drought alerts and drought emergencies thereunder, in any portion of the border region, is vested in the Commission.

6. The Commission is authorized to modify or terminate a declaration of Drought Alert or Drought Emergency when the hydrometeorological conditions so warrant.

7. Declarations of Drought Alert and Drought Emergency, and modifications to or termination of the same, shall be immediately communicated to the Governments and published so as to come to the attention of all water users in the border region.

8.   The Governments shall provide the indicated information, data, studies and reports concerning drought as set forth in Paragraphs 2 and 3 of Article IV.

[Omitted: Comment]

Article XIII - Inquiry in the public interest

1.   The Commission shall by general notice invite written statements and information from all persons professing interest in the groundwater-related conditions and activities in the portion of the border region for which a Transboundary Groundwater Conservation Area declaration, a Comprehensive Management Plan, a Depletion Plan, a transboundary transfer, or a Drought Alert or emergency declaration is under consideration.

2.   All submissions received pursuant to Paragraph 1 shall be taken into account by the Commission.

3.   Whenever the Commission deems that public interest warrants, it shall schedule and conduct hearings open to the public in appropriate places and facilitates in the border region, and shall make and publish a record of such hearings.

4.   Any person professing an interest may also petition the Commission at any time requesting the Commission to schedule a hearing or to invite written statements and information concerning groundwater conditions in the border region, or urging the Commission to take a particular action under this Agreement.

5.   When deemed useful by the Commission, technical meetings, workshops and briefings relating to transboundary groundwater matters may be held under the auspices of the Commission or in cooperation with authorities and organizations concerned with the welfare of the border region.

[Omitted: Comment]

Article XIV - Existing rights and obligations

The rights and obligations of the Parties as set forth in prior agreements between the Parties shall not be permanently altered by this Agreement or any measures taken hereunder.

[Omitted: Comment]
[Omitted: Article XV - Accommodation of differences, Article XVI - Resolution of disputes, Article XVII - Amendment, Article XVIII - Entry into force, Article XIX - Authentic texts, Article XX - Reservations and exceptions]

46. International Law Association (ILA) - The Berlin Rules on Water Resources [2004]*

[Omitted: Preface, Usage note]

Chapter 1 - Scope

Article 1 - Scope

1.   These Rules express international law applicable to the management of the waters of international drainage basins and applicable to all waters, as appropriate.

2.   Nothing in these Rules affects rights or obligations created by treaty or special custom.

[Omitted: Article 2 - Implementation of these rules]

---

* Adopted by the International Law Association (ILA) at its Seventy-First Conference, held in Berlin in 2004. ILA, Report of the Seventy-First Conference held in Berlin, 16– 21 August 2004 (forthcoming, 2005).

Article 3 - Definitions

For the purposes of these Articles, these terms have the following meanings:

1.   "Aquatic environment" means all surface waters and groundwater,
      the lands and subsurface geological formations connected to those
      waters, and the atmosphere related to those waters and lands.

2.   "Aquifer" means a subsurface layer or layers of geological strata of
      sufficient porosity and permeability to allow either a flow of or the
      withdrawal of usable quantities of groundwater.

3.   A "basin State" is a State the territory of which includes any portion
      of an international drainage basin.

      ...

5.   "Drainage basin" means an area determined by the geographic limits
      of a system of interconnected waters, the surface waters of which
      normally share a common terminus.

      ...

7.   "Environment" includes the waters, land, air, flora, and fauna that
      exist in a particular region at a particular time.

      ...

11.   "Groundwater" means water beneath the surface of the ground
      located in a saturated zone and in direct contact with the ground or
      soil.

      ...

13.   An "international drainage basin" is a drainage basin extending over
      two or more States.

14.   "Management of waters" and "to manage waters" includes the
      development, use, protection, allocation, regulation, and control of
      waters.

      ...

16. "Pollution" means any detrimental change in the composition or quality of waters that results directly or indirectly from human conduct.

17. "Regional economic integration organization" means an organization constituted by sovereign States of a given region, to which its member States have transferred competence in respect of matters governed by these Rules.

18. "State" means a sovereign State or a regional economic integration organization.

19. "Sustainable use" means the integrated management of resources to assure efficient use of and equitable access to waters for the benefit of current and future generations while preserving renewable resources and maintaining non-renewable resources to the maximum extent reasonably possible.

...

21. "Waters" means all surface water and groundwater other than marine waters.

Chapter II - Principles of international law governing the management of all waters

[Omitted: Article 4 - Participation by persons]

Article 5 - Conjunctive management

States shall use their best efforts to manage surface waters, groundwater, and other pertinent waters in a unified and comprehensive manner.

Article 6 - Integrated management

States shall use their best efforts to integrate appropriately the management of waters with the management of other resources.

[Omitted: Article 7 – Sustainability; Article 8 - Minimization of environmental harm, Article 9 - Interpretation of these rules; Chapter III - Internationally shared waters: Article 10 - Participation by basin states,

Article 11 - Cooperation, Article 12 - Equitable utilization, Article 13 - Determining an equitable and reasonable use, Article 14 - Preferences among uses, Article 15 - Using allocated water in other basin states, Article 16 - Avoidance of transboundary harm; Chapter IV - The rights of persons: Article 17 - The right of access to water, Article 18 - Public participation and access to information, Article 19 - Education, Article 20 - Protection of particular communities, Article 21 - The right to compensation; Chapter V - Protection of the aquatic environment: Article 22 - Ecological integrity, Article 23 - The precautionary approach, Article 24 - Ecological flows, Article 25 - Alien species, Article 26 - Hazardous substances, Article 27 - Pollution, Article 28 - Establishing water quality standards; Chapter VI - Impact assessments: Article 29 - The obligation to assess impacts, Article 30 - Participation in impact assessments in another state, Article 31 - The impact assessment process; Chapter VII - Extreme situations: Article 32 - Responses to extreme conditions, Article 33 - Highly polluting accidents, Article 34 - Floods, Article 35 - Droughts]

Chapter VIII - Groundwater

Article 36 - Application of these Rules to aquifers

1. The Rules of this Chapter apply to all aquifers, including aquifers that do not contribute water to, or receive water from, surface waters or receive no significant contemporary recharge from any source.

2. States, in managing aquifers, are subject to all Rules expressed in these Articles, taking into account the special characteristics of groundwater.

Article 37 - Managing aquifers generally

States shall manage groundwater conjunctively with the surface waters of any basin of which it is a part, taking into account any interconnections between aquifers or between and [sic] an aquifer and a body of surface water, as well as any impact on aquifers caused by activities within the State's jurisdiction or control.

Article 38 - Precautionary management of aquifers

States, in accordance with the precautionary approach, shall take early action and develop long-term plans to ensure the sustainable use of groundwater and of the aquifers in which the groundwater is contained.

Article 39 - Duty to acquire information

In order to comply with this Chapter, States shall take all appropriate steps to acquire the information necessary to manage groundwater and aquifers efficiently and effectively, including:

(a)   Monitoring groundwater levels, pressures, and quality;

(b)   Developing aquifer vulnerability maps;

(c)   Assessing the impacts on groundwater and aquifers of industrial, agricultural, and other activities; and

(d)   Any other measures appropriate to the circumstances of the aquifer.

Article 40 - Sustainability applied to groundwater

1.   States shall give effect to the principle of sustainability in managing aquifers, taking into account natural and artificial recharge.

2.   The rule in paragraph 1 does not preclude the withdrawal of groundwater from an aquifer that is receiving no significant contemporary recharge.

Article 41 - Protecting aquifers

1.   States shall take all appropriate measures to prevent, insofar as possible, any pollution of, and the degradation of the hydraulic integrity of, aquifers.

2.   States in fulfilling their obligation to prevent pollution of an aquifer shall take special care to prevent, eliminate, reduce, or control:

    (a)   The direct or indirect discharge of pollutants, whether from point or non-point sources;

    (b)   The injection of water that is polluted or would otherwise degrade an aquifer;

    (c)   Saline water intrusion; or

(d)   Any other source of pollution.

3.   States shall take all appropriate measures to abate the effects of the
        pollution of aquifers.

4.   States shall integrate aquifers into their programs of general
        environmental protection, including but not limited to:

        (a)   The management of other waters;

        (b)   Land use planning and management; and

        (c)   Other programs of general environmental protection.

5.   States shall specially protect sites where groundwater is withdrawn
        from or recharged to an aquifer.

Article 42 - Transboundary aquifers

1.   The Rules applicable to internationally shared waters apply to an
        aquifer if:

        (a)   It is connected to surface waters that are part of an
                international drainage basin; or

        (b)   It is intersected by the boundaries between two or more
                States even without a connection to surface waters that form
                an international drainage basin.

2.   Whenever possible and appropriate, basin States sharing an aquifer
        referred to in paragraph 1 shall manage an aquifer in its entirety.

3.   In managing the waters of an aquifer referred to in paragraph 1,
        basin States shall consult and exchange information and data at the
        request of any one of them and shall cooperate in the collection
        and analyzing additional needed information pertinent to the
        obligations under these Rules.

4.   Basin States shall cooperate according to the procedures in Chapter
        XI to set drawdown rates in order to assure the equitable
        utilization of the waters of an aquifer referred in paragraph 1,

having due regard for the obligation not to cause significant harm to other basin States and to the obligation to protect the aquifer.

5.   Basin States sharing an aquifer referred to in paragraph 1 shall cooperate in managing the recharge of the aquifer.

6.   Basin States sharing an aquifer referred to in paragraph 1 shall refrain from and prevent acts or omissions within their territory that cause significant harm to another basin State, having due regard to the right of each basin State to make equitable and reasonable use of the waters.

[Omitted: Chapter IX - Navigation: Article 43 - Freedom of navigation, Article 44 - Limitations on freedom of navigation, Article 45 - Regulating navigation, Article 46 - Maintaining navigation, Article 47 - Granting the right to navigate to nonriparian states, Article 48 - Exclusion of public vessels, Article 49 - Effect of war or other emergencies on navigation; Chapter X - Protection of waters and water installations during war or armed conflict: Article 50 - Rendering water unfit for use, Article 51 - Targeting waters or water installations, Article 52 - Ecological targets, Article 53 - Dams and dykes, Article 54 - Occupied territories, Article 55 - Effect of war on water treaties; Chapter XI - International cooperation and administration: Article 56 - Exchange of information, Article 57 - Notification of programs, projects, or activities, Article 58 - Consultations, Article 59 - Failure to consult, Article 60 - Requests for impact assessments, Article 61 - Urgent implementation of programs, plans, projects, or activities, Article 62 - Harmonization of national laws and policies, Article 63 - Protection of installations, Article 64 - Establishment of basin wide or other joint management mechanisms, Article 65 - Minimal requirements for basin wide management mechanisms, Article 66 - Compliance review, Article 67 - Sharing expenses; Chapter XII - State responsibility: Article 68 - Responsibility for injuries to other states; Chapter XIII - Legal remedies: Article 69 - Access to courts, Article 70 - Remedies for damage to persons, Article 71 - Remedies for persons in other states; Chapter XIV - Settlement of international disputes: Article 72 - Peaceful settlement of international water management disputes, Article 73 - Arbitration and litigation]

APPENDIX

List of treaties and other documents contained in:
Ludwik A. Teclaff and Albert E. Utton (eds.), *International Groundwater Law* (London, Rome, New York: Oceana Publishers, Inc., 1981), reproduced with permission of Oceana Publishers, Inc.

LIST OF TREATIES AND OTHER DOCUMENTS

Albania - Yugloslavia
Agreement . . . concerning water economy questions
(1956). UN LEG. SER.44.

Allied Powers - Italy
Peace treaty (1947) (Commune of Gorizia water supply)
UN LEG. SER. 415.

Austria - Bavaria
Frontier line treaty (1862). UN LEG. SER. 468.

Austria - Germany (Federal Republic)
Agreement concerning water diversion (1950).
UN LEG. SER. 469.

Austria - Switzerland
Treaty for the regulation of the Rhine (1892).
UN. LEG. SER. 489.

Bavaria - Austria
Frontier line treaty (1862). UN LEG. SER. 468.

Belgium - Germany
Arrangement concerning the frontier (1929)
(Kalterherberg water supply). UN LEG. SER. 529.

(Belgium - Germany)
Frontier dispositions of the Delimitation Commission
(1922). UN LEG. SER. 411.

Belgium - United Kingdom
Agreement on boundary water rights, Tanganyika-Ruanda
Urundi (1934). UN LEG. SER. 97.

Big Blue River Compact (1972). See under United States —
Kansas-Nebraska

Bulgaria - Yugoslavia
Agreement concerning water-economy questions (1958).
UN LEG. SER. 558.

Canada - United States
Great Lakes water quality agreement (1978).
TIAS 9257

Czechoslovakia - Poland
Agreement . . . concerning . . . frontier waters
(1958). 538 UNTS 108 (1965).

Delaware River Basin Compact (1961). See under United States.

Dominican Republic - Haiti
Treaty of peace . . . (1929). UN LEG. SER. 225.

Egypt - Italy
Agreement on the Cyrenaica-Egypt frontier (Ramla
well) (1925). UN LEG. SER. 99.

Eritrea - Sudan (River Gash). See under Italy - United Kingdom.

European Economic Community (E.E.C.)
> Proposal for Council Directive on water pollution from wood pulp mills (20 Jan. 1975). OJ No.C 99/2, 2.5.1975.
>
> Council Directive on disposal of waste oils (16 June 1975). OJ No.L 194/23, 25.7.1975.
>
> Proposal for Council Directive relating to quality of water for human consumption (31 July 1975). OJ No.C 214/2, 18.9.1975.
>
> Council Directive on waste from the titanium dioxide industry (20 Feb. 1978). OJ No. L 54/19, 25.2.1978.
>
> Council Directive on toxic and dangerous waste (20 Mar. 1978). OJ No. L 84/43, 31.3.1978.
>
> Proposal for Council Directive on protection of ground-water against pollution caused by dangerous substances (27 Jan. 1978). OJ No. C 37/3, 14.2.1978.
>
> Amendments to proposal for Council Directives on protection of groundwater ... (30 Dec. 1978). OJ No. C 27/2, 31.1.1979.
>
> Council Directive on the protection of groundwater against pollution caused by dangerous substances (17 Dec. 1979). OJ No. L 20/43, 26.1.1980.
>
> Written Question No. 1687/79 (Transport and storage of specialized waste in border areas). OJ No. C 126/82, 27.5.1980.
>
> Written Question No. 785/79 (Risk of radioactive pollution of springs of Roya River from uranium mine). OJ No. C 86/11, 8.4.1980.

Finland - Sweden
> Agreement concerning frontier rivers (1971). 825 UNTS 272 (1972).

France - Germany
> Frontier delimitation treaty (1925). UN LEG. SER. 657.

France - Germany (Federal Republic)
> Convention concerning development of the Rhine .... (1970). 760 UNTS 346 (1970).
>
> Convention for development of the upper course of the Rhine (1956). UN LEG. SER. 660.

France - Switzerland (Canton of Neufchâtel)
> Procès-verbal on frontier delimitation (1824). UN LEG. SER. 700.

France - Switzerland
> Convention on protection of Lake Leman waters against pollution (1962). OECD 418 (1978).
>
> Arrangement relating to the ... Franco-Swiss Genevese aquifer (1977). Unpublished.

France - United Kingdom
　　Agreement regarding the Somali Coast (wells of Hadou)
　　(1888). UN LEG. SER. 118.

　　Exchange of Notes relating to the Gold Coast-French
　　Soudan boundary (1904). UN LEG. SER. 121.

Geneva - Haute Savoie. See France - Switzerland (1977)

Germany - Belgium
　　Arrangement concerning the frontier (1929)
　　(Kalterherberg water supply). UN LEG. SER. 529

　　Frontier dispositions of the Delimitation Commission
　　(1922). UN. LEG. SER. 411.

Germany - France
　　Frontier delimitation treaty (1925). UN LEG. SER. 657.

Germany (Federal Republic) - Austria
　　Agreement concerning water diversion (1950).
　　UN LEG. SER. 469.

Germany (Federal Republic) - France
　　Convention concerning development of the Rhine (1970)
　　760 UNTS 346 (1970).

　　Convention for development of the upper course of the
　　Rhine (1956). UN LEG. SER. 660.

Germany (Federal Republic) - Luxembourg
　　Treaty concerning the construction of a hydro-electric
　　power-plant on the Sauer (1950). UN LEG. SER. 721.

　　Treaty . . . concerning . . . hydro-electric power installations
　　on the Our (1958). UN LEG. SER. 726.

Gorizia, Commune of, water supply. See Allied Powers -
　　Italy (1947); and, Italy - Yugoslavia (1957)

Greece - Yugoslavia
　　Procès-verbal . . . concerning hydro-economic studies of
　　the Lake Dojran basin (1957). UN LEG. SER. 813

Hadou wells. See France - United Kingdom (1888)

Haiti - Dominican Republic
　　Treaty of peace . . . (1929). UN LEG. SER. 225.

Hanover - Netherlands
　　Frontiers treaty (1824). UN LEG. SER. 740.

Haute Savoie - Geneva. See France - Switzerland (1977)

Hungary - Yugoslavia
　　Agreement concerning water economy questions (1955).
　　UN LEG. SER. 830.

Italy - Allied Powers
　　Peace treaty (1947) (Commune of Gorizia water supply).
　　UN LEG. SER. 415.

　　See also Italy - Yugoslavia (1957)

Ruanda Urundi - Tanganyika. See Belgium - United Kingdom
(1934)

Susquehanna River Basin Compact. See under United States

Sweden - Finland
Agreement concerning frontier rivers (1971).
825 UNTS 272 (1972).

Switzerland
Federal law on ... pollution (1971). FF II (1971) 909.

Switzerland - Austria
Treaty for the regulation of the Rhine (1892).
UN LEG. SER. 489.

Switzerland (Canton of Neufchâtel) - France
Procès-verbal on frontier delimitation (1824).
UN LEG. SER. 700.

Switzerland - France
Convention on protection of Lake Leman waters against
pollution (1962). OECD 418 (1978).

(Geneva - Haute Savoie). Arrangement relating to the ...
Franco-Swiss Genevese aquifer (1977). Unpublished.

Syria - Jordan
Agreement ... concerning ... the Yarmuk (1953).
UN LEG. SER. 378.

Tanganyika - Ruanda Urundi. See Belgium - United Kingdom
(1934)

Turkey - Persia
Frontier line agreement (1932). UN LEG. SER. 370.

Multipartite frontier delimitation protocol (1913).
UN LEG. SER. 266.

U.S.S.R. - Persia
Frontier waters convention (1926). UN LEG. SER. 371.

U.S.S.R. - Poland
Agreement ... concerning ... frontier waters (1964).
552 UNTS 188 (1966).

United Kingdom - Belgium
Agreement on boundary water rights, Tanganyika - Ruanda
Urundi (1934). UN LEG. SER. 97.

United Kingdom - France
Agreement regarding the Somali Coast (wells of Hadou)
(1888). UN LEG. SER. 118.

Exchange of Notes relating to the Gold Coast - French
Soudan boundary (1904). UN LEG. SER. 121.

United Kingdom - Italy
(Eritrea - Sudan) Exchange of Notes respecting the ...
River Gash (1925). UN LEG. SER. 128.

United Nations, Conference on Desertification (1977) Trans-
  national Project: the Management of the Major Regional
  Aquifers in Northeast Africa and the Arabian Peninsula.
  A/CONF.74/24 (1977).

United States
  Delaware River Basin Compact (1961). P.L. 87-328,
  75 Stat. 688.

  Susquehanna River Basin Compact (1967). P.L. 91-575,
  84 Stat. 1509.

  Nebraska-Kansas. Big Blue River Compact (1972).
  P.L. 92-308, 86 Stat. 193.

  Nebraska-South Dakota. Lower Niobrara River and Ponca
  Creek Compact (1961). Nebr. Session Laws 1961, ch. 288.

  Nebraska-Wyoming. Upper Niobrara River Compact (1969).
  P.L. 91-50, 83 Stat. 86.

United States, Environmental Protection Agency
  Proposed Ground Water Protection Strategy. 45 Fed. Reg.
  77514 (Nov. 24, 1980).

United States - Canada
  Great Lakes water quality agreement (1978).
  TIAS 9257.

United States - Mexico
  Treaty relating to the utilization of the Colorado,
  Tijuana and Rio Grande (1944). UN LEG. SER. 236.

  Minute No. 242 (1973). Dept. State Bull. 395 (1973).

Upper Niobrara River Compact (1969). See under United States

Yugoslavia - Albania
  Agreement . . . concerning water economy questions (1956).
  UN LEG. SER. 441.

Yugoslavia - Bulgaria
  Agreement concerning water-economy questions (1958).
  UN LEG. SER. 558.

Yugoslavia - Greece
  Procès-verbal . . . concerning hydro-economic studies
  of the Lake Dojran basin (1957). UN LEG. SER. 813.

Yugoslavia - Hungary
  Agreement concerning water economy questions (1955).
  UN LEG. SER. 830.

Yugoslavia - Italy (Commune of Gorizia water supply)
  (Allied Powers - Italy) Peace Treaty (1947).
  UN LEG. SER. 415

  Agreement concerning water supply to the Commune of
  Gorizia (1957). UN LEG. SER. 866.

1. Wildlife and national park legislation in Asia, 1971 (E*)
2. Wildlife and national park legislation in Latin America, 1971 (E* S*)
3. Vicuña conservation legislation, 1971 (E* S*)
4. Legal systems for environment protection: Japan, Sweden, United States, 1973 (E*)
5. Agrarian law and judicial systems, 1975 (E* F* S*)
6. Agricultural credit legislation in selected developing countries, 1974 (E*)
7. An outline of food law, 1983 (E* F S*)
8. Legislación de aguas en América Central, Caribe y México – Vol. I, 1983 (S)
9. A legal and institutional framework for natural resources management, 1983 (E S)
10. Water law in selected European countries (Belgium, England and Wales, France, Israel, Italy, Spain, Turkey) – Vol. I, 1979 (E* F S*)
11. Fundamentos teóricos para una legislación tributaria en el sector agropecuario, 1976 (S*)
12. International food standards and national laws, 1976 (E F*)
13. Derecho agrario y desarrollo agrícola: estado actual y perspectivas en América Latina, 1978 (S*)
14. Legal and institutional responses to growing water demand, 1977 (E* F* S*)
15. Systematic index of international water resources treaties, declarations, acts and cases by basin – Vol. I, 1978 (E/F/S*)
16. Seed legislation, 1980 (E F* S)
17. Water law in selected African countries, 1980 (E* F S)
18. Reforma agraria y desarrollo rural integrado, 1979 (S*)
19. Water legislation in South American countries, 1983 (E* F S*)
20. Legislation on wildlife, hunting and protected areas in some European countries, 1980 (E* F* S*)
21. Coastal state requirements for foreign fishing has been replaced by FISHLEX database published in the FAO Legal Office home page: www.fao.org/Legal
22. Agricultural insurance legislation, 1981 (E* S*)
23. The law of international water resources, 1980 (E* F S)
24. Irrigation users' organizations in the legislation and administration of certain Latin American countries, 1983 (E S)
25. Legislation on wildlife and protected areas in Africa, 1984 (E F)
26. The UN Convention on the Law of the Sea: impacts on tuna regulation, 1982 (E F)
27. Regional compendium of fisheries legislation – West Africa (CECAF Region), 1983 (E/F*)
28. Plant protection legislation, 1984 (E* F S)
29. Legislation on foods for infants and small children, 1983 (E*)
30. Water law in selected European countries (Cyprus, Finland, the Netherlands, Union of Soviet Socialist Republics, Yugoslavia) – Vol. II, 1983 (E)
31. The role of legislation in land use planning for developing countries, 1985 (E)
32. Agricultural census legislation, 1984 (E*)
33. Legislation on productivity in agriculture: a comparative outline, 1985 (E F S)
34. Systematic index of international water resources treaties, declarations, acts and cases by basin – Vol. II, 1984 (E/F/S*)
35. Regional compendium of fisheries legislation (Western Pacific Region) – Vols. I and II, 1984 (E)
36. Legislation controlling the international beef and veal trade, 1985 (E* F S)
37. La législation forestière au Cap-Vert, en Ethiopie, en Gambie, au Mali et en Mauritanie, au Niger, au Rwanda et au Sénégal, 1986 (F)
38. The environmental impact of economic incentives for agricultural production: a comparative law study, 1990 (E F S)
39. Propiedad, tenencia y redistribución de tierras en la legislación de América Central y México, 1986 (S)
40. International groundwater resources law, 1986 (E F S)
41. Land tenure systems and forest policy, 1987 (E F)
42. Regional compendium of fisheries legislation (Indian Ocean Region) – Vols I and II, 1987 (E)
43. Pesticide labelling legislation, 1988 (E F S)
44. La réforme du droit de la terre dans certains pays d'Afrique francophone, 1987 (F)
45. Legal aspects of international joint ventures in agriculture, 1990 (E)

46. The freshwater-maritime interface: legal and institutional aspects, 1990 (E)

47. The regulation of driftnet fishing on the high seas: legal issues, 1991 (E F)

48. Les périmètres irrigués en droit comparé africain (Madagascar, Maroc, Niger, Sénégal, Tunisie), 1992 (F)

49. Analyse préliminaire de certains textes législatifs régissant l'aquaculture, 1993 (F S)

50. Treaties concerning the non-navigational uses of international watercourses – Europe, 1993 (E/F/S)

51. Pesticide registration legislation, 1995 (E F)

52. Preparing national regulations for water resources management, 1994 (E)

53. Evaluation des impacts sur l'environnement pour un développement rural durable: étude juridique, 1994 (F)

54. Legislation governing food control and quality certification – The authorities and procedures, 1995 (E F)

55. Treaties concerning the non-navigational uses of international watercourses – Asia, 1995 (E/F)

56. Tendances d'évolution des législations agrofroncières en Afrique francophone, 1996 (F)

57. Coastal State requirements for foreign fishing, 1996 (E), has been replaced by FISHLEX database published in the FAO Legal Office home page:www.fao.org/Legal

58. Readings in African customary water law, 1996 (E/F)

59. Cadre juridique de la sécurité alimentaire, 1996 (F)

60. Le foncier-environnement – Fondements juridico-institutionnels pour une gestion viable des ressources naturelles renouvelables au Sahel, 1997 (F)

61. Treaties concerning the non-navigational uses of international watercourses – Africa, 1997 (E/F)

62. New principles of phytosanitary legislation, 1999 (E F S)

63. The burden of proof in natural resources legislation – Some critical issues for fisheries law, 1998 (E)

64. Política y legislación de aguas en el Istmo centroamericano – El Salvador, Guatemala, Honduras, 1998 (S)

65. Sources of international water law, 1998 (E)

66. Trends in Forestry Law in America and Asia, 1998 (E F S)

67. Issues in water law reform, 1999 (E)

68. Extracts from international and regional instruments and declarations, and other authoritative texts addressing the right to food, 1999 (E/F/S)

69. Élaboration des réglementations nationales de gestion des ressources en eau – Principes et pratiques, 1999 (F)

70. Water rights administration – Experience, issues and guidelines, 2001 (E)

71. Fisheries enforcement – Related legal and institutional issues: national, subregional or regional perspectives, 2001 (E)

72. Trends in forestry law in Europe and Africa, 2003 (E F)

73. Law and sustainable development since Rio – Legal trends in agriculture and natural resource management, 2002 (E)

74. Legal trends in wildlife management, 2002 (E S)

75. Mountains and the law – Emerging trends, 2003 (E F S)

76. Gender and law – Women's rights in agriculture, 2002 (E)

77. The right to adequate food in emergencies, 2003 (E)

78. Law and modern biotechnology – Selected issues of relevance to food and agriculture, 2003 (E)

79. Legislation on water users' organizations – A comparative analysis, 2003 (E)

80. Preparing national regulations for water resources management – Principles and practice, 2003 (E)

81. Administración de derechos de agua, 2003 (S)

82. Administrative sanctions in fisheries law, 2003 (E)

83. Legislating for property rights in fisheries, 2004 (E)

84 Land and water – The rights interface, 2004 (E)

85 Intellectual property rights in plant varieties – International legal regimes and policy options for national governments, 2004 (E)

86 Groundwater in international law – Compilation of treaties and other legal instruments, 2005 (E)

ANNUAL PUBLICATION

Food and Agricultural Legislation (E/F/S) - A selection of significant and illustrative laws and regulations governing food and agriculture in

FAO Member Nations has been replaced by the
FAOLEX database published on the FAO Legal
Office Web site: www.fao.org or directly at http:
//faolex.fao.org/faolex

Availability: March 2005

Ar	– Arabic	Multil –	Multilingual
C	– Chinese	*	Out of print
E	– English	**	In preparation
F	– French		
P	– Portuguese		
S	– Spanish		

The FAO Technical Papers are available through
the authorized FAO Sales Agents or directly
from Sales and Marketing Group, FAO, Viale
delle Terme di Caracalla, 00100 Rome, Italy.